Maybe You Should Talk to Someone

BOOKS BY LORI GOTTLIEB

Stick Figure

Inside the Cult of Kibu
(with Jesse Jacobs)

I Love You, Nice to Meet You
(with Kevin Bleyer)

Marry Him

Maybe You Should Talk to Someone

* * *

A Therapist, *Her* Therapist, and Our Lives Revealed

Lori Gottlieb

Houghton Mifflin Harcourt

BOSTON   NEW YORK

For information about permission to reproduce selections
from this book, write to trade.permissions@hmhco.com or to
Permissions, Houghton Mifflin Harcourt Publishing Company,
3 Park Avenue, 19th Floor, New York, New York 10016.

hmhco.com

Library of Congress Cataloging-in-Publication Data
Names: Gottlieb, Lori, author.
Title: Maybe you should talk to someone : a therapist, HER
therapist, and our lives revealed / Lori Gottlieb.
Description: Boston : Houghton Mifflin Harcourt, 2019.
Identifiers: LCCN 2018042562 (print) | LCCN 2018045914 (ebook) |
ISBN 9781328663047 (ebook) | ISBN 9781328662057 (hardback)
Subjects: LCSH: Gottlieb, Lori,—Health. | Psychotherapists—Biography. |
Therapist and patient—Biography. | BISAC: PSYCHOLOGY / Psychotherapy /
General. | BIOGRAPHY & AUTOBIOGRAPHY / Personal Memoirs. |
SELF-HELP / Personal Growth / Happiness. | FAMILY & RELATIONSHIPS /
Love & Romance. Classification: LCC RC480.8 (ebook) |
LCC RC480.8 .G68 2019 (print) | DDC 616.89/14092 [B]— DC23
LC record available at https://lccn.loc.gov/2018042562

Book design by Chrissy Kurpeski

Printed in the United States of America
DOC 10 9 8 7 6

4500786061

Illustrations on page 42 copyright © 2019 by Arthur Mount. Emoji art on page
49, from left to right: Standard Studio via Shutterstock; Sovenko Artem via
Shutterstock; Park Ji Sun via Shutterstock; Rvector via Shutterstock.

"Welcome to Holland," copyright © 1987 by Emily Perl Kingsley. Reprinted by
the permission of the author. All rights reserved.

It is proposed that happiness be classified as a psychiatric disorder and be included in future editions of the major diagnostic manuals under the new name: major affective disorder, pleasant type. In a review of the relevant literature it is shown that happiness is statistically abnormal, consists of a discrete cluster of symptoms, is associated with a range of cognitive abnormalities, and probably reflects the abnormal functioning of the central nervous system. One possible objection to this proposal remains—that happiness is not negatively valued. However, this objection is dismissed as scientifically irrelevant.

— RICHARD BENTALL,
JOURNAL OF MEDICAL ETHICS, 1992

The eminent Swiss psychiatrist Carl Jung said this:
*"People will do anything, no matter how absurd,
to avoid facing their own souls."*

But he also said this:
"Who looks inside, awakes."

Author's Note

This is a book that asks, "How do we change?" and answers with "In relation to others." The relationships I write about here, between therapists and patients, require a sacred trust for any change to occur. In addition to attaining written permission, I have gone to great lengths to disguise identities and any recognizable details, and in some instances, material and scenarios from a few patients have been attributed to one. All changes were carefully considered and painstakingly chosen to remain true to the spirit of each story while also serving the greater goal: to reveal our shared humanity so that we can see ourselves more clearly. Which is to say, if you see yourself in these pages, it's both coincidental and intentional.

A note on terminology: Those who come to therapy are referred to in various ways, most commonly as *patients* or *clients*. I don't believe that either word quite captures the relationship I have with the people I work with. But *the people I work with* is awkward, and *clients* might be confusing, given that term's many connotations, so for simplicity and clarity, I use *patients* throughout this book.

Contents

Part One

Nothing is more desirable than to be released from
an affliction, but nothing is more frightening
than to be divested of a crutch.

—James Baldwin

1

Idiots

CHART NOTE, JOHN:

Patient reports feeling "stressed out" and states that he is having difficulty sleeping and getting along with his wife. Expresses annoyance with others and seeks help "managing the idiots."

Have compassion.

Deep breath.

Have compassion, have compassion, have compassion . . .

I'm repeating this phrase in my head like a mantra as the forty-year-old man sitting across from me is telling me about all of the people in his life who are "idiots." Why, he wants to know, is the world filled with so many idiots? Are they born this way? Do they become this way? Maybe, he muses, it has something to do with all the artificial chemicals that are added to the food we eat nowadays.

"That's why I try to eat organic," he says. "So I don't become an idiot like everyone else."

I'm losing track of which idiot he's talking about: the dental hygienist who asks too many questions ("None of them rhetorical"), the coworker who *only* asks questions ("He never makes *statements,* because that would imply that he had something to say"), the driver in front of him who stopped at a yellow light ("No sense of *urgency!*"), the Apple technician at the Genius Bar who couldn't fix his laptop ("Some genius!").

"John," I begin, but he's starting to tell a rambling story about his wife. I can't get a word in edgewise, even though he has come to me for help.

I, by the way, am his new therapist. (His previous therapist, who lasted just three sessions, was "nice, but an idiot.")

"And then Margo gets angry—can you believe it?" he's saying. "But she doesn't *tell* me she's angry. She just *acts* angry, and I'm supposed to *ask* her what's wrong. But I know if I ask, she'll say, 'Nothing,' the first three times, and then maybe the fourth or fifth time she'll say, 'You *know* what's wrong,' and I'll say, 'No, I don't, or I wouldn't be *asking!*'"

He smiles. It's a huge smile. I try to work with the smile—anything to change his monologue into a dialogue and make contact with him.

"I'm curious about your smile just now," I say. "Because you're talking about being frustrated by many people, including Margo, and yet you're smiling."

His smile gets bigger. He has the whitest teeth I've ever seen. They're gleaming like diamonds. "I'm smiling, Sherlock, because I know *exactly* what's bothering my wife!"

"Ah!" I reply. "So—"

"Wait, wait. I'm getting to the best part," he interrupts. "So, like I said, I really *do* know what's wrong, but I'm not that interested in hearing another complaint. So this time, instead of asking, I decide I'm going to—"

He stops and peers at the clock on the bookshelf behind me.

I want to use this opportunity to help John slow down. I could comment on the glance at the clock (does he feel rushed in here?) or the fact that he just called me Sherlock (was he irritated with me?). Or I could stay more on the surface in what we call "the content"—the narrative he's telling—and try to understand more about why he equates Margo's feelings with a complaint. But if I stay in the content, we won't connect at all this session, and John, I'm learning, is somebody who has trouble making contact with the people in his life.

"John," I try again. "I wonder if we can go back to what just happened—"

"Oh, good," he says, cutting me off. "I still have twenty minutes left." And then he's back to his story.

I sense a yawn coming on, a strong one, and it takes what feels like superhuman strength to keep my jaw clenched tight. I can feel my muscles resisting, twisting my face into odd expressions, but thankfully the yawn stays inside. Unfortunately, what comes out instead is a burp. A loud one. As though I'm drunk. (I'm not. I'm a lot of unpleasant things in this moment, but drunk isn't one of them.)

Because of the burp, my mouth starts to pop open again. I squeeze my lips together so hard that my eyes begin to tear.

Of course, John doesn't seem to notice. He's still going on about Margo. *Margo did this. Margo did that. I said this. She said that. So then I said—*

During my training, a supervisor once told me, "There's something likable in everyone," and to my great surprise, I found that she was right. It's impossible to get to know people deeply and not come to like them. We should take the world's enemies, get them in a room to share their histories and formative experiences, their fears and their struggles, and global adversaries would suddenly get along. I've found something likable in literally everyone I've seen as a therapist, including the guy who attempted murder. (Beneath his rage, he turned out to be a real sweetheart.)

I didn't even mind the week before, at our first session, when John explained that he'd come to me because I was a "nobody" here in Los Angeles, which meant that he wouldn't run into any of his television-industry colleagues when coming for treatment. (His colleagues, he suspected, went to "well-known, *experienced* therapists.") I simply tagged that for future use, when he'd be more open to engaging with me. Nor did I flinch at the end of that session when he handed me a wad of cash and explained that he preferred to pay this way because he didn't want his wife to know he was seeing a therapist.

"You'll be like my mistress," he'd suggested. "Or, actually, more like my hooker. No offense, but you're not the kind of woman I'd choose as a mistress . . . if you know what I mean."

I *didn't* know what he meant (someone blonder? Younger? With whiter, more sparkly teeth?), but I figured that this comment was just one of John's defenses against getting close to anybody or acknowledging his need for another human being.

"Ha-ha, my hooker!" he said, pausing at the door. "I'll just come here each week, release all my pent-up frustration, and nobody has to know! Isn't that funny?"

Oh, yeah, I wanted to say, *super-funny.*

Still, as I heard him laugh his way down the hall, I felt confident that I could grow to like John. Underneath his off-putting presentation, something likable—even beautiful—was sure to emerge.

But that was last week.

Today he just seems like an asshole. An asshole with spectacular teeth.

Have compassion, have compassion, have compassion. I repeat my silent mantra then refocus on John. He's talking about a mistake made by one of the crew members on his show (a man whose name, in John's telling, is simply The Idiot) and just then, something occurs to me: John's rant sounds eerily familiar. Not the situations he's describing, but the feelings they evoke in him—and in *me.* I know how affirming it feels to blame the outside world for my frustrations, to deny ownership of whatever role I might have in the existential play called *My Incredibly Important Life.* I know what it's like to bathe in self-righteous outrage, in the certainty that I'm completely right and have been terribly wronged, because that's *exactly* how I've felt all day.

What John doesn't know is that I'm reeling from last night, when the man I thought I was going to marry unexpectedly called it quits. Today I'm trying to focus on my patients (allowing myself to cry only in the ten-minute breaks between sessions, carefully wiping away my running mascara before the next person arrives). In other words, I'm dealing with my pain the way I suspect John has been dealing with his: by covering it up.

As a therapist, I know a lot about pain, about the ways in which pain is tied to loss. But I also know something less commonly understood: that change and loss travel together. We can't have change without loss, which is why so often people say they want change but nonetheless stay exactly the same. To help John, I'm going to have to figure out what his loss would be, but first, I'm going to have to understand mine. Because right now, all I can think about is what my boyfriend did last night.

The idiot!

I look back at John and think: *I hear you, brother.*

Wait a minute, you might be thinking. *Why are you telling me all this? Aren't therapists supposed to keep their personal lives private? Aren't they supposed to be blank slates who never reveal anything about themselves, objective observers who refrain from calling their patients names—even in their heads? Besides, aren't therapists, of all people, supposed to have their lives together?*

On the one hand, yes. What happens in the therapy room should be done on behalf of the patient, and if therapists aren't able to separate their own struggles from those of the people who come to them, then they should, without question, choose a different line of work.

On the other hand, this—right here, right now, between you and me —isn't therapy, but a story about therapy: how we heal and where it leads us. Like in those National Geographic Channel shows that capture the embryonic development and birth of rare crocodiles, I want to capture the process in which humans, struggling to evolve, push against their shells until they quietly (but sometimes loudly) and slowly (but sometimes suddenly) crack open.

So while the image of me with mascara running down my tear-streaked face between sessions may be uncomfortable to contemplate, that's where this story about the handful of struggling humans you are about to meet begins—with my own humanity.

Therapists, of course, deal with the daily challenges of living just like everyone else. This familiarity, in fact, is at the root of the connection we forge with strangers who trust us with their most delicate stories and secrets. Our training has taught us theories and tools and techniques, but whirring beneath our hard-earned expertise is the fact that we know just how hard it is to be a person. Which is to say, we still come to work each day as ourselves—with our own sets of vulnerabilities, our own longings and insecurities, and our own histories. Of all my credentials as a therapist, my most significant is that I'm a card-carrying member of the human race.

But revealing this humanity is another matter. One colleague told me that when her doctor called with the news that her pregnancy wasn't viable, she was standing in a Starbucks, and she burst into tears. A patient happened to see her, canceled her next appointment, and never came back.

I remember hearing the writer Andrew Solomon tell a story about a married couple he'd met at a conference. During the course of the day, he said, each spouse had confessed independently to him to taking antidepressants but didn't want the other to know. It turned out that *they were hiding the same medication in the same house.* No matter how open we as a society are about formerly private matters, the stigma around our emotional struggles remains formidable. We'll talk with almost anyone about our physical health (can anyone imagine spouses hiding their reflux medication from each other?), even our sex lives, but bring up anxiety or depression or an intractable sense of grief, and the expression on the face looking back at you will probably read, *Get me out of this conversation, pronto.*

But what are we so afraid of? It's not as if we're going to peer in those darker corners, flip on the light, and find a bunch of cockroaches. Fireflies love the dark too. There's beauty in those places. But we have to look in there to see it.

My business, the therapy business, is about looking.

And not just with my patients.

A little-discussed fact: Therapists go to therapists. We're required, in fact, to go during training as part of our hours for licensure so that we know firsthand what our future patients will experience. We learn how to accept feedback, tolerate discomfort, become aware of blind spots, and discover the impact of our histories and behaviors on ourselves and others.

But then we get licensed, people come to seek *our* counsel and . . . we still go to therapy. Not continuously, necessarily, but a majority of us sit on somebody else's couch at several points during our careers, partly to have a place to talk through the emotional impact of the kind of work we do, but partly because life happens and therapy helps us confront our demons when they pay a visit.

And visit they will, because everyone has demons—big, small, old, new, quiet, loud, whatever. These shared demons are testament to the fact that we aren't such outliers after all. And it's with this discovery that we can create a different relationship with our demons, one in which we no longer try to reason our way out of an inconvenient inner voice or numb our feelings with distractions like too much wine or food or hours spent surfing the internet (an activity my colleague calls "the most effective short-term nonprescription painkiller").

One of the most important steps in therapy is helping people take responsibility for their current predicaments, because once they realize that they can (and must) construct their own lives, they're free to generate change. Often, though, people carry around the belief that the majority of their problems are circumstantial or situational—which is to say, external. And if the problems are caused by everyone and everything else, by stuff *out there,* why should they bother to change themselves? Even if they decide to do things differently, won't the rest of the world still be the same?

It's a reasonable argument. But that's not how life generally works.

Remember Sartre's famous line "Hell is other people"? It's true—the world is filled with difficult people (or, as John would have it, "idiots"). I'll bet you could name five truly difficult people off the top of your head right now—some you assiduously avoid, others you would assiduously avoid if they didn't share your last name. But sometimes—more often than we tend to realize—those difficult people are us.

That's right—sometimes hell is us.

Sometimes *we* are the cause of our difficulties. And if we can step out of our own way, something astonishing happens.

A therapist will hold up a mirror to patients, but patients will also hold up a mirror to their therapists. Therapy is far from one-sided; it happens in a parallel process. Every day, our patients are opening up questions that we have to think about for ourselves. If they can see themselves more clearly through our reflections, we can see ourselves more clearly through theirs. This happens to therapists when we're providing therapy, and it happens to our own therapists too. We are mirrors reflecting mirrors reflecting mirrors, showing one another what we can't yet see.

• • •

Which brings me back to John. Today, I'm not thinking about any of this. As far as I'm concerned, it's been a difficult day with a difficult patient, and to make matters worse, I'm seeing John right after a young newlywed who's dying of cancer—which is never an ideal time to see anyone, but especially not when you haven't gotten much sleep, and your marriage plans have just been canceled, and you know that your pain is trivial compared to that of a terminally ill woman, and you also sense (but aren't yet aware) that it's not trivial at all because something cataclysmic is happening inside you.

Meanwhile, about a mile away, in a quaint brick building on a narrow one-way street, a therapist named Wendell is in his office seeing patients too. One after another, they're sitting on his sofa, adjacent to a lovely garden courtyard, talking about the same kinds of things that my patients have been talking to me about on an upper floor of a tall glass office building. Wendell's patients have seen him for weeks or months or perhaps even years, but I have yet to meet him. In fact, I haven't even heard of him. But that's about to change.

I am about to become Wendell's newest patient.

2

If the Queen Had Balls

CHART NOTE, LORI:

Patient in her mid-forties presents for treatment in the aftermath of an unexpected breakup. Reports that she seeks "just a few sessions to get through this."

It all starts with a presenting problem.

By definition, the *presenting problem* is the issue that sends a person into therapy. It might be a panic attack, a job loss, a death, a birth, a relational difficulty, an inability to make a big life decision, or a bout of depression. Sometimes the presenting problem is less specific—a feeling of "stuckness" or the vague but nagging notion that something just isn't quite right.

Whatever the problem, it generally "presents" because the person has reached an inflection point in life. *Do I turn left or right? Do I try to preserve the status quo or move into uncharted territory?* (Be forewarned: therapy will always take you into uncharted territory, even if you choose to preserve the status quo.)

But people don't care about inflection points when they come for their first therapy session. Mostly, they just want relief. They want to tell you their stories, beginning with their presenting problem.

So let me fill you in on the Boyfriend Incident.

• • •

The first thing I want to say about Boyfriend is that he's an extraordinarily decent human being. He's kind and generous, funny and smart, and when he's not making you laugh, he'll drive to the drugstore at two a.m. to get you that antibiotic you just can't wait until morning for. If he happens to be at Costco, he'll text to ask if you need anything, and when you reply that you just need some laundry detergent, he'll bring home your favorite meatballs and twenty jugs of maple syrup for the waffles he makes you from scratch. He'll carry those twenty jugs from the garage to your kitchen, pack nineteen of them neatly into the tall cabinet you can't reach, and place one on the counter, accessible for the morning.

He'll also leave love notes on your desk, hold your hand and open doors, and never complain about being dragged to family events because he genuinely enjoys hanging out with your relatives, even the nosy or elderly ones. For no reason at all, he'll send you Amazon packages full of books (books being the equivalent of flowers to you), and at night you'll both curl up and read passages from them aloud to each other, pausing only to make out. While you're binge-watching Netflix, he'll rub that spot on your back where you have mild scoliosis, and when he stops, and you nudge him, he'll continue rubbing for exactly sixty more delicious seconds before he tries to weasel out without your noticing (you'll pretend not to notice). He'll let you finish his sandwiches and sentences and sunscreen and listen so attentively to the details of your day that, like your personal biographer, he'll remember more about your life than you will.

If this portrait sounds skewed, it is. There are many ways to tell a story, and if I've learned anything as a therapist, it's that most people are what therapists call "unreliable narrators." That's not to say that they purposely mislead. It's more that every story has multiple threads, and they tend to leave out the strands that don't jibe with their perspectives. Most of what patients tell me is absolutely true—from their current points of view. Ask about somebody's spouse while they're both still in love, then ask about that same spouse post-divorce, and each time, you'll get only half the story.

What you just heard about Boyfriend? That was the good half.

• • •

And now for the bad: It's ten o'clock on a weeknight. We're in bed, talking, and we've just decided which movie tickets to preorder for the weekend when Boyfriend goes strangely silent.

"You tired?" I ask. We're both working single parents in our mid-forties, so ordinarily an exhausted silence would mean nothing. Even when we aren't exhausted, sitting in silence together feels peaceful, relaxing. But if silence can be heard, tonight's silence sounds different. If you've ever been in love, you know the kind of silence I'm talking about: silence on a frequency only your significant other can perceive.

"No," he says. It's one syllable but his voice shakes subtly, followed by more unsettling silence. I look over at him. He looks back. He smiles, I smile, and a deafening silence descends again, broken only by the rustling sound his twitching foot is making under the covers. Now I'm alarmed. In my office I can sit through marathon silences, but in my bedroom I last no more than three seconds.

"Hey, is something up?" I ask, trying to sound casual, but it's a rhetorical question if ever there was one. The answer is obviously yes, because in the history of the world, nothing reassuring has ever followed this question. When I see couples in therapy, even if the initial response is no, in time the true answer is revealed to be some variation of *I'm cheating, I maxed out the credit cards, my aging mother is coming to live with us,* or *I'm not in love with you anymore.*

Boyfriend's response is no exception.

He says: "I've decided that I can't live with a kid under my roof for the next ten years."

I've decided that I can't live with a kid under my roof for the next ten years?

I burst out laughing. I know there's nothing funny about what Boyfriend has said, but given that we're planning to spend our lives together and I have an eight-year-old, it sounds so ridiculous that I decide it has to be a joke.

Boyfriend says nothing, so I stop laughing. I look at him. He looks away.

"What in the world are you *talking* about? What do mean, you can't live with a kid for the next ten years?"

"I'm sorry," he says.

"Sorry for what?" I ask, still catching up. "You mean you're serious? You don't want to be together?"

He explains that he *does* want to be together, but now that his teenagers are leaving for college soon, he's come to realize that he doesn't want to wait another ten years for the nest to be empty.

My jaw drops. Literally. I feel it open and hang in the air for a while. This is the first I'm hearing of this, and it takes a minute before my jaw is able to snap back into position so I can speak. My head is saying, *Whaaaaaat?* but my mouth says, "How long have you felt this way? If I hadn't just asked if something was up, when were you going to *tell* me?" I think about how this can't possibly be happening because just five minutes ago, we picked our movie for the weekend. We're supposed to be *together* this weekend. *At a movie!*

"I don't know," he says sheepishly. He shrugs without moving his shoulders. His entire body is a shrug. "It never felt like the right time to bring it up." (When my therapist friends hear this part of the story, they immediately diagnose him as "avoidant." When my nontherapist friends hear it, they immediately diagnose him as "an asshole.")

More silence.

I feel as though I'm viewing this scene from above, watching a confused version of myself move at incredible speed through the famous stages of grief: denial, anger, bargaining, depression, and acceptance. If my laughter was denial and my when-the-hell-were-you-going-to-tell-me was anger, I'm moving on to bargaining. How, I want to know, can we make this work? Can I take on more of the childcare? Add an extra date night?

Boyfriend shakes his head. His teenagers don't wake up at seven a.m. to play Legos, he says. He's looking forward to finally having his freedom, and he wants to relax on weekend mornings. Never mind that my son plays independently with his Legos in the mornings. The problem, apparently, is that my son occasionally says this: "Look at my Lego! Look what I made!"

"The thing is," Boyfriend explains, "I don't want to have to look at the Legos. I just want to read the paper."

I consider the possibility that an alien has invaded Boyfriend's body or that he has a burgeoning brain tumor of which this personality shift is the first symptom. I wonder what Boyfriend would think of me if I broke up with him because his teenage daughters wanted me to look at their new leggings from Forever 21 when I was trying to relax and read a book. *I don't want to look at the leggings. I just want to read my book.* What kind of person gets away with simply not wanting to look?

"I thought you wanted to marry me," I say, pathetically.

"I *do* want to marry you," he says. "I just don't want to live with a kid."

I think about this for a second, like a puzzle I'm trying to solve. It sounds like the riddle of the Sphinx.

"But I *come with a kid*," I say, my voice getting louder. I'm furious that he's bringing this up now, that he's bringing this up at all. "You can't order me up à la carte, like a burger without the fries, like a . . . a—" I think about patients who present ideal scenarios and insist that they can only be happy with that exact situation. *If he didn't drop out of business school to become a writer, he'd be my dream guy (so I'll break up with him and keep dating hedge-fund managers who bore me). If the job wasn't across the bridge, it would be the perfect opportunity (so I'll stay in my dead-end job and keep telling you how much I envy my friends' careers). If she didn't have a kid, I'd marry her.*

Certainly we all have our deal-breakers. But when patients repeatedly engage in this kind of analysis, sometimes I'll say, "If the queen had balls, she'd be the king." If you go through life picking and choosing, if you don't recognize that "the perfect is the enemy of the good," you may deprive yourself of joy. At first patients are taken aback by my bluntness, but ultimately it saves them months of treatment.

"The truth is, I didn't want to date somebody with a kid," Boyfriend is saying. "But then I fell in love with you, and I didn't know what to do."

"You didn't fall in love with me *before* our first date, when I told you I had a six-year-old," I say. "You knew what to do *then*, didn't you?"

More suffocating silence.

As you've probably guessed, this conversation goes nowhere. I try to understand if it's about something else—how could it not be about something else? After all, his wanting his freedom is the ultimate "It's not you, it's me" (always code for *It's not me, it's you*). Is Boyfriend unhappy with something in the relationship that he's afraid to tell me about? I ask him calmly, my voice softer now, because I'm mindful of the fact that Very Angry People aren't Very Approachable. But Boyfriend insists that it's only about his wanting to live without kids, not without me.

I'm in a state of shock mixed with bewilderment. I don't understand how this has never come up. How do you sleep soundly next to a person and plan a life with her when you're secretly grappling with whether to leave? (The answer is simple—a common defense mechanism called compartmentalization. But right now I'm too busy using another defense mechanism, denial, to see it.)

Boyfriend, by the way, is an attorney, and he lays it all out as he would in front of a jury. He really does want to marry me. He really does love me. He just wants much more time with me. He wants to be able to leave spontaneously together for the weekend or come home from work and go out to eat without worrying about a third person. He wants the privacy of a couple, not the communal feel of a family. When he learned I had a young child, he told himself it wasn't ideal, but he said nothing to me because he thought he could adjust. Two years later, though, as we're about to merge our homes, just as his freedom is in sight, he's realized how important this is. He knew things had to end, but he also didn't want them to—and even when he thought about telling me, he didn't know how to bring it up because of how far in we were already and how angry I'd likely be. He hesitated to tell me, he says, because he didn't want to be a jerk.

The defense rests and is also very sorry.

"You're sorry?" I spit out. "Well, guess what. By trying NOT to be a jerk, you've made yourself into the world's BIGGEST jerk!"

He goes quiet again, and it hits me: His eerie silence earlier *was* his way of bringing this up. And although we go round and round on this until the sun peeks through the shutters, we both know in a bone-deep way that there's nothing else to say.

I have a kid. He wants freedom. Kids and freedom are mutually exclusive.

If the queen had balls, she'd be the king.

Voilà—I had my presenting problem.

3

The Space of a Step

Telling somebody you're a psychotherapist often leads to a surprised pause, followed by awkward questions like these: "Oh, a therapist! Should I tell you about my childhood?" Or "Can you help me with this problem with my mother-in-law?" Or "Are you going to psychoanalyze me?" (The answers, by the way, are "Please, don't"; "Possibly"; and "Why would I do that *here?* If I were a gynecologist, would you ask if I was about to give you a pelvic exam?")

But I understand where these responses come from. It boils down to fear—of being exposed, of being found out. *Will you spot the insecurities that I'm so skillful at hiding? Will you see my vulnerabilities, my lies, my shame?*

Will you see the human *in my being?*

It strikes me that the people I'm talking to at a barbecue or dinner party don't seem to wonder whether *they* might see *me* and the qualities I, too, try to hide in polite company. Once they hear that I'm a therapist, I morph into somebody who might peer into their psyches if they aren't careful to deflect the conversation with therapist jokes or walk away to refill a drink as soon as possible.

Sometimes, though, people will ask more questions, like "What kind of people do you see in your practice?" I tell them I see people just like any of us, which is to say, just like whoever is asking. Once I told a curious couple at a Fourth of July gathering that I see a good number of couples in my practice, and they proceeded to get into an argument right in front of me. He wanted to know why she seemed so interested in what a couples therapist does—after all, *they* weren't having problems (uncomfortable chuckle). She wanted to know why he had no interest in the emotional lives of couples—after all, maybe they could use some help (glare). But was I thinking about them as a therapy case? Not at all. This time, I was the one who left the conversation to "get a refill."

Therapy elicits odd reactions because, in a way, it's like pornography. Both involve a kind of nudity. Both have the potential to thrill. And both have millions of users, most of whom keep their use private. Though statisticians have attempted to quantify the number of people in therapy, their results are thought to be skewed because many people who go to therapy choose not to admit it.

But those underreported numbers are still high. In any given year, some thirty million American adults are sitting on clinicians' couches, and the United States isn't even the world leader in therapy. (Fun fact: the countries with the most therapists per capita are, in descending order, Argentina, Austria, Australia, France, Canada, Switzerland, Iceland, and the United States.)

Given that I'm a therapist, you'd think that the morning after the Boyfriend Incident, it might occur to me to see a therapist myself. I work in a suite of a dozen therapists, my building is full of therapists, and I've belonged to several consultation groups in which therapists discuss their cases together, so I'm well versed in the therapy world.

But as I lie paralyzed in the fetal position, that's not the call I make.

"He's trash!" my oldest friend, Allison, says after I tell her the story from my bed before my son wakes up. "Good riddance! What kind of person *does* that—not just to you, but to your kid?"

"Right!" I agree. "Who *does* this?" We spend about twenty minutes bashing Boyfriend. During an initial burst of pain, people tend to lash out either at others or at themselves, to turn the anger outward or inward. Allison and I are choosing outward, baby! She's in the Midwest, commuting to work, two hours ahead of me here on the West Coast, and she gets right to the point.

"You know what you should do?" she says.

"What?" I feel like I've been stabbed in the heart, and I'll do anything to stop the pain.

"You should go sleep with somebody! Go sleep with somebody and forget about the Kid Hater." I instantly love Boyfriend's new name: the Kid Hater. "Clearly he wasn't the person you thought he was. Go take your mind off of him."

Married for twenty years to her college sweetheart, Allison has no idea how to give guidance to single people.

"It might help you bounce back faster, like falling off a bike and then getting right back on," she continues. "And don't roll your eyes."

Allison knows me well. I'm rolling my red, stinging eyes.

"Okay, I'll go sleep with someone," I squeak out, knowing she's trying to make me laugh. But then I'm sobbing again. I feel like a sixteen-year-old going through her first breakup, and I can't believe I'm having this reaction in my forties.

"Oh, hon," Allison says, her voice like a hug. "I'm here, and you'll get through this."

"I know," I say, except that in a strange way, I don't. There's a popular saying, a paraphrase of a Robert Frost poem: "The only way out is through." The only way to get to the other side of the tunnel is to go *through* it, not *around* it. But I can't even picture the entrance right now.

After Allison parks her car and promises to call at her first break, I look at the clock: 6:30 a.m. I call my friend Jen, who's a therapist with a practice across town. She picks up on the first ring and I hear her husband in the background asking who it is. Jen whispers, "I *think* it's Lori?" She must have seen the caller ID, but I'm crying so hard I haven't even said hello yet. If it weren't for caller ID, she'd think I was some sicko prank-calling.

I catch my breath and tell her what happened. She listens attentively. She keeps saying that she can't believe it. We also spend twenty minutes trashing Boyfriend, and then I hear her daughter enter the room and say that she needs to get to school early for swim practice.

"I'll call you at lunch," Jen says. "But in the meantime, I don't know that this is the end of the story. Something's screwy. Unless he's a sociopath, it doesn't jibe at all with what I saw for the past two years."

"Exactly," I say. "Which means he's a sociopath."

I hear her take a sip of water and put the glass down.

"In that case," she says, swallowing, "I have a great guy for you—one who's not a kid hater." She also likes Boyfriend's new name. "In a few weeks, when you're ready, I want to introduce you."

I almost smile at the preposterousness of this. What I really need just hours into this breakup is for somebody to sit with me in my pain, but I also know how helpless it feels to watch a friend suffer and do nothing to fix it. Sitting-with-you-in-your-pain is one of the rare experiences that people get in the protected space of a therapy room, but it's very hard to give or get outside of it—even for Jen, who *is* a therapist.

When we're off the phone, I think about her "in a few weeks" comment. Could I really go on a date in just a few weeks? I imagine being out with a well-meaning guy who's doing his best to make first-date conversation; without knowing it, he'll make a reference to something that reminds me of Boyfriend (pretty much everything will remind me of Boyfriend, I'm convinced), and I won't be able to hold back tears. Crying on a first date is decidedly a turnoff. A therapist crying on a first date is both a turnoff and alarming. Besides, I have the bandwidth to focus only on the immediate present.

Right now it's all about one foot, then the other.

That's one thing I tell patients who are in the midst of crippling depression, the kind that makes them think, *There's the bathroom. It's about five feet away. I see it, but I can't get there.* One foot, then the other. Don't look at all five feet at once. Just take a step. And when you've taken that step, take one more. Eventually you'll make it to the shower. And you'll make it to tomorrow and next year too. *One step.* They may not be able to imagine their depression lifting anytime soon, but they don't need to. Doing something prompts you to do something else, replacing a vicious cycle with a virtuous one. Most big transformations come about from the hundreds of tiny, almost imperceptible, steps we take along the way.

A lot can happen in the space of a step.

Somehow I manage to wake my son, prepare breakfast, pack his lunch, make conversation, drop him at school, and drive to work, all without shedding a tear. *I can do this,* I think as I ride the elevator up to my office. *One foot, then the other.* One fifty-minute session at a time.

I enter my suite, say hello to colleagues in the hallway, unlock the door to my office, and go through my routine: I put away my belongings, turn off the phone ringers, unlock the files, and fluff the pillows on the couch. Then, uncharacteristically, I take a seat on it myself. I look at my empty therapist chair and consider the view from this side of the room. It's oddly comforting. I stay there until the tiny green light by the door flicks on, letting me know that my first patient is here.

I'm ready, I think. One foot, then the other. *I'm going to be fine.*

Except that I'm not.

4

The Smart One or
the Hot One

I've always been drawn to stories—not just what happens, but how the story is told. When people come to therapy, I'm listening to their narratives but also for their *flexibility* with them. Do they consider what they're saying to be the only version of the story—the "accurate" version—or do they know that theirs is just one of many ways to tell it? Are they aware of what they're choosing to leave in or out, of how their motivation in sharing this story affects how the listener hears it?

I thought a lot about those questions in my twenties—not in relation to therapy patients, but in relation to movie and TV characters. That's why, as soon as I graduated from college, I got a job in the entertainment business, or what everyone called, simply, "Hollywood."

This job was at a large talent agency, and I worked as the assistant to a junior film agent who, like many people in Hollywood, wasn't much older than me. Brad represented screenwriters and directors, and he was so boyish-looking, with his smooth cheeks and mop of floppy hair he'd constantly swat from his eyes, that his fancy suits and expensive shoes always seemed too mature for him, like he was wearing his father's clothing.

Technically, my first day on the job was a trial. I'd been told by Gloria in human resources (I never learned her last name; everyone called her

"Gloria-in-human-resources") that Brad had narrowed down his assistant candidates to two finalists, and each of us would work for a day as a test run. On the afternoon of mine, returning from the Xerox room, I overheard my prospective boss and another agent, his mentor, talking in his office.

"Gloria-in-human-resources wants an answer by tonight," I heard Brad say. "Should I pick the smart one or the hot one?"

I froze, appalled.

"Always pick the smart one," the other agent replied, and I wondered which one Brad considered me to be.

An hour later, I got the job. And despite finding the question outrageously inappropriate, I felt perversely hurt.

Still, I wasn't sure why Brad had pegged me as smart. All I'd done that day was dial a string of phone numbers (repeatedly disconnecting calls by pressing the wrong buttons on the confusing phone system), make coffee (which was sent back twice), Xerox a script (I pushed *10* instead of *1* for number of copies, then hid the nine extra screenplays under a couch in the break room), and trip over a lamp cord in Brad's office and fall on my ass.

The hot one, I concluded, must have been particularly stupid.

Technically, my position was "motion-picture literary assistant," but really I was a secretary who rolled the call list all day, dialing the numbers of studio executives and filmmakers, telling each person's assistant that my boss was on the line, then patching my boss through. It was widely known in the industry that assistants were expected to listen in silently on these calls so that we'd know what scripts had to be sent where without the need for instructions later. Sometimes, though, the parties on the calls would forget about us, and we'd hear all kinds of juicy gossip about our bosses' famous friends—who'd had an argument with a spouse or which studio executive was "very confidentially" about to be sent to "producers pasture," shorthand for being given a vanity production deal on the studio lot. If the person my boss was trying to reach wasn't available, I'd "leave word" and move on to the next name on the hundred-person call sheet, sometimes being instructed to strategically return calls at inopportune times (before nine thirty a.m., because nobody in Hollywood arrived at work before ten, or, less subtly, during lunch) in order to miss the person on purpose.

Although the movie world was glamorous—Brad's Rolodex was filled with the home numbers and addresses of people I'd admired for years—the job of an assistant was its opposite. As an assistant, you fetched coffee, made haircut and pedicure appointments, picked up dry cleaning, screened calls from parents or exes, Xeroxed and messengered documents, took cars to the mechanic, ran personal errands, and always, without fail, brought chilled bottled water into every meeting (never saying a word to the writers or directors present, whom you were dying to meet).

Finally, late at night, you'd type up ten pages of single-spaced notes on scripts that came in from the agency's clients so that your boss could make insightful comments in meetings the next day without having to read anything. We assistants put a lot of effort into those script notes in order to demonstrate that we were bright and capable and could one day (please, God!) stop doing assistant work, with its mind-numbing duties, long hours, minimal pay, and no overtime compensation.

A few months into the job, it became apparent that while the hot ones at my agency got all the attention—and there were many hot ones in the assistant pool—the smart ones got assigned all the extra work. In my first year there, I slept very little because I was reading and writing comments on a dozen scripts a week—all after hours and on weekends. But I didn't mind. In fact, that was my favorite part of the job. I learned how to craft stories and fell in love with fascinating characters with complicated inner lives. As the months went by, I got slightly more confident in my instincts, less worried about sharing a silly story idea.

Soon I was hired as an entry-level film executive at a production company, with the title story editor; here I got to participate in meetings while another assistant brought in the bottled water. I worked closely with writers and directors, hunkering down in a room and going over material scene by scene, helping to make changes the studio wanted without having the writers, who often felt protective of their material, fly into a rage or threaten to quit the project. (These negotiations would turn out to be great practice for couples therapy.)

Sometimes, to avoid distractions at the office, I'd work with filmmakers early in the morning in my tiny starter apartment, picking up breakfast snacks the night before while thinking, *John Lithgow is going to be eating this bagel in my crappy living room with the hideous wall-to-wall carpet and popcorn ceilings tomorrow! Could it get any better than this?*

And then it did—or so I thought. I got promoted. It was a promotion I'd worked hard for and wanted very badly. Until I actually got it.

The irony of my job was that a lot of the creative work happens when you don't have much experience. When you're just starting out, you're the behind-the-scenes person, the one who does all the script work at the office while the higher-level people are out wooing talent, lunching with agents, or stopping by movie sets to check in on the company's productions. When you become a development executive, you go from being what's known as an internal executive to an external one, and if you were the social kid in high school, this is the job for you. But if you were the bookish kid who was happiest working intently with a couple of friends in the library, be careful what you wish for.

Now I was out awkwardly attempting to socialize at lunches and meetings all day. On top of that, the pace of the process began to feel glacial. It could take ages—literally years—for a film to be made, and I got the sinking feeling that I was in the wrong job. I'd moved into a duplex with a friend, and she pointed out that I'd been watching a lot of TV every night. Like, in a pathological way.

"You seem depressed," she said with concern. I said I wasn't depressed; I was just bored. I hadn't considered that if the only thing that keeps you going all day is knowing you'll get to turn on the TV after dinner, you probably *are* depressed.

One day around this time, I was sitting at lunch in a perfectly nice restaurant with a perfectly lovely agent who was talking about a perfectly good deal she had made when I noticed that four words kept running through my mind: *I. Just. Don't. Care.* No matter what the agent said, these four words played in a loop, and they didn't stop when the check came, nor did they stop on the drive back to the office. They rattled around in my head the next day, too, and for the next several weeks, until finally I had to admit, months later, that they weren't going away. *I. Just. Don't. Care.*

And since the only thing I *did* seem to care about was watching TV — since the only time I felt anything (or, perhaps more accurately, the only time I felt the absence of something unpleasant that I couldn't quite put my finger on) was when I was immersed in these imaginary worlds with new episodes arriving weekly like clockwork — I applied for a job in television. Within a few months, I began working in series development at NBC.

It felt like a dream come true. I thought, *I'll get to help tell stories again. Even better, instead of developing self-contained films with neatly crafted endings, I'll get to work on series. Over the course of multiple episodes and seasons, I'll have a hand in helping audiences get to know their favorite characters, layer by layer — characters as flawed and contradictory as the rest of us, with stories that are just as messy.*

It seemed like the perfect solution to my boredom. It would take years for me to realize that I'd solved the wrong problem.

5

Namast'ay in Bed

CHART NOTE, JULIE:

Thirty-three-year-old university professor presents for help in dealing with cancer diagnosis upon returning from her honeymoon.

"Is that a pajama top?" Julie asks as she walks into my office. It's the afternoon after the Boyfriend Incident, right before my appointment with John (and his idiots), and I've almost made it through the day.

I give her a quizzical look.

"Your shirt," she says, settling onto the couch.

I flash back to the morning, to the gray sweater I intended to wear and then, with a sinking feeling, to the image of the sweater laid out on my bed next to the gray pajama top I'd taken off before stepping into the shower in my post-breakup daze.

Oh God.

On one of his Costco runs, Boyfriend had gotten me a pack of PJs, their fronts emblazoned with sayings like AREN'T I JUST A FUCKING RAY OF SUNSHINE and TALK NERDY TO ME and ZZZZZZZZZZ SNORE (*not* the message a therapist wants to send her patients). I'm trying to remember which one I wore last night.

I brace myself and glance down. My top says NAMAST'AY IN BED. Julie is looking at me, waiting for an answer.

Whenever I'm not sure what to say in the therapy room—which happens to therapists more often than patients realize—I have a choice: I can say nothing until I understand the moment better, or I can attempt an answer, but whatever I do, I must tell the truth. So while I'm tempted to say that I do yoga and that my top is simply a casual T-shirt, both would be lies. Julie does yoga as part of her Mindful Cancer program, and if she starts talking about various poses, I'd have to lie further and pretend that I'm familiar with them—or admit that I lied.

I remember when, during my training, a fellow intern told a patient he would be out of the clinic for three weeks, and she asked where he was going.

"I'm going to Hawaii," the intern said truthfully.

"For vacation?" the patient asked.

"Yes," he replied, even though, technically, he was going for his wedding, which was to be followed by a two-week island honeymoon.

"That's a long vacation," the patient remarked, and the intern, believing that sharing the news of his wedding would be too personal, decided instead to focus on the patient's comment. What would it be like for her to miss three weeks of sessions? What did her feelings about his absence remind her of? Both of which might be fruitful avenues to explore, but so would the patient's indirect question: *Since it's neither summer nor a holiday season, why are you really taking three weeks off?* And sure enough, when the intern returned to work, the patient noticed his wedding ring and felt betrayed: "Why didn't you just tell me the truth?"

In retrospect, the intern wished he had. So what if a patient learned that he was getting married? Therapists get married and patients have reactions to that. Those can be worked through. Loss of trust is harder to repair.

Freud argued that "the physician should be impenetrable to the patient, and like a mirror, reflect nothing but what is shown to him." Nowadays, though, most therapists use some form of what's known as self-disclosure in their work, whether it's sharing some of their own reactions that come up during the session or acknowledging that they watch the TV show that a patient keeps referring to. (Better to admit that you watch *The Bachelor* than to feign ignorance and slip up by naming a cast member the patient hasn't mentioned yet.)

Inevitably, though, the question of what to share gets tricky. One therapist I know told a patient whose child was diagnosed with Tourette's syndrome that she, too, had a son with Tourette's—and it deepened their relationship. Another colleague treated a man whose father had committed suicide but never revealed to the patient that his own father had also committed suicide. In each situation, there's a calculation to make, a subjective litmus test we use to assess the value of the disclosure: Is this information helpful for the patient to have?

When done well, self-disclosure can bridge some distance with patients who feel isolated in their experiences, and it can encourage more openness. But if it's perceived as inappropriate or self-indulgent, the patient will feel uncomfortable and start to shut down—or simply flee.

"Yes," I tell Julie. "It's a pajama top. I guess I put it on by mistake."

I wait, wondering what she'll say. If she asks why, I'll tell the truth (although not the specifics): I wasn't paying attention this morning.

"Oh," she says. Then her mouth twitches the way it does when she's about to cry, but instead, she starts laughing.

"I'm sorry, I'm not laughing at you. *Namast'ay in Bed* . . . that's exactly how I feel!"

She tells me about a woman in her Mindful Cancer program who's convinced that if Julie doesn't take yoga seriously—along with the famous pink ribbons and the optimism—her cancer will kill her. Never mind that Julie's oncologist has already informed her that her cancer will kill her. This woman still insists it can be cured with yoga.

Julie despises her.

"Imagine if I walked into yoga wearing that top and—"

Now she's laughing uncontrollably, reining it in and then bursting out with another round. I haven't seen Julie laugh once since she learned she was dying. This must be what she was like in what she calls "B.C." or "Before Cancer," when she was happy and healthy and falling in love with her soon-to-be husband. Her laughter is like a song, and it's so contagious that I start laughing too.

We both sit there laughing, her at the sanctimonious woman, and me at my mistake—at the ways in which our minds betray us as much as our bodies do.

Julie discovered her cancer while having sex with her husband on a beach in Tahiti. She didn't suspect it was cancer, though. Her breast felt tender, and later, in the shower, the tender spot felt funky, but often she had areas that felt funky and her gynecologist always found them to be glands that changed size at certain times of the month. Anyway, she thought, maybe she was pregnant. She and her new husband, Matt, had been together for three years and both had talked about wanting to start a family as soon as they got married. In the weeks before the wedding, they hadn't been vigilant about birth control.

It was a good time to have a baby too. Julie had just gotten tenure at her university, and after years of hard work, she could finally take a breath. Now there would be more time for her passions: running marathons and climbing mountains and baking silly cakes for her nephew. There would also be time for marriage and parenthood.

When Julie got back from her honeymoon, she peed on a stick and showed it to Matt, who picked her up and danced around the room with her. They decided that the song that happened to be on the radio—"Walking on Sunshine"—would be their baby's theme song. Excited, they went to the obstetrician for their first prenatal appointment, and when her doctor felt the "gland" that Julie had noticed on her honeymoon, his smile faded slightly.

"It's probably nothing," he said, "but let's get it checked out."

It wasn't nothing. Young, newly married, and pregnant, with no family history of breast cancer, Julie had been struck by the randomness of the universe. Then, while grappling with how to handle the cancer treatment and the pregnancy, she had a miscarriage.

This was when Julie landed in my office.

It was an odd referral, given that I wasn't a therapist who specialized in treating people with cancer. But my lack of expertise was exactly why Julie wanted to see me. She had told her physician that she didn't want a therapist from "the cancer team." She wanted to feel normal, to be part of the living. And since her doctors seemed confident that she'd be fine after surgery and chemo, she wanted to focus on both getting through the treatment and being newly married. (What should she say in her wedding-gift thank-you notes? *Thanks so much for the lovely bowl . . . I keep it by my bed to vomit in?*)

The treatment was brutal but Julie got better. The day after her doctors declared her "tumor-free," she and Matt went on a hot-air balloon ride with their closest friends and family. It was the first week of summer, and as they joined arms and watched the sunset from a thousand feet above the earth, Julie no longer felt cheated, as she had during the treatment, but lucky. Yes, she'd gone through hell. But it was behind her, and her future lay ahead. In six months, she would get a final scan, a sign-off, to clear her for pregnancy. That night, she dreamed that she was in her sixties and holding her first grandchild.

Julie was in good spirits. Our work was done.

I didn't see Julie between the hot-air balloon ride and the scan. But I did start getting calls from other cancer patients who'd been referred by Julie's oncologist. There's nothing like illness to take away a sense of control, even if we often have less of it than we imagine. What people don't like to think about is that you can do everything right—in life or in a treatment protocol—and still get the short end of the stick. And when that happens, the only control you have is how you deal with that stick—*your* way, not the way others say you should. I'd let Julie do it her way—I was so inexperienced that I didn't have a strong sense of what a "way" should look like —and it seemed to help.

"Whatever you did with her," Julie's oncologist said, "she seemed pleased with the outcome."

I knew that I hadn't done anything brilliant with Julie. Mostly, I worked hard not to flinch from her rawness. But that rawness went only so far because we weren't even thinking about death then. Instead, we discussed wigs versus scarves, sex and postsurgery body image. And I helped her think through how to manage her marriage, parents, and work, much the way I might with any patient.

Then one day I checked my messages and heard Julie's voice. She wanted to see me right away.

She came in the next morning, ashen. The scan that was supposed to show nothing had instead found a rare form of cancer, different from the original. In all likelihood, this cancer was going to kill her. It might take a year or five or, if things went very well, ten. Of course, they would explore experimental treatments, but they were just that—experimental.

"Will you stay with me until I die?" Julie asked, and though my instinct was to do what people tend to do whenever somebody brings up death, which is to deny death completely (*Oh, hey, let's not go there yet. Those experimental treatments might work*), I had to remember that I was there to help Julie, not comfort myself.

Still, at the moment she asked, I was stunned, still absorbing the news. I wasn't sure I was the best person for this. What if I said or did the wrong thing? Would I offend her if my feelings—discomfort, fear, sadness—came across in my facial expressions or body language? She was going to get only one chance at doing this the way she wanted. What if I let her down?

She must have seen my hesitation.

"*Please*," she said. "I know it's not a picnic, but I can't go to those cancer people. It's like a cult. They call everyone 'brave,' but what choice do we have, and besides, I'm terrified and still cringe at the sight of the needles like I did as a kid getting my shots. I'm not brave and I'm not a warrior fighting a battle. I'm just an ordinary college professor." She leaned forward on the couch. "They have *affirmations* on their walls. So, please?"

Looking at Julie, I couldn't say no. More important, now I didn't want to.

And right then, the nature of our work together changed: I was going to help her come to terms with her death.

This time, my inexperience might matter.

6

Finding Wendell

"Maybe you should talk to someone," Jen suggests two weeks after the breakup. She has just called to check on me at work. "You need to find a place where you're not being a therapist," she adds. "You need to go where you can completely fall apart."

I look at myself in the mirror that hangs by the door in my office, the one I use to make sure I don't have lipstick on my teeth when I'm about to retrieve a patient from the waiting room after a quick snack between sessions. I appear normal, but I feel dizzy and disoriented. I'm fine with patients—seeing patients is a relief, a full fifty minutes of respite from my own life—but outside of sessions, I'm losing it. In fact, as each day goes by, I seem worse, not better.

I can't sleep. I can't concentrate. Since the breakup, I've left my credit card at Target, driven out of the gas station with my tank's cap hanging off, and fallen off a step in my garage, badly bruising my knee. My chest hurts as if my heart has been crushed, though I know it hasn't been, because if anything, my heart is working harder, beating rapidly 24/7—a sign of anxiety. I obsess about Boyfriend's state of mind, which I imagine is calm and unconflicted, while I lie on my bedroom floor at night and miss him. Then I obsess about whether I really miss him—did I even *know* him? Do I miss him, or do I miss the idea of him?

So when Jen says I should see a therapist, I know she's right. I need someone to help me through this crisis.

But who?

Finding a therapist is a tricky thing. It's not like looking for, say, a good internist or dentist because pretty much everyone needs an internist or dentist. A therapist, though? Consider:

1. If you ask somebody for a therapist recommendation and that person isn't seeing a therapist, he or she might be offended that you'd made that assumption. Similarly, if you ask somebody for a therapist recommendation and that person *is* seeing a therapist, he or she might be upset that it was so apparent to you. *Of all the people she knows,* this person might wonder, *why did she think to ask* me?

2. When you inquire, you risk this person asking why you want to see a therapist. "What's wrong?" this person might say. "Is it your marriage? Are you depressed?" Even if people don't ask this aloud, every time they see you, they might be silently wondering, *What's wrong? Is it your marriage? Are you depressed?*

3. If your friend does give you her therapist's name, there might be unexpected checks and balances to what you say in the therapy room. If, for instance, your friend recounts to this therapist a not-so-flattering incident that involves you, and you give a different version of this same incident—or omit it altogether—the therapist will see you in a way you haven't chosen to present. But you won't know what the therapist knows about you, because the therapist can't mention anything said in somebody else's session.

These caveats notwithstanding, word of mouth is often an effective way to find a therapist. You can also go on PsychologyToday.com and sort through profiles in your area. But however you do it, you may need to meet with a few before you find the right one. That's because clicking with your therapist matters in a way that it doesn't with other clinicians (as another therapist said: "It's not the same as choosing a good cardiologist who sees you maybe twice a year and will never know about your massive insecurity"). Study after study shows that *the* most important factor in the success of your treatment is your relationship with the therapist, your experience of "feeling felt." This matters more than the therapist's training, the kind of therapy they do, or what type of problem you have.

But I have unique constraints in finding a therapist. To avoid an ethical breach known as a dual relationship, I can't treat or receive treatment from any person in my orbit—not a parent of a kid in my son's class, not the sister of my coworker, not a friend's mom, not my neighbor. The relationship in the therapy room needs to be its own, distinct and apart. These rules don't hold for other health-care clinicians. You can play tennis or be in a book club with your surgeon, dermatologist, or chiropractor, but not with your therapist.

This narrows my prospects dramatically. I'm friendly with, refer patients to, go to conferences with, or otherwise associate with numerous therapists in town. On top of that, my friends who are therapists, like Jen, know many of the same therapists I do. Even if Jen referred me to one of her colleagues that I don't know, there would be something awkward about her being friendly with my therapist—it's too close. And as for my asking my colleagues? Well, there's this: I don't want my colleagues to know I'm seeking urgent therapy. Might they hesitate, consciously or not, to send referrals my way?

So while I'm surrounded by therapists, my predicament conjures that Coleridge line "Water, water, everywhere / Nor any drop to drink."

But by the end of the day, I have an idea.

My colleague Caroline isn't in my suite, or even in my building. She's not a friend, although we're professionally friendly. Sometimes we share cases —I'll see a couple, and she'll see one of the members of the couple individually, or vice versa. Any referral she'd have, I'd trust.

I dial her cell at ten to the hour, and she picks up.

"Hi, how are you?" she asks.

I say I'm great. "Absolutely *great*," I repeat enthusiastically. I don't mention the fact that I've barely slept or eaten and feel like I might faint. I ask how she is, then get right to the point.

"I need a referral," I say, "for a friend."

I quickly explain that this "friend" is looking specifically for a male therapist to keep Caroline from wondering why I'm not referring my friend to her.

Through the phone, I can almost hear the gears turning in her head. About three-fourths of clinicians who do therapy (as opposed to research, psychological testing, or medication management) are women, so it takes some thought for her to find a man. I add that the one male therapist in my office suite, who happens to be one of the most talented therapists I know, won't work out for this friend because this friend doesn't feel comfortable doing therapy at my office, where we share a waiting room.

"Hmm," Caroline says. "Let me think. It's a male patient who wants the referral?"

"Yes, he's in his forties," I say. "High-functioning."

High-functioning is therapist code for "a good patient," the kind most therapists enjoy working with, often to balance out the patients we also want to work with but who are less high-functioning. High-functioning patients are those who can form relationships, manage adult responsibilities, and have a capacity for self-reflection. The kind who don't call daily between sessions with emergencies. Studies show, and common sense dictates, that most therapists prefer to work with patients who are verbal, motivated, open, and responsible—these are the patients who improve more quickly. I include the high-functioning bit with Caroline because it broadens the range of therapists who might be interested in this case, and, well, I consider myself to be relatively high-functioning. (At least, I did until recently.)

"I think he'd feel more comfortable with a male therapist who's also married with kids," I continue.

I add this for a reason too. I know this isn't a fair assumption, but I'm afraid that a female therapist might be predisposed to empathize with me post-breakup and that a male therapist who's neither married nor a father won't understand the nuances of the kid part of the situation. In short, I want to see if an *objective male professional who has firsthand experience of marriage and kids*—a man just like Boyfriend—will be as appalled at Boyfriend's behavior as I am, because then I'll know that my reaction is normal and I'm not going insane after all.

Yes, I'm seeking objectivity, but only because I'm convinced that objectivity will rule in my favor.

I hear Caroline clicking away on her keyboard. *Tap, tap, tap.*

"How about—no, scratch that, he thinks much too highly of himself," she says of some unnamed therapist. She goes back to her keyboard.

Tap, tap, tap.

"There's a colleague who used to be in my consultation group," she begins. "But I'm not sure. He's great. Very skilled. He always has insightful things to say. It's just—"

Caroline hesitates.

"Just what?"

"He's so *happy* all the time. It feels . . . *unnatural.* Like, what the hell is he so happy about? But some patients like that. Do you think your friend would do well with him?"

"Definitely not," I say. I, too, am suspicious of chronically happy people.

Next Caroline names a good therapist I also know relatively well, so I tell her that he won't work out for my friend because there's a *conflict* —therapist shorthand for "Their worlds collide, but I can't reveal more."

She clicks around again—*tap, tap, tap*—then stops.

"Oh, hey, there's a psychologist named Wendell Bronson," Caroline says. "I haven't talked to him in years, but we trained together and he's smart. Married with kids. Late forties or so, been doing this a long time. Do you want his info?"

I say I do. I mean, "my friend" does. We exchange some pleasantries and then hang up.

At this point, all I know about Wendell is what Caroline has just told me and that there's two-hour free parking in the lot across the street from his office. I know about the parking because when Caroline texts me his phone number and address a minute after our call, I realize that my bikini-wax place happens to be on the same street (*Not that I'll be needing those services for the foreseeable future,* I think, which makes me start crying again).

I pull it together long enough to dial Wendell's number, and of course I get voicemail. Therapists rarely answer their office phones so that patients won't feel rebuffed if they call in a crisis and their therapists have only a few minutes between sessions to speak. Colleague-to-colleague calls are made via cell phone or pager.

I hear a generic outgoing recording ("Hi, you've reached the office of Wendell Bronson. I return my calls during business hours Monday through Friday. If this is an emergency, please call . . ."), and after the beep I leave a concise message with exactly the information a therapist wants—name, one-liner about why I'm calling, and return phone number. I'm doing well until, thinking it might get me in to see him sooner, I add that I'm also a therapist, but my voice cracks as I say the word *therapist*. Mortified, I cover with a cough and quickly hang up.

When Wendell calls me back an hour later, I try to sound as together as possible as I explain that I just need a little crisis management, a few weeks to "process" an unexpected breakup, and then I'll be good to go. I've done therapy before, I say, so I come "preshrunk." He doesn't laugh at my joke so I'm pretty sure he has no sense of humor, but it doesn't matter because I don't need a sense of humor for crisis management.

This is, after all, just about getting me back on my feet.

Wendell says about five words the entire call. I use the term *words* loosely because it's more like a bunch of *Uh-huh*s before he offers a nine o'clock appointment the next morning. I accept and we're done.

Although Wendell didn't say much, our conversation provides me with immediate relief. I know this is a common placebo effect: patients often feel hopeful after making that first appointment, before even setting foot in the therapy room. I'm no different. *Tomorrow*, I think, *I'll get help with this. Yes, I'm a mess now because this whole thing is a shock, but soon I'll make sense of it* (that is, Wendell will confirm that Boyfriend is a sociopath). *When I look back, this breakup will be a blip on the radar screen of my life. It will be a mistake that I will have learned from, the kind of mistake my son calls "a beautiful oops."*

That night before I go to sleep, I gather up Boyfriend's things—his clothes, toiletries, tennis racket, books, and electronics—and pack them in a box that I'll give back to him. I take the Costco pajamas out of my drawer and find a Post-it with a flirtatious note that Boyfriend had stuck on one of them. When he wrote that, I wonder, did he already know he was leaving?

At a case consultation I went to the week before the breakup, a colleague brought up a patient who found out that her husband had been leading a double life. Not only had he been having an affair for years, but he'd gotten the woman pregnant and she was about to have his baby. When his wife discovered all of this (was he ever going to tell her?), she no longer knew what to make of her life with him. Were her memories real? For example, that romantic vacation—was her version of the trip accurate or was it some fiction, given that he was having his affair at that time? She felt robbed of her marriage but also of her memories. Likewise, when Boyfriend put the Post-it on my pajamas—when he bought me the pajamas in the first place—was he also secretly planning his kid-free life? I frown at the note. *Liar,* I think.

I walk the box out to the car and place it on the front seat so I'll remember to drop it off. Maybe I'll even do it in the morning, on the way to my appointment with Wendell.

I can't wait for him to tell me what a sociopath Boyfriend is.

7

The Beginning
of Knowing

I'm standing in the doorway of Wendell's office, trying to figure out where to sit. I see a lot of therapy offices in my profession—my supervisors' offices during training, my colleagues' offices that I visit—but I've never seen one like Wendell's.

Yes, there are the usual diplomas on the walls and therapy-related books on the shelves, along with the conspicuous absence of anything that might give away his personal life (no family photos on the desk, for instance; just a lone laptop). But instead of the standard setup of the therapist's chair in the middle of the room with seating against the walls (during internship, we learned to sit close to the door in case "things escalated" and we needed an escape route), Wendell's office has two long sofas on the far walls arranged in an L-shape with a side table between them—and no therapist chair at all.

I'm flummoxed.

Here's a diagram of my office:

My Office

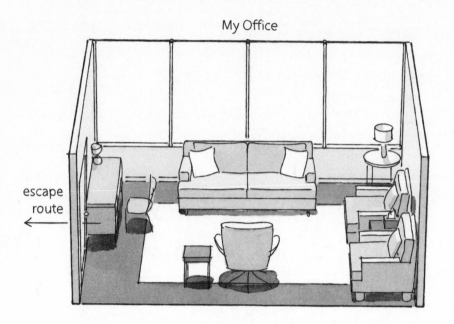

escape
route
←

And here's a diagram of Wendell's office.

Wendell's Office

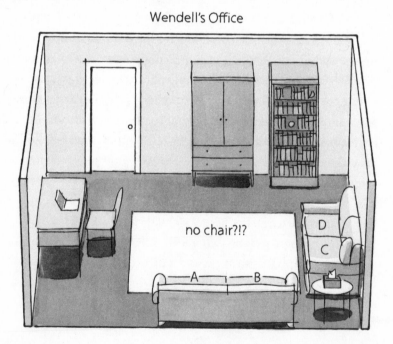

Wendell, who is very tall and very thin with a balding head and the stooped posture of our profession, stands there waiting for me to take a seat. I consider the possibilities. I assume we won't sit side by side on the same sofa, but which sofa does he typically take? The one by the window (so he can escape through *that* if things escalate)? Or the one by the wall? I decide to take a seat by the window, position A, before he closes the door, walks across the room, and relaxes into position C.

Generally when I see a new patient, I'll open the conversation with an icebreaker like "So, tell me what brings you here today."

Wendell, however, says nothing. He just looks at me, his green eyes questioning. He's wearing a cardigan, khakis, and loafers, like he came straight from Therapist Central Casting.

"Hi," I say.

"Hi," he replies. And he waits.

About a minute passes, which is longer than it sounds, and I try to gather my wits so that I can clearly lay out the Boyfriend situation. The truth is, every day since the breakup has been worse than the night of the breakup itself because now a glaring void has opened up in my life. For the past couple of years, Boyfriend and I had been in constant contact throughout our days, had said good night every bedtime. Now what was he doing? How had *his* day gone? Did his presentation at work go well? Was he thinking about me? Or was he glad to have gotten the truth off his chest so he could go search for somebody who was kid-free? I've felt his absence in every cell of my body, so by the time I get to Wendell's office this morning, I'm a wreck—but I don't want that to be his first impression of me.

Or, to be honest, his second or hundredth.

An interesting paradox of the therapy process: In order to do their job, therapists try to see patients as they really are, which means noticing their vulnerabilities and entrenched patterns and struggles. Patients, of course, want to be helped, but they also want to be liked and admired. In other words, they want to hide their vulnerabilities and entrenched patterns and struggles. That's not to say that therapists don't look for a patient's strengths and try to build on those. We do. But while we aim to discover

what's not working, patients try to keep the illusion going to avoid shame
—to seem more together than they really are. Both parties have the well-
being of the patient in mind but often work at cross-purposes in the service of a mutual goal.

As calmly as possible, I begin to tell Wendell the Boyfriend story, but
almost immediately, my dignity's gone and I'm sobbing. I go through the
entire story play-by-play and by the time I'm done, my hands are covering
my face, my body is shaking, and I think about what Jen said on the phone
when she called to check on me yesterday: "You need to find a place where
you're not being a therapist."

I'm definitely not being a therapist right now. I'm making the case for
why Boyfriend must be blamed for all of this: If he hadn't been so avoidant (Jen's diagnosis), I wouldn't have been so blindsided. And, I add, he
must be a sociopath (again quoting Jen; this is exactly the reason therapists
can't see their friends for therapy), because I had no idea that he felt this
way—he was such a good actor! And even if he's not a certifiable sociopath, he's clearly missing a few marbles, because who keeps something this
big to himself for God knows how long? After all, I know what normal
communication looks like, especially because I see so many couples in my
practice, and besides . . .

I look up and I think I see Wendell suppress a smile (I imagine his
thought bubble: *This wacko's a therapist . . . who treats couples?*) but it's hard
to tell because I can't see very well. It's like looking through the windshield
of a car without its wipers on during a rainstorm. In a strange way, I'm relieved to be able to cry this hard in front of another person, even if that
person is a stranger who doesn't say much.

After a bunch of empathetic *Mmm*s, Wendell asks a question: "Is this a
typical breakup reaction for you?" His tone is kind, but I know what he's
getting at. He's trying to determine what's known as my attachment style.
Attachment styles are formed early in childhood based on our interactions
with our caregivers. Attachment styles are significant because they play out
in people's adult relationships too, influencing the kinds of partners they
pick (stable or less stable), how they behave during the course of a relationship (needy, distant, or volatile), and how their relationships tend to end

(wistfully, amiably, or with a huge explosion). The good news is that maladaptive attachment styles can be modified in adulthood—this, in fact, is a lot of the work of therapy.

"No, this isn't typical," I insist, using my sleeve to dry my tears. I let him know that I've had long-term relationships and I've gone through breakups but not like this. And, I reiterate, the only reason I'm having this reaction is that this particular breakup was such a shock, so out of left field, and isn't what Boyfriend did the most *confusing* and *bizarre* and . . . UNETHICAL thing to do to someone?

I'm sure that this married professional with kids is going to say something supportive right now about how painful it is to be blindsided but that in the long run, thank goodness this happened, because I dodged a bullet—not just for me, but for my son. I sit back, take a breath, and wait for the validation to pour in.

But Wendell doesn't offer any. Of course, I didn't expect him to call Boyfriend trash, as Allison had; a therapist would use more neutral language, such as "It sounds like he had a lot of feelings that he didn't communicate directly to you." Still, Wendell says nothing.

My tears are starting to spill onto my pants again when out of the corner of my eye, I see an object flying through the air toward me. At first it looks like a football, and I wonder if I'm hallucinating (from the zero hours of restful sleep I've gotten since the breakup), but then I realize that it's a brown box of tissues—the one that was on the end table between the sofas, next to the seat I didn't take. Instinctively, my hands fly up to catch it, but I miss. It lands with a thud on the cushion next to me, and I grab a bunch of tissues and blow my nose. Having the box there seems to narrow the space between Wendell and me, as if he just threw me a lifeline. Over the years, I've handed tissue boxes to patients countless times, but I'd forgotten how cared for that simple gesture can make someone feel.

A phrase I first heard in graduate school pops into my head: "the therapeutic *act,* not the therapeutic word."

I take more tissues and wipe my eyes. Wendell is watching me, waiting.

I continue talking about Boyfriend and his avoidance issues, building a case using details from his past, including the way his marriage ended, which wasn't dissimilar to how our relationship ended in terms of shock value for his wife and kids. I'm telling Wendell everything I knew about Boyfriend's history of avoidance without realizing that what I'm unintentionally illustrating is *my* avoidance of his avoidance—about which apparently I knew quite a bit.

Wendell tilts his head slightly, a questioning smile on his face. "It's curious, isn't it, given what you knew about his history, that this is such a shock to you?"

"But it *is* a shock," I say. "He'd never said anything about not wanting a kid in the house! In fact, he'd just talked to HR at his firm to make sure that he could put my son on his benefits policy once we were married!" I go over the entire chronology again, adding more evidence to support my story, then notice that Wendell's face is starting to cloud over.

"I know I'm being repetitive," I say. "But you have to understand, I was expecting that we would spend the rest of our lives together. This was how things were supposed to go, and now it's all up in the air. Half my life is *over*, and I have no idea what's going to happen. What if Boyfriend was the last person I fall in love with? What if he was the end of the line?"

"The end of the line?" Wendell perks up.

"Yeah, the end of the line," I say.

He waits for me to continue, but instead my tears return. Not the wild sobs of the past week, but something both calmer and deeper.

Quieter.

"I know that you feel caught by surprise," Wendell says. "But I'm also interested in something else you said. *Half your life is over.* Maybe what you're grieving isn't just the breakup, though I know this experience feels devastating." He pauses, and when he speaks again, his voice is softer. "I wonder if you're grieving something bigger than the loss of your boyfriend."

He looks at me meaningfully, like he just said something incredibly important and profound, but I kind of want to punch him.

What a load of garbage, I think. I mean, really? I was *fine*—more than fine; I was *fine-plus*—before this turn of events. I have a child I adore beyond measure. I have a career I enjoy immensely. I have a supportive family and amazing friends whom I care about and who care about me. I'm grateful for this life . . . okay, *sometimes* I'm grateful. I certainly *try* to be grateful. And now I'm frustrated. I'm paying this therapist to help me with a painful breakup and this is what he has to offer?

Grieving something bigger, my ass.

Before I can say this, I notice that Wendell is looking at me in a way I'm not used to being looked at. His eyes are like magnets, and every time I glance away, they seem to find me. His expression is intense but gentle, a combination of a wise elder and a stuffed animal, and it comes with a message: *In this room, I'm going to see you, and you'll try to hide, but I'll still see you, and it's going to be okay when I do.*

But I'm not here for that. As I told Wendell when I called to schedule the appointment, I just need some crisis management.

"I'm really just here to get through the breakup," I say. "I feel like I've been tossed in a blender and can't get out, and that's all I'm here for—to find a way out."

"Okay," Wendell says, graciously backing off. "Help me understand more about the relationship." He's trying to establish what's known as a therapeutic alliance, a trust that has to develop before any work can get done. In the early sessions, it's always more important for patients to feel heard and understood than it is for them to gain any insight or make any changes.

Relieved, I go back to talking about Boyfriend, rehashing the whole thing.

But he knows.

He knows what all therapists know: That the presenting problem, the issue somebody comes in with, is often just one aspect of a larger problem, if not a red herring entirely. He knows that most people are brilliant at finding ways to filter out the things they don't want to look at, at using distractions or defenses to keep threatening feelings at bay. He knows that pushing aside emotions only makes them stronger, but that before he goes in and destroys somebody's defense—whether that defense is obsessing about another person or pretending not to see what's in plain sight—he needs to help the patient replace the defense with something else so that he doesn't leave the person raw and exposed with no protection whatsoever. As the term implies, *defenses* serve a useful purpose. They shield people from injury . . . until they no longer need them.

It's in this ellipsis that therapists work.

Meanwhile, back on my couch, clutching the tissue box, a small part of me knows something too. As much as I want validation, somewhere inside, I know that Wendell's load of garbage is *precisely* what I'm paying him for, because if I just want to complain about Boyfriend, I can do that for free, with my family and friends (at least until their patience runs out). I know that often people create faulty narratives to make themselves feel better in the moment even though it makes them feel worse over time— and that sometimes, they need somebody else to read between the lines.

But I also know this: Boyfriend is a *goddamn motherfucking selfish sociopath.*

I'm in that space between knowing and not knowing.

"That's all we can do with this today," Wendell says, and following his gaze, I notice for the first time that his clock has been resting on the windowsill over my shoulder. He lifts his arms and gives his legs two loud pats as if to punctuate the session's end, a gesture that I'll soon come to recognize as his signature sign-off. Then he rises and escorts me to the door.

He says to let him know if I'd like to come back next Wednesday. I think about the week ahead, the void where Boyfriend used to be, and the comfort of, as Jen said, having a place to completely fall apart.

"Sign me up," I say.

I walk across the street to the lot where I used to park for my bikini waxes, and I feel both lighter and like I might vomit. A supervisor once likened doing psychotherapy to undergoing physical therapy. It can be difficult and cause pain, and your condition can worsen before it improves, but if you go consistently and work hard when you're there, you'll get the kinks out and function so much better.

I check my phone.

A text from Allison:

Remember, he's trash.

An email from a patient needing to move her session.

A voicemail from my mom wondering if I'm okay.

No message from Boyfriend. I'm still hoping he'll call. I can't understand how he could be fine while I'm suffering so much. At least, he seemed fine when we coordinated my returning his belongings this morning. Had he gotten through his sadness months ago, knowing that eventually he was going to end things? If so, how could he have kept talking about our future together? How could he send *I love you* emails just hours before what was to become our last conversation, at the start of which we made movie plans for the weekend? (Did he go see the movie? I wonder.)

I start to stew again on the drive to the office. By the time I pull into my building's parking garage, I'm thinking about the fact that not only has Boyfriend wasted two years of my life, but now I'm going to have to deal with the fallout by going to therapy, and I don't have time for any of this because I'm in my forties now and half my life is over and . . . oh my God, there it is again! *Half my life is over.* I've never said that to myself or anyone else before. Why does it keep popping up?

You're grieving something bigger, Wendell had said.

But I forget all about this as soon as I step into the elevator at work.

8

Rosie

"Well, it's official," John says after slipping off his shoes and sitting cross-legged on the sofa. "I'm surrounded by idiots."

His phone vibrates. As he reaches for it, I raise my eyebrows. In return, John gives me an exaggerated eye roll.

It's our fourth session together, and I've started to form some initial impressions. I get the sense that, despite all the people surrounding him, John is desperately isolated—and that this is by design. Something in his life has made getting close seem dangerous, so dangerous that he does everything in his power to prevent it. His arsenal is effective: He insults me, goes on long tangents, changes the subject, and interrupts whenever I attempt to speak. But unless I can find a way to get past his defenses, we'll have no chance of making headway.

One of these defenses is his cell phone.

Last week, after John began texting in session, I brought his attention to my experience of feeling dismissed when he texts. This is called working in the here-and-now. Instead of focusing on a patient's stories from the outside world, the here-and-now is about what's occurring in the room. You can bet that whatever a patient does with his therapist, he also does with others, and I wanted John to begin to see the impact he had on people. I knew I ran the risk of pushing too far too soon, but I remembered a detail about his earlier therapy: It had lasted just three sessions, exactly where we were. I didn't know how long I'd have with him.

I was guessing that John had left his previous therapist for one of two reasons: either she didn't call him on his bullshit, which makes patients feel unsafe, like children whose parents don't hold them accountable; or she *did* call him on his bullshit, but she moved too fast and committed the same mistake I was potentially about to make. I was willing to risk it, though. I wanted John to feel comfortable in therapy but not so comfortable that I wasn't helping him.

Above all, I didn't want to fall into the trap that Buddhists call *idiot compassion*—an apt phrase, given John's worldview. In idiot compassion, you avoid rocking the boat to spare people's feelings, even though the boat needs rocking and your compassion ends up being more harmful than your honesty. People do this with teenagers, spouses, addicts, even themselves. Its opposite is *wise compassion,* which means caring about the person but also giving him or her a loving truth bomb when needed.

"You know, John," I'd said the week before as he texted away, "I'm curious if you have any reaction to my feeling dismissed when you do this."

He held up a finger—*Hang on*—but continued to text. When he finished, he looked up at me. "Sorry, what was I saying?"

I loved that. Not "What were *you* saying" but "What was *I* saying."

"Well—" I began, but his phone pinged, and off he went, responding to another text.

"See, this is what I mean," he grumbled. "I can't delegate anything if I want it done right. Just a sec."

Judging by the pings coming in, he seemed to be having multiple conversations. I wondered if we were reenacting a scene that played out with his wife.

Margo: Pay attention to me.

John: Who, you?

It was profoundly annoying. What to do with my annoyance? I could sit and wait (and become more irritated), or I could do something else.

I stood up, walked over to my desk, searched through a file, picked up my cell phone, walked back to my chair, and started texting.

It's me, your therapist. I'm over here.

John's phone pinged. I watched him read my text, surprised. "Jesus Christ! You're texting me now?"

I smiled. "I wanted to get your attention."

"You have my attention," he said, but he kept on texting.

I don't feel like I have your attention.
I feel ignored, and a bit insulted.

Ping.

John sighed dramatically, then resumed his texting.

And I don't think I can help you unless we're
able to give each other our full attention.
So if you'd like to try to work together, I'm going
to ask that you not use your phone in here.

Ping.

"*What?*" John said, looking up at me. "You're banning my cell phone? Like I'm on an airplane? You can't do that. It's *my* session!"

I shrugged. "I don't want to waste your time."

I didn't tell John that our sessions aren't, in fact, his alone. Every therapy session belongs to both patient and therapist, to the interaction between them. It was the psychoanalyst Harry Stack Sullivan who, in the early twentieth century, developed a theory of psychiatry based on interpersonal relationships. Breaking away from Freud's position that mental disorders were *intrapsychic* in origin (meaning "in one's mind"), Sullivan believed that our struggles were *interactional* (meaning "relational"). He went so far as to say, "It's the mark of a senior clinician that he or she is the same person in their living room that they are in their office." We can't teach patients to be relational if we aren't relational with them.

John's phone pinged again, but this time it wasn't me. He looked between me and his phone, deliberating. As his internal battle waged, I waited it out. I was half prepared for him to get up and leave, but I also knew that if he didn't want to be here, he wouldn't have come. Whether he understood it or not, he was getting something out of this. I was likely the only person in his life right now who would listen to him.

"Oh, for God's sake!" he said, tossing his cell onto the chair across the room. "Okay, I'll put down the *goddamned phone.*" Then he changed the subject.

I expected his anger, but for a second it looked as if his eyes had moistened. Was that sadness? Or was that a reflection from the sun streaming in the window? I toyed with inquiring, but there was only a minute left in the session, a time usually reserved for putting people back together rather than opening them up. I decided to file it away for a more opportune moment.

Like a miner spotting a glimmer of gold, I suspected that I'd hit on something.

Today, with much restraint, John stops mid-reach, leaving his vibrating phone alone and continues his story about being officially surrounded by idiots.

"Even Rosie's being idiotic," he says. I'm surprised to hear him talk this way about his daughter, who's four. "I tell her not to go near my laptop, and what does she do? She jumps on the bed, which is fine, but it's not fine to jump *on the laptop* that's on the bed. Idiot! And then as soon as I yell, '*No!*' she pees on the bed. Ruined the mattress. She hasn't peed on anything since she was a baby."

This story concerns me. There's a myth that therapists are trained to be neutral, but how can we be? We're humans, not robots. In fact, instead of being neutral, we therapists strive to notice our very un-neutral feelings and biases and opinions (what we call *countertransference*), so that we can step back and figure out what to do with them. We use, rather than suppress, our feelings to help guide the treatment. And this story about Rosie raises my hackles. Many parents have yelled at their kids in their less-than-glorious parenting moments, but I wonder about John's relationship with his daughter. When working with couples on empathy, often I'll say, "Before you speak, ask yourself, *What is this going to feel like to the person I'm speaking to?*" I make a mental note to share this with John one day.

"That sounds frustrating," I say. "Do you think you might have scared her? A loud voice can be frightening."

"Nah, I yell at her all the time," he says. "The louder the better. Only way she listens."

"The only way?" I ask.

"Well, when she was younger I would go outside and run around with her, let her blow off some steam. Sometimes she just needed to be outside. But lately she's been a real pain in the ass. She even tried to bite me."

"Why?"

"She wanted to play with me, but . . . oh, you'll love this."

I know what's coming.

"I was texting, so she had to wait, and she just lost her shit. Margo was out of town, so Rosie was spending her days with her Danny, and—"

"Remind me, who's Danny?"

"Not Danny. Her *danny*. You know, a dog nanny?"

I stare back blankly.

"A dog sitter. A nanny for the dog. A danny."

"Oh, so Rosie is your dog," I say.

"Well, who the hell did you *think* I was talking about?"

"I thought your daughter's name was—"

"*Ruby,*" he says. "The little one is Ruby. Wasn't it *obvious* that I was talking about a dog here?" He sighs and shakes his head as if I'm the biggest idiot in his kingdom of idiots.

He never mentioned having a dog before. The fact that I remembered the first letter of his daughter's name, which was referenced only in passing two sessions ago, feels like a victory to me. But more than John's entitlement, what strikes me is this: he's showing me a softer side I haven't seen yet.

"You really love her," I say.

"Of course I do. She's my daughter."

"No, I mean Rosie. You care about her deeply." I'm trying to touch him in some way, to bring him closer to his emotions, which I know are there but atrophied, like a neglected muscle.

He waves me away with his hand. "She's a dog."

"What kind of dog is she?"

His face brightens. "A mix. She's a rescue dog. She was a mess when we got her because of those idiots who were *supposed* to be taking care of her, but now she's—I'll show you a photo if you'll let me use my goddamned phone."

I nod.

As he scrolls through his pictures, he smiles to himself. "I'm looking for a good one," he says. "So you can see how cute she really is." With each photo, he beams a bit more, and I glimpse his perfect teeth again.

"Here she is!" he says proudly, handing me the phone.

I look down at the picture. I happen to love dogs, but Rosie, God bless her, is one of the ugliest dogs I've ever seen. She has sagging jowls, uneven eyes, multiple bald patches, and a missing tail. John is still beaming, smitten.

"I can see how much you love her," I say, handing back the phone.

"I don't *love* her. She's a fucking dog." He sounds like a fifth-grade boy denying a crush on a classmate. *John and Rosie sitting in a tree . . .*

"Oh," I say gently. "The way you talk about her, I hear a lot of love there."

"Would you stop saying that?" His tone is irritated, but I see pain in his eyes. I think back to our previous session—something about love or caring must feel painful for him. With a different patient, I might ask why what I'm saying is so upsetting. But I know that John will avoid the topic by arguing with me about whether he loves his dog. Instead, I say, "Most people who have pets care about them deeply." I lower my voice so that he almost has to lean in to hear me. Neuroscientists discovered that humans have brain cells called mirror neurons that cause them to mimic others, and when people are in a heightened state of emotion, a soothing voice can calm their nervous systems and help them stay present. "Whether it's called love or something else, it doesn't really matter."

"This is a ridiculous conversation," John says.

He's looking down at the floor, but I can see that I've got his full attention. "You brought up Rosie for a reason today. She matters to you, and now she's acting in a way that concerns you—because you care."

"People matter to me," John says. "My wife, my kids. *People.*"

He glances toward his cell, which is vibrating again, but I don't follow his gaze. I stay with him, trying to hold on so he won't get pulled away whenever an unwanted feeling appears and go numb. People often mistake numbness for nothingness, but numbness isn't the absence of feelings; it's a response to being overwhelmed by too many feelings.

John looks from his cell back to me.

"You know what I love about Rosie?" he says. "She's the only one who doesn't ask things of me. The only one who isn't, in one way or another, disappointed with me—or at least, she wasn't before she bit me! Who wouldn't love that?"

He laughs loudly, like we're at a bar and he's just tossed out a breezy one-liner. I try to talk about the disappointment—who's disappointed with him and why?—but he claims it was just a joke and can't I take a joke? And though we get nowhere with this today, we both know what he told me: he has a heart under those quills, and the capacity for love.

For starters, he adores that hideous dog.

9

Snapshots of Ourselves

People who come to therapy present snapshots of themselves, and from these snapshots, a therapist has to extrapolate. Patients arrive, if not at their worst, then certainly not at their best. They might be despairing or defensive, confused or chaotic. Generally, they're in very bad moods.

So they sit on the therapist's couch and look up expectantly, hoping to find some understanding and, eventually (but preferably immediately), a cure. But therapists don't have an immediate cure because these people are complete strangers to us. We need time to acquaint ourselves with their hopes and dreams, their feelings and behavior patterns, sometimes more deeply than even they have. If it takes from birth to the day they arrive in our offices to develop whatever is troubling them or if a problem has been incubating for many months, it makes sense that they might need more than a couple of fifty-minute sessions to attain the desired relief.

But when people are in extremis, they want their therapists, these professionals, to *do* something. Patients want our patience but may not have much patience themselves. Their demands can be overt or tacit, and—especially in the beginning—they can weigh heavily on the therapist.

Why would we choose a profession that requires us to meet unhappy, distressed, abrasive, or unaware people and sit with them, one after the other, alone in a room? The answer is this: Because therapists know that at first, each patient is simply a snapshot, a person captured in a particular moment. It's like a photo of you taken from an unfortunate angle and with a sour expression on your face. There might also be a photo in which you're glowing, caught opening a present or mid-laugh with a lover. Both are you in that fraction of time, and neither is you in your entirety.

So therapists listen, suggest, nudge, guide, and occasionally cajole our patients to bring other snapshots into view, to shift their experience of what's happening inside and around them. We sort through the snapshots, and before long it becomes apparent that these seemingly discrete images all revolve around a common theme, one that might not have been in our patients' fields of vision when they decided to come in.

Some snapshots are disturbing, and glimpsing them reminds me that we all have a dark side. Others are blurry. People don't always remember events or conversations clearly, but they do remember with great accuracy how an experience made them feel. Therapists have to be interpreters of these blurry snapshots, aware that patients *need* to be fuzzy to some extent, because those first snapshots help to gloss over painful feelings that might be invading their peaceful inner territory. In time, they find out that they aren't at war after all, that the path to peace is to call a truce with themselves.

Which is why when people first come in, we're imagining them down the line. We do this not just on that first day but in every single session, because that image allows us to hold for them the hope that they can't yet muster themselves, and it informs how the treatment unfolds.

I once heard creativity described as being the ability to grasp the essence of one thing and the essence of some very different thing and smash them together to create some entirely new thing. That's what therapists do too. We take the essence of the initial snapshot and the essence of an imagined snapshot and smash them together to create an entirely new one.

I have this in mind each time I meet a new patient.

I hope that Wendell does too, because in those early sessions, my snapshots are, well—not flattering.

10

The Future Is Also
the Present

Today I'm early for my appointment, so I sit in Wendell's waiting room and take a look around. Turns out his waiting room is as unusual as his therapy room. Instead of professional-looking furniture and the usual art —a framed poster of an abstract painting; maybe an African mask—the aesthetic in here is Grandma's hand-me-downs. There's even a musty smell to go with it. In a corner are two worn, high-backed dining chairs in an outdated paisley gold-brocade fabric, an equally worn and outdated rug on top of the beige wall-to-wall carpet, and a credenza covered by a stained lace tablecloth topped with doilies—doilies!—and a vase of fake flowers. On the floor between the chairs is a white-noise machine, and in front of them, in lieu of a coffee table, is what probably used to be a living-room side table now nicked and chipped and covered by a mess of magazines. A paper folding screen shields this seating area from the path leading in and out of Wendell's office so that patients have some privacy, but you can still see clearly through the hinged openings.

I know I'm not here for the décor, but I find myself wondering: *Can somebody with such bad taste help me? Is this a reflection of his judgment?* (An acquaintance told me that she'd been profoundly distracted by the crooked pictures hanging in her therapist's office; why wouldn't she just straighten the damn things?)

For about five minutes, I glance at the magazine covers— *Time, Parents, Vanity Fair*—and then the door to the therapy room opens and out walks a woman. She whizzes behind the screen, but I can tell in the split second I see her that she's pretty, well dressed, and tearful. Then Wendell appears in the waiting area.

"I'll just be a minute," he says, and he heads into the hallway, presumably to use the restroom.

As I wait, I wonder what the pretty woman was crying about.

When Wendell returns, he gestures for me to enter his office. There's no hesitation at the doorway now. I go straight to position A, by the window, he to position C, by the side table, and I launch right in.

"Blah-blah-blah-blah," I begin. "And if you can believe *this,* Boyfriend said, 'Blah-blah-blah-blah-blah,' so I said, 'Well, blah-blah-blah?'"

Or at least, that's what I'm sure it sounds like to Wendell. This goes on for a while. I've brought in pages of notes for this session, numbered, annotated, and in chronological order, just like I organized the interviews I did as a journalist before I became a therapist.

I confess to Wendell that I'd caved and phoned Boyfriend and that he'd let it go to voicemail. Humiliated, I had to wait a full day for him to call me back, knowing the entire time that the last thing anyone wants to do is talk to the person he's just broken up with but who still wants to be together.

"You're probably going to ask what I wanted to get out of calling him," I say, anticipating his next question.

Wendell raises his right eyebrow—just the one, I notice, and I wonder how he does that—but before he can respond, I plow ahead. First, I explain, I wanted Boyfriend to tell me that he missed me and this was all a big mistake. But barring that "unlikely possibility" (added so that Wendell knows I have self-awareness, even though I'd believed that Boyfriend *would* tell me he'd reconsidered), I wanted to get clear on how we had arrived at this point. If I could just get my questions answered, I'd stop going over the breakup in my head ad nauseam, in an infinite loop of confusion. Which is why, I tell Wendell, I subjected Boyfriend to a several-hour interrogation—I mean *conversation*—in which I tried to solve the mystery of What the Fuck Led to Our Sudden Breakup.

"And then he says, 'Being around a kid is limiting and distracting,'" I go on, reading verbatim quotes. "'It never would have been enough alone time with you. And I realized that no matter how great the kid, I'm never going to want to live with any child other than my own.' So then I said, 'Why did you hide all this from me?' and he said, 'Because I needed to figure it out before I said anything.' And then I said, 'But don't you think we should have *discussed* this?' and he said, 'What's to discuss? It's binary. Either I could live with a kid or I couldn't, and only I could figure that out.' And just as my brain is about to burst, he says, 'I really love you, but love doesn't conquer all.'

"It's binary!" I say to Wendell, shaking my papers in the air. I'd put an asterisk next to this word in my notes. "*Binary!* If it's so *binary,* why get into the *binary* situation in the first place?"

I'm insufferable and I know it, but I can't stop.

For the next several weeks, I come to Wendell's office and report the details of my circular conversations with Boyfriend (admittedly, there are several more) while Wendell tries to interject something useful (that he's not sure how this is helping me; that this feels masochistic; that I keep telling the same story hoping for a different outcome). He says that I want Boyfriend to explain himself to me—and that he *is* explaining himself to me—but that I keep going back because his explanation isn't what I want to hear. Wendell says that if I've been taking such copious notes during our phone calls, I probably haven't been able to listen to Boyfriend, and if my goal is to be open to understanding his perspective, that's hard to do when I'm trying to prove a point rather than have an interaction in earnest. And, he adds, I'm doing the same thing to *him* in our sessions.

I agree, then go right back to railing against Boyfriend.

In one session, I explain with excruciating specificity the arrangements for getting Boyfriend's belongings returned to him. In another, I repeatedly ask, Am I crazy or is he? (Wendell says neither of us is crazy, which infuriates me.) Another consists of an analysis of what kind of person says, "I want to marry you, just not you with a kid." For this session, I've created an infographic on gender differences. A man can say "I don't want to have to look at the Legos" and "I'll never love a kid who's not mine" and get away with it. A woman who said that would be crucified.

I also pepper our sessions with reports of what I've discovered in my daily Google-stalking: the women Boyfriend must be dating (based on elaborate stories I create from social media Likes); how fabulous his life is without me (based on his Tweets about his business trip); how he isn't even sad about the breakup (because he photographs salads in restaurants—how can he even *eat*?). I'm convinced that Boyfriend has quickly transitioned into his post-me life completely unscathed. It's a refrain I recognize from divorcing couples I see in which one person is struggling mightily and the other seems fine, happy even, to be moving on.

I tell Wendell that, like these patients, I want some sign of the scar tissue left behind. I want to know, in the end, that I mattered.

"Did I matter?" I ask over and over.

I continue like this, letting my freak flag fly, until finally Wendell kicks me.

One morning, as I drone on about Boyfriend, Wendell scoots to the edge of his couch, stands up, walks over to me, and, with his very long leg, lightly kicks my foot. Smiling, he returns to his seat.

"Ouch!" I say reflexively, even though it didn't hurt. I'm startled. "What was *that?*"

"Well, you seem like you're enjoying the experience of suffering, so I thought I'd help you out with that."

"What?"

"There's a difference between pain and suffering," Wendell says. "You're going to have to feel pain—everyone feels pain at times—but you don't have to suffer so much. You're not choosing the pain, but you're choosing the suffering." He goes on to explain that all of this perseverating I'm doing, all of this endless rumination and speculation about Boyfriend's life, is adding to the pain and causing me to suffer. So, he suggests, if I'm clinging to the suffering so tightly, I must be getting something out of it. It must be serving some purpose for me.

Is it?

I think about why I might be obsessively Google-stalking Boyfriend despite how bad I know it makes me feel. Is it a way to stay connected to Boyfriend and his daily routine, even if it's only one-sided? Maybe. Is it a way to numb out so I don't have to think about the reality of what happened? Possibly. Is it a way of avoiding what I should be paying attention to in my life but don't want to?

Earlier, Wendell had pointed out that I'd kept my distance from Boyfriend—ignoring clues that would have made his revelation less shocking—because if I'd inquired about them, Boyfriend might have said something I didn't want to hear. I told myself it meant nothing that he seemed irritated by kids in public places, that he'd happily run errands for us rather than attend my son's basketball games, that he said it was more important to his ex-wife than to him to have children when they were having fertility problems, and that his brother and sister-in-law stayed in a hotel when they came to visit because Boyfriend didn't want the commotion of their three kids in his house. And yet, neither he nor I had ever discussed our feelings about children directly. I figured: *He's a dad, he likes kids.*

Wendell and I talked about my pretending away certain parts of Boyfriend's history and comments and body language to quiet the alarm that might have gone off if I'd paid them heed. And now Wendell wonders if I've been keeping my distance from *him* as well, obsessing over my notes and sitting far away from him in order to protect myself here too.

I glance at the L-shaped sofa configuration. "Don't most people sit here?" I ask from my seat under the window. I'm certain that nobody shares a sofa with him, so that rules out position D. And as for position B, catty-corner to him, who would sit that close to the therapist? Again, nobody.

"Some do," Wendell says.

"Really? Where?"

"Anywhere along here." Wendell gestures from where I'm sitting all the way to position B.

Suddenly the distance between us seems vast, but I still can't believe that people sit that close to Wendell.

"So somebody walks into your office for the very first time, scans the room, and then plops down right there, even though you're going to be sitting just inches away?"

"They do," Wendell says simply. I think about the tissue box that Wendell had tossed to me and how he kept it on the table next to position B because, it occurs to me now, most people must sit *there*.

"Oh," I say. "Should I move?"

Wendell shrugs. "It's up to you."

I get up and sit down perpendicular to Wendell. I have to adjust my legs to the side so that they don't touch his. I notice a bit of gray at the roots of his dark hair. The wedding ring on his finger. I remember asking Caroline to refer me—or my "friend"—to a married male therapist, but now that I'm here, I realize it doesn't really matter. He hasn't sided with me or declared Boyfriend a sociopath.

I adjust the pillows and try to get comfortable. This feels strange. I look down at my notes, but I have no interest in reading them right now. I feel exposed, and I have the urge to run.

"I can't sit here," I say.

Wendell asks why, and I tell him I don't know.

"Not knowing is a good place to start," he says, and this feels like a revelation. I spend so much time trying to figure things out, chasing the answer, but it's okay to *not know.*

We're both quiet for a while, then I get up and move farther away, about midway between positions A and B. I can breathe again.

I think of a Flannery O'Connor quote: "The truth does not change according to our ability to stomach it." What am I protecting myself from? What do I not want Wendell to see?

All along, I'd been telling Wendell that I didn't wish ill upon Boyfriend —like having his next girlfriend blindside *him*—I just wanted our relationship back. I said with a straight face that I didn't want revenge, that I didn't hate Boyfriend, that I wasn't angry, just confused.

Wendell listened but said he wasn't buying it. Obviously, I *did* want revenge, I *did* hate Boyfriend, I *was* furious.

"Your feelings don't have to mesh with what you think they should be," he explained. "They'll be there regardless, so you might as well welcome them because they hold important clues."

How many times had I said something similar to my own patients? But here I feel as if I'm hearing this for the first time. *Don't judge your feelings; notice them. Use them as your map. Don't be afraid of the truth.*

My friends, my family—like me, they've had trouble considering the possibility that Boyfriend is a decent guy who was confused and conflicted. Instead, he was either selfish or a liar. They've also never considered that, even though Boyfriend told himself that he couldn't live with a kid, maybe he also couldn't live with *me*. Maybe, in ways he didn't realize, I reminded him too much of his parents or ex-wife or the woman he once mentioned who had hurt him deeply in graduate school. "I made a decision never to go through anything like that again," he had said early in our relationship. I'd asked him to explain more, but he didn't want to talk about it, and I, colluding with his avoidance, didn't push it.

Wendell, though, has been asking me to look at the ways we avoided each other by hiding behind romance and banter and plans for our future. And now I'm in pain and creating my own suffering—and my therapist is literally trying to kick some sense into me.

He switches his crossed legs from right over left to left over right, something therapists do when their legs start to fall asleep. His striped socks match his striped cardigan today, as if they came as a set. He points with his chin to the papers in my hand. "I don't think you're going to get the answers you're looking for from these notes."

You're grieving something bigger pops into my head, like a song lyric I can't shake. "But if I don't talk about the breakup, I won't have anything to say," I insist.

Wendell tilts his head. "You'll have the important things to say."

I hear him and I don't. Whenever Wendell implies that this is bigger than Boyfriend, I push back, so I suspect that he must be onto something. The things we protest against the most are often the very things we need to look at.

"Maybe," I say. But I feel antsy. "Right now I feel like I need to finish telling you what Boyfriend said. Can I just tell you one last thing?"

He takes in a breath and then stops, hesitating, like he was about to say something but decided against it. "Sure," Wendell says. He's pushed me enough and knows it. He's taken away my drug—talking about Boyfriend—for a minute too long, and I need another fix.

I start rifling through the pages, but now I can't remember where I was. I'm scanning the notes to see which damning quote I should share next, but there are so many asterisks and so many notes, and I can feel Wendell's eyes on me. I wonder what I would be thinking if somebody like me were sitting in my therapy room right now. Actually, I know. I'd be thinking of the laminated sign that my office mate posted inside the files at work: *There is a continuing decision to be made as to whether to evade pain, or to tolerate it and therefore modify it.*

I put down the notes.

"Okay," I say to Wendell. "What did you want to say?"

Wendell explains that my pain feels like it's in the present, but it's actually in both the past and the future. Therapists talk a lot about how the past informs the present—how our histories affect the ways we think, feel, and behave and how at some point in our lives, we have to let go of the fantasy of creating a better past. If we don't accept the notion that there's no redo, much as we try to get our parents or siblings or partners to fix what happened years ago, our pasts will keep us stuck. Changing our relationship to the past is a staple of therapy. But we talk far less about how our relationship to the *future* informs the present too. Our notion of the future can be just as powerful a roadblock to change as our notion of the past.

In fact, Wendell continues, I've lost more than my relationship in the present. I've lost my relationship in the future. We tend to think that the future happens later, but we're creating it in our minds every day. When the present falls apart, so does the future we had associated with it. And having the future taken away is the mother of all plot twists. But if we spend the present trying to fix the past or control the future, we remain stuck in place, in perpetual regret. By Google-stalking Boyfriend, I've been watching his future unfold while I stay frozen in the past. But if I live in the present, I'll have to accept the loss of my future.

Can I sit through the pain, or do I want to suffer?

"So," I say to Wendell, "I guess I should stop interrogating Boyfriend —and Google-stalking him."

He smiles indulgently, the way one would at a smoker who announces that she'll quit cold turkey but doesn't realize how overly ambitious that is.

"Or at least try," I say, backtracking. "Spend less time on his future, more on my present."

Wendell nods, then pats his legs twice and stands. The session is over but I want to stay.

I feel like we just got started.

11

Goodbye, Hollywood

My first week working at NBC, I was assigned to two shows that were about to premiere: *ER,* a medical drama, and *Friends,* a sitcom. These shows would catapult the network to number one and establish its Thursday-night dominance for years to come.

The series were set to air in the fall, following a much faster cycle than in the film world. Within months, casts and crews were hired, sets were built, and production began. I was in the room when Jennifer Aniston and Courteney Cox auditioned for starring roles in *Friends.* I weighed in on whether Julianna Margulies's character in *ER* should die at the end of episode one, and I was on the set with George Clooney before anyone knew how famous this series would make him.

Energized by this new job, I watched less TV at home. I had stories I was passionate about and colleagues who were equally passionate about those stories, and I felt connected to my work again.

One day *ER*'s writers called up a local emergency department with a medical question, and a physician named Joe happened to take the call. It seemed like kismet—in addition to his medical degree, he had a master's in film production.

When the writers learned of Joe's background, they began to consult him regularly. Before long, they hired him as a technical adviser to block out the highly choreographed trauma-bay scenes, teach the actors how to pronounce medical terms, and make the procedures look as accurate as possible (flush out the syringe; wipe the skin with alcohol before starting an IV; hold the patient's neck in this position when inserting a breathing tube). Of course, sometimes we skipped the surgical masks the characters should have worn, because everyone wanted to see George Clooney's face.

On set, Joe was a study in competence and calm, the same qualities that served him in a real ER. During breaks, he would talk about patients he'd seen recently, and I'd want to hear every detail. *What stories!* I thought. One day I asked Joe if I could visit him on the job—"Research," I said—and he offered me access to his ER, where, in borrowed baggy scrubs, I followed him around during his shift.

"The drunk drivers and gang shootings don't start pouring in until dark," he explained when I arrived on a Saturday afternoon and not much was going on. But soon we were rushing from room to room, patient to patient, as I tried to keep the names and charts and diagnoses straight. In the span of an hour, I watched Joe do a lumbar puncture, see inside a pregnant woman's uterus, and hold the hand of a thirty-nine-year-old mother of twins as she was told that her migraine was really a brain tumor.

"No, you see, we just wanted more migraine medicine" was her only response—denial that would soon give way to a rush of tears. Her husband excused himself to go to the restroom but vomited on the way. For a second I pictured this drama on TV—an ingrained instinct when your work is coming up with stories—but I had a sense that finding TV material wasn't only what being here was about for me. And Joe sensed that, too. Week after week, I kept going back to the ER.

"You seem more interested in what we're doing here than in your day job," Joe said one evening months later as we looked at an x-ray together and he showed me where the fracture was. Then, almost as an afterthought, he said, "You could still go to medical school, you know."

"Medical school?" I said. I looked at him like he was nuts. I was twenty-eight years old and had been a language major in college. It was true that in high school I'd competed in math and science tournaments, but outside of school, I'd always been drawn to words and stories. And now my work was a great job at NBC that I felt incredibly lucky to have.

Even so, I kept sneaking away from tapings to go back to the ER—not just with Joe but with other doctors who let me shadow them too. I knew that my being there had gone from research to hobby, but so what? Didn't everyone have hobbies? And, okay, sure, maybe spending my evenings in the ER had become the new equivalent of obsessively watching TV every night when I was restless in my film job. Again, so what? I certainly wasn't about to give all this up and start over in medical school. Besides, I wasn't bored by the work at NBC. I just felt that something real and big and meaningful was happening in the ER that couldn't happen in the same way on television. And my hobby could fill in those blanks—that's what hobbies were *for.*

But sometimes I'd be standing in the ER, and, during a lull in the action, I'd realize how at home I felt, and more and more I wondered if Joe was onto something.

Before long, my hobby led me out of the ER and into a neurosurgery suite. The case I'd been invited to see was that of a middle-aged man with a pituitary tumor that was likely benign but had to be removed to keep it from pressing on his cranial nerves. Gowned and masked and wearing running shoes for comfort, I stood over Mr. Sanchez, peering into his skull. After sawing through the bone (using a tool like something you'd buy at Home Depot), the surgeon and his team meticulously pulled aside layer after layer of fascia until they reached his naked brain.

Finally, there it was, looking just like the images I'd seen in a book the night before, but as I stood there, my own brain inches from Mr. Sanchez's, I felt a sense of awe. Everything that made this man himself—his personality, his memories, his experiences, his likes and dislikes, his loves and losses, his knowledge and abilities—was contained in this three-pound organ. You lose a leg or a kidney, you're still you, but lose a part of your brain—literally, *lose your mind*—and who are you then?

I had a perverse thought: *I've gotten inside a person's head!* Hollywood tried to get into people's heads all the time via market research and ads, but I was actually there, deep inside this man's skull. I wondered if those slogans the network bombarded viewers with ever made it to their destinations: *It's Must See TV!*

As classical music played softly in the background and two neurosurgeons picked away at the tumor, carefully depositing pieces of it onto a metal tray, I thought of the frenetic sets in Hollywood with all of their commotion and commands.

"Come on, people! Let's go!" An actor would be rushed down a hallway on a stretcher, red liquid drenching his clothes, but then someone would turn the corner too quickly. "Shit!" the director would say. "Jesus, people, let's get it right this time!" Burly men with cameras and lights would rush around in a frenzy, resetting the scene. I'd see a producer pop a pill—Tylenol or Xanax or Prozac?—and down it with sparkling water. "I'm gonna have a heart attack if we don't get this shot today." He'd sigh. "I swear, I'm gonna die."

In the OR with Mr. Sanchez, there was no yelling, no one feeling as if a coronary was imminent. Even Mr. Sanchez, with his head sawed open, seemed less stressed out than the people on the set. As the surgical team worked, "Please" and "Thank you" peppered each request, and if it weren't for the steady stream of blood dripping out of a man's head and into a bag near my leg, I might have mistaken this place for fantasy. And in a way it was. It was at once more real than anything I had ever seen and also galaxies away from what I considered to be my actual life back in Hollywood, a place I had no intention of leaving.

But months later, everything changed.

I'm following an ER doctor in a county hospital on a Sunday. As we approach a curtain, he says, "Forty-five-year-old with complications from diabetes." He pulls back the curtain and I see a woman lying on the table under a sheet. That's when the smell hits my nostrils—an assault so vile I worry I might faint. I can't identify the odor because I've never smelled anything this nauseating in my life. Has she defecated? Vomited?

I see no signs of either, but the smell becomes so powerful that I feel the lunch I ate an hour ago rise into my throat, and I swallow hard to keep it down. I hope she can't see how pale I must be or sense the queasiness taking over my gut. I'm thinking: *Maybe it's coming from the next bed over. Maybe if I move more to this side of the room, I won't smell it so strongly.* I concentrate on the woman's face—watery eyes, reddish cheeks, bangs over her sweaty forehead. The doctor is asking her questions and I can't understand how he manages to breathe. I've been trying to hold my breath this entire time, but I have to come up for air.

Okay, I tell myself. *Here goes.*

I take in some air and the smell seizes my body. Steadying myself against the wall, I look on as the doctor lifts the sheet covering the woman's legs. Only there are no lower legs. Her diabetes has caused severe vasculitis, and all that remain are two stumps above the knees. One has gangrene, and I can't decide if the sight of this infected stump, all black and moldy like a rotten fruit, is worse than its smell.

The space is small, and I move closer to the woman's head, as far away from the infected stump as possible, and that's when something extraordinary happens. This woman takes my hand and smiles at me as if to say, *I know this is hard to watch, but it's okay.* Even though I'm the one who should be holding *her* hand, even though she's the one with the missing appendages and a massive infection, she's reassuring me. And though this could make a great story line on *ER,* in that millisecond, I know I won't be working on that show much longer.

I am going to medical school.

Maybe that's an impulsive reason to change careers—the fact that this graceful stranger with a blackened stump is holding my hand as I try not to barf—but something is happening inside me that I've never felt at any of my Hollywood jobs. I still love TV, but there's something about the real stories I'm experiencing in person that seduce me and make the imaginary ones feel thin. *Friends* is about community, but a fake one. *ER* is about life and death, but they're fictional. Instead of taking these stories I witness and folding them back into my world at the network, I want real life—real people—to *be* my world.

As I drive home from the hospital that day, I don't know how or when this might happen or what kind of medical-school loans I can get or even if I can get in. I don't know how many science classes I'll have to take to meet the requirements and prepare for the MCAT or where to take those courses, since I graduated from college six years ago.

But somehow, I decide, I'm going to make this happen, and I can't do that while working sixty-hour weeks on Must See TV.

12

Welcome to Holland

After Julie learned that she was dying, her best friend, Dara, wanting to be helpful, sent her the well-known essay "Welcome to Holland." Written by Emily Perl Kingsley, the parent of a child with Down syndrome, it's about the experience of having your life's expectations turned upside down:

> When you're going to have a baby, it's like planning a fabulous vacation trip—to Italy. You buy a bunch of guide books and make your wonderful plans. The Coliseum. The Michelangelo David. The gondolas in Venice. You may learn some handy phrases in Italian. It's all very exciting.
>
> After months of eager anticipation, the day finally arrives. You pack your bags and off you go. Several hours later, the plane lands. The flight attendant comes in and says, "Welcome to Holland."
>
> "Holland?!?" you say. "What do you mean Holland?? I signed up for Italy! I'm supposed to be in Italy. All my life I've dreamed of going to Italy."
>
> But there's been a change in the flight plan. They've landed in Holland and there you must stay.
>
> The important thing is that they haven't taken you to a horrible, disgusting, filthy place, full of pestilence, famine and disease. It's just a different place.
>
> So you must go out and buy new guide books. And you must

learn a whole new language. And you will meet a whole new group of people you would never have met.

It's just a different place. It's slower-paced than Italy, less flashy than Italy. But after you've been there for a while and you catch your breath, you look around . . . and you begin to notice that Holland has windmills . . . and Holland has tulips. Holland even has Rembrandts.

But everyone you know is busy coming and going from Italy . . . and they're all bragging about what a wonderful time they had there. And for the rest of your life, you will say "Yes, that's where I was supposed to go. That's what I had planned."

And the pain of that will never, ever, ever, ever go away . . . because the loss of that dream is a very, very significant loss.

But . . . if you spend your life mourning the fact that you didn't get to Italy, you may never be free to enjoy the very special, the very lovely things . . . about Holland.

"Welcome to Holland" made Julie furious. After all, there was nothing special or lovely about her cancer. But Dara, whose son had severe autism, said that Julie was missing the point. She agreed that Julie's prognosis was devastating and unfair and a complete departure from how her life was supposed to go. But she didn't want Julie to spend the time she had remaining—perhaps as long as ten years—missing out on what she might still have while alive: Her marriage. Her family. Her work. She could still have a version of those things in Holland.

To which Julie thought, *Screw you.*

And also, *You're right.*

Because Dara would know.

I'd already heard about Dara from Julie, the same way I hear about all of my patients' close friends. I knew from Julie that when Dara was at her wits' end with worry and grief over her son's endless hitting and head-banging, his tantrums, his inability to have a conversation or feed himself at four years old, his need for multiple weekly therapies that had taken over her life but also didn't seem to be helping, Dara would call Julie, despondent.

"Now, I'm embarrassed by this," Julie said after she explained her initial anger toward Dara, "but when I saw what Dara was going through with her son, my biggest fear was to end up in her situation. I love her so much, and I also felt like any hope for the life she wanted had died."

"Like you feel now," I said.

Julie nodded.

She told me that for a long while, Dara would say, "I didn't sign up for this!" and catalog all the ways in which her life had been irrevocably changed. She and her husband would never have cuddles and carpools and reading stories before bed. They would never have a child who would grow into an independent adult. Dara would look at her husband, Julie said, and think, *He's an amazing father to our son,* but she couldn't help contemplate the amazing father he would have been to a child who could fully interact with him. She couldn't help the sadness that would descend when she let herself think about the kinds of experiences they wouldn't be able to have with their child, ever.

Dara felt selfish and guilty for her sadness, because she wished most of all that her son's life could be easier for *his* sake, that *he* could live a fulfilling life, one with friends and lovers and work. She felt enveloped by both pain and envy when she saw other moms playing with their four-year-olds at the park, knowing that in that situation, her son would likely lose control and be asked to leave. That her son would continue to be shunned as he grew older, and so would she. The looks she got from the other moms, the ones who had typical kids with typical problems, added to her sense of isolation.

Dara phoned Julie often that year, each call more hopeless than the previous one. Depleted financially, emotionally, and practically, she and her husband decided not to add a sibling to the mix—how could they afford and have time for another, and what if that child also had autism? She'd already stopped working in order to manage their son's life while her husband took on an extra job, and she didn't know how to cope. Until one day she came across "Welcome to Holland" and realized that she would have to not only cope in this strange land but find joy there where she could. There were still pleasures to be had, if she could let them in.

In Holland, Dara found friends who understood her family's situation. She found ways to connect with her son, to enjoy him and love him for who he was and not focus on who he wasn't. She found ways to stop obsessing about what she did and did not know about tuna and soy and chemicals in cosmetics during her pregnancy that might have harmed her developing baby. She got care for her son so that she could care for herself and do meaningful part-time work and have meaningful downtime too. She and her husband found each other and their marriage again while also struggling with the challenges they couldn't change. Instead of sitting in their hotel room the whole trip, they decided to venture out and see the country.

Now Dara was inviting Julie to do the same, to look at the tulips and Rembrandts. And after Julie's anger about "Welcome to Holland" subsided, it occurred to her that there would always be somebody whose life seemed more—or less—enviable. Would Julie trade places with Dara now? Her first instinct: yes, in a heartbeat. Her second: maybe not. She'd come up with various scenarios: If she could have ten great years with a healthy child, would she take that over a longer life? Is it more difficult to be sick yourself or to have a child who is? She felt horrible even having these thoughts, but she couldn't deny them either.

"Do you think I'm a bad person?" she'd ask, and I'd assure her that everyone who comes to therapy worries that what they think or feel might not be "normal" or "good," and yet it's our honesty with ourselves that helps us make sense of our lives with all of their nuances and complexity. Repress those thoughts, and you'll likely behave "badly." Acknowledge them, and you'll grow.

In this way, Julie started to see that we're all in Holland, because most people don't have lives that go exactly as planned. Even if you're lucky enough to be traveling to Italy, you might experience canceled flights and horrible weather. Or your spouse might have a fatal heart attack in the shower ten minutes after the two of you have glorious sex in a luxurious Rome hotel room during a trip to celebrate your anniversary, as happened to an acquaintance of mine.

So Julie was going to Holland. She didn't know how long her stay would be, but we were booking her trip for ten years and would change the itinerary as needed.

Meanwhile, we'd work together to figure out what she wanted to do there.

Julie had just one stipulation.

"Will you promise to tell me if I'm doing something crazy? I mean, now that I'm going to die sooner than I ever imagined, I don't have to be so . . . *sensible*, right? So if I'm going overboard, and things get a little over-the-top, you'll tell me?"

I said I would. Julie had spent her entire life being conscientious and responsible, doing everything by the book, and I couldn't imagine what her version of over-the-top would look like. I figured if anything, it would be the equivalent of the goody-goody student who went a little crazy by having one too many beers at a party.

But I'd forgotten that people are often at their most interesting when they've got a proverbial gun to their head.

"Bucket list," Julie said in session as we tried to envision her Holland. "It's such a funny term, isn't it?" I had to agree. What do we want to do before we kick the bucket?

Often people think about bucket lists when somebody close to them dies. That's what happened for Candy Chang, an artist who, in 2009, created a space on a public wall in New Orleans with the prompt *Before I die* _____. Within days the wall was completely filled. People wrote things like *Before I die, I want to straddle the international dateline. Before I die, I want to sing for millions. Before I die, I want to be completely myself.* Soon the idea spawned over a thousand such walls all over the world: *Before I die, I would like to have a relationship with my sister. Be a great dad. Go skydiving. Make a difference in someone's life.*

I don't know if people followed through, but based on what I've seen in my office, a good number may have had momentary awakenings, done a little soul-searching, added more to their lists—and then neglected to tick things off. People tend to dream without doing, death remaining theoretical.

We think we make bucket lists to ward off regret, but really they help us to ward off death. After all, the longer our bucket lists are, the more time we imagine we have left to accomplish everything on them. Cutting the list down, however, makes a tiny dent in our denial systems, forcing us to acknowledge a sobering truth: Life has a 100 percent mortality rate. Every single one of us will die, and most of us have no idea how or when that will happen. In fact, as each second passes, we're all in the process of coming closer to our eventual deaths. As the saying goes, none of us will get out of here alive.

I'll bet right now you're glad that I'm not your therapist. Who wants to think about this? How much easier it is to become death procrastinators! Many of us take for granted the people we love and the things we find meaningful, only to realize, when our deadline is announced, that we'd been skating by on the project: our lives.

But now Julie needed to grieve all the things she'd have to leave *off* her list. Unlike older people, who grieve for what they'll be losing and leaving behind, Julie was grieving for what she would never have—all of the milestones and firsts that people in their thirties just assume will happen. Julie had, as she put it, "a concrete deadline" ("*Dead* being the operative part of the word," she said), a deadline so unforgiving that most of what she'd expected would never come to pass.

One day Julie told me that she'd begun to notice how often in casual conversation people talked about the future. *I'm going to lose weight. I'm going to start exercising. We're going to take a vacation this year. In three years, I'll get that promotion. I'm saving to buy a house. We want to have a second baby in a couple of years. I'll go to my next reunion in five years.*

They plan.

It was hard for Julie to plan a future not knowing how much time there was. What do you do when the difference between a year and ten is enormous?

• • •

Then something miraculous happened. Julie's experimental treatment seemed to be shrinking her tumors. In a matter of weeks, they were almost gone. Her doctors were optimistic—maybe she had longer than they'd thought. Maybe these drugs would work not just now or for a few years but for the long term. There were a lot of maybes. So many maybes that when the tumors disappeared completely, she and Matt began, very tentatively, to become the kind of people who plan.

When Julie examined her bucket list, she and Matt talked about having a baby. Should they have their own child if Julie might not be around for middle school—or, if things went very badly, preschool? Was Matt up for that? What about the child? Was it fair for Julie to become a mother under these circumstances? Or would Julie's greatest motherly act be the decision not to become one, even if it would be the hardest sacrifice she'd ever make?

Julie and Matt decided that they had to live their lives, even in the face of such uncertainty. If they had learned anything, it was that life is the very definition of uncertainty. What if Julie remained cautious and they didn't have a baby because they were waiting for the cancer to return—but it never did? Matt assured Julie that he would be a committed father no matter what happened with Julie's health. He would always be there for their child.

So it was decided. Looking death in the eye would force them to live more fully—not in the future, with some long list of goals, but *right now*.

Julie kept her bucket list lean: they were going to start their family.

It didn't matter if they ended up in Italy or Holland or someplace else entirely. They would hop on a plane and see where they landed.

13

How Kids Deal with Grief

Shortly after the breakup, I told Zach, my eight-year-old, the news. We were eating dinner, and I tried to keep it simple: Boyfriend and I had both decided (poetic license) that we weren't going to be together after all.

His face fell. He looked both surprised and confused. (*Welcome to the club!* I thought.)

"Why?" he asked. I told him that before two people got married, they needed to figure out if they'd make good partners, not just for the moment, but for the rest of their lives, and even though Boyfriend and I loved each other, both of us realized (again, poetic license) that we wouldn't and that it was better for us to find other people who would.

This was, basically, the truth—minus some details and plus a few pronoun changes.

"Why?" Zach asked again. "Why wouldn't you be good partners?" His face was a wrinkle. My heart ached for him.

"Well," I said. "You know how you used to hang out with Asher and then he got really into soccer and you got really into basketball?"

He nodded.

"You guys still like each other, but now you spend more time with people who have similar interests."

"So you like different things?"

"Yeah," I said. *I like kids, and he's a Kid Hater.*

"What things?"

I took a breath. "Well, things like I want to be home more and he wants to travel more." *Kids and freedom are mutually exclusive. If the queen had balls . . .*

"Why can't you both compromise? Why can't sometimes you stay home and sometimes you go traveling?"

I mulled this over. "Maybe we could, but it's like that time you were assigned to work with Sonja on that poster and she wanted to put pink butterflies all over it, and you wanted it to have Clone troopers, and in the end, you ended up with yellow dragons, which was pretty cool, but not really what either of you wanted. Then on the next project you worked with Theo and even though you had different ideas, they were similar enough, and you still both compromised, but not as much as you had to do with Sonja."

He was staring at the table.

"Everyone has to compromise to get along," I said, "but if you have to compromise *too much,* it might be hard to be married to each other. If one of us wanted to travel a lot and one of us wanted to stay home a lot, we both might get frustrated a lot. Does that make sense?"

"Yeah," he said. We sat together for a minute, and then suddenly he looked up and blurted out, "Are we killing a banana if we eat it?"

"What?" I said, thrown by the non sequitur.

"You know how you kill a cow to get the meat and that's why vegetarians don't eat meat?"

"Uh-huh."

"Well," he continued, "if we pull the banana off the tree, aren't we also killing the banana?"

"I guess it's like hair," I said. "Hair falls off our heads when it's ready to die, and then new hair grows in its place. New bananas grow where the old ones used to be."

Zach leaned forward in his chair. "But we pull the bananas *before* they fall off, when they're still alive. What if somebody PULLED YOUR HAIR OUT before it was ready to fall off? So doesn't it kill the banana? And doesn't it hurt the tree when we pull the banana off?"

Oh. This was Zach's way of dealing with the news. He was the tree here. Or the banana. Either way, he was hurting.

"I don't know," I said. "Maybe we don't intend to hurt the tree or the banana, but it's possible that sometimes we hurt it anyway, even though we really, *really* don't want to."

He went quiet for a while. Then: "Am I going to see him again?"

I told him I didn't think so.

"So we're not going to play Goblet anymore?" Goblet was a board game that belonged to Boyfriend's kids when they were young, and Zach and Boyfriend sometimes played it together.

I told him no, not with Boyfriend. But if he felt like it, I'd play it with him.

"Maybe," he said quietly. "But he was really good at it."

"He *was* really good at it," I agreed. "I know this is a big change," I added, and then I stopped talking because nothing I said would help him right then. He was going to have to feel sad. I knew that over the next few days and weeks and even months, we'd have many conversations to help him through this (the upside of being a therapist's child is that nothing gets shoved under the rug; the downside is that you'll be totally screwed up anyway). Meanwhile, the news would have to marinate.

"Okay," Zach mumbled. Then he got up from the table, went over to the fruit bowl on the counter, picked up a banana, ripped it open, and with dramatic flair, sunk his teeth into it.

"Yummmm," he said, a strangely gleeful look on his face. Was he murdering the banana? He devoured the entire thing in three big bites and then went to his room.

Five minutes later, he came out carrying the Goblet game.

"Let's give this to Goodwill," he said, placing the box by the door. Then he walked over to me for a hug. "I don't like it anymore anyway."

14

Harold and Maude

At medical school, my cadaver's name was Harold. Or, rather, that's what my lab partners and I named him after the group next to us named theirs Maude. We were in gross anatomy, the traditional first-year human-dissection course, and each student team at Stanford worked on the cadaver of a generous person who had donated his or her body to science.

Our professors gave us two instructions before we set foot in the lab. One: Pretend that the bodies belonged to our grandmothers and show respect accordingly. ("Do normal people slice up their grandmothers?" one freaked-out student replied.) Two: Pay attention to any emotions that came up during what we were told would be an intense process.

We weren't given any information about our cadavers—names, ages, medical histories, causes of death. The names were withheld for privacy, and the rest because the goal was to solve a mystery, not a *who*dunnit but a *why*dunnit. Why did this person die? Was he a smoker? A red-meat lover? A diabetic?

Over the semester, I discovered that Harold had had a hip replacement (clue: the metal staples in his side); his mitral valve had been leaky (clue: enlargement on the left side of the heart); he'd been constipated, probably from lying in a hospital bed, at the end of his life (clue: the backed-up feces in his colon). He had pale blue eyes, straight yellowing teeth, a circle of white hair, and the muscular fingers of a builder, pianist, or surgeon. Later,

I learned that he'd died of pneumonia at ninety-two, which surprised us all, including our professor, who declared, "He had the organs of a sixty-year-old."

Maude, however, had lungs full of tumors, and her nicely painted pink nails belied the nicotine stains on her fingers from her habit. She was the opposite of Harold; her body had aged prematurely, making her organs seem like those of someone much older. One day, the Maude Squad, as we called Maude's lab group, carved out her heart. One of the students lifted it gingerly and held it up for the others to examine, but it slipped off her glove, fell to the floor with a thud, and split apart. We all gasped—a broken heart. *How easy it is,* I thought, *to break someone's heart, even when you take great care not to.*

Pay attention to your emotions, we'd been instructed, but it was far more convenient to close them off as we scalped our cadaver and sawed open his skull like a cantaloupe. ("It's another Black and Decker day," our professor said when he greeted us on the second morning of that unit. A week later, we'd do a "gentle dissection" of the ear—meaning chisels and hammers, but no saws.)

We opened each lab session by unzipping the bag containing our cadaver and pausing as a class for a minute of silence to honor the people who were letting us take their bodies apart. We started below the neck, keeping their heads covered as a sign of respect, and when we moved up to their faces, we kept their eyelids closed, again out of respect, but also to make them seem less human to us—less real.

Dissection showed us that living is a precarious thing, and we did our best to distance ourselves from this fact by lightening the mood with obscene mnemonics passed down from class to class, like the one for the cranial nerves (olfactory, optic, oculomotor, trochlear, trigeminal, abducens, facial, vestibulocochlear, glossopharyngeal, vagus, accessory, and hypoglossal): Oh, Oh, Oh, To Touch And Feel Virginia's Greasy Vagina, AH. While dissecting the head and neck, the class would shout this out in unison. Then we'd hit the books and prepare for the next day's lab.

Our hard work paid off. We aced each unit, but I'm not sure that any of us were paying attention to our emotions.

. . .

When exams rolled around, we did our first walkabout. A walkabout is just that—you walk about a roomful of skin and bone and viscera as if examining the wreckage from a horrific plane crash, except your job is to identify not the victims but the individual parts. Instead of "I think this is John Smith," you try to figure out if the fleshy thing sitting by itself on a table is part of a hand or a foot, then say, "I think this is extensor carpi radialis longus." But even that wasn't the goriest experience we had.

The day we dissected Harold's penis—cold, leathery, lifeless—the students at Maude's table, having a cadaver with female organs, joined us to observe. Kate, my lab partner, was meticulous in her dissections (her focus, the professor liked to say, was as "sharp as a nine blade") but now she was distracted by shouts from the Maude Squad watching her work. The deeper she sliced, the louder the shouts became.

"Ouch!"

"Eww!"

"I think I'm gonna puke!"

More classmates came over to watch, and a bunch of male students started dancing in circles and guarding their crotches with their plastic-protected textbooks.

"Drama queens," Kate muttered. She had no patience for squeamishness—she was going to be a surgeon. Refocusing, Kate used a probe to locate the spermatic cord, then grabbed the scalpel again and made a vertical incision along the entire base of the penis, so that it split open into two neat halves, like a hotdog.

"Okay, that's it, I'm outta here!" one of the guys announced, and then he and several of his friends ran from the room.

The final day of the course, there was a ceremony in which we paid our respects to the people who had let us learn from their bodies. We all read personal thank-you notes to them, played music, and offered blessings, hoping that even though their bodies had been dismantled, their souls were intact and open to receiving our gratitude. We talked a lot about the vulnerability of our cadavers, exposed and at our mercy, cut open and scrutinized, millimeter by millimeter, samples of them literally put under a microscope as we removed their tissues. But we were the truly vulnerable ones, made more so by our unwillingness to admit it—we were first-years wondering if we could hack it in this field; young people seeing death up close; students not knowing what to make of the tears we'd sometimes shed at the most unexpected moments.

They had told us to pay attention to our emotions, but we weren't sure what our emotions were or what to do with them, anyway. Some people took meditation classes offered by the medical school. Some thrived on exercise. Others buried themselves in their studies. One student on the Maude Squad took up smoking, sneaking out for quick cigarette breaks and refusing to believe he'd end up tumor-ridden like his cadaver. I volunteered for a literacy program and read to kindergartners—how healthy they were! How alive! How intact their body parts!—and when I wasn't doing that, I wrote. I wrote about my experiences, and I became curious about other people's experiences, and then I started writing about these experiences for magazines and newspapers.

At one point, I wrote about a class called Doctor-Patient that taught us how to interact with the people we would one day treat. As part of our final exam, each student was videotaped taking a medical history, and my professor commented that I was the only student who'd asked the patient how she was feeling. "That should be your first question," he told the class.

Stanford emphasized the need to treat patients as people, not cases, but at the same time, our professors would say, this was becoming harder to do because of the way the practice of medicine was changing. Gone were the long-term personal relationships and meaningful encounters, replaced by some newfangled system called "managed care" with its fifteen-minute visits, factory-like treatment, and restrictions on what a doctor could do for each patient. As I moved on from gross anatomy, I thought a lot about what specialty I might choose—was there one in which the older model of the family doctor survived? Or would I not know the names of many of my patients, much less anything about their lives?

I shadowed doctors in various specialties, ruling out the ones with the least amount of patient interaction. (Emergency medicine: exciting, but you rarely see your patients again. Radiology: you see pictures, not people. Anesthesiology: your patients are asleep. Surgery: ditto.) I liked internal medicine and pediatrics, but the physicians I followed warned me that those practices were becoming far less personal—to stay afloat, they had to cram in thirty patients each day. If they were starting out now, a few even said, they might consider another field.

"Why become a doctor if you can write?" one professor asked after he had read something I'd written for a magazine.

When I was at NBC, I worked with stories but wanted real life. Now that I had real life, I wondered if, in the modern daily practice of medicine, there'd be no room for people's stories. What was satisfying, I discovered, was immersing myself in other people's lives, and the more I wrote as a journalist, the more I found myself doing just that.

One day, I talked to a professor about my dilemma, and she suggested that I do both—journalism and medicine together. If I could bring in extra income as a writer, she said, I could have a smaller practice and see patients the way doctors used to. But, she added, I'd still have to answer to insurance companies with their time-consuming mounds of paperwork, which would take me away from patient care. *Has it really come to this?* I thought. *Writing as a way to support a living as a doctor? Didn't it used to be the other way around?*

I considered her idea anyway. At that point, though, I was thirty-three years old, with two more years of medical school, at least three years of residency, maybe a fellowship after that—and I knew that I wanted a family. The more I saw the effects of managed care up close, the less I could imagine myself taking the years-long risk of finishing my training and then trying to find out if it was possible to concoct the kind of practice I wanted while also being a writer. Besides, I wasn't sure I *could* do both—not well, at least—and also have room for a personal life. By the end of the term, I felt like I had to choose: journalism or medicine.

I chose journalism, and over the next several years, I published books and wrote hundreds of magazine and newspaper stories. *Finally,* I thought, *I've found my professional calling.*

As for the rest of my life—the family—that, too, would fall into place. At the time I left medical school, I was absolutely sure of it.

15

Hold the Mayo

"Seriously? Is that all you shrinks care about?"

John is back on my couch, sitting cross-legged and barefoot. He's come in wearing flip-flops because the pedicurist was at the studio today. His toenails, I notice, are as perfect as his teeth.

I've just asked something about his childhood, and he's not happy about it.

"How many times do I have to tell you? I had a great childhood," he continues. "My parents were saints. Saints!"

Whenever I hear about saintly parents, I get suspicious. It's not that I'm looking for problems. It's just that no parent is a saint. Most of us end up being the "good-enough" parents that Donald Winnicott, the influential English pediatrician and child psychiatrist, believed was sufficient to raise a well-adjusted child.

Even so, the poet Philip Larkin put it best: "They fuck you up, your mum and dad, / They may not mean to, but they do."

It wasn't until I became a parent that I could truly understand two crucial things about therapy:

1. The purpose of inquiring about people's parents isn't to join them in blaming, judging, or criticizing their parents. In fact, it's not about their parents at all. It's solely about understanding how their early experiences

inform who they are as adults so that they can separate the past from the present (and not wear psychological clothing that no longer fits).

2. Most people's parents did their absolute best, whether that "best" was an A-minus or a D-plus. It's the rare parent who, however limited, deep down doesn't want his or her child to have a good life. That doesn't mean people can't have feelings about their parents' limitations (or mental-health challenges). They just need to figure out what to do with them.

Here's what I know about John so far: He's forty years old, married for twelve years, and has two daughters, ages ten and four, and a dog. He writes and produces popular television shows, and when I learn which ones, I'm not surprised; he's won Emmys precisely because his characters are so brilliantly wicked and insensitive. He complains that his wife is depressed (although, as the saying goes, "Before diagnosing people with depression, make sure they're not surrounded by assholes"), his kids don't respect him, his colleagues waste his time, and everyone demands too much of him.

His father and two older siblings live in the Midwest, where John grew up; he was the only one to move away. His mother died when he was six and his brothers were twelve and fourteen. She was a drama teacher, and she had been leaving the high school after rehearsal when she saw one of her students in the path of a speeding car. She ran and pushed the student out of the way, but she was hit herself and died at the scene. John told me this part with no emotion, as if he were matter-of-factly recounting the plot of one of his TV shows. His father, an English professor with aspirations to be a writer, took care of the boys alone until he married a widowed neighbor with no children three years later. John described his stepmom as "vanilla, but I have nothing against her."

While John has had a lot to say about the various idiots in his life, his parents have been largely absent from our conversations. During my internship, a supervisor suggested that with very defended patients, one way to get a sense of their pasts is by asking them, "Without thinking about it, what three adjectives come immediately to mind in relation to your mom's [or dad's] personality?" These off-the-cuff answers have always given me (and my patients) helpful insights into their parental relationships.

But nothing comes of this with John. "Saint, saint, and *saint*—that's three words for both of them!" he replies, using nouns instead of adjectives despite his writerly facility with words. (I'll learn later that his father "might have" had a drinking problem after his wife died and "possibly" still does and that John's oldest brother once told John that their mother "might have" had "a light version of bipolar disorder," but, John said, his brother was just "being dramatic.")

I'm curious about John's childhood because of his narcissism. His self-involvement, defensiveness, demeaning treatment of others, need to dominate the conversation, and sense of entitlement—basically, his being an asshole—all fall under the diagnostic criteria for narcissistic personality disorder. I noticed these traits at our very first session, and while some therapists might have referred John out (narcissistic personalities aren't considered good candidates for introspective, insight-oriented therapy due to their struggle to see themselves and others clearly), I was game.

I didn't want to lose the person behind the diagnosis.

Yes, John had likened me to a prostitute, acted as though he were the only person in the room, and felt that he was better than everyone else. But underneath all that, how different, really, was he from the rest of us?

The term *personality disorder* evokes all kinds of associations, not just for therapists, who consider these patients to be a handful, but in the popular culture as well. There's even a Wikipedia entry that catalogs movie characters and the personality disorders they exemplify.

The most recent version of the *Diagnostic and Statistical Manual of Mental Disorders,* the clinical bible of psychological conditions, lists ten types of personality disorders, broken into three groups, called clusters:

Cluster A (odd, bizarre, eccentric):
   Paranoid PD, Schizoid PD, Schizotypal PD
Cluster B (dramatic, erratic):
   Antisocial PD, Borderline PD, Histrionic PD, Narcissistic PD

Cluster C (anxious, fearful):
Avoidant PD, Dependent PD, Obsessive-Compulsive PD

In outpatient practice, we mostly see patients in cluster B. People who are untrusting (paranoid), loners (schizoid), or oddballs (schizotypal) don't tend to seek out therapy, so there goes cluster A. People who shun connection (avoidant), struggle to function like adults (dependent), or are rigid workaholics (obsessive-compulsive) also don't look for help very often, so there goes cluster C. The antisocial folks in cluster B generally won't be calling us either. But the people who experience difficulty in relationships and are either extremely emotional (histrionics and borderlines) or married to people like this (narcissists) do make their way to us. (Borderline types tend to couple up with narcissists, and we see that pairing often in couples therapy.)

Until very recently, most mental-health practitioners believed that personality disorders were incurable because unlike mood disorders, such as depression and anxiety, personality disorders consist of long-standing, pervasive patterns of behavior that are very much a part of one's *personality*. In other words, personality disorders are ego-*syn*tonic, which means the behaviors seem in sync with the person's self-concept; as a result, people with these disorders believe that others are creating the problems in their lives. Mood disorders, on the other hand, are ego-*dys*tonic, which means the people suffering from them find them distressing. They don't like being depressed or anxious or needing to flick the lights on and off ten times before leaving the house. They know something's off with them.

But personality disorders lie on a spectrum. People with borderline personality disorder are terrified of abandonment, but for some, that might mean feeling anxious when their partners don't respond to texts right away; for others, that might mean choosing to stay in volatile, dysfunctional relationships rather than being alone. Or consider the narcissist. Who doesn't know somebody who fits the bill to varying degrees—accomplished, charismatic, smart, and witty but alarmingly egocentric?

Most important, having *traits* of a personality disorder doesn't necessarily mean that a person meets the criteria for an official diagnosis. From time to time—on a doozy of a bad day or when pushed until a fragile nerve is struck—*everyone* exhibits a tad of this or that personality disorder, because each is rooted in the very human wish for self-preservation, acceptance, and safety. (If you don't think this applies to you, just ask your spouse or best friend.) In other words, just as I always try to see the whole person and not just the snapshot, I also try to see the underlying struggle and not just the five-digit diagnosis code I can put on an insurance form. If I rely on that code too much, I start to see every aspect of the treatment through this lens, which interferes with forming a real relationship with the unique individual sitting in front of me. John may be narcissistic, but he's also just . . . John. Who can be arrogant and, to use a nonclinical description, incredibly fucking annoying.

And yet.

Diagnosis has its usefulness. I know, for example, that people who are demanding, critical, and angry tend to suffer from intense loneliness. I know that a person who acts this way both wants to be seen and is terrified of being seen. I believe that for John, the experience of being vulnerable feels pathetic and shameful—and I'm guessing that he somehow got the message not to show "weakness" at six years old when his mother died. If he spends any time at all with his emotions, they likely overwhelm him, so he projects them onto others as anger, derision, or criticism. That's why patients like John are especially challenging: they're masters at getting your goat—all in the service of deflection.

My job is to help both of us understand what feelings he's hiding from. He's got fortresses and moats to keep me out, but I know that part of him is in the turret calling for help, hoping to be saved—from what, I don't know yet. And I'll apply my knowledge of diagnosis without getting lost in it to help John see that the way he acts in the world might be causing more problems for him than the so-called idiots around him are.

"Your light is on."

John and I are discussing his irritation with my questions about his childhood when he announces that the green light on the wall near my door that's connected to a button in the waiting room is illuminated. I glance at the light, then at the clock. It's just five minutes past the hour, so I figure that my next patient must be uncharacteristically early.

"It is," I say, wondering if John is trying to change the subject or if he might even have some feelings about the fact that he's not my only patient. Many patients secretly wish to be their therapist's only patient. Or, at least, the favorite—the funniest, most entertaining and, above all, most beloved.

"Can you get it?" John says, nodding toward the light. "It's my lunch."

I'm confused. "Your lunch?"

"The food delivery guy is out there. You said no cell phones, so I told him to press the button. I haven't had time for lunch yet, and now I have a free hour—I mean, *fifty minutes*. I need to eat."

I'm floored. People don't generally eat in therapy, but if they do, they'll say something along the lines of "Is it okay if I eat in here today?" And they bring their own food. Even my patient with hypoglycemia brought food into this room only once, and that was to avoid going into shock.

"Don't worry," John says, registering the look on my face. "You can have some if you want." Then he gets up, walks down the hall, and retrieves his lunch from the delivery person in the waiting room.

When John comes back, he unpacks the bag, puts a napkin on his lap, unwraps his sandwich, takes a bite, then loses it.

"Jesus Christ, I said no mayo! Look at this!" He opens up the sandwich to show me the mayonnaise, and with his free hand he reaches for his cell phone—presumably to call about his order—but I give him a look reminding him of the no-cell-phone policy.

His face turns bright red, and I wonder if he might yell at me too, but instead he just explodes with "*Idiot!*"

"Me?" I ask.

"You what?"

"I remember you once described your last therapist as nice, but an idiot. Am I also nice, but an idiot?"

"No, not at all," he says, and I'm pleased that he's able to acknowledge that somebody in his life isn't an idiot.

"Thank you," I say.

"For what?"

"For saying I'm not an idiot."

"That's not what I meant," he replies. "I meant no, you're not *nice.* You won't let me use my phone to call the idiot who put mayonnaise on my sandwich."

"So I'm mean *and* an idiot?"

He grins, and when he does, his eyes twinkle and his dimples appear. For a second I can see how some people might find him charming.

"Well, you're mean, that's for sure. I don't know about the idiot part yet." He's being playful, and I smile back.

"Phew," I say. "At least you're giving me the benefit of getting to know me first. I appreciate that." He begins fidgeting, uncomfortable with my attempt to engage. He's so desperate to escape from this moment of human contact that he starts munching on his mayonnaise-y sandwich and looks away. But he's not fighting me, and I'll take it. I sense a microscopic opening.

"I'm sorry that you experience me as being mean," I say. "Is that why you made that comment about the fifty minutes?" The mistress insult—that I'm more like his hooker—was more complicated, but I'm guessing he made the fifty-minutes crack for the same reason most people do—they wish they could stay longer but don't know how to say this directly. Acknowledging their attachment makes them feel too vulnerable.

"No, I'm glad it's fifty minutes!" he says. "God knows, if I stayed for an hour, you'd keep asking me about my childhood."

"I just want to get to know you better," I say.

"What's to know? I'm anxious and I can't sleep. I'm juggling three shows, my wife's complaining all the time, my ten-year-old is acting like a teenager, my four-year-old misses the nanny who left for graduate school, the fucking dog is acting out, and I'm surrounded by idiots who make my life harder than it needs to be. And, frankly, I'm pissed off at this point!"

"That's a lot," I say. "You're dealing with a lot."

John says nothing. He's chewing his food and studying a spot on the floor near his flip-flops.

"Damn right," he says finally. "What's so hard to understand about three words? *Hold. The. Mayo.* That's it!"

"You know, about those idiots," I say. "I have a thought about that. What if the people who are pissing you off aren't trying to piss you off? What if these people aren't idiots but reasonably intelligent people who are just doing the best they can on a given day?"

John lifts his eyes slightly, as if considering this.

"And," I add softly, thinking that as hard as he is on others, he's probably triply hard on himself, "what if you are too?"

John starts to say something, then stops. He looks back toward his flip-flops, lifts a napkin, and pretends to wipe the crumbs from his mouth. But I see it happen anyway. He quickly maneuvers the napkin upward and below his eye.

"Goddamn sandwich," he says, stuffing the napkin into the food bag along with the rest of the meal before tossing the whole thing into the trash can under my desk. *Swish.* A perfect shot.

He looks at the clock. "This is nuts, you know. I'm starving, it's my one break to eat, and I can't even use my phone to order a proper lunch. You call this therapy?"

I want to say *Yes, this is therapy*—face-to-face, without phones or sandwiches, so that two people can sit together and connect. But I know John will just offer a sardonic rebuttal. I think about what Margo must go through and wonder what her own psychological history must be for her to have chosen John.

"I'll make you a deal," John says. "I'll tell you something about my childhood if I can order some lunch from the place up the street. I'll order for *both* of us. Let's just be civilized and have a conversation over a goddamn Chinese chicken salad, okay?" He looks at me, waiting.

Normally I wouldn't do this, but therapy isn't by the numbers. We need professional boundaries, but if they're too open, like an ocean, or too constricting, like a fishbowl, we run into trouble. An aquarium seems just right. We need space for spontaneity—which is why when Wendell kicked me, it was effective. And if John needs some distance between us in the form of food to feel comfortable talking to me right now, so be it.

I tell him we can order lunch but he doesn't have to talk about his childhood. It's not a quid pro quo. He ignores me and dials a restaurant to place the order, a process that, of course, frustrates him.

"Right, no dressing. Not drinks, *dressing!*" He's yelling into the phone, which is on speaker. "D-r-e-s-s-i-n-g." He sighs loudly, rolls his eyes.

"Extra dressing?" the guy at the restaurant says in broken English, and John becomes apoplectic as he tries to communicate that the dressing should be on the side. Everything's a problem—they have Diet Pepsi, not Diet Coke; they can be here in twenty minutes, not fifteen. I watch, horrified and bemused. *It must be so hard to be John,* I think. As they wrap up, John says something in Chinese, and the guy doesn't understand. John doesn't understand why the guy doesn't understand his "own language" and the guy explains that he speaks Cantonese.

They hang up and John looks at me, incredulous. "What, they don't use *Mandarin?*"

"If you know Chinese, why didn't you use it to place the order?" I ask.

John gives me a withering look. "Because I speak *English.*"

Yikes.

John grumbles until lunch arrives, but once we set out our salads, he lets down the drawbridge a bit. I've already had lunch but I eat some salad anyway to join him; there's something innately bonding about sharing a meal together. I hear some stories about his father and older brothers and how he thinks it's strange that while he doesn't remember much about his mom, he began dreaming about her a few years ago. He keeps having versions of the same dream, like *Groundhog Day,* and he can't make it stop. He wants it to stop. Even in his sleep, he says, he's being bothered. He just wants peace.

I inquire about the dream but he says it will upset him to talk about it and he's not paying me to upset him. Didn't he just tell me that he wanted peace? Don't they teach "listening skills" to therapists? I want to talk about what he just said—to challenge his beliefs that he shouldn't be uncomfortable in therapy and that he can find peace without also experiencing discomfort—but I need time for that, and there are just a couple of minutes left.

I ask when he has peace.

"Walking the dog," he says. "Until Rosie started acting out. That used to be peaceful."

I think about how he doesn't want to bring the dream into this room. Could it be that this room has become something of a sanctuary for him, away from his job, wife, kids, dog, the world's idiots, and the ghost of his mom that appears in his sleep?

"Hey, John," I try. "Are you feeling peaceful right now?"

He chucks his chopsticks into the bag where he's just packed away the remains of his salad. "Of course not," he says, adding an impatient eye roll.

"Oh," I say, letting it go. But John hasn't. Our time is up and he stands to leave.

"Are you kidding?" he continues as he heads to the door. "In *here?* Peace?" His eye roll has been replaced by a smile now—not a condescending smirk, but a secret he's sharing with me. It's a lovely smile, luminous, and not because of those dazzling teeth.

"I thought so," I say.

16

The Whole Package

Spoiler: After I left medical school, the rest of my life did not fall into place as planned.

Three years later, when I was nearly thirty-seven, a two-year relationship ended. It was sad but amicable and not a surprise the way the breakup with Boyfriend later turned out to be. But still, it was the worst timing imaginable for someone who wanted to have a baby.

I'd always known, in the surest possible way, that I wanted to be a parent. I'd spent my adulthood volunteering with kids and assumed that I would one day have my own. Now, though, with forty looming, I was *dying* to have a baby, but not so much that I would just marry the next guy who came along. This left me in a tricky predicament—desperate, but picky.

It was then that a friend suggested I could do things in reverse order: baby first, partner later. One night, she emailed me links for some sperm-donor sites. I'd never heard of such a thing and wasn't sure at first how I felt about it, but after considering my options, I made the decision to move forward.

Now I just needed to choose a donor.

Of course I wanted a donor with a good health history, but on these sites there were other qualities to consider, and not just things like hair color or height. Did I want a lacrosse player or a literature major? A Truf-faut buff or a trombonist? An extrovert or an introvert?

I was surprised to see that in many ways, these donor profiles resembled dating profiles—except that most of the candidates were college students and provided their SAT scores. And there were a few other key differences, chief among them the comments of the so-called lab girls. These were the women (they all seemed to be female) who worked at the banks and met the donors when they came in to give a "release." (Not in the sense of "contract.") The lab girls would then write what they termed *staff impressions* and add them to the donors' profiles, but there was no rhyme or reason as to what kinds of impressions they'd share. Their comments varied wildly from *He has amazing biceps!* to *He tends to procrastinate, but eventually gets his stuff done.* (I was wary of any male college student whose procrastination extended to masturbation.)

I relied heavily on these staff impressions because the more profiles I read, the more I realized that I wanted to feel some intangible connection to the donor who would have a connection to my child. I wanted to *like* him, whatever that meant—to feel that if he were sitting at our family dinner table, I would enjoy his company. But as I read the staff impressions and listened to the audio of the interviews that the lab girls conducted with the donors ("What's the funniest thing that's ever happened to you?," "How would you describe your personality?," and, weirdly, "What's your idea of a romantic first date?"), it still felt clinical, impersonal.

Then one day I called up the sperm bank with a question about a donor's health history and was transferred to a lab girl named Kathleen. As Kathleen looked up his medical records, I began chatting with her and learned that *she* had been the lab girl who'd met this particular donor. I couldn't help myself. "Is he cute?" I asked, trying to sound casual. I didn't know if I was allowed to be asking.

"Well . . ." Kathleen hedged, drawing out the word in her thick New York accent. "He's not *un*attractive. But I wouldn't look twice at him on the subway."

After that, Kathleen became my sperm concierge, suggesting donors and answering my questions. I trusted her because while some of the lab girls inflated their assessments—they were trying to sell sperm, after all —Kathleen was honest to a fault. Her standards were very high, and so were mine, which was a problem, because nobody made it through our filters.

To be fair, it seemed reasonable to assume that my future child would want me to be picky. And there were multiple factors to juggle. If I found a donor who seemed to share my sensibilities, there would be other problems, like his family's health history wasn't a good match with mine (breast cancer under age sixty, kidney disease). Or I'd find a donor with a pristine health history but who was a six-foot-four Danish guy with Nordic features, a look that would stick out—and might make my child feel self-conscious—in my family of short, brown-haired Ashkenazi Jews. Other donors seemed to have good health, intelligence, and similar physical features, but something else would raise a red flag, like the donor who wrote that his favorite color was black, his favorite book *Lolita,* and his favorite movie *A Clockwork Orange.* I tried to imagine my child reading this profile one day and looking at me like, "And you chose *this* one?" I had the same reaction if the donor couldn't spell or use punctuation correctly.

This process continued for three exhausting months, during which I began to lose hope that I'd find a healthy donor I'd be proud to tell my child about.

And then—finally!—I found him.

I came home late one evening to a message on my voicemail from Kathleen. She told me to check out a donor she described as looking like "a young George Clooney." She added that she especially liked this donor because he was always friendly and in a great mood when he arrived at the bank to donate. I rolled my eyes. After all, if you're a guy in his twenties who's about to go watch porn and have an orgasm—and you're getting *paid* for that—what's not to be in a great mood about? But Kathleen gushed about this guy—he had good health, good looks, strong intelligence, and a winning personality.

"He's the whole package," she said confidently.

Kathleen had never sounded so enthusiastic, so I logged on to take a look. I clicked on his profile, pored over his health history, read his essays, listened to his audio interview, and instantly knew, in the same way that people talk about love at first sight, that I'd found The One. Everything about him—his likes and dislikes, his sense of humor, his interests and values—felt like family. Elated but exhausted, I figured I'd get some sleep and handle the details in the morning. The next day happened to be my birthday, and overnight I had vivid dreams about my baby for what felt like eight hours straight. For the first time, I pictured an actual baby coming from two specific people instead of some hazy idea of a baby with half its heritage blank.

In the morning, I jumped out of bed with a burst of excitement, the song "Child of Mine" playing in my head. *Happy birthday to me!* I'd been wanting a baby for the past several years, and finding a donor I felt so comfortable with seemed like the best birthday present ever. Heading to the computer, I smiled at my good fortune—I was really going to *do* this. I typed in the sperm bank's URL, found the donor's profile, and read it all over again. I was just as certain as I'd been the night before that he was The One—the one that would make sense to my child when he or she asked why, of all the possible donors, I chose *this* guy.

I placed the donor in my online shopping cart—just as I might with a book on Amazon—double-checked the order, then clicked Purchase Vials. *I'm having a baby!* I thought. The moment felt monumental.

As the order processed, I planned what I had to do next: Make an appointment for the insemination, buy prenatal vitamins, put together a baby registry, get the baby's room set up. Between thoughts, I noticed that my order was taking a while to complete. The rotating circle on my screen, known as the "spinning wheel of death," seemed to be spinning for an unusually long time. I waited, waited some more, and finally tried using the back button in case my computer was crashing. But nothing happened. Finally, the spinning wheel of death disappeared and a message popped up: *Out of stock.*

Out of stock? I figured there must be some computer glitch—maybe when I pressed the back button?—so I speed-dialed the sperm bank and asked for Kathleen, but she was out and I got transferred to a customer-service rep named Barb.

Barb looked into the matter and determined that this was no glitch. I'd selected a very popular donor, she said. She went on to explain that popular donors went quickly and that, while the company tried to "restock" their "inventory" often, there was a six-month hold for it so it could get quarantined and tested. Even when the inventory was made available, she said, there still might be a long wait, because some people had placed it on back order. As Barb spoke, I thought of how Kathleen had called just yesterday. Now it occurred to me that maybe she'd suggested this donor to several women. Like me, maybe *many* women had bonded with Kathleen over her honest appraisals of semen.

Barb placed me on the waitlist ("Don't be foolish and waste your time waiting," she'd said ominously), then I put down the phone and felt numb. After months of fruitless searching, I'd found my donor, and my future baby had finally seemed like a reality, more than just an idea in my head. But now, on my birthday, I had to let that baby go. I was all the way back at square one.

I slumped over my laptop, staring into space. I sat there for a long while until I noticed, on the corner of my desk, a business card that I'd gotten the week before at a professional networking event. It was from a twenty-seven-year-old filmmaker named Alex. I'd spoken to Alex for only about five minutes, but he was kind and smart and seemed healthy, and I thought, with the impulsivity of somebody running out of options, that maybe I could skip the online banks and try to find my donor out in the real world. Alex fit the profile of the kind of donor I sought. Why not ask if he'd consider it? After all, the worst he could say was no.

I chose my subject line carefully (*An Unusual Question*) and left the email vague (*Hey, remember me, from that networking event?*). Then I invited him to meet for coffee so that I could ask my "unusual question." Alex responded, wondering if I could email him the question. I replied that I'd prefer to discuss it in person. He wrote, *Sure*. And the next thing I knew, we were set to meet for coffee Sunday at noon.

· · ·

I was, to put it mildly, nervous when I arrived at Urth Caffé. After sending my impulsive email, I was certain that Alex would say no and then tell ten of his friends what I'd done, leaving me so humiliated that I'd never be able to go to a networking event again. I'd considered backing out, but I wanted a baby so badly that I felt I had to do this, just in case. *The answer to an unasked question is always no,* I repeated to myself over and over.

Alex greeted me warmly and the small talk came easily—so easily that, before I knew it, we were having a great time. After about an hour, in fact, I'd almost forgotten what we were doing there when Alex leaned across the table, looked me in the eye, and asked flirtatiously, as if he'd concluded we were on a date, "So, what was your 'unusual question'?"

Instantly my face felt hot and my palms sweaty, and I did what any normal person would do under the circumstances—I went mute. The gravity and lunacy of what I was about to do rendered me speechless.

Alex waited until I began forming words, flailing, using incoherent analogies to explain my request. I was saying things like "I don't have all the ingredients for the recipe" and "It's like donating a kidney, but without removing the organ." The second I said the word *organ,* I got even more flustered and tried changing course. "It's like giving blood," I said, "except there's sex instead of needles!" With that, I willed myself to shut up. Alex was staring back with a strange look on his face, and I thought, *Life does not get more humiliating than this.*

But then it did. Because it quickly became apparent that Alex had no idea what I was trying to ask.

"Look," I managed to say. "I'm thirty-seven years old and I want to have a baby. I'm not having luck with the sperm banks, and I'm wondering if you'd consider—"

This time Alex clearly got it, because his entire body froze; even his mocha chai latte stayed suspended in midair. Other than one catatonic patient in medical school, I'd never seen a person sit so still before in my life. Finally Alex's lips moved and out came one word: "Wow."

Then, slowly, more words came out. "I wasn't expecting *that* at all."

"I know," I said. I felt terrible for having put him in such an awkward situation, for bringing this up at all, and I was just about to say so when, to my amazement, Alex added: "But I'd be willing to talk about it."

Now it was my turn to freeze before eventually saying "Wow." The next few hours flew by: Alex and I discussed about everything from our childhoods to future dreams. It seemed that talking about sperm had broken down all the emotional walls, the way having sex with somebody for the first time can open the emotional floodgates. When we finally got up to leave, Alex said that he needed to do some thinking, and I said okay, and he said he'd be in touch. I was sure, though, that once he actually thought this through, I'd never hear from him again.

But that night, Alex's name appeared in my inbox. I clicked on his message, expecting a nice rejection. Instead he wrote: *So far I am a yes, but with more questions.* So we set up another meeting.

Over the next couple of months we met at Urth so often that I started calling the café my "sperm office," and my friends started calling it simply Spurth. At Spurth, we talked about everything from semen samples and medical histories to contracts and contact with the child. Eventually we got to the point where we talked about how to do the transfer—whether we should have the doctor do the insemination or have sex to increase the odds of conception.

He picked sex.

Honestly, I had no objection. And more honestly? I was *thrilled* with this development! After all, I imagined that in my future life as a mom, there wouldn't be much opportunity to have sex with a gorgeous twenty-seven-year-old like Alex, with his ripped abs and chiseled cheekbones.

Meanwhile, I began obsessively monitoring my menstrual cycles. One day at Spurth, I mentioned to Alex that I was about to ovulate, so if we were going to try this month, he had exactly one week to make a decision. In other circumstances that might have seemed like a lot of pressure to put on a guy, but by now it felt like a done deal and I didn't have time to waste. We'd already looked at our plan from every possible angle: legal, emotional, ethical, practical. By this point, too, we had inside jokes and nicknames for each other and had bonded over what a blessing this child would be. The week before, he had even asked if, like any other business opportunity, I had "gone out to others" or if this was an exclusive offer. I had the fleeting impulse to invent a bidding war to seal the deal (*Pete is circling and there's also interest from Gary, so you better get back to me by Friday. There's a lot of heat around this*). But I wanted our relationship to be based in complete truthfulness, and anyway, I was sure that Alex would say yes.

The day after I issued the deadline, we decided to take a walk on the beach to discuss one last time the final details in the contract we'd had drawn up. As we strolled along the shore, drizzle appeared out of nowhere. We looked at each other—should we head back?—but then the drizzle turned into a veritable storm. We were both in short sleeves, and Alex took the jacket from around his waist and placed it over my shoulders, and as we faced each other, getting drenched in the rain on the beach, he gave me the official green light. After all the negotiations, all the getting to know each other, all the questions about what this would mean for us and the child, we were ready.

"Let's make you a baby!" he said, and there we were, hugging and smiling, me in an oversize jacket that went down to my knees, embracing this man who was going to give me his sperm, and I thought about how I couldn't *wait* to tell my child this story one day.

When we got back to his car, Alex gave me his executed copy of the contract.

And then he disappeared.

I didn't hear from him for another three days. This might not seem long, but if you're in your late thirties and about to ovulate and your only other baby option is on indefinite back order, three days is an eternity. I tried not to read into it (stress is bad for conception), but when Alex finally resurfaced, he left me a message saying, "We need to talk." I sank to the floor. Like every adult on the planet, I knew exactly what that meant: I was about to be dumped.

The next morning, as we sat at our regular table at Spurth, Alex looked away and began issuing the usual breakup clichés: "It's not you, it's me"; "I'm so unsettled in my life right now that I don't know if I can commit, so for your sake, I don't want to string you along." And the perennial favorite "I hope we can still be friends."

"It's okay, there are other fish in the sea," I said, protecting myself with a bad pun. I hoped to lighten the mood, to let Alex know that the rational part of me understood why he felt that he couldn't go through with the donation. But inside I was gutted, because now this was the second baby I'd so clearly imagined and that I would never get to hold in my arms. A friend who had her second miscarriage around this time said that she felt exactly the same way. I went home and decided to take a break from the sperm-donor search because the heartbreak was too much to bear. And like my friend who had miscarried, I avoided babies as much as possible. Even diaper commercials sent me lunging for the remote so I could change the channel.

After a few months, I knew I had to get back online and resume my search. But just as I was about to sign on again, I got an unexpected call.

It was Kathleen, my lab girl at the sperm bank.

"Lori, good news!" she announced in her heavy Brooklyn accent. "Somebody returned a vial of the Clooney kid."

The Clooney kid . . . my guy. The one who was "the whole package."

"Returned?" I asked. I wasn't sure how I felt about *returned* semen. I thought about how at Whole Foods, you couldn't return any personal-hygiene items, even with a receipt. But Kathleen assured me that the vial hadn't left its sealed nitrogen tank and that there was nothing wrong with the "product." Somebody had simply gotten pregnant some other way and no longer needed the backup. If I wanted it, I had to buy it now.

"Clooney has a waiting list, you know—" she began, but before she finished her sentence, I had already said yes.

Late that fall, I was out to dinner with a group of people after my baby shower when my mother noticed the real George Clooney sitting at a table nearby. Everyone at our table knew about Kathleen's "young George Clooney" description, and one by one, my friends and family pointed at my enormous belly, then turned their heads toward the movie star.

He looked much more grown up than he had as a young actor starring in *ER*. I, too, felt much more grown up than I'd been as a young executive working at NBC. So much had happened in both of our lives. He was about to win an Oscar. I was about to have my son.

A week later, "the Clooney kid" got a new name: Zachary Julian. ZJ. He is love and joy and wonder and magic. He is, as Kathleen might say, "the whole package."

Flash-forward eight years: a déjà vu, of sorts. When Boyfriend says, "I can't live with a kid under my roof for the next ten years," I'll be transported back to that day at Urth when Alex told me he couldn't be my donor after all. I'll remember how shattered I was, but also how Kathleen called soon after, resurrecting what had felt like the death of a dream.

The situations will seem similar enough—the blindsiding twist, plans dashed—that underneath my pain in the wake of Boyfriend's announcement, I might expect to have hope that things will work themselves out again.

But something feels very different this time.

17

Without Memory or Desire

In the mid-twentieth century, the British psychoanalyst Wilfred Bion posited that therapists should approach their patients "without memory or desire." In his view, therapists' memories were prone to subjective interpretation, morphing over time, while their desires might run counter to what their patients wanted. Taken together, memories and desires can create biased notions that therapists hold about the treatment (known as formulated ideas). Bion wanted clinicians to enter each session committed to hearing the patient in the present moment (rather than being influenced by memory) and remaining open to various outcomes (rather than being influenced by desire).

Early in my internship, I trained under a Bion enthusiast, and I challenged myself to start each session with "no memory, no desire." I loved the idea of not getting sidetracked by preconceived notions or agendas. There also seemed to be a Zen flavor to this kind of relinquishment, similar to the Buddhist notion of letting go of attachment. In practice, though, it felt more like trying to emulate the neurologist Oliver Sacks's famous patient H.M., whose brain injury confined him to live only in the moment, with no ability to remember the immediate past or conceptualize the future. With my frontal lobes intact, I couldn't will myself into that kind of amnesia.

I know, of course, that Bion's concept was more nuanced and that there's value in checking the distracting aspects of memory and desire at the door. But I bring up Bion here because when I drive to my sessions with Wendell, I think about how, from the patient's side of the room—from *my* side—"no memory (of Boyfriend), no desire (for Boyfriend)" would be close to grace.

It's Wednesday morning and I'm on Wendell's couch, sitting halfway between positions A and B, having just arranged the pillows behind my back.

I fully intend to open with what happened at work the day before when I was in the communal kitchen and spotted a copy of *Divorce* magazine on top of a pile of reading material that was to be placed in the waiting room. I pictured the people who subscribed to this magazine coming home at the end of the day and finding, among all the bills and store catalogs, this magazine with the word DIVORCE in bright yellow letters on the cover. Then I imagined these people walking into their empty houses, each one turning on the lights, heating up a frozen dinner or ordering takeout for one, sitting down to eat, and flipping through this magazine's pages, wondering, *How did this become my life?* I figured the people who had moved on from their divorces were doing something other than reading this magazine and that the majority of subscribers would be people like me, newly smarting and trying to make sense of it all.

Of course, I hadn't married Boyfriend, so this wasn't a divorce. But we were *supposed to get married,* which, according to my thinking at that moment, put me in a similar category. I even felt that this breakup might be worse than a divorce in one particular aspect. In a divorce, things have gone badly already, thus leading to the split. If you're going to mourn a loss, isn't it better to have an arsenal of unpleasant memories—stony silences, screaming fights, infidelity, massive disappointment—to temper the good ones? Isn't it harder to let go of a relationship filled with happy memories?

It seemed to me the answer was yes.

So I was sitting at the table eating a yogurt and scanning the magazine's headlines ("Healing from Rejection"; "Managing Negative Thoughts"; "Creating the New You!") when my phone beeped, indicating that an

email had come in. It was not, as I still (delusionally) hoped, from Boyfriend. The subject line read *Prepare for the best night ever!* Spam, I assumed
—but if it wasn't, who was I to turn down the best night ever, given how
bad I felt?

I clicked on it and saw that the email was a confirmation for the concert tickets I'd ordered months in advance as a surprise for Boyfriend's up-
coming birthday. We both loved this band, and their music had been like
a soundtrack to our relationship. On our first date, we discovered that
we had the same all-time-favorite song. I couldn't imagine going to this
concert with anyone but Boyfriend—especially on his birthday. Should
I go? With whom? And wouldn't I be thinking about him on his birthday? Which raised the questions: Would he be thinking about me? And if
not, didn't I mean anything to him? I looked back at the *Divorce* headline:
"Managing Negative Thoughts."

I was finding it hard to manage my negative thoughts because, outside of Wendell's office, they didn't have much of an outlet. Breakups tend
to fall into the category of silent losses, less tangible to other people. You
have a miscarriage, but you didn't lose a baby. You have a breakup, but
you didn't lose a spouse. So friends assume that you'll move on relatively
quickly, and things like these concert tickets become an almost welcome
external acknowledgment of your loss—not only of the person but of the
time and company and daily routines, of the private jokes and references,
and of the shared memories that now are yours alone to carry.

I fully intend to say all this to Wendell as I get comfortable on the
couch, but instead all that comes out is a torrent of tears.

Through the blur, I see the tissue box soaring toward me. Once again,
I miss the catch. (In addition to being dumped, I think, I've become un-
coordinated.)

I'm both surprised by and ashamed of my outburst—we haven't even
greeted each other yet—and every time I try to pull it together, I get in a
quick "I'm sorry" before I lose it again. For about five minutes, my session
goes like this: Cry. Try to stop. Say, *I'm sorry.* Cry. Try to stop. Say, *I'm sorry.*
Cry. Try to stop. Say, *Oh God, I'm really sorry.*

Wendell wants to know what I'm apologizing for.

I point to myself. "Look at me!" I make loud honking noises into a tissue.

Wendell shrugs as if to say, *Well, yeah—and so what?*

And then I don't even pause to say "I'm sorry"; it's just cry. Try to stop. Cry. Try to stop. Cry. Try to stop.

This goes on for another few minutes.

While I'm crying, I think about how the morning after the breakup, after a sleepless night, I got out of bed and went on with my daily life.

I remember how I dropped Zach off at school and said, "Love you," as he jumped out of the car, and he looked around to make sure nobody could hear and then said, "Love you!" before running off to join his friends.

I think about how on the drive to work, I replayed Jen's comment over and over in my mind: *I don't know that this is the end of the story.*

I think about how, riding up to my office in the elevator, I actually laughed when I remembered the old pun *Denial is not a river in Egypt*—and how even so, I went right back into denial: *Maybe he'll change his mind*, I thought. *Maybe this is all a big misunderstanding.*

Of course it wasn't all a big misunderstanding because here I am, crying in front of Wendell and telling him again how lame I am to be doing this, to still be such a wreck.

"Let's make a deal," Wendell says. "How about we agree that you'll be kind to yourself while you're in here? You can go ahead and beat yourself up all you want as soon as you leave, okay?"

Be kind to myself. This hadn't occurred to me.

"But it's just a breakup," I say, immediately forgetting to be kind to myself.

"Or I could just leave a pair of boxing gloves at the door so you could hit yourself with them all session. Would that be easier?" Wendell smiles, and I feel myself take in some air, let it out, relax into the kindness. I flash on a thought I often have when seeing my own self-flagellating patients: *You are not the best person to talk to you about you right now.* There is a difference, I point out to them, between self-blame and self-responsibility, which is a corollary to something Jack Kornfield said: "A second quality of mature spirituality is kindness. It is based on a fundamental notion of self-acceptance." In therapy we aim for self-compassion (*Am I human?*) versus self-esteem (a judgment: *Am I good or bad?*).

"Maybe not the boxing gloves," I say. "It's just that I was doing better and now I can't stop crying again. I feel like I'm going backward, like I'm back where I was the week of the breakup."

Wendell tilts his head. "Let me ask you something," he says, and, assuming it's going to be about my relationship, I wipe my eyes and wait expectantly.

"In your work as a therapist," he begins, "have you ever sat with somebody who's grieving?"

His question stops me cold.

I have sat with people dealing with all kinds of grief—the loss of a child, the loss of a parent, the loss of a spouse, the loss of a sibling, the loss of a marriage, the loss of a dog, the loss of a job, the loss of an identity, the loss of a dream, the loss of a body part, the loss of youth. I've sat with people whose faces close in on themselves, whose eyes become slits, whose open mouths resemble the image in Munch's *The Scream.* I've sat with patients who describe their grief as "monstrous" and "unbearable"; one patient, quoting something she had heard, said it made her feel "alternately numb and in excruciating pain."

I've also seen grief from afar, like the time in medical school when I was transporting blood samples in the emergency room and heard a sound so startling that I almost dropped the tubes. It was a wail, more animal-like than human, so piercing and primal that it took me a minute to find its source. Out in the hallway was a mother whose three-year-old had drowned after running out the back door and falling in the swimming pool during the two minutes in which the mother had gone upstairs with her infant to change his diaper. As I listened to the wail, I saw her husband arrive and receive the news, heard his shock erupting into shrieks as if in chorus with his wife's roar-moan. It was my first time hearing this particular music of sorrow and anguish, but I have heard it countless times since.

Grief, not surprisingly, can resemble depression, and for this reason, until a few years ago, there was something termed the *bereavement exclu-*

sion in our profession's diagnostic manual. If a person experienced the symptoms of depression in the first two months after a loss, the diagnosis was bereavement. But if those symptoms persisted past two months, the diagnosis became depression. This bereavement exclusion no longer exists, partly because of the timeline: Are people really supposed to be done griev-ing after two months? Can't grief last six months or a year or, in some form or another, an entire lifetime?

Then there's the fact that losses tend to be multilayered. There's the actual loss (in my case, of Boyfriend), and the underlying loss (what it represents). That's why for many people the pain of a divorce is only par-tially about the loss of the other person; often it's just as much about what the change *represents*—failure, rejection, betrayal, the unknown, and a dif-ferent life story than the one they'd expected. If the divorce happens at midlife, the loss might involve coping with the limitations of knowing someone and being known again with the same degree of intimacy. I re-member reading a divorced woman's experience of getting to know a new lover after her decades-long marriage ended: "I will never lock eyes in the delivery room with David," she wrote. "I've never met his mother."

And that's also why Wendell's question is so important. In asking me to remember what it's like to sit with people who are grieving, he's show-ing me what he can do for me right now. He can't fix my broken relation-ship. He can't change the facts. But he can help because he knows this: We all have a deep yearning to understand ourselves and be understood. When I see couples in therapy, often one or the other will complain, not "You don't love me" but "You don't *understand* me." (One woman said to her husband, "You know what three words are even more romantic to me than 'I love you'?" "You look beautiful?" he tried. "No," his wife said. "I *understand* you.")

My tears start again, and I'm thinking about what it might be like for Wendell to sit here with me. Everything we therapists do or say or feel as we sit with our patients is mediated by our histories; everything I've ex-perienced will influence how I am in any given session at any given hour. The text I just received, the conversation I had with a friend, the interac-tion I had with customer service while trying to resolve a mistake on my bill, the weather, how much sleep I've gotten, what I dreamed of before my first session of the day, a memory inspired by a patient's story, will all influence my behavior with my patient. Who I was before Boyfriend is different from who I am now. Who I was when my son was an infant is different from who I am in sessions now, including in this one with Wendell. And he is different in this session with me because of whatever has happened in his life up to this point. Maybe my tears are bringing up whatever grief he's experienced and it's painful for him to sit through this too. He's as mysterious to me as I am to him, and yet here we are, joining forces to unravel the story of how I ended up here.

It's Wendell's job to help me edit my story. All therapists do this: What material is extraneous? Are the supporting characters important or a distraction? Is the story advancing or is the protagonist going in circles? Do the plot points reveal a theme?

The techniques we use are a bit like the type of brain surgery in which the patient remains awake throughout the procedure; as the surgeons operate, they keep checking in with the patient: *Can you feel this? Can you say these words? Can you repeat this sentence?* They're constantly calibrating how close they are to sensitive regions of the brain, and if they hit one, they back off so as not to damage it. Therapists delve into a mind rather than a brain, and we can see from the subtlest gesture or expression if we've hit a nerve. But unlike neurosurgeons, we gravitate *toward* the sensitive area, pressing delicately on it, even if it makes the patient feel uncomfortable.

That's how we get to the deeper meaning of the story, and often at the core is some form of grief. But a lot of plot stands in between.

A patient named Samantha came to therapy in her twenties to understand the story of her beloved father's death. She'd been told as a child that he had died in a boating accident, but as an adult, she began to suspect that he had killed himself. Suicide often leaves the survivors with an unsolved mystery: *Why? What could have been done to prevent this?*

Meanwhile, Samantha was always looking for problems in her relationships, searching for issues that would inevitably provide her with a reason to leave. In not wanting her boyfriends to be the enigma that her father was, she'd unwittingly re-create a story of abandonment—only in this version, she was the one doing the abandoning. She had control, but ended up alone. In therapy, she learned that the mystery she was trying to solve was larger than whether or not her father committed suicide. It was also the mystery of who her father was *when he was alive*—and who *she* became as a result of that.

People want to be understood and to understand, but for most of us, our biggest problem is that we don't know what our problem is. We keep stepping in the same puddle. *Why do I do the very thing that will guarantee my own unhappiness over and over again?*

I cry and cry, wondering how it's possible that I can cry so long. I wonder if I've become massively dehydrated. And still more tears appear. Before I know it, Wendell is patting his legs to indicate that our session is over. I take a breath and notice that I feel strangely calm now. Sobbing freely in Wendell's office was like being wrapped in a blanket, warm and safe and separate from everything happening out there. I think about the Jack Kornfield quote again, the part about self-acceptance, but still I start to judge: *Did I just pay somebody to watch me cry for forty-five minutes straight?*

Yes and no.

Wendell and I had a conversation, even if no words were exchanged. He watched me grieve, and he didn't try to make things more comfortable by interrupting or analyzing the issue. He let me tell my story in whatever way I needed to today.

As I dry my tears and stand to leave, I think about how whenever Wendell has asked about other aspects of my life—what else was happening while Boyfriend and I were dating, what my life was like before I met Boyfriend—I've given a pat response (family, work, friends; *nothing to see here, folks!*), always returning the topic to Boyfriend. But now, tossing my tissues in the trash can, I realize that what I've told Wendell isn't really complete.

I haven't lied, exactly. But I haven't told the whole story either.

Let's just say that I left out some details.

Part Two

Honesty is stronger medicine than sympathy,

which may console but often conceals.

—Gretel Ehrlich

18

Fridays at Four

We're in my colleague Maxine's office—skirted chairs, distressed wood, vintage fabrics, and soft shades of cream. It's my turn to present a case in today's consultation group, and I want to talk about a patient I can't seem to help.

Is it her? Is it me? That's what I'm here to find out.

Becca is thirty years old, and she came to me a year ago because of difficulty with her social life. She did well at her work but felt hurt that her peers excluded her, never inviting her to join them for lunch or drinks. Meanwhile, she'd just dated a string of men who seemed excited at first but broke it off after two months.

Was it her? Was it them? That's what she'd come to therapy to find out.

This isn't the first time I've brought up Becca on a Friday at four, when our weekly group meets. Though not required, consultation groups are a fixture of many therapists' lives. Working alone, we don't have the benefit of input from others, whether that's praise for a job well done or feedback on how to do better. Here we examine not just our patients but *ourselves in relation to our patients.*

In our group, Andrea can say to me, "That patient sounds like your brother. That's why you're responding that way." I can help Ian manage his feelings about the patient who begins her sessions by reporting her horoscope ("I can't stand this woo-woo shit," he says). Group consultation is a system—imperfect, but valuable—of checks and balances to ensure that we're maintaining objectivity, homing in on the important themes, and not missing anything obvious in the treatment.

Admittedly, there's also banter on these Friday afternoons—often along with food and wine.

"It's the same dilemma," I tell the group—Maxine, Andrea, Claire, and Ian, our lone male. Everyone has blind spots, I add, but what's notable about Becca is that she seems to have so little curiosity about herself.

The members of the group nod. Many people begin therapy more curious about others than about themselves— *Why does my husband do this?* But in each conversation, we sprinkle seeds of curiosity, because therapy can't help people who aren't curious about themselves. At some point I might even say something like "I wonder why I seem to be more curious about you than you are about yourself?" and see where the patient takes this. Most people will start to get curious about my question. But not Becca.

I take a breath and go on. "She's not satisfied with what I'm doing, she's not moving forward, and instead of seeing somebody else, she comes each week—almost to show that she's right and I'm wrong."

Maxine, who's been in practice for thirty years and is the matriarch of the group, swirls the wine in her glass. "Why do you keep seeing her?"

I consider this as I slice some cheese from the wedge on the tray. In fact, all of the ideas the group has offered in the past several of months have fallen flat. If, for instance, I asked Becca what her tears were about, she'd shoot back with "That's why I'm coming to you—if *I* knew what was going on, I wouldn't need to be here." If I talked about what was happening between us in the moment—her disappointment in me, her feeling misunderstood by me, her perception that I wasn't helpful—she'd go off on a tangent about how this kind of impasse didn't happen with anybody else, just me. When I attempted to keep the conversation focused on us—did she feel accused of something, or criticized?—she'd get angry. When I tried to talk about the anger, she'd shut down. When I wondered if the shutting down was a way of keeping out what I had to say for fear it might hurt her, she'd say again that I misunderstood. If I asked why she kept coming to see me if she felt so misunderstood, she'd say I was abandoning her and that I wished she would leave—just like her boyfriends or her peers at work. When I tried to help her consider why those people pulled away from her, she'd say the boyfriends were commitment-phobes and her coworkers were snobby.

Generally what happens between therapist and patient also plays out between the patient and people in the outside world, and it's in the safe space of the therapy room that the patient can begin to understand why. (And if the dance between therapist and patient doesn't play out in the patient's outside relationships, it's often because the patient doesn't have any deep relationships—precisely for this reason. It's easy to have smooth relationships on a surface level.) It seemed that Becca was reenacting with me and everyone else a version of her relationship with her parents, but she wasn't willing to discuss that either.

Of course, there are times when something just isn't right between therapist and patient, when the therapist's countertransference is getting in the way. One sign: having negative feelings about the patient.

Becca *does* irritate me, I tell the group. But is it because she reminds me of somebody from my past, or because she's genuinely difficult to interact with?

Therapists use three sources of information when working with patients: What the patients say, what they do, and *how we feel while we're sitting with them.* Sometimes a patient will basically be wearing a sign around her neck saying I REMIND YOU OF YOUR MOTHER! But as a supervisor drilled into us during training, "What you feel on the receiving end of an encounter with a patient is real—use it." Our experiences with this person are important because we're probably feeling something pretty similar to what everyone else in this patient's life feels.

Knowing that helped me empathize with Becca, to see how deep her struggles were. The late reporter Alex Tizon believed that every person has an epic story that resides "somewhere in the tangle of the subject's burden and the subject's desire." But I couldn't get there with Becca. I felt increasingly fatigued in our sessions—not from mental exertion, but from boredom. I made sure to have chocolate and do jumping jacks before she came in to wake myself up. Eventually, I moved her evening session to first thing in the morning. The minute she sat down, though, the boredom set in and I felt helpless to help her.

"She needs to make you feel incompetent so she can feel more powerful," Claire, a sought-after analyst, says today. "If you fail, then she doesn't have to feel like such a failure."

Maybe Claire is right. The hardest patients aren't the ones like John, people who are changing but don't seem to realize it. The hardest patients are the ones, like Becca, who keep coming but don't change.

Recently Becca had started dating someone new, a guy named Wade, and last week, she told me about an argument they'd had. Wade had noticed that Becca seemed to complain about her friends quite a bit. "If you're so unhappy with them," he said, "why do you keep them as friends?"

Becca "couldn't believe" Wade's response. Didn't he understand that she was just venting? That she wanted to talk it through with him and not be "shut down"?

The parallels here seemed obvious. I asked Becca if she was just trying to vent with me and that, as with her friends, she found some value in our relationship, even though sometimes she also felt frustrated. No, Becca said, I'd gotten it wrong again. She was here to talk about Wade. She couldn't see that she had shut Wade down just as she had shut me down, which left her feeling shut down herself. She wasn't willing to look at what she was doing that made it difficult for people to give her what she wanted. Though Becca came to me wanting aspects of her life to change, she didn't seem open to actually changing. She was stuck in a "historical argument," one that predated therapy. And just as Becca had her limitations, so did I. Every therapist I know has come up against theirs.

Maxine asks again why I'm still seeing Becca. She points out that I've tried everything I know from my training and experience, everything I've gleaned from the therapists in my consultation group, and Becca is making no progress.

"I don't want her to feel emotionally stranded," I say.

"She already feels emotionally stranded," Maxine says. "By everyone in her life, including you."

"Right," I say. "But I'm afraid that if I end therapy with her, it's going to further cement her belief that nobody can help her."

Andrea raises her eyebrows.

"What?" I say.

"You don't need to prove your competence to Becca," she says.

"I know that. It's Becca I'm worried about."

Ian coughs loudly, then pretends to gag. The entire group bursts out laughing.

"Okay, maybe I *do*." I put some cheese on a cracker. "It's like this other patient I have who's in a relationship with a guy who doesn't treat her very well, and she won't leave because on some level, she wants to prove to him that she deserves to be treated better. She's never going to prove it to him, but she won't stop trying."

"You need to concede the fight," Andrea says.

"I've never broken up with a patient before," I say.

"Breakups are awful," Claire says, popping some grapes in her mouth. "But we'd be negligent if we didn't do them."

A collective *Mm-hmm* fills the room.

Ian watches, shaking his head. "You're all going to jump down my throat over this" — Ian's famous in our group for making generalizations about men and women — "but here's the thing. Women put up with more crap than men do. If a girlfriend's not treating a guy well, he has an easier time leaving. If a patient isn't benefiting from what I have to offer, and I've made sure I'm doing my very best but nothing's working, I'll break it off."

We give him our familiar stare-down: Women are just as good at letting go as men are. But we also know there might be a grain of truth here.

"To breaking it off," Maxine says, raising her glass. We clink glasses but not in a joyful way.

It's heartbreaking when a patient invests hope in you and, in the end, you know you've let her down. In those cases, a question stays with you: *If I'd done something differently, if I'd found the key in time, could I have helped?* The answer you give yourself: *Probably.* No matter what my consultation group says, I wasn't able to reach Becca in just the right way, and in that sense, I failed her.

• • •

Therapy is hard work—and not just for the therapist. That's because the responsibility for change lies squarely with the patient.

If you expect an hour of sympathetic head-nodding, you've come to the wrong place. Therapists will be supportive, but our support is for your growth, not for your low opinion of your partner. (Our role is to understand your perspective but not necessarily to endorse it.) In therapy, you'll be asked to be both accountable and vulnerable. Rather than steering people straight to the heart of the problem, we nudge them to arrive there on their own, because the most powerful truths—the ones people take the most seriously—are those they come to, little by little, on their own. Implicit in the therapeutic contract is the patient's willingness to tolerate discomfort, because some discomfort is unavoidable for the process to be effective.

Or as Maxine said one Friday afternoon: "I don't do 'you go, girl' therapy."

It may seem counterintuitive, but therapy works best when people start getting better—when they feel less depressed or anxious, or the crisis has passed. Now they're less reactive, more present, more able to engage in the work. Unfortunately, sometimes people leave just as their symptoms lift, not realizing (or perhaps knowing all too well) that the work is just beginning and that staying will require them to work even harder.

Once, at the end of a session with Wendell, I told him that sometimes, on days when I left more upset than when I came in—tossed out into the world, having so much more to say, holding so many painful feelings—I hated therapy.

"Most things worth doing are difficult," he replied. He said this not in a glib way but in a tone and with an expression that made me think he spoke from personal experience. He added that while everyone wants to leave each session feeling better, I, of all people, should know that that's not always how therapy works. If I wanted to feel good in the short term, he said, I could eat a piece of cake or have an orgasm. But he wasn't in the short-term-gratification business.

And neither, he added, was I.

Except that I was—as a patient, that is. What makes therapy challenging is that it requires people to see themselves in ways they normally choose not to. A therapist will hold up the mirror in the most compassionate way possible, but it's up to the patient to take a good look at that reflection, to stare back at it and say, "Oh, isn't that interesting! Now what?" instead of turning away.

I decide to take my consultation group's advice and end my sessions with Becca. Afterwards, I feel both disappointed and liberated. When I tell Wendell about it at my next session, he says he knows exactly how it felt to be with her.

"You have patients like her?" I ask.

"I do," he says, and he smiles broadly, holding my gaze.

It takes a minute, but then I get it: He means *me*. Yikes! Does he do jumping jacks or down caffeine before our sessions too? Many patients wonder if they bore us with what feels to them like their unremarkable lives, but they're not boring at all. The patients who are boring are the ones who won't *share* their lives, who smile through their sessions or launch into seemingly pointless and repetitive stories every time, leaving us scratching our heads: *Why are they telling me this? What significance does this have for them?* People who are aggressively boring want to keep you at bay.

It's what I've done with Wendell when talking incessantly about Boyfriend; he can't quite reach me because I'm not allowing him to. And now he's laying it out there: I'm doing with him what Boyfriend and I did with each other—and I'm not so different from Becca after all.

"I'm telling you this by way of invitation," Wendell says, and I think about how many invitations of mine Becca had rebuffed. I don't want to do that with Wendell.

If I wasn't able to help Becca, maybe she'll be able to help me.

19

What We Dream Of

One day, a twenty-four-year-old woman I'd been seeing for a few months came in and told me about the previous night's dream.

"I'm at the mall," Holly began, "and I run into this girl, Liza, who was horrible to me in high school. She didn't tease me to my face, like some other girls did. She just completely ignored me! Which would have been okay, except that if I ran into her outside of school, she'd pretend she had no idea who I was. Which was *crazy*, because we'd been at the same school for three years, and we had several classes together.

"Anyway, she lived a block away, so I'd run into her a lot—you know, around the neighborhood—and I'd have to pretend I didn't see her, because if I said hi or waved or acknowledged her in any way, she'd scrunch up her forehead and give me this look like she was trying to place me but couldn't. And then she'd say, in this fake-sweet voice, 'I'm sorry, do I know you?' or 'Have we met before?' or, if I was lucky, 'This is so embarrassing, but what's your name again?'"

Holly's voice faltered for a second, then she continued.

"So in the dream, I'm at the mall, and Liza is there. I'm no longer in high school and I look different—I'm thin, wearing the perfect outfit, blow-dried hair. I'm flipping through some clothes on a rack when Liza comes over to browse through the same rack, and she starts making small talk about the clothes, the way you might with a stranger. At first I'm pissed, like here we go again—she's *still* pretending not to recognize me. Except then I realize that now it's real—she *doesn't* recognize me because I look so good."

Holly shifted on the couch, covering herself with the blanket. We've talked in the past about how she uses that blanket to cover up her body, to hide her size.

"So I play innocent, and we start chatting about the clothes and what our jobs are, and as I'm talking, I see this look of recognition dawning on her face. It's like she's trying to reconcile her image of me from twelfth grade—you know, pimply, fat, frizzy hair—with me now. I see her brain connecting the dots, and then she says, 'Oh my God! Holly! We went to high school together!'"

Holly was starting to laugh now. She was tall and striking, with long chestnut hair and eyes the color of a tropical ocean, and she was still a good forty pounds overweight.

"So," she continued, "I scrunch up my forehead and say, in the same fake-sweet voice she used to use on me, 'Wait, I'm so sorry. Do I know you?' And she says, 'Of course you know me—it's Liza! We had geometry and ancient history and French together—remember Ms. Hyatt's class?' And I say, 'Yeah, I had Ms. Hyatt, but, gosh, I don't remember you. You were in that class?' And she says, '*Holly!* We lived a block away from each other. I used to see you at the movies and the yogurt place and that one time in Victoria's Secret by the dressing rooms—'"

Holly laughed some more.

"She's totally giving away that she *did* know me all those times. But I say, 'Wow, how weird, I don't remember you, but it's nice to meet you.' And then my phone rings and it's her high-school boyfriend telling me to hurry up, we'll be late for our movie. So I give her that condescending smile she used to give me, and I walk away, leaving her feeling how I felt in high school. And then I realize that the ringing phone is actually my alarm and it was all a dream."

Later, Holly would call this her "poetic-justice dream," but to me it was about a common theme that comes up in therapy, and not just in dreams—the theme of exclusion. It's the fear that we'll be left out, ignored, shunned, and end up unlovable and alone.

Carl Jung coined the term *collective unconscious* to refer to the part of the mind that holds ancestral memory, or experience that is common to all humankind. Whereas Freud interpreted dreams on the *object level*, meaning how the content of the dream related to the dreamer in real life (the cast of characters, the specific situations), in Jungian psychology, dreams are interpreted on the *subject level*, meaning how they relate to common themes in our collective unconscious.

It's no surprise that we often dream about our fears. We have a lot of fears.

What are we afraid of?

We are afraid of being hurt. We are afraid of being humiliated. We are afraid of failure and we are afraid of success. We are afraid of being alone and we are afraid of connection. We are afraid to listen to what our hearts are telling us. We are afraid of being unhappy and we are afraid of being too happy (in these dreams, inevitably, we're punished for our joy). We are afraid of not having our parents' approval and we are afraid of accepting ourselves for who we really are. We are afraid of bad health and good fortune. We are afraid of our envy and of having too much. We are afraid to have hope for things that we might not get. We are afraid of change and we are afraid of not changing. We are afraid of something happening to our kids, our jobs. We are afraid of not having control and afraid of our own power. We are afraid of how briefly we are alive and how long we will be dead. (We are afraid that after we die, we won't have mattered.) We are afraid of being responsible for our own lives.

Sometimes it takes a while to admit our fears, especially to ourselves.

I've noticed that dreams can be a precursor to self-confession—a kind of pre-confession. Something buried is brought closer to the surface, but not in its entirety. A patient dreams that she's lying in bed hugging her roommate; initially she thinks it's about their strong friendship but later she realizes she's attracted to women. A man has a recurring dream that he's been caught speeding on the freeway; a year into this dream, he begins to consider that his decades of cheating on his taxes — of positioning himself above the rules — might catch up with him.

After I've been seeing Wendell for a few months, my patient's dream about her high-school classmate seeps into mine. I'm at the mall, looking through a rack of dresses, when Boyfriend appears at the same rack. Apparently, he's shopping for a birthday gift for his new girlfriend.

"Oh, which birthday?" I ask in the dream.

"Fiftieth," he says. At first I'm relieved in the pettiest way — not only is she not the clichéd twenty-five-year-old, but she's actually older than I am. It makes sense. Boyfriend wanted no kids in the house, and she's old enough to have kids in college. Boyfriend and I are having a pleasant conversation — friendly, innocuous — until I happen to catch a glimpse of myself in the mirror adjacent to the rack. That's when I see that I'm actually an old lady — late seventies, maybe eighties. It turns out that Boyfriend's fifty-year-old girlfriend is, in fact, decades younger than I am.

"Did you ever write your book?" Boyfriend asks.

"What book?" I say, watching my wrinkled, prune-like lips move in the mirror.

"The book about your death," he replies matter-of-factly.

And then my alarm goes off. All day, as I hear other patients' dreams, I can't stop thinking about mine. It haunts me, this dream.

It haunts me because it's my pre-confession.

20

The First Confession

Allow me to get defensive for a minute. You see, when I told Wendell that everything was just fine until the breakup, I was telling the absolute truth. Or, rather, the truth as I knew it. Which is to say, the truth as I wanted to see it.

And now let me remove the defense: I was lying.

One thing I haven't told Wendell is that I'm supposed to be writing a book—and that it hasn't been going very well. By "not going very well," I mean that I haven't actually been writing it. This wouldn't be a problem if I weren't under contract and therefore legally obligated to either produce a book or return the advance that I no longer have in my bank account. Well, it would still be a problem even if I could return the money, because in addition to being a therapist, I am a writer—it's not just what I do but *who I am*—and if I can't write, then a crucial part of me goes missing. And if I don't turn in this book, my agent says that I won't get the opportunity to write another.

It isn't that I haven't been able to write at all. In fact, during the time I was supposed to be writing my book, I was crafting fabulously witty and flirtatious emails to Boyfriend, all while telling friends and family and even Boyfriend that I was busy writing my book. I was like the closet gambler who gets dressed for work and kisses his family goodbye each morning and then drives to the casino instead of the office.

I've been meaning to talk to Wendell about this situation, but I've been so focused on getting through the breakup that I haven't had a chance.

Obviously that, too, is a big fat lie.

I haven't told Wendell about the book-I'm-not-writing because every time I think about it, I'm filled with panic, dread, regret, and shame. Whenever the situation pops into my head (which is constantly; as Fitzgerald put it, "In a real dark night of the soul, it is always three o'clock in the morning, day after day"), my stomach tightens and I feel paralyzed. Then I question every bad decision I've made at various forks in the road because I'm convinced that I'm in this current situation due to what ranks as one of the most colossally bad decisions of my life.

Perhaps you're thinking, *Really? You were lucky enough to get a book contract, and now you're not writing the book? Boo-hoo! Try working twelve hours a day in a factory, for God's sake!* I understand how this comes across. I mean, who do I think I am, Elizabeth Gilbert at the beginning of *Eat, Pray, Love* when she's crying on the bathroom floor as she thinks about leaving the husband who loves her? Gretchen Rubin in *The Happiness Project* who has the loving, handsome husband, the healthy daughters, and more money than most people will ever see but still has that niggling feeling of something missing?

Which reminds me—I left out an important detail about the book-I'm-not-writing. The topic? Happiness. No, the irony hasn't been lost on me: the happiness book has been making me miserable.

I should never have been writing a happiness book in the first place, and not just because, if Wendell's grieving-something-bigger theory holds water, I've been depressed. When I made the decision to write this book, I'd recently begun my private practice, and I'd just written a cover story for the *Atlantic* called "How to Land Your Kid in Therapy: Why Our Obsession with Our Kids' Happiness May Be Dooming Them to Unhappy Adulthoods," which, at the time, was the most emailed piece in the hundred-plus-year history of the magazine. I talked about it on national television and radio; media from around the world called me for interviews; and overnight, I became a "parenting expert."

Next thing I knew, publishers wanted the book version of "How to

Land Your Kid in Therapy." By *wanted,* I mean they wanted it for—I don't know how else to say this—a dizzying sum of money. It was the kind of money that a single mom like me only dreamed of, the kind of money that would provide our one-income family with some financial room to breathe for a long time. A book like this would have led to speaking engagements (which I enjoy) at schools across the country and a steady flow of patients (which would have helped, as I was starting out). The article was even optioned for a television series (which might have gotten made had there also been a best-selling book to go along with it).

But when given the opportunity to write the book version of "How to Land Your Kid in Therapy," a book that could potentially change the entire landscape of my professional and financial future, I said, with an astonishing lack of forethought: *Thanks very much, that's so kind, but . . . I'd rather not.*

I hadn't had a stroke. I just said no.

I said no because something felt wrong about it. Mainly, I didn't think that the world needed another helicopter-parenting book. Dozens of smart, thoughtful books had already covered overparenting from every conceivable angle. After all, *two hundred years* ago, the philosopher Johann Wolfgang von Goethe succinctly summarized this sentiment: "Too many parents make life hard for their children by trying, too zealously, to make it easy for them." Even in recent history—2003, to be exact—one of the early modern overparenting books, aptly named *Worried All the Time,* put it this way: "The cardinal rules of good parenting—moderation, empathy, and temperamental accommodation with one's child—are simple and are not likely to be improved upon by the latest scientific findings."

As a mom myself, I wasn't immune to parental anxiety. I wrote my original article, in fact, with the hope that it would be useful to parents in the way that a therapy session might be. But if I eked a book out of it in order to jump on the commercial bandwagon and join the ranks of insta-experts, I thought I'd be part of the problem. What parents needed, I believed, wasn't another book about how they had to calm down and take a break. What they needed was an *actual* break from the deluge of parenting books. *(The New Yorker* later ran a humor piece about the proliferation of parenting manifestos, saying that "another book at this point would just be cruel.")

So like Bartleby the Scrivener (and with similarly tragic results), I said, "I would prefer not to." Then I spent the next several years watching more and more overparenting books hit the market and beating myself up with a rotating roster of self-flagellating questions: Had I been a responsible adult by turning down that kind of money? I'd recently finished an unpaid internship, I had graduate-school loans to repay, and I was the sole provider for my family; why couldn't I have just written the parenting book quickly, reaped the professional and financial benefits, and gone my merry way? After all, how many people have the luxury of working only on what matters most to them?

The regret I felt about having not done the parenting book was compounded by the fact that I continued to get weekly reader mail and speaking-engagement queries about the "How to Land Your Kid in Therapy" article. "Will there be a book?" person after person asked. *No,* I wanted to reply, *because I'm a moron.*

I did feel like a moron, because in the interest of not selling out and cashing in on the parenting craze, I agreed instead to write the now-dreaded, depression-inducing happiness book. To make ends meet as I launched my practice, I still had to write *a* book, and I thought at the time that I could provide a service to readers. Instead of showing how we parents were trying too hard to make our kids happy, I was going to show how we were trying too hard to make *ourselves* happy. This idea seemed closer to my heart.

But whenever I sat down to write, I felt as disconnected from the topic as I had from the subject of helicopter parenting. The research didn't— *couldn't*—reflect the subtleties of what I was seeing in the therapy room. Some scientists had even come up with a complex mathematical equation to predict happiness based on the premise that happiness stems not from how well things go but whether things go *better than expected.* It looks like this:

$$\text{Happiness } (t) = w_0 + w_1 \sum_{j=1}^{t} \gamma^{t-j} CR_j + w_2 \sum_{j=1}^{t} \gamma^{t-j} EV_j + w_3 \sum_{j=1}^{t} \gamma^{t-j} RPE_j$$

Which all boils down to: Happiness equals reality minus expectations. Apparently, you can make people happy by delivering bad news and then taking it back (which, personally, would just make me mad).

Still, I knew I could put together some interesting studies, but I felt I'd just be scratching the surface of something else I wanted to say but couldn't quite put my finger on. And in my new career, and in my life more generally, scratching the surface no longer felt satisfying. You can't go through psychotherapy training and not be changed in some way, not become, without even noticing, oriented toward the core.

I told myself it didn't matter. *Just write the book and be done with it.* I'd already botched things up with the parenting book; I couldn't botch up this happiness book too. And yet, day after day, I couldn't get myself to write it. Just like I couldn't get myself to write the parenting book. How had I gotten here again?

In graduate school, we used to watch therapy sessions through one-way mirrors, and sometimes when I'd sit down to write the happiness book, I'd think about a thirty-five-year-old patient I'd observed. He'd come to therapy because he very much loved and was attracted to his wife but he couldn't stop cheating on her. Neither he nor his wife understood how his behavior could be so at odds with what he believed he wanted — trust, stability, closeness. In his session, he explained that he hated the turmoil his cheating put his wife and their marriage through and knew that he wasn't the husband or father he wanted to be. He talked for a while about how desperately he wanted to stop cheating and how he had no idea why he kept doing it.

The therapist explained that often different parts of ourselves want different things, and if we silence the parts we find unacceptable, they'll find other ways to be heard. He asked the guy to sit in a different chair, across the room, and see what happened when the part of him that chose to cheat wasn't shoved aside but got to say its piece.

At first the poor guy was at a loss, but gradually, he began to give voice to his hidden self, the part that would goad the responsible, loving husband into engaging in self-defeating behavior. He was torn between these two aspects of himself, just as I was torn between the part of me that wanted to provide for my family and the part of me that wanted to do something meaningful—something that touched my soul and hopefully others' souls as well.

Boyfriend appeared on the scene just in time to distract me from this internal battle. And once he was gone, I filled the void by Google-stalking him when I should have been writing. So many of our destructive behaviors take root in an emotional void, an emptiness that calls out for something to fill it. But now that Wendell and I have talked about not Google-stalking Boyfriend, I feel accountable. I have no excuse not to sit down and write this misery-inducing happiness book.

Or at least tell Wendell the truth about the mess I'm in.

21

Therapy with a Condom On

"Hi, it's me," I hear as I listen to my voicemails between sessions. My stomach lurches; it's Boyfriend. Though it's been three months since we've spoken, his voice instantly transports me back in time, like hearing a song from the past. But as the message continues, I realize it's *not* Boyfriend because (a) Boyfriend wouldn't call my office number and (b) Boyfriend doesn't work on a TV show.

This "me" is John (eerily, Boyfriend and John have similar voices, deep and low) and it's the first time a patient has called my office without leaving a name. He does this as if he's the only patient I have, not to mention the only "me" in my life. Even suicidal patients will leave their names. I've never gotten *Hi, it's me. You told me to call if I was feeling like killing myself.*

John says in his message that he can't make our session today because he's stuck at the studio, so he'll be Skyping in instead. He gives me his Skype handle, then says, "Talk to you at three."

I note that he doesn't *ask* if we can Skype or inquire whether I do Skype sessions in the first place. He just assumes it will happen because that's how the world works for him. And while I'll Skype with patients under certain circumstances, I think it's a bad idea with John. So much of what I'm doing to help him relies on our in-the-room interaction. Say what you will about the wonders of technology, but screen-to-screen is, as a colleague once said, "like doing therapy with a condom on."

It's not just the words people say or even the visual cues that therapists notice in person—the foot that shakes, the subtle facial twitch, the quivering lower lip, the eyes narrowing in anger. Beyond hearing and seeing, there's something less tangible but equally important—the energy in the room, the *being together*. You lose that ineffable dimension when you aren't sharing the same physical space.

(There's also the issue of glitches. I was once on a Skype session with a patient who was in Asia temporarily, and just as she began crying hysterically, the volume went out. All I saw was her mouth moving, but she didn't know that I couldn't hear what she was saying. Before I could get that across, the connection dropped entirely. It took ten minutes to restore the Skype, and by then not only was the moment lost but our time had run out.)

I send John a quick email offering to reschedule, but he types back a message that reads like a modern-day telegram: *Can't w8. Urgent. Please.* I'm surprised by the *please* and even more by his acknowledgment of needing urgent help—of needing me, rather than treating me as dispensable. So I say okay, we'll Skype at three.

Something, I figure, must be up.

At three, I open Skype and click Call, expecting to find John sitting in an office at a desk. Instead, the call connects and I'm looking into a familiar house. It's familiar to me because it's one of the main sets of a TV show that Boyfriend and I used to binge-watch on my sofa, arms and legs entwined. Here, camera and lighting people are moving about, and I'm staring at the interior of a bedroom I've seen a million times. John's face comes into view.

"Hang on a second" is how he greets me, and then his face disappears and I'm looking at his feet. Today he's wearing trendy checkered sneakers, and he seems to be walking somewhere while carrying me with him. Presumably he's looking for privacy. Along with his shoes, I see thick electrical wires on the floor and hear a commotion in the background. Then John's face reappears.

"Okay," he says. "I'm ready."

There's a wall behind him now, and he starts rapid-fire whispering.

"It's Margo and her idiot therapist. I don't know how this person has a license but he's making things worse, not better. She was supposed to be getting help for her depression but instead she's getting more upset with me: I'm not available, I'm not listening, I'm distant, I avoid her, I forgot something on the calendar. Did I tell you that she created a shared Google calendar to make sure I won't forget things that are 'important'" — with his free hand, John does an air quote as he says the word *important* — "so now I'm even *more* stressed because my calendar is filled with Margo's things and I've already got a packed schedule!"

John has gone over this with me before so I'm not sure what the urgency is about today. Initially he had lobbied Margo to see a therapist ("So she can complain to *him*") but once she started going, John often told me that this "idiot therapist" was "brainwashing" his wife and "putting crazy ideas in her head." My sense has been that the therapist is helping Margo gain more clarity about what she will and will not put up with and that this exploration has been long overdue. I mean, it can't be easy being married to John.

At the same time, I empathize with John because his reaction is common. Whenever one person in a family system starts to make changes, even if the changes are healthy and positive, it's not unusual for other members in this system to do everything they can to maintain the status quo and bring things back to homeostasis. If an addict stops drinking, for instance, family members often unconsciously sabotage that person's recovery, because in order to regain homeostasis in the system, *somebody* has to fill the role of the troubled person. And who wants that role? Sometimes people even resist positive changes in their friends: *Why are you going to the gym so much? Why can't you stay out late — you don't need more sleep! Why are you working so hard for that promotion? You're no fun anymore!*

If John's wife becomes less depressed, how can John keep his role as the sane one in the couple? If she tries to get close in healthier ways, how can he preserve the comfortable distance he has so masterfully managed all of these years? I'm not surprised that John is having a negative reaction to Margo's therapy. Her therapist seems to be doing a good job.

"So," John continues, "last night, Margo asks me to come to bed, and

I tell her I'll be there in a minute, I have to answer a few emails. Normally after about two minutes she'll be all over me—*Why aren't you coming to bed? Why are you always working?* But last night, she doesn't do any of that. And I'm amazed! I think, Jesus Christ, something's *finally* working in her therapy, because she's realizing that nagging me about coming to bed isn't going to get me in bed any faster. So I finish my emails, but when I get in bed, Margo's asleep. Anyway, this morning, when we wake up, Margo says, 'I'm glad you got your work done, but I miss you. I miss you a lot. I just want you to know that I miss you.'"

John turns to his left and now I hear what he hears—a nearby conversation about lighting—and without his saying a word, I'm staring at John's sneakers again as they move across the floor. When I see his face appear this time, the wall behind him is gone, and now the star of the TV series is in the distant background in the upper-right corner of my screen, laughing with his on-camera nemesis along with the love interest he verbally abuses on the show. (I'm sure John is the one who writes this character.)

I love these actors, so now I'm squinting at the three of them through my screen like I'm one of those people behind the ropes at the Emmys trying to get a glimpse of a celebrity—except this isn't the red carpet and I'm watching them take sips from water bottles while they chat between scenes. *The paparazzi would kill for this view,* I think, and it takes massive willpower to focus solely on John.

"Anyway," he whispers, "I *knew* it was too good to be true. I thought she was being understanding last night, but of course the complaining starts up again first thing this morning. So I say, 'You miss me? What kind of guilt trip is that?' I mean, I'm right here. I'm here *every night.* I'm one hundred percent loyal. Never cheated, never will. I provide a nice living. I'm an involved father. I even take care of the dog because Margo says she hates walking around with plastic bags of poop. And when I'm not there, I'm *working.* It's not like I'm off in Cabo all day. So I tell her I can quit my job and she can miss me less because I'll be twiddling my thumbs at home, or I can keep my job and we'll have a roof over our heads." He yells "I'll just be a minute!" to someone I can't see and then continues. "And you know what she does when I say this? She says, all Oprah-like"—here he does a dead-on impression of Oprah—"'I know you do a lot, and I appreciate that, but I also miss you even when you're here.'"

I try to speak but John plows on. I haven't seen him this stirred up before.

"So for a second I'm relieved, because normally she'd yell at this point, but then I realize what's going on. This sounds *nothing* like Margo. She's up to something! And sure enough, she says, 'I really need you to hear this.' And I say, 'I hear it, okay? I'm not deaf. I'll try to come to bed earlier but I have to get my work done first.' But then she gets this sad look on her face, like she's about to cry, and it kills me when she gets that look, because I don't want to make her sad. The last thing I want to do is disappoint her. But before I can say anything, she says, 'I need you to hear how much I miss you because if you don't hear it, I don't know how much longer I can keep telling you.' So I say, 'We're threatening each other now?' and she says, 'It's not a threat, it's the truth.'" John's eyes become saucers and his free hand juts into the air, palm up, as if to say, *Can you believe this shit?*

"I don't think she'd actually do it," he goes on, "but it shocked me because neither of us has ever threatened to leave before. When we got married we always said that no matter how angry we got, we would never threaten to leave, and in twelve years, we haven't." He looks to his right. "Okay, Tommy, let me take a look—"

John stops talking and suddenly I'm staring at his sneakers again. When he finishes with Tommy, he starts walking somewhere. A minute later his face pops up; he's in front of another wall.

"John," I say. "Let's take a step back. First, I know you're upset by what Margo said—"

"What *Margo* said? It's not even her! It's her idiot therapist acting as her ventriloquist! She loves this guy. She quotes him all the time, like he's her fucking guru. He probably serves Kool-Aid in the waiting room, and women all over the city are divorcing their husbands because they're drinking this guy's bullshit! I looked him up just to see what his credentials are and, sure enough, some *moron therapy board* gave him a license. Wendell Bronson, P-h-fucking-D."

Wait.

Wendell Bronson?

!

!!

!!!!

!!!!!!!

Margo is seeing *my* Wendell? The "idiot therapist" is Wendell? My mind explodes. I wonder where on the couch Margo chose to sit on her first day. I wonder if Wendell tosses her tissue boxes or if she sits close enough to reach them herself. I wonder if we've ever passed each other on the way in or out (the pretty crying woman from the waiting room?). I wonder if she's ever mentioned my name in her own therapy—"John has this awful therapist, Lori Gottlieb, who said . . ." But then I remember that John is keeping his therapy a secret from Margo—I'm the "hooker" he pays in cash—and right now, I'm tremendously grateful for this circumstance. I don't know what to do with this information, so I do what therapists are taught to do when we're having a complicated reaction to something and need more time to understand it. I do nothing—for the moment. I'll get consultation on this later.

"Let's stay with Margo for a second," I say, as much to myself as to John. "I think what she said was sweet. She must really love you."

"Huh? She's threatening to leave!"

"Well, let's look at it another way," I say. "We've talked before about how there's a difference between a criticism and a complaint, how the former contains judgment while the latter contains a request. But a complaint can also be an unvoiced compliment. I know that what Margo says often feels like a series of complaints. And they are—but they're sweet complaints because inside each complaint, she's giving you a compliment. The presentation isn't optimal, but she's saying that she loves you. She wants more of you. She misses you. She's asking you to *come closer.* And now she's saying that the experience of wanting to be with you and not having that reciprocated is so painful that she might not be able to tolerate it *because she loves you so much.*" I wait to let him absorb that last part. "That's quite a compliment."

I'm always working with John on identifying his in-the-moment feelings, because feelings lead to behaviors. Once we know what we're feeling, we can make choices about where we want to go with them. But if we push them away the second they appear, often we end up veering off in the wrong direction, getting lost yet again in the land of chaos.

Men tend to be at a disadvantage here because they aren't typically raised to have a working knowledge of their internal worlds; it's less socially acceptable for men to talk about their feelings. While women feel cultural pressure to keep up their physical appearance, men feel that pressure to keep up their emotional appearance. Women tend to confide in friends or family members, but when men tell me how they feel in therapy, I'm almost always the first person they've said it to. Like my female patients, men struggle with marriage, self-esteem, identity, success, their parents, their childhoods, being loved and understood—and yet these topics can be tricky to bring up in any meaningful way with their male friends. It's no wonder that the rates of substance abuse and suicide in middle-aged men continue to increase. Many men don't feel they have any other place to turn.

So I let John take his time to sort out his feelings about Margo's "threat" and the softer message that might be behind it. I haven't seen him sit with his feelings this long before, and I'm impressed that he's able to do so now.

John's eyes have darted down and to the side, which is what usually happens with someone when what I'm saying touches someplace vulnerable, and I'm glad. It's impossible to grow without first becoming vulnerable. It looks like he's still really taking this in, that for the first time, his impact on Margo is resonating.

Finally John looks back up at me. "Hi, sorry, I had to mute you back there. They were taping. I missed that. What were you saying?"

Un-fucking-believable. I've been, quite literally, talking to myself. No wonder Margo wants to leave! I should have listened to my gut and had John reschedule an in-person session, but I got sucked in by his urgent plea.

"John," I say, "I really want to help you with this but I think this is too important to talk about on Skype. Let's schedule a time for you to come in so there aren't so many distract—"

"Oh, no, no, no, no, no," he interrupts. "This can't wait. I just had to give you the background first so you can talk to him."

"To . . ."

"The idiot therapist! Clearly he's only hearing one side of the story, and not a very accurate side at that. But you *know* me. You can vouch for me. You can give this guy some perspective before Margo really goes nuts."

I noodle this scenario around in my head: *John wants me to call my own therapist to discuss why my patient isn't happy with the therapy my therapist is doing with my patient's wife.*

Um, no.

Even if Wendell weren't my therapist, I wouldn't make this call. Sometimes I'll call another therapist to discuss a patient if, say, I'm seeing a couple and a colleague is seeing one member of the couple, and there's a compelling reason to exchange information (somebody is suicidal or potentially violent, or we're working on something in one setting that it would be helpful to have reinforced in another, or we want to get a broader perspective). But on these rare occasions, the parties will have signed releases to this effect. Wendell or no Wendell, I can't call up the therapist of my patient's wife for no clinically relevant reason and without both patients signing consent forms.

"Let me ask you something," I say to John.

"What?"

"Do you miss Margo?"

"Do *I* miss *her?*"

"Yes."

"You're not going to call Margo's therapist, are you?"

"I'm not, and you're not going to tell me how you really feel about Margo, are you?" I have a feeling that there's a lot of buried love between John and Margo because I know this: love can often look like so many things that don't seem like love.

John smiles as I see somebody who I assume is Tommy again enter the frame holding a script. I'm flipped toward the ground with such speed that I get dizzy, as if I'm on a roller coaster that just took a quick dive. Staring at John's shoes, I hear some back-and-forth about whether the character—

my favorite!—is supposed to be a complete asshole in this scene or maybe have some awareness that he's being an asshole (interestingly, John picks awareness) and then Tommy thanks John and leaves. To my amusement, John seems perfectly pleasant, apologizing to Tommy for his absence and explaining to him that he's busy "putting out a fire with the network." (I'm "the network.") Maybe he's polite to his coworkers after all.

Or maybe not. He waits for Tommy to leave, then lifts me up to face level again and mouths, *Idiot,* rolling his eyes in Tommy's direction.

"I just don't understand how her therapist, who's *a guy,* can't see both sides of this," he continues. "Even *you* can see both sides of this!"

Even me? I smile. "Was that a compliment you just gave me?"

"No offense. I just meant . . . you know."

I do know, but I want him to say it. In his own way, he's becoming attached to me, and I want him to stay in his emotional world a bit longer. But John goes back to his tirade about Margo pulling the wool over her therapist's eyes and how Wendell is a quack because his sessions are only forty-five minutes, not the typical fifty. (This bugs me too, by the way.) It occurs to me that John is talking about Wendell the way a husband might talk about a man his wife has a crush on. I think he's jealous and feels left out of whatever goes on between Margo and Wendell in that room. (I'm jealous too! Does Wendell laugh at Margo's jokes? Does he like her better?) I want to bring John back to that moment when he almost connected with me.

"I'm glad that you feel understood by me," I say. John gets a deer-in-the-headlights look on his face for a second, then moves on.

"All I want to know is how to deal with Margo."

"She already told you," I say. "She misses you. I can see from our experience together how skilled you are at pushing away people who care about you. I'm not leaving, but Margo's saying she might. So maybe you'll try something different with her. Maybe you'll let her know that you miss her too." I pause. "Because I might be wrong, but I think you do miss her."

He shrugs, and this time when he looks down, I'm not on mute. "I miss the way we were," he says.

His expression is sad instead of angry now. Anger is the go-to feeling for most people because it's outward-directed—angrily blaming others can feel deliciously sanctimonious. But often it's only the tip of the iceberg, and if you look beneath the surface, you'll glimpse submerged feelings you either weren't aware of or didn't want to show: fear, helplessness, envy, loneliness, insecurity. And if you can tolerate these deeper feelings long enough to understand them and listen to what they're telling you, you'll not only manage your anger in more productive ways, you also won't be so angry all the time.

Of course, anger serves another function—it pushes people away and keeps them from getting close enough to see you. I wonder if John needs people to be angry at him so that they won't see his sadness.

I start to speak, but somebody yells John's name, startling him. The phone slips out of his hand and careens toward the floor, but just as I feel like my face might hit the ground, John catches it, bringing himself back into view. "Crap—gotta go!" he says. Then, under his breath: "Fucking morons." And the screen goes blank.

Apparently, our session is over.

With time to spare before my next session, I head into the kitchen for a snack. Two of my colleagues are there. Hillary is making tea. Mike's eating a sandwich.

"Hypothetically," I say, "what would you do if your patient's wife was seeing your therapist, and your patient thought your therapist was an idiot?"

They look up at me, eyebrows raised. Hypotheticals in this kitchen are never hypothetical.

"I'd switch therapists," Hillary says.

"I'd keep my therapist and switch patients," Mike says.

They both laugh.

"No, really," I say. "What would you do? It gets worse: He wants me to talk to my therapist about his wife. His wife doesn't know he's in therapy yet, so it's a non-issue now, but what if at some point he tells her and then wants me to consult with my therapist about his wife, and his wife consents? Do I have to disclose that he's my therapist?"

"Absolutely," Hillary says.

"Not necessarily," Mike says at the same time.

"Exactly," I say. "It's not clear. And you know why it's not clear? Because this kind of thing NEVER HAPPENS! When has something like this ever happened?"

Hillary pours me some tea.

"I once had two people come to me individually for therapy right after they'd separated," Mike says. "They had different last names and listed different addresses because of the separation, so I didn't know they were married until the second session with each of them, when I realized I was hearing the same stories from different sides. Their mutual friend, who was a former patient, gave both of them my name. I had to refer them out."

"Yeah," I say, "but this isn't two patients with a conflict of interest. My therapist is mixed up in this. What are the odds of *that?*"

I notice Hillary looking away. "What?" I say.

"Nothing."

Mike looks at her. She blushes. "Spill it," he says.

Hillary sighs. "Okay. About twenty years ago, when I was first starting out, I was seeing a young guy for depression. I felt like we were making progress, but then the therapy seemed to stall. I thought he wasn't ready to move forward, but really I just didn't have enough experience and was too green to know the difference. Anyway, he left, and about a year later, I ran into him at my therapist's."

Mike grins. "Your patient left you for your own therapist?"

Hillary nods. "The funny thing is, in therapy, I talked about how stuck I was with this patient and how helpless I felt when he left. I'm sure the patient later told my therapist about his inept former therapist and used my name at some point. My therapist had to have put two and two together."

I think about this in relation to the Wendell situation. "But your therapist never said anything?"

"Never," Hillary says. "So one day I brought it up. But of course she can't say that she sees this guy, so we kept the conversation focused on how I deal with the insecurities of being a new therapist. *Pfft. My* feelings?

Whatever. I was just dying to know how *their* therapy was going and what she did differently with him that worked better."

"You'll never know," I say.

Hillary shakes her head. "I'll never know."

"We're like vaults," Mike says. "You can't break us."

Hillary turns to me. "So, are you going to tell your therapist?"

"Should I?"

They both shrug. Mike glances at the clock, tosses his trash into the can. Hillary and I take our last sips of tea. It's time for our next sessions. One by one, the green lights on the kitchen's master panel go on, and we file out to retrieve our patients from the waiting room.

22

Jail

"Hmm," Wendell says after I make my book confession well into our session. It's taken me a while to get up the courage to tell him.

For two weeks I've moved over to position B planning to confess all, but once we're face-to-face, catty-corner on the couches, I stall. I talk about my son's teacher (pregnant), my dad's health (poor), a dream (freaky), chocolate (a tangent, I'll admit), my emerging forehead wrinkles (not a tangent, surprisingly), and the meaning of life (mine). Wendell tries to focus me, but I'm skating so quickly from one thing to the next that I outmaneuver him. Or so I think.

Out of the blue, Wendell yawns. It's a fake yawn, a strategic one, a big, dramatic, gaping yawn. It's a yawn that says, *Until you tell me what's really on your mind, you'll stay stuck exactly where you are.* Then he sits back and studies me.

"I have something to tell you," I say.

He looks at me like *No shit.*

And out comes the entire story in one fell swoop.

"Hmm," he says again. "So you don't want to write this book."

I nod.

"And if you don't turn in the book, there will be serious financial and professional repercussions?"

"Right." I shrug as if to say, *See how screwed I am?* "If I'd just done the parenting book," I say, "I wouldn't be in this situation." It's the refrain I've been repeating to myself daily—sometimes hourly—for the past few years.

Wendell does his shrug-smile-wait routine.

"I know." I sigh. "I made a colossal, irrevocable mistake." I feel the panic well up again.

"That's not what I'm thinking," he says.

"Then, what?"

He starts singing. "'Half my life is over, oh yeah. Half my life has passed me by.'"

I roll my eyes, but he keeps going. It's a bluesy tune and I'm trying to place it. Etta James? B. B. King?

"'I wish I could go back, change the past. Have more years, to get it right . . .'"

And then I realize it's not a famous song. It's Wendell Bronson, impromptu lyricist. His lyrics are awful, but he surprises me with his strong, resonant voice.

The song goes on, and he's getting really into it. Tapping his feet. Snapping his fingers. If we were out in the world, I'd think he was a nerdy guy in a cardigan, but in here, it's his confidence and spontaneity that strike me, his willingness to be fully himself, entirely unconcerned that he'll come across as foolish or unprofessional. I can't imagine doing this in front of my patients.

"''Cause half my life is o-o-o-o-over.'" He arrives at the finale, complete with jazz hands.

Wendell stops singing and looks at me seriously. I want to tell him that he's being annoying, that he's trivializing what is realistically and practically an anxiety-provoking problem. But before I can say that, I feel a heavy sadness descend, seemingly out of nowhere. His tune is going through my head.

"It's like that Mary Oliver poem," I say to Wendell. "'What is it you plan to do with your one wild and precious life?' I thought I knew what I planned to do, but now everything has changed. I was going to be with Boyfriend. I was going to write what mattered to me. I never expected—"

"—to be in this situation." Wendell gives me a look. *Here we go again.* We're like an old married couple by now, finishing each other's sentences.

But then Wendell is silent, and it doesn't seem like the intentional kind of silence I'm used to. It occurs to me that maybe Wendell is stumped, the way I sometimes get stumped in sessions when my patients are stuck and I get stuck too. He's tried yawning and singing and redirecting me and asking important questions. But still, I'm back to where I usually go—the saga of my losses.

"I was just thinking about what you want in here," he says. "How do you think I can help you?"

I'm thrown by his question. I don't know if he's enlisting my help as a fellow therapist or asking me as his patient. Either way, I'm not sure; what *do* I want from therapy?

"I don't know," I say, but as soon as I say it, I'm scared. Maybe Wendell *can't* help me. Maybe nothing can. Maybe I just have to learn to live with my choices.

"I think I can help," he says, "but maybe not in the way you imagine. I can't bring your boyfriend back, and I can't give you a redo. And now you're in this book situation and you want me to save you from that too. And I can't do that either."

I let out a snort at how preposterous this is. "I don't want you to *save* me," I say. "I'm a head of household, not a damsel in distress."

He locks his eyes on mine. I look away.

"Nobody is going to save you," he says quietly.

"But I don't want to be *saved!*" I insist, though this time part of me wonders, *Wait, do I?* On some level, don't we all? I think about how people come to therapy expecting to feel better, but what does *better* really mean?

There's a magnet that somebody stuck on the refrigerator in our office's kitchen: PEACE. IT DOES NOT MEAN TO BE IN A PLACE WHERE THERE IS NO NOISE, TROUBLE, OR HARD WORK. IT MEANS TO BE IN THE MIDST OF THOSE THINGS AND STILL BE CALM IN YOUR HEART. We can help patients find peace, but maybe a different kind than they imagined they'd find when they started treatment. As the late psychotherapist John Weakland famously said, "Before successful therapy, it's the same damn thing over and over. After successful therapy, it's one damn thing after another."

I know that therapy won't make all my problems disappear, prevent new ones from developing, or ensure that I'll always act from a place of enlightenment. Therapists don't perform personality transplants; they just help to take the sharp edges off. A patient may become less reactive or critical, more open and able to let people in. In other words, therapy is about understanding the self that you *are*. But part of getting to know yourself is to *unknow* yourself—to let go of the limiting stories you've told yourself about who you are so that you aren't trapped by them, so you can live your life and not the story you've been telling yourself about your life.

But how to help people do this is another matter.

I go through the problem again in my mind. *Must write book to have roof over head. Turned down opportunity to write book that would have put roof over head for years to come. Can't seem to write stupid book about stupid topic that's making me miserable. Will force myself to write stupid miserable happiness book. Have tried to force myself to write stupid miserable happiness book but end up on Facebook, feeling envious of all the people who manage to have their shit together.*

I remember a quote from Einstein: "No problem can be solved from the same level of consciousness that created it." I've always felt that made sense, but, like most of us, I also believe that I should be able to think my way out of my problem by going over and over how I thought myself into it.

"I just see no way out of this," I say. "And I don't just mean the book. I mean the whole *this*—everything that's happened."

Wendell leans back, uncrosses and recrosses his legs, then closes his eyes, something he does when he seems to be gathering his thoughts.

When he opens his eyes again, we sit there for a while, saying nothing, two therapists comfortable together in a long silence. I lean back and luxuriate in it, and I think about how I wish everyone could do this more in daily life, simply be together with no phones, laptops, TVs, or idle chitchat. Just presence. Sitting like this makes me feel relaxed and energized at the same time.

Finally, Wendell speaks up.

"I'm reminded," he begins, "of a famous cartoon. It's of a prisoner, shaking the bars, desperately trying to get out—but to his right and left, it's open, no bars."

He pauses, allowing the image to sink in.

"All the prisoner has to do is *walk around*. But still, he frantically shakes the bars. That's most of us. We *feel* completely stuck, trapped in our emotional cells, but there's a way out—as long as we're willing to see it."

He lets that last part linger between us. *As long as we're willing to see it.* He gestures to an imaginary prison cell with his hand, inviting me to see it.

I look away, but I feel Wendell's eyes on me.

I sigh. *Okay.*

I close my eyes and take a breath. I start by picturing the prison, a tiny cell with drab beige walls. I picture the metal bars, thick and gray and rusty. I picture myself in an orange jumpsuit, furiously shaking those bars, pleading for release. I picture my life in this tiny cell with nothing but the pungent smell of urine and the prospect of a dismal, constrained future. I imagine screaming, "Get me out of here! *Save me!*" I envision myself frantically looking to my right, then to my left, then doing one hell of a double take. I notice my whole body respond; I feel lighter, like a thousand-pound weight has been lifted, as the realization hits me: *You are your own jailer.*

I open my eyes and glance at Wendell. He raises his right eyebrow as if to say, *I know—you see. I saw you see.*

"Keep looking," he whispers.

I close my eyes again. Now I'm walking around the bars and heading toward the exit, moving tentatively at first, but as I get closer to it, I start to run. Outside, I can feel my feet on the ground, the breeze on my skin, the sun's warmth on my face. I'm free! I run as fast as I can, then after a while I slow down and check behind me. No prison guards are giving chase. It occurs to me that there were no prison guards to begin with. Of course!

Most of us come to therapy feeling trapped—imprisoned by our thoughts, behaviors, marriages, jobs, fears, or past. Sometimes we imprison ourselves with a narrative of self-punishment. If we have a choice between believing one of two things, both of which we have evidence for— *I'm unlovable, I'm lovable*—often we choose the one that makes us feel bad. Why do we keep our radios tuned to the same static-ridden stations (the everyone's-life-is-better-than-mine station, the I-can't-trust-people station, the nothing-works-out-for-me station) instead of moving the dial up or down? Change the station. Walk around the bars. Who's stopping us but ourselves?

There is a way out—*as long as we're willing to see it.* A cartoon, of all things, has taught me the secret of life.

I open my eyes and smile, and Wendell smiles back. It's a conspiratorial smile, one that says, *Don't be fooled. It may seem as though you've had an earth-shattering breakthrough, but this is just the beginning.* I know full well what challenges lie ahead, and Wendell knows that I know, because we both know something else: freedom involves responsibility, and there's a part of most of us that finds responsibility frightening.

Might it feel safer to stay in jail? I picture the bars and the open sides again. A part of me lobbies to stay, another to go. I choose to go. But walking around the bars in my mind is different from walking around them in real life.

"Insight is the booby prize of therapy" is my favorite maxim of the trade, meaning that you can have all the insight in the world, but if you don't change when you're *out* in the world, the insight—and the therapy —is worthless. Insight allows you to ask yourself, *Is this something that's being done to me or am I doing it to myself?* The answer gives you choices, but it's up to you to make them.

"Are you ready to start talking about the fight you're in?" Wendell asks.

"You mean the fight with Boyfriend?" I begin. "Or with myself—"

"No, your fight with death," Wendell says.

For a second I'm confused, but then I flash to my dream about running into Boyfriend at the mall. Him: *Did you ever write your book?* Me: *What book?* Him: *The book about your death.*

Oh. My. God.

Typically therapists are several steps ahead of our patients—not because we're smarter or wiser but because we have the vantage point of being outside their lives. I'll say to a patient who has bought the ring but can't seem to find the right time to propose to his girlfriend, "I don't think you're sure you want to marry her," and he'll say, "What? Of course I am! I'm doing it this weekend!" And then he goes home and doesn't propose, because the weather was bad and he wanted to do it at the beach. We'll have the same dialogue for weeks, until one day he'll come back and say, "Maybe I don't want to marry her." Many people who say, "No, that's not me," find themselves a week or a month or a year later saying, "Yeah, actually, that's me."

I have a feeling that Wendell has been storing up this question, waiting for just the right moment to float it out there. Therapists are always weighing the balance between forming a trusting alliance and getting to the real work so the patient doesn't have to continue suffering. From the outset, we move both slowly and quickly, slowing the content down, speeding up the relationship, planting seeds strategically along the way. As in nature, if you plant the seeds too early, they won't sprout. If you plant too late, they might make progress, but you've missed the most fertile ground. If you plant at just the right time, though, they'll soak up the nutrients and grow. Our work is an intricate dance between support and confrontation.

Wendell asks about my fight with death at exactly the right moment—but for more reasons than he could possibly know.

23

Trader Joe's

It's a busy Saturday morning at Trader Joe's, and I'm scanning the lines to see which is shortest while my son darts off to look at the display of chocolate bars. Despite the chaos, the cashiers seem unfazed. A young guy whose arms are covered in tattoos rings a bell, and a bagger in leggings dances over and packs up a customer's groceries, jiving to the canned music. In the next aisle a hipster with a Mohawk calls for a price check, and at the end of the row, a pretty blond cashier juggles some oranges to amuse a toddler having a meltdown in her stroller.

It takes me a minute before I realize that the juggling cashier is my patient Julie. I haven't seen her new blond wig yet, though she had mentioned it in therapy.

"Too crazy?" she'd asked about the idea of being a blonde, holding me to my promise to tell her if she was going overboard. She'd asked the same thing about answering an ad for a singer in a local band, going on a game show, and signing up for a Buddhist retreat that required a full week of no talking. This was all before the miracle drug had worked its miracle on her tumors.

I'd enjoyed watching her stretch from the risk-averse stance she'd embraced all her life. She had always thought that achieving tenure would give her freedom, but now she was tasting a completely unexpected kind of freedom.

"Is this too off-the-wall?" she'd sometimes say before presenting a new idea to me. She was eager to veer from her mapped-out course, but not so far that she'd get lost. Yet nothing she proposed surprised me.

Then, finally, Julie had an idea that caught me off guard. She told me that at one point during those weeks when she believed she was about to die, she was waiting in line at Trader Joe's and found herself mesmerized by the cashiers. They seemed so *themselves* in the ways they interacted with their customers and one another, making conversation about the small daily things that are really the big things in people's lives—food, traffic, the weather. How different she imagined this job from her own, which she loved but which also came with a constant pressure to produce and publish, to position herself for advancement. With a shortened future, she imagined doing work where she could see tangible results in the moment—you pack groceries, you cheer up customers, you stock items. At the end of the day, you've done something concrete and useful.

Julie decided that if she had only, say, a year to live, she'd apply to be a weekend cashier at Trader Joe's. She knew she was idealizing the job. But she still wanted to experience that sense of purpose and community, of being a small part of lots of different people's lives—even if just for the time it took to ring up their groceries.

"Maybe Trader Joe's can be part of my Holland," she mused.

I could feel myself push against the idea, and I sat for a minute, trying to understand why. It might have had something to do with a dilemma I'd been facing in treating Julie. If Julie hadn't had cancer, I'd try to help her look at the part of her that had felt inhibited for so long. She seemed to be opening the lid on aspects of herself that hadn't had space to breathe.

But with someone who's dying, did it make sense to do therapy or simply offer support? Should I treat Julie like a healthy patient in terms of more ambitious goals, or should I just offer comfort and not upset the apple cart? I wondered if Julie would ever have asked herself the questions about risk and safety and identity that had been hiding beneath her awareness had she not faced the terror of imminent death. And now that she had, how far should we delve into them?

These are questions we all deal with in a quieter way: How much do we want to know? How much is too much? And how much is too much when you're dying?

The Trader Joe's fantasy seemed to represent an escape of some sort—like a child saying, "I'm running away to Disneyland!"—and I wondered how this fantasy related to Julie's pre-cancer self. But mostly, I wondered if she could handle the job physically. The experimental treatment had added to her fatigue. She needed rest.

Her husband, she told me, thought she was insane.

"You have a limited time to live, and your dream is to work at Trader Joe's?" he'd asked.

"Why, what would *you* do if you only had a year or so to live?" Julie countered.

"I'd work less," he said, "not more."

As Julie told me about Matt's reaction, it occurred to me that he and I both seemed unsupportive, even though we wanted Julie to experience joy. Sure, there were some practical concerns, but could our hesitation also be that we were both, in a strange way, *envious* of Julie and her conviction to follow her dream, no matter how odd it sounded? Therapists tell their patients: Follow your envy—it shows you what you want. Did watching Julie's blossoming highlight the fact that we were too afraid to act on our own equivalents of working at Trader Joe's—and that we wanted Julie to remain like us, dreaming without doing, constrained by nothing more than the open bars on our prison cells?

Or maybe that was just me.

"Besides," Matt had said in his conversation with Julie, "don't you want to spend that time together?"

Julie said that of course she did. But she also wanted to work at Trader Joe's, and it became a kind of obsession. So she applied for a job there, and on the day that she learned she was tumor-free, she was offered a Saturday-morning shift.

In my office, Julie got out her cell phone and played both phone messages for me: one from her oncologist, one from a manager at Trader Joe's. She was grinning as if she'd won not just any lottery, but the Powerball of all Powerballs.

"I told them yes," she said after the Trader Joe's message ended. She explained that nobody knew if the tumors would come back, and she didn't want to just add things to her bucket list; she wanted to cross things off too.

"You have to pare it down," she said, "or else it's just a useless exercise in what could have been."

So here I am, standing in the market, and I'm not sure which checkout line to choose. I knew, of course, that Julie had started working at Trader Joe's, but I had no idea it was *this* Trader Joe's.

She hasn't seen me yet, and I can't help but watch her from afar. She rings the bell for a bagger, gets a child some stickers, laughs with a customer over something I can't hear. She's like the Queen of Cashiers, the party everyone wants to be at. People seem to know her and, not surprisingly, she's incredibly efficient, moving the line along quickly. I feel my eyes get wet and the next thing I know my son calls out, "Mom, over here!" and I see that he has negotiated his way into Julie's line.

I hesitate. After all, Julie might feel awkward ringing up her therapist. And, truth be told, I might feel awkward too. She knows so little about me that even displaying the contents of my shopping cart feels somehow too revealing. But mostly, I'm thinking about how Julie talks about the sadness she experiences whenever she sees her friends' kids while she and her husband are trying to find a way to become parents themselves. What will it be like for her to see me with my son?

"Over here!" I reply, gesturing for Zach to move to a different line.

"But this one's shorter!" he yells back, and of course it is, because Julie's so goddamned *efficient*, and that's when Julie looks over at my son and then follows his gaze to me.

Busted.

I smile. She smiles. I start to head to the other line, but Julie says, "Hey, lady, listen to the boy. This line's shorter!" I join Zach in Julie's line.

I try not to stare as we wait our turn, but I can't help it. I'm watching the real-life version of the vision she described in her therapy session—her dream literally come true. When Zach and I get to the register, Julie banters with us as she does with her other customers.

"Joe's O's," she says to my son. "A good breakfast."

"They're for my mom," he answers. "No offense, but I like Cheerios better."

Julie looks around to make sure nobody's in earshot, gives him a sly wink, and whispers, "Don't tell anyone, but me too."

They spend the rest of the time discussing the merits of the various chocolate bars my son selected. When we're all bagged up and rolling our cart away, Zach examines the stickers from Julie.

"I like that lady," he says.

"I do too," I say.

It isn't until half an hour later, as I'm unpacking the bags in my kitchen, that I see something scrawled on my credit card receipt.

I'm pregnant! it says.

24

Hello, Family

CHART NOTE, RITA:

Patient is a divorced woman who presents with depression. Expresses regret over what she believes to be "bad choices" and a life poorly lived. Reports that if her life doesn't improve in one year, she plans to "end it."

"I have something to show you," Rita says.

In the hallway between the waiting room and my office, she hands me her cell phone. Rita has never handed me her phone before, much less begun speaking to me before we're settled in my office with the door closed, so I'm surprised by the gesture. She indicates that I should take a look.

On her screen is a profile from the dating app called Bumble. Rita recently started using Bumble because, unlike more hookup-oriented apps like Tinder ("Revolting!" she said), Bumble allows only women to contact men. Coincidentally, my friend Jen had just seen an article about it and forwarded it to me with the message *For whenever you're ready to date again.* I'd texted back, *Whenever isn't here yet.*

I glance from the phone to Rita.

"Well?" she says expectantly as we enter my office.

"Well what?" I ask, handing her back the phone. I'm not sure what she's getting at.

"Well *what?*" she replies incredulously. "He's *eighty-two!* I'm no spring chicken, but please! I know what eighty looks like naked, and *that* gave me nightmares for a week. I'm sorry, but seventy-five is as far as I'll go. And don't try to talk me out of it!"

Rita, I should mention, is sixty-nine.

A few weeks ago, after months of encouragement, Rita had decided to try a dating app. After all, in her daily life, she wasn't encountering any single older men, much less those who met her requirements: intelligent, kind, financially stable ("I don't want anyone looking for a nurse and a purse"), and physically fit ("Somebody who can still get an erection in a timely manner"). Hair was optional, but teeth, she insisted, were not.

Before the eighty-year-old, there had been a same-age gentleman who was not so gentle. They had gone out to dinner, and the night before what was supposed to be their second date, Rita had texted him the recipe and photo of a dish he said he wanted to try. *Mmmm,* he texted back. *Sounds delicious.* Rita was about to respond, but then another *Mmmm* popped up, followed by *You're killing me here . . .* , followed by *If you don't stop, I won't be able to stand up,* followed a minute later by *Sorry, I was texting my daughter about my bad back.*

"Bad back, my eye, the pervert!" Rita exclaimed. "He was doing who knows what with who knows who, and he certainly wasn't talking about my salmon dish!" There was no second date, and no dates at all until she met the eighty-year-old.

Rita had come to me at the beginning of spring. At our very first session, she was so depressed that when she gave me an account of her situation, it seemed as if she were reading an obituary. The final line had been written, and her life, she believed, was a tragedy. Thrice-divorced and the mother of four troubled adults (due to her own bad mothering, she explained), grandchildless and living alone, retired from a job she disliked, Rita saw no reason to get up in the morning.

Her list of mistakes was long: choosing the wrong husbands, failing to put her children's needs above her own (including not protecting them from their alcoholic father), not using her skills in a professionally fulfilling way, not making an effort when she was younger to form a community. She had numbed herself with denial for as long as that worked. Recently, it had lost its efficacy. Even painting—the one activity she enjoyed and excelled at—barely held her interest.

Now her seventieth birthday was coming up and she had struck a deal with herself to make her life better by then or stop living it.

"I think I'm beyond help," she concluded. "But I want to give it one last try, just to be certain."

No pressure, I thought. While suicidal thoughts—known as suicidal ideation—are commonplace with depression, most people respond to treatment and never act on those hopeless impulses. In fact, it's as patients begin to get *better* that the risk for suicide increases. During this short window, they're no longer so depressed that eating or dressing seem like monumental efforts but they're still in enough pain to want to end it all —a dangerous mix of residual distress and newfound energy. But once the depression lifts and suicidal thoughts subside, a new window opens. That's when the person can make changes that improve life significantly over the long term.

Whenever suicide comes up—either because the patient or the therapist broaches the topic (bringing it up does not, as some worry, "plant" the idea in a person's head), the therapist has to assess the situation. Does the patient have a concrete plan? Is there a means to carry out the plan (a gun in the house, a spouse out of town)? Have there been previous attempts? Are there particular risk factors (lack of social support or being male; men commit suicide three times more often than women)? Often people talk about suicide not because they want to be dead but because they want to end their pain. If they can just find a way to do that, they very much want to be alive. We make the best assessment we can, and as long as there's no imminent danger, we monitor the situation closely and work with the depression. If the person is set on suicide, though, there are a series of steps to take right away.

Rita was telling me that she would kill herself, but she was very clear that she would wait out the year and not do anything before her seventieth birthday. She wanted change, not death—as it was, she was already dead inside. For now, suicide wasn't my concern.

What *was* concerning to me, though, was Rita's age.

I'm ashamed to admit this, but at first I worried that I might secretly agree with Rita's grim perspective. Maybe she really *was* beyond help—or at least beyond the kind of help she wanted. A therapist is supposed to be a container for the hope that a depressed person can't yet hold, and I wasn't seeing much hope here. Typically I see possibility because the people who are depressed have something to keep them going—it might be a job that gets them out of bed (even if they don't love that particular job), a network of friends (just one or two people they can talk to), or contact with some family members (problematic but present). Having children in the house or a beloved pet or religious faith can also protect against suicide.

But most notably, the depressed people I saw were younger. More malleable. Their lives might seem bleak now, but they had time to turn things around and create something new.

Rita, however, seemed like a cautionary tale: a senior citizen, utterly alone, lacking in purpose and full of regret. By her account, she had never truly been loved by anybody. The only child of older and distant parents, she had messed up her own children so badly that none of them spoke to her, and she had no friends or relatives or social life. Her father had been dead for decades, and her mother had died at ninety after suffering for years with Alzheimer's.

She looked me in the eye and presented me with a challenge. Realistically, she asked, what could change at this late date?

About a year earlier, I'd gotten a call from a well-respected psychiatrist in his late seventies. He asked if I would see his patient, a woman in her thirties who was considering freezing her eggs while she continued to look for a partner. He thought that this woman might benefit from consultation with me because, he said, he didn't know enough about the dating and baby-making landscape for today's thirty-somethings. Now I knew how he felt. I wasn't sure that I fully understood the aging landscape for today's senior citizens.

I'd learned in my training about the unique challenges faced by older adults, and yet this age group gets short shrift when it comes to mental-health services. For some, therapy is a foreign concept, like TiVo, and besides, their generation grew up largely believing that they could "get through it" (whatever "it" was) on their own. Others, living on retirement savings and seeking help at low-cost clinics, don't feel comfortable seeing the twenty-something therapy interns who predominantly staff them. Before long, these patients drop out. Still other older people assume that what they're feeling is a normal part of aging and don't realize that treatment might help. The result is that many therapists see relatively few seniors in their practices.

At the same time, old age is a proportionately larger percentage of the average person's life than it used to be. Unlike the sixty-year-olds of a few generations ago, the sixty-year-olds of today are often at the top of their games in terms of skill, knowledge, and experience, but they're still pushed out professionally for younger employees. The average life expectancy in the United States now hovers around eighty, and it's becoming common to live into one's nineties, so what happens to these sixty-year-olds' identities during the decades they still have left? With aging comes the potential to accrue many losses: health, family, friends, work, and purpose.

But Rita, I realized, wasn't experiencing loss primarily *as a result of* aging. Instead, as she aged, she was becoming aware of the losses she had been living with her entire life. Here she was, wanting a second chance, a chance she was giving herself only a year to realize. As she saw it, she had lost so much that she had nothing left to lose.

That part I agreed with too—mostly. She could still lose her health and beauty. Tall and slim, with large green eyes and high cheekbones, her thick naturally red hair flecked with just a few strands of gray, Rita was genetically blessed with the complexion of a forty-year-old. (Terrified of living as long as her mother had and running out of retirement funds, she refused to pay for what she called "modern beauty expenses," her euphemism for Botox.) She also attended an exercise class at the Y every morning, "just to have a reason to get out of bed." Her physician, who had sent her to me, said that she was "one of the healthiest people her age I've seen."

But in every other way, Rita seemed dead, lifeless. Even her movements were listless, like the way she sauntered to the sofa in slow motion, a sign of depression known as psychomotor retardation. (This slowing down of coordinated efforts between the brain and the body might also explain why I kept missing the tissue box in Wendell's office.)

Often at the beginning of therapy, I'll ask patients to recount the past twenty-four hours in as much detail as possible. In this way I get a good sense of the current situation—their level of connectedness and sense of belonging, how their lives are peopled, what their responsibilities and stressors are, how peaceful or volatile their relationships might be, and how they choose to spend their time. It turns out that most of us aren't aware of how we actually spend our time or what we really do all day until we break it down hour by hour and say it out loud.

Here's how Rita's days went: Get up early ("Menopause ruined my sleep"), drive to the Y. Come home, eat breakfast while watching *Good Morning America*. Paint or nap. Eat lunch while reading the paper. Paint or nap. Heat up frozen dinner ("It's too much trouble cooking for one"), sit on her building's stoop ("I like to look at the babies and puppies that people walk at dusk"), watch "junk" on TV, fall asleep.

Rita seemed to have almost no contact with other human beings. Many days, she talked to nobody. But what struck me most about her life wasn't just how solitary it was, but how nearly everything she said or did conjured for me an image of death. As Andrew Solomon wrote in *The Noonday Demon:* "The opposite of depression isn't happiness, but vitality."

Vitality. Yes, Rita had had lifelong depression and a complicated history, but I wasn't sure that her past should be our initial focus. Even if she hadn't given herself a one-year deadline, there was another deadline that neither of us could change: mortality. As with Julie, I wondered what the goal should be in treating her. Did she just need somebody to talk to, to ease the pain and loneliness, or was she willing to understand her role in creating it? It was also the question I was struggling with in Wendell's office: What should be accepted and what should be changed in my own life? But I was more than two decades younger than Rita. Was it too late for her to redeem herself—is it ever too late for that? And what degree of emotional discomfort would she be willing to endure to find out? I thought about how regret can go one of two ways: it can either shackle you to the past or serve as an engine for change.

Rita said that she wanted her life to improve by her seventieth birthday. Instead of dredging up the past seven decades, I thought, maybe we should start with trying to inject her life with a little vitality—now.

"*Companionship?*" Rita says today after I tell her that I won't try to talk her out of finding companionship with men under seventy-five. "Oh, honey, please don't be so naive—I want more than companionship. I'm not dead *yet*. Even *I* know how to order something on the internet from the privacy of my apartment."

It takes me a minute to connect the dots: *She buys vibrators? Good for her!*

"Do you know," Rita adds, "how long it's been since I've been touched?"

Rita goes on to describe how disheartening she finds the dating scene —and in this regard, at least, she's not alone. It's the most common refrain I hear from single women of all ages: *Dating sucks.*

Marriage, though, hasn't been much better for her. She'd met the man who would be husband number one when she was twenty years old, eager to escape her dreary home. She commuted to college each day and went from "dying of boredom and silence" to "a world of interesting ideas and people." But she also had to hold down a job, and while she sat in a real estate agent's office typing up mind-numbing correspondence after class, she missed out on the social life she craved.

Enter Richard, a charming, sophisticated upperclassman in her English seminar with whom she had deep conversations and who swept her off her feet and into the life she wanted—until their first child was born a couple of years later. That's when Richard started working longer hours and drinking; soon, Rita was just as bored and lonely as she had been in her childhood home. After four kids, countless fights, and too many drunken episodes during which Richard struck both her and their children, Rita wanted out.

But how? What could she do? She had dropped out of college; how would she support herself and the kids? With Richard, the kids had clothes and food and good schools and friends. What could she, by herself, offer them? In many ways, Rita felt like a child herself, helpless. Soon Richard wasn't the only one who drank.

It wasn't until a particularly terrifying incident that Rita screwed up the courage to leave, but by then her children were well into their teens and the family was a shambles.

She married husband number two five years later. Edward was Richard's opposite: a kind and caring widower who'd recently lost his wife. After her divorce at age thirty-nine, Rita had returned to tedious secretarial work (her only marketable skill, despite her keen intelligence and artistic talent). Edward was a client of the insurance agent Rita worked for. They married six months after they met, but Edward was still grieving his wife's death, and Rita felt envious of his love for her. They argued constantly. The marriage lasted two years and then Edward called it quits. Husband number three left his wife for Rita, and five years later, he left Rita for someone else.

Each time, Rita was shocked to find herself alone, but her history didn't surprise me. We marry our unfinished business.

For the next decade, Rita steered clear of dating. Not that she met men anyway, holed up in her apartment or aerobicizing at the Y. Then came the recent reality of an eighty-year-old's body—so withered and saggy compared to the body of her last husband, who had been only fifty-five at the time of their divorce. Rita had met Mr. Saggy, as she called him, through the dating app, and "because I wanted to be touched," she said, "I thought I could give it a try." He had looked young for his age, she explained ("more like seventy") and handsome—in clothing, that is.

After they had sex, she told me, he had wanted to cuddle but she'd escaped to the bathroom, where she discovered "an entire pharmacy of medications," including Viagra. Finding the whole scene "revolting" (Rita found many things revolting), she waited until her date was fast asleep ("His snores sounded as revolting as his orgasm"), and took a taxi home.

"Never again," she says now.

I try to imagine sleeping with an eighty-year-old and wonder if most elderly people are put off by their partners' bodies. Is it jarring only to those who haven't been with an older body before? Do people who have been together fifty years not notice because they acclimate to the gradual changes over time?

I remember reading a news story in which a couple, married for more than sixty years, was asked for tips on happy marriages. After the usual advice about communication and compromise, the husband added that oral sex was still in their repertoire. Naturally, this story spread like wildfire online, and most of the commenters were disgusted. Given the public's visceral reactions to aging bodies, it's no wonder old people don't get touched much.

But it's a deep human need. It's well documented that touch is important for well-being throughout our lifetimes. Touch can lower blood pressure and stress levels, boost moods and immune systems. Babies can die from lack of touch, and so can adults (adults who are touched regularly live longer). There's even a term for this condition: skin hunger.

Rita tells me that she splurges on pedicures not because it matters if her toenails are painted ("Who's going to see them?"), but because the only human touch she gets is from a woman named Connie. Connie has been doing her toes for years and doesn't speak a lick of English. But her foot massages, Rita says, "are heaven."

When she got divorced for the third time, Rita didn't know how to live without being touched even for a week. She'd get antsy, she says. Then it was a month. Then years turned to a decade. She doesn't like to spend the money on a pedicure nobody will see, but what choice does she have? The pedicures are a necessity because she'll go crazy with no human contact at all.

"It's like going to a prostitute, paying to be touched," Rita says.

Like John does with me, I think—*I'm his emotional hooker.*

"The point," Rita is saying about the eighty-year-old, "is that I thought it would feel good to be touched by a man again, but I think I'll just stick with my pedicures."

I tell her that the choices aren't necessarily limited to either Connie or an eighty-year-old, but Rita shoots me a look and I know what she's thinking.

"I don't know who you'll meet," I concede. "But maybe you'll be touched—both physically and emotionally—by somebody you care about and who cares about you. Maybe you'll be touched in an entirely new way, one that's more satisfying than your other relationships have been."

I'm expecting a click of the tongue, which I've come to recognize as Rita's version of an eye roll, but she goes quiet, her green eyes filling with tears.

"Let me tell you a story," she says, fishing out a crumpled, used-looking tissue from the depths of her purse, even though a fresh box sits right beside her on the end table. "There's a family in the apartment across from mine," she begins. "Moved in about a year ago. New to town, saving up for a house. Two small children. The husband works from home and plays with the kids in the courtyard, hoisting them onto his shoulders and giving them piggyback rides and tossing a ball with them. All the things I never had."

She reaches into her purse for more tissues, can't find any, and dabs her eyes with the one she's just blown her nose into. I always wonder why she doesn't take a clean tissue from the box a few inches from her.

"Anyway," she says, "every day around five p.m., the mother comes home from work. And every day the same thing happens."

Rita chokes up here, stops. More nose-blowing and eye dabbing. *Take the damn tissues!* I want to scream. This pained woman, whom nobody talks to or touches, won't even let herself have a clean tissue. Rita squeezes what's left of the snot ball in her hand, wipes her eyes, and takes a breath.

"Every day," she continues, "the mother unlocks the front door, opens it up, and calls out, 'Hello, family!' That's how she greets them: 'Hello, family!'"

Her voice falters and she takes a minute to compose herself. The children, Rita explains, come running, squealing with joy, and her husband gives her a big, excited kiss. Rita tells me that she watches all this through the peephole that she secretly had enlarged for spying purposes. ("Don't judge," she says.)

"And do you know what I do?" she asks. "I know it's horribly ungenerous, but I *seethe* with anger." She's sobbing now. "There's never been a 'Hello, family!' for me."

I try to imagine the kind of family Rita might fashion for herself at this point in her life—perhaps with a partner or a rapprochement with her adult children. But I wonder about other possibilities too—what she might do with her passion for art or how she might form some new friendships. I think about the abandonment she experienced as a child and the trauma her own children experienced. How all of them must feel so ripped off and full of resentment that none of them can see what's actually there and what kind of lives they might still be able to create. And how for a while, I haven't been able to see it for Rita either.

I walk over to the tissue box, hand it to Rita, then sit down next to her on the couch.

"Thank you," she says. "Where did those come from?"

"They've been there all along," I say. But instead of taking a fresh tissue, she continues to wipe her face with the snot ball.

In the car on the way home, I call Jen. I know she's probably also in the car driving home.

When she picks up, I say, "Please tell me that I won't still be dating in retirement."

She laughs. "I don't know. *I* might be dating in retirement. People used to hang it up once their spouses died. Now they date." I hear the blare of horns before she continues. "And there are so many divorced people out there too."

"Are you trying to tell me you're having marital problems?"

"Yes."

"He's farting again?"

"Yes."

It's their ongoing joke. Jen has warned her husband that she's moving into the next room at night if he keeps eating dairy, but he loves dairy and she loves him, so she never moves.

I pull into the driveway and tell Jen I have to go. I park the car and unlock the front door to our house, where my son is being cared for by his babysitter, Cesar. Technically, Cesar works for us, but really, he's like an older brother to my son and a second son to me. We're close with his parents and sibling and his multitude of cousins, and I've watched him grow up through the years into the college student he is now, taking care of my son as he grows too.

I open the door and yell, "Hello, family!"

Zach shouts from his room, "Hey, Mom!" Cesar takes off an earbud and calls out from the kitchen, where he's preparing dinner, "Hey!"

Nobody runs up excitedly to greet me, nobody squeals with delight, but I don't feel deprived the way Rita does—just the opposite. I go to my bedroom to change into sweatpants, and when I come back out, we all start talking at once, sharing our days, teasing one another, vying for airtime, putting plates on the table and pouring the drinks. The boys bicker over setting the table and race to get the bigger portions. *Hello, family.*

I once told Wendell that I'm a terrible decision maker, that often what I think I want doesn't turn out the way I'd imagined. But there were two notable exceptions, and both proved to be the best decisions of my life. In each case, I was nearly forty.

One was my decision to have a baby.

The other was my decision to become a therapist.

25

The UPS Guy

The year Zach was born, I began acting inappropriately with my UPS delivery guy.

I don't mean that I tried to seduce him (it's hard to be seductive with milk stains on your T-shirt). I mean that whenever he delivered a package—which was often, given the need for baby supplies—I would try to detain him with conversation simply because I craved adult company. I'd strain to make small talk about the weather, a news headline, even the weight of a package ("Wow, who knew diapers were so *heavy!* Do you have kids?") while the UPS driver fake-smiled and nodded as he not-so-subtly backed away from me to the safety of his truck.

At the time I was working from home as a writer, which meant that all day, I sat alone in my pajamas at a computer when I wasn't feeding, changing, bouncing, or otherwise engaging with an adorable but demanding ten-pound human with a talent for screaming like a banshee. Basically, I interacted with what I called, in my darkest moments, "a gastrointestinal tract with lungs." Before having a baby, I'd relished the freedom of a non-office job. But now I longed to get dressed every day and be in the company of verbal grownups.

It was during this perfect storm of isolation and plummeting estrogen that I started to wonder if I'd made a mistake by leaving medical school. Journalism suited me well—I got to cover hundreds of topics for dozens of publications, and they all revolved around a common thread that fasci-nated me: the human psyche. I didn't want to stop writing, but now, while reeking of spit-up in the middle of the night, I reconsidered the possibility of a dual career. If I became a psychiatrist, I reasoned, I could interact with people in a meaningful way, helping them to be happier, but I could also have the flexibility to write and spend time with my family.

I sat on the idea for a few weeks, until one spring morning I called up my former dean at Stanford and floated my plan by her. A renowned re-searcher, she was also the med-school version of a camp mom—warm, wise, intuitive. I had run her mother-daughter book group when I was in medical school and knew her well. I was sure that after I explained my thought process, she would be supportive of my plan.

Instead she said: "Why would you do that?"

And then: "Besides, psychiatrists don't make people happy!"

I remembered the old medical-school quip: "Psychiatrists don't make people happy—prescriptions do!" Suddenly sobered, I knew what she meant. It wasn't that she didn't respect psychiatrists; it was that psychiatry today tends to be more about the nuances of medication and neurotrans-mitters than the subtleties of people's life stories—all of which she knew I knew.

Anyway, she asked, did I really want to do three years of residency with a toddler? Did I want to spend time with my son before he started kinder-garten? Did I remember talking with her as a medical student about my desire to have more substantial relationships with patients than the con-temporary medical model afforded?

Then—just as I imagined my former dean shaking her head on the other end of the phone, just when I wished I could turn back time so that this conversation had never happened—she said something that would change the course of my life: "You should go to graduate school and get a degree in clinical psychology." By going the clinical psychology route, she said, I could work with people in the way I'd always talked about—the ap-pointments would be fifty minutes instead of fifteen, and the work would be deeper and longer term.

I got chills. People often use that expression loosely, but I actually did get chills, goose bumps and all. It was shocking how right this felt, as if my life's plan had finally been revealed. In journalism, I thought, I could tell people's stories, but I wasn't *changing* their stories. As a therapist, I could help people change their stories. And with *this* dual career, I could have the perfect combination.

"Being a therapist is going to require a blend of the cognitive and the creative," the dean continued. "There's an artistry in combining the two. What could be a better mix of your abilities and interests?"

Not long after that conversation, I sat in a room with college seniors and took the GRE, the graduate-school version of the SAT. I applied to a local graduate program, and over the next few years, I worked toward my degree. And I continued to write, hearing stories and sharing them, while learning to help people change as my life changed too.

During this time, my son began to talk and walk, and the UPS guy's deliveries gradually evolved from diapers to Legos. "Oh, the Jedi Starfighter!" I'd say. "Are you a Star Wars fan?" And when I was finally ready to graduate, I told the UPS guy the news.

For the first time, he didn't try to run for his truck. Instead, he leaned over and hugged me.

"Congratulations!" he said, his arms wrapped around my back. "Wow, you did all that already, and with a kid too? I'm proud of you."

I stood there, shocked and moved, embracing my UPS guy. When we finally let go, he told me that he had news too: He wouldn't be on my route anymore. Like me, he'd decided to go back to school. And to save on rent, he needed to move in with his family, who lived a few hours away. He wanted to become a contractor.

"Congratulations to *you!*" I said, throwing my arms around him. "I'm proud of you too."

We probably looked odd ("That must have been *some* package!" I imagined the neighbors murmuring), but we stayed that way for what felt like a long time, delighted by how far we'd both come.

"I'm Sam, by the way," he said, after we finished hugging.

"I'm Lori, by the way," I said. He'd always called me "Ma'am" before.

"I know." He gestured with his chin to the package with my name on the address label.

We both laughed.

"Well, Sam, I'll be rooting for you," I said.

"Thanks," he replied. "I'll need it."

I shook my head. "I have a feeling you'll do just fine, but I'll root for you anyway."

Then Sam asked for my signature one last time and left, giving me a thumbs-up from the driver's seat as he pulled away in his big brown truck.

A couple of years later, I received a business card from Sam. *I saved your address,* he wrote on a Post-it attached to the card. *If you have any friends who need my services, I would appreciate the business.* I was midway through my internship, and I placed his card in my drawer for later, knowing exactly when I'd use it.

The bookshelves in my office?

Built by Sam.

26

Embarrassing Public Encounters

Early in our relationship, Boyfriend and I were standing in line at the frozen-yogurt place when one of my therapy patients walked in.

"Wow, hi!" Keisha said, taking her place in line behind us. "It's so funny running into you here." She turned to her right. "This is Luke."

Luke, who was thirtyish and attractive like Keisha, smiled and shook my hand. Although we'd never met, I knew exactly who he was. I knew that Luke was the boyfriend who had recently cheated on Keisha and that she'd figured this out because he'd been unable to get an erection with her. Each time he cheated, the same thing happened. ("His guilt," she once said, "is in his penis.")

I also knew that Keisha was preparing to leave him. She'd come to understand what had drawn her to him in the first place and wanted to be more intentional about choosing a trustworthy partner. In our last session, she had said that she planned to break up with him this weekend. It was now Saturday. Had she decided to stay with him, I wondered, or was she going to break it off on Sunday so that she'd have the structure of Monday's workday to help her stay the course? She'd told me that she wanted to tell Luke in a public place so that he wouldn't make a scene and beg her to stay, which he'd done when she attempted the conversation at her apartment twice before. She didn't want to cave again just because he said all the right things to convince her to change her mind.

In the yogurt line, Boyfriend was standing next to me expectantly, waiting to be introduced. I hadn't yet explained to him that if I see therapy patients outside the office, in order to protect their privacy, I won't acknowledge them if they don't acknowledge me first. It could be upsetting, for instance, if I said hello to a patient and the person accompanying her asked, "Who's that?," leaving the patient in the awkward position of having to hedge or explain on the spot. What if I were to say hello to a patient who was with a coworker or boss or who was on a first date?

Even if patients said hello to me first, I didn't introduce them to whomever I was with. That would also be breaking confidentiality—unless I were to lie when asked about how I know the patient.

So Boyfriend was looking at me, and Luke was looking at Boyfriend, and Keisha glanced at my hand, which Boyfriend was holding.

Unbeknownst to Boyfriend, I'd already run into a patient while he and I were together. A few days before, the husband in a couple I was seeing walked by us on the street. Without stopping, he said hi, I said hi back, and we both kept going in opposite directions.

"Who was that?" Boyfriend had asked then.

"Oh, just somebody I know through work," I said casually. Never mind that I knew more about his sexual fantasies than I knew about Boyfriend's.

At the yogurt place that Saturday night, I smiled at Keisha and Luke, then turned around to face the counter. The line was long, and Boyfriend took the hint and made small talk with me about yogurt flavors as I tried to tune out Luke's voice while he excitedly discussed vacation plans with Keisha. He was trying to pin down dates, and Keisha was being cagey, and Luke asked if she'd rather go next month, and Keisha asked if they could talk about it later and changed the subject.

I cringed for both of them.

After Boyfriend and I got our yogurts, I led him to a far table by the exit and took a seat with my back to the rest of the crowded room so that Keisha and I could both have our space.

A few minutes later, Luke stormed past our table and out the door, Keisha trailing behind him. Through the glass walls, we could see Keisha making apologetic gestures to Luke and then Luke getting in his car and driving away, nearly running Keisha over.

Boyfriend seemed to be putting it all together. "So *that's* how you know her." He joked that dating a therapist was like dating a CIA agent.

I laughed and said that being a therapist sometimes felt more like having an affair with your entire caseload, past and present, simultaneously. We're always pretending not to know the people we know most intimately.

But often it's therapists who feel uncomfortable when our outside worlds collide. After all, we've seen our patients' real lives. They haven't seen ours. Outside of our offices, we're like Z-list celebrities, meaning that hardly anyone knows who we are, but for those few who do, a sighting is significant.

Here are some things you can't do in public as a therapist: Cry to a friend in a restaurant; argue with your spouse; hit the building's elevator button relentlessly like it's a morphine pump. If you're in a rush on your way into the office, you can't honk at the slow car blocking the entrance to the parking garage in case your patient sees (or because the person you're honking at might *be* your patient).

If you're a respected child psychologist, like a colleague of mine, you don't want to be standing in the bakery when your four-year-old has a meltdown about not getting another cookie, culminating with the ear-piercing proclamation "YOU'RE THE WORST MOM EVER!" while your six-year-old patient and her mother look on, aghast. Nor, as happened to me, do you want to run into a former patient in the bra section of a department store as the salesperson announces loudly, "Good news, ma'am! I was able to find the Miracle Bra in the thirty-four *A*."

When you're making a restroom run between sessions, it's best to avoid the stall adjacent to your next patient, especially if either of you is taking a malodorous dump. And if you use the pharmacy across the street from your office, you don't want to be seen in the aisles buying condoms, tampons, constipation aids, adult diapers, creams for yeast infections and hemorrhoids, or prescriptions for STDs or mental disorders.

One day, while feeling flu-like and weak, I went to the CVS across from my office to pick up a prescription. The pharmacist handed me what was supposed to be an antibiotic, but when I looked at the label, I saw it was an antidepressant. A few weeks earlier, a rheumatologist had prescribed the antidepressant off-label for fibromyalgia, which she thought might explain some lingering fatigue, but then we decided I should hold off due to its potential side effects. I never picked up that prescription, and the rheumatologist canceled it; nevertheless, for some reason, it still sat in the computer, and every time I got a medication, the pharmacist would bring out the antidepressant and announce its name loudly while I prayed that none of my patients were in line behind me.

Often when patients see our humanity, they leave us.

Soon after John began seeing me, I ran into him at a Lakers game. It was halftime, and my son and I were waiting to buy a jersey.

"Jesus Christ," I heard somebody mutter, and I followed the voice and spotted John ahead of us in the line next to ours. He was with another man and two girls who looked to be around John's older daughter's age, ten. A dad-daughter outing, I figured. John was complaining to his friend about the couple in front of them who were taking a while to make their purchase—they kept losing track of which sizes the cashier had said were sold out.

"Oh, for God's sake," John said to the couple, his booming voice catching the attention of everyone around us. "They're out of the black Kobe in all sizes but the small—which is clearly not *your* size—and they only have the white Kobe in a kid's size, which is also clearly not your size. But it *is* the size of these girls here who came to watch a Lakers game, which is starting up in"—here he made a great show of holding up his watch—"four minutes."

"Chill, buddy," the guy in the couple said to John.

"Chill?" John said. "Maybe you're *too* chill. Maybe you should think about the fact that halftime is fifteen minutes and there's a sizable crowd behind you. Let's see, twenty people, fifteen minutes, less than a minute per person—*Oh shit, maybe I shouldn't be so chill!*"

He flashed his gleaming smile at the guy, and that's when John noticed me looking at him. He froze, stunned to see his mistress-hooker-therapist standing there, the one whom he didn't want his wife or, probably, his friend or daughter to know about.

We both looked away, ignoring each other.

But after my son and I made our purchase, as we were running hand in hand back to our seats, I noticed John watching us from afar, an inscrutable expression on his face.

Sometimes when I see people out in the world, particularly the first time it happens, I ask back in session what the experience was like for them. Some therapists wait for their patients to bring it up, but often, not mentioning it makes it bigger, the elephant in the room, and acknowledging the encounter feels like a relief. So the following week in therapy, I asked John what it was like to see me at the Lakers game.

"What the fuck kind of question is that?" John said. He let out a sigh, followed by a groan. "Do you know how many people were at the game?"

"A lot," I said, "but sometimes it's strange seeing your therapist outside of the office. Or seeing their children."

I'd been thinking about the look on John's face as he watched me run off with Zach. I privately wondered what it was like for him to see a mother hand in hand with her son, given the loss of his own mother when he was a boy.

"You know what it was like seeing my therapist and her kid?" John asked. "It was upsetting."

I was surprised that John was willing to share his reaction. "How so?"

"Your son got the last Kobe jersey in my daughter's size."

"Oh?"

"Yeah, so that was upsetting."

I waited to see if he'd say more, if he'd stop with the jokes. We were both quiet for a bit. Then John began counting. "One Mississippi, two

Mississippi, *three* Mississippi . . ." He shot me an exasperated look. "How long are we going to sit here saying nothing?"

I understood his frustration. In movies, therapist silences have become a cliché, but it's only in silence that people can truly hear themselves. Talking can keep people in their heads and safely away from their emotions. Being silent is like emptying the trash. When you stop tossing junk into the void—words, words, and more words—something important rises to the surface. And when the silence is a shared experience, it can be a gold mine for thoughts and feelings that the patient didn't even know existed. It's no wonder that I spent an entire session with Wendell saying virtually nothing and simply crying. Even great joy is sometimes best expressed through silence, as when a patient comes in after landing a hard-won promotion or getting engaged and can't find the words to express the magnitude of what she's feeling. So we sit in silence together, beaming.

"I'm listening for whatever you have to say," I told John.

"Fine," he said. "In that case, I have a question for you."

"Mmm?"

"What was it like for you to see *me?*"

Nobody had ever asked me that before. I thought for a minute about my reaction and how I would convey it to John. I remembered my irritation with the way he was talking to that couple at the front of the line and also my guilt at silently cheering him on. I, too, wanted to get back in the stadium before the second half started. I also remembered, when I was back at my seat, glancing down and noticing that John and his group were sitting courtside. I saw his daughter showing him something on his phone, and as they were looking at it together, he put his arm around her and they laughed and laughed, and I was so touched that I couldn't take my eyes off them. I wanted to share that with him.

"Well," I began, "it was—"

"Oh, Jesus, I was kidding!" John interrupted. "Obviously I don't care what it was like for you. That's my *point*. It was a Lakers game! We were there to see the Lakers."

"Okay."

"Okay what?"

"Okay, you don't care."

"Damn right, I don't." I saw that look on John's face again, the one I noticed when he was watching me run with Zach. No matter how I tried to engage with John that day—by helping him to slow down and notice his feelings, by talking about his experience with me in the room, by sharing some of my experience in our conversation—he remained closed off.

It wasn't until he was leaving that he turned back to me from the hallway and said, "Cute kid, by the way. Your son. The way he held your hand. Boys don't always do that."

I waited for the punch line. Instead, he looked me right in the eye and said, almost pensively, "Enjoy it while it lasts."

I stood there for a second. *Enjoy it while it lasts.*

I wondered if he was thinking about his daughter—maybe she'd outgrown letting John hold her hand in public. But he'd also said, "*Boys* don't always do that." What did he know about raising boys, being the father of two girls?

It was about him and his mother, I decided. I tucked away the exchange for when he'd be ready to talk about her.

27

Wendell's Mother

When Wendell was a boy, every August he and his four siblings would pile into the family station wagon and drive with their parents from their Midwestern suburb to a cabin on a lake for a vacation with their large extended family. There were about twenty cousins in all, and the kids would wander as a pack, taking off in the morning, checking back in with the adults for lunch (which they ate ravenously while sitting on blankets spread over a verdant field), and disappearing again until dinnertime.

Sometimes the cousins would go for bike rides, but Wendell, the youngest, was afraid to ride a bike. Whenever his parents and older siblings offered to teach him, he feigned indifference, but everyone knew that the story of an older boy in town who had fallen off his bike, hit his head, and gone deaf from the blow had stuck in Wendell's mind.

Fortunately, bikes didn't matter all that much at the cabin. Even when some of the cousins went out on their bikes, there were always enough kids with whom he could swim in the lake, climb trees, and play epic games of capture the flag.

Then one summer, just after Wendell turned thirteen, he went missing. The clan of cousins had returned for lunch, and while they were munching on watermelon, somebody noticed that Wendell wasn't there. They checked inside the cabins. Empty. Groups dispersed to search for him at the lake, in the woods, around town. But Wendell was nowhere to be found.

After four terrifying hours for his family, Wendell returned—riding a bike. Apparently, a cute girl he'd met by the lake had asked him to go on a bike ride with her, so he went to the bike shop and explained his problem. The owner looked at this eager, skinny thirteen-year-old and instantly understood. He shut down the store, took Wendell to an abandoned lot, and taught him how to ride. Then he gave him a free day's rental.

Now there he was, riding a bike toward the cabins. His parents cried in relief.

Wendell and the girl from the lake rode together every day for the rest of the trip, and when it was over, they wrote letters back and forth for the next several months. But one day Wendell got a letter from her saying that she was very sorry, but she had found a new boyfriend at her school and would no longer be writing to Wendell. His mom found the ripped page while emptying the trash.

Wendell pretended not to care.

"That year was a crash course in biking and love," Wendell's mother later remarked. "You take a risk, you fall down, and you get back up and do it all over again."

Wendell did get back up. And in time, he stopped pretending not to care. After graduating from college and joining the family business, he couldn't pretend any longer that his interest in psychology was just a hobby. So Wendell quit and got a doctorate in psychology instead. Now it was his father's turn to pretend not to care. And like Wendell, eventually his father got back up on that metaphorical bike and embraced his son's decision.

At least, that's how Wendell's mother tells the story.

Of course, she didn't tell *me* this story. I know all of this courtesy of the internet.

I wish I could say that I accidentally stumbled on this information, that I needed Wendell's address to send in a check and typed in his name and — *Oh, wow, look what popped up*—right there, on the very first page of results, was an interview with his mother. But the only part that would be true is the part where I typed in his name.

A small comfort: I wasn't alone in Googling my therapist.

Julie once said something to me about a scientist at her university that I'd written about, as if we'd previously mentioned that we both knew him (we hadn't). Rita once alluded to the fact that she and I had both grown up in Los Angeles, though I'd never told her where I'd grown up. John finished one of his "idiot" rants about a just-out-of-college hire who'd graduated from Stanford with "The Harvard of the West, my ass." Then, looking sheepishly at me, he added, "I mean, no offense." He must have known I'd gone to Stanford. I also know that John Googled Wendell to check out his wife's therapist, because once he complained that Wendell had no website or photo, which immediately made John suspicious. "What's the idiot trying to hide?" he'd said. "Oh, right—his incompetence."

So patients do Google their therapists, but that wasn't my excuse. In fact, it had never occurred to me to Google Wendell until he suggested that by Google-stalking Boyfriend I was holding on to a future that had been canceled. I was watching Boyfriend's future unfold while I stayed locked in the past. I'd need to accept that his future and mine, his present and mine, were now separate and that all we had left in common was our history.

Sitting at my laptop, I remembered the way Wendell had made this all so clear. Then I thought about how I knew nearly nothing about Wendell other than the fact that he'd trained with Caroline, the colleague who gave me his name. I didn't know where he'd gotten his degree or what he specialized in or any of the basic information people tend to gather online before seeing a therapist. I'd been so eager for help that I took Caroline's referral for my "friend" sight unseen.

If something isn't working, do something different, therapists are taught in training when they're hitting a wall with a patient, and we also suggest it to our patients: Why continue doing the same unhelpful thing over and over? If following Boyfriend online was keeping me stuck, Wendell implied, I should do something different. But what? I tried closing my eyes and taking some breaths, an intervention that can disrupt a compulsive urge. And it worked—sort of. When I opened my eyes, I didn't type Boyfriend's name into Google.

I typed in Wendell's.

John had been right; Wendell was virtually invisible. No website. No LinkedIn. No *Psychology Today* listing or public Facebook or Twitter. Just a single link with his office address and phone number. For a practitioner of my generation, Wendell was unusually old-school.

I scanned the search results again. There were several Wendell Bronsons, but none was my therapist. I kept looking, and two pages in, I noticed a Yelp listing for Wendell. It had one review. I clicked.

The reviewer, who went by the name Angela L., had been named an "elite" reviewer for five years in a row, and no wonder. She had posted about restaurants, dry cleaners, mattress warehouses, dog parks, dentists (a revolving door of them), gynecologists, manicurists, roofers, florists, clothing stores, hotels, pest-control companies, movers, pharmacies, car dealers, tattoo parlors, a personal injury lawyer, and even a criminal defense attorney (something about being "falsely accused" of a parking violation, which had somehow become a criminal offense).

But most striking about Angela L. wasn't the sheer number of reviews; it was how aggressively negative nearly all of them were.

FAIL! she'd write. Or *DUMBASSES!* Angela L. seemed to be horribly disappointed with everything. The way her cuticles were cut. The way a receptionist spoke to her. Even when she was on vacation, nothing escaped her scrutiny. She'd post reviews while at the rental-car booth, at the hotel check-in, upon arrival in her room, in seemingly every place she ate and drank during her trip, and even out at the beach (where she'd once stepped on a rock in what was supposed to be silky white sand and claimed that it had injured her foot). Invariably, everyone she encountered was lazy or incompetent or stupid.

She reminded me of John. And then it occurred to me that maybe Angela L. was Margo! Because the one person in the world that Angela L. didn't feel pissed off at or treated unfairly by was Wendell.

He got Angela L.'s very first five-star review.

I've been to many therapists—no surprise there—*but this time I feel like I'm making real strides,* she wrote. She went on to gush about Wendell's compassion and wisdom, adding that he was helping her to see how her behaviors were contributing to her marital difficulties. Because of Wendell, she added, she had been able to reconcile with her husband after they'd separated. (So *not* Margo.)

The review had been posted a year ago. Scanning her subsequent entries, I noticed a trend. Gradually, her string of one- and two-star pans became three- and then four-star praise. Angela L. was becoming less angry at the world, less prone to blaming others for her unhappiness (what we call externalizing). There was less raging at customer-service reps, fewer perceived slights (personalization), more self-awareness (acknowledging, in one review, that she could be difficult to please). The quantity of posts had dropped off too, making the endeavor seem less obsessive. She was approaching "emotional sobriety"—the ability to regulate one's feelings without self-medicating, whether that medication comes in the form of substances, defenses, affairs, or the internet.

Kudos to Wendell, I thought. I could see Angela L.'s emotional evolution through the progression of her Yelp reviews.

But just as I was admiring Wendell's skill, I came across another irate one-star review from Angela L. It was for a shuttle service, a downgrade from an earlier four-star review she'd given the company. Angela L. seemed livid that the bus played loud Muzak and the driver couldn't turn it off. How could they "attack" riders like this? Three paragraphs later, punctuated by multiple ALL CAPS and exclamation marks, Angela L. ended the review with *I've used this company for months, but no more. Our relationship is over!!!*

Her dramatic breakup with the shuttle service after all those more balanced reviews might have been expected. Like many people, she'd probably backslid, regretted it, realized she'd hit bottom, and decided that moderation wasn't enough; she had to quit Yelp entirely. And so far she had—that had been Angela L.'s final review, posted six months ago.

But I wasn't ready to quit my Google-stalking. Half an hour later, my cursor hovered over the interview with Wendell's mother. The therapist I knew seemed both grounded and unconventional, tough and gentle, confident and awkward. Who had raised him? I felt like I'd found the mother lode—so to speak.

Of course, I clicked.

The Q&A, which turned out to be a ten-page family history, appeared on the blog of a local organization that was documenting the lives of notable families who had lived in that Midwestern town for half a century.

Both of Wendell's parents, I learned, had grown up poor. His maternal grandmother died in childbirth, so his mom went to live with her father's sister in a small apartment, and their family became hers. Wendell's father, meanwhile, had become a self-made man, the first in his family to go to college. It was at this large state university that he met Wendell's mother, the first woman in her family to get a college degree. After they married, he started a business, she gave birth to a brood of five, and by the time Wendell was a teenager, the family had become spectacularly wealthy—one of the reasons for the interview I was reading. Apparently, Wendell's parents gave away much of their wealth to charitable causes.

By the time I got to the names of Wendell's siblings and their spouses and children, I had become as unhinged as Angela L. I researched Wendell's entire family—what they did for a living, what cities they were in, how old their kids were, who was divorced. None of this was easy to find; my mission involved extensive cross-referencing and hours of time.

Admittedly, I knew a few things about Wendell from comments he'd strategically dropped into our sessions. Once, after I said, "But it's not fair!" about the Boyfriend situation, Wendell looked at me and replied, kindly, "You sound like my ten-year-old. What makes you think life is supposed to be fair?"

I took in his point, but I also thought, *Oh, he has a kid around my son's age.* When he tossed me these morsels, they felt like unexpected gifts.

But that night on the internet, there was always another lead, another link. He'd met his wife through a mutual friend; his family lived in a Spanish-style house that, according to Zillow, had doubled in value since they'd bought it; recently, when he'd needed to reschedule our appointment, it was because he was presenting at a conference.

By the time I finally shut down my laptop, the night was over and I felt guilty, empty, and exhausted.

The internet can be both a salve and an addiction, a way to block out pain (the salve) while simultaneously creating it (the addiction). When the cyber-drug wears off, you feel worse, not better. Patients think they want to know about their therapists, but often, once they find out, they wish they hadn't, because this knowledge has the potential to contaminate the relationship, leaving patients to edit, consciously or not, what they say in their sessions.

I knew that what I'd done had been destructive. And I also knew that I wouldn't tell Wendell about it. I understood why, when a patient inadvertently reveals knowing more about me than I've shared and I ask about it, there's a slight hesitation while the person decides whether to be honest or lie. It's hard to confess to stalking your therapist. I was ashamed—of invading Wendell's privacy, of wasting away the evening—and I vowed (perhaps like Angela L.) never to do it again.

Still, the damage had been done. When I went back to Wendell the following Wednesday, I felt weighed down by my newfound knowledge. I couldn't help thinking that it was only a matter of time before I'd slip up —just like my own patients did.

28

Addicted

CHART NOTE, CHARLOTTE:

Patient, age twenty-five, reports feeling "anxious" for the past few months, though nothing of note has recently occurred. States that she is "bored" at her job. Describes difficulty with parents and a busy social life but no history of significant romantic relationships. Reports that to relax, she drinks "a couple glasses of wine" nightly.

"You're going to *kill* me," Charlotte says as she saunters in and slowly settles herself into the oversize chair diagonally to my right, arranges a pillow on her lap, then tosses the throw blanket over it. She has never sat on the couch, not even at the first session, instead making the chair her throne. As usual, she takes her belongings out of her bag, one by one, unpacking for her fifty-minute stay. On the left arm of the chair, she places her phone and pedometer; on the right, her water bottle and sunglasses.

Today she's wearing blush and lipstick, and I know what that means: she's been flirting again with the guy in the waiting room.

Our suite has a large reception area where patients wait to be seen. Leaving their appointments is more private—there's an exit through an interior corridor that leads to the building's hallway. Patients generally keep to themselves in the waiting room—but Charlotte has something going on.

The Dude, as Charlotte calls the object of her flirtation (neither of us knows his name), is my colleague Mike's patient, and he and Charlotte have their sessions at the same time. According to Charlotte, the first time the Dude showed up, they noticed each other immediately, stealing glances over their respective phones. This went on for weeks, and after their sessions, which also ended at the same time, they'd exit through the interior door only to steal more glances at each other in the elevator before going their separate ways.

Finally, one day, Charlotte came in with news.

"The Dude just talked to me!" she whispered, as if the Dude could hear her through the walls.

"What did he say?" I asked.

"He said, 'So, what's *your* issue?'"

Great line, I thought, impressed despite its cheesiness.

"So here's the part where you're going to kill me," she said that day. She took a big breath, but I'd heard this refrain before. If Charlotte drank too much the previous week, she'd open the session with "You're going to kill me." If she'd hooked up with a guy and regretted it (as happened often), she'd open with "You're going to kill me." I was even going to kill her when she put off researching graduate-school options and missed the application deadlines. We'd talked before about how underneath the projection was a deep sense of shame.

"Okay, you don't want to kill me," she conceded. "But, *ugh*. I didn't know what to say, so I froze. I completely ignored him and pretended to text. God, I hate myself."

I imagined the Dude at that very moment sitting in my colleague's therapy room just a few doors away and recounting the same incident: *I finally spoke to that girl in the waiting room, and she completely rejected me. Ugh! I sounded like an idiot. God, I hate myself.*

Still, the next week, the flirtation continued. When the Dude walked into the waiting room, Charlotte told me, she opened with a line she'd been rehearsing all week.

"You want to know what my issue is?" Charlotte asked him. "I freeze when strangers in waiting rooms ask me questions." That made the Dude laugh, and they were both laughing when I opened the door to greet Charlotte.

Upon seeing me, the Dude blushed. *Guilty?* I wondered.

As we walked toward my office, Charlotte and I passed Mike, who was approaching to collect the Dude. Mike and I met each other's eyes then immediately looked away. *Yup,* I thought. *The Dude has told him about Charlotte too.*

By the following week, the waiting-room banter was in full swing. Charlotte told me that she asked the Dude his name, and he replied, "I can't tell you."

"Why not?" she asked.

"Everything in here is confidential," he said.

"Okay, Confidential," she shot back. "My name's Charlotte. I'm going to go talk about you with my therapist now."

"Hope you get your money's worth," he said with a sexy grin.

I'd seen the Dude a few times, and Charlotte was right, he had a killer smile. And while I didn't know the first thing about him, something in me sensed danger for Charlotte. Given her history with men, I had a feeling the whole thing would end badly—and two weeks later, Charlotte walked in with an update. The Dude had come to his session with a woman.

Of course, I thought. *Unavailable.* Just Charlotte's type. Charlotte, in fact, had used that same expression every time she mentioned the Dude. *He's so my type.*

What most people mean by *type* is a sense of attraction—a *type* of physical appearance or a *type* of personality turns them on. But what underlies a person's type, in fact, is a sense of familiarity. It's no coincidence that people who had angry parents often end up choosing angry partners, that those with alcoholic parents are frequently drawn to partners who drink quite a bit, or that those who had withdrawn or critical parents find themselves married to spouses who are withdrawn or critical.

Why would people do this to themselves? Because the pull toward that feeling of "home" makes what they want as adults hard to disentangle from what they experienced as children. They have an uncanny attraction to people who share the characteristics of a parent who in some way hurt them. In the beginning of a relationship, these characteristics will be barely perceptible, but the unconscious has a finely tuned radar system inaccessible to the conscious mind. It's not that people want to get hurt again. It's that they want to master a situation in which they felt helpless as children. Freud called this "repetition compulsion." *Maybe this time,* the unconscious imagines, *I can go back and heal that wound from long ago by engaging with somebody familiar—but new.* The only problem is, by choosing familiar partners, people guarantee the opposite result: they reopen the wounds and feel even more inadequate and unlovable.

This happens completely outside of awareness. Charlotte, for instance, said that she wanted a reliable boyfriend capable of intimacy, but every time she met somebody who was her type, chaos and frustration ensued. Conversely, after a recent date with a guy who seemed to possess many of the qualities she said she wanted in a partner, she came to therapy and reported: "It's too bad, but there just wasn't any chemistry." To her unconscious, his emotional stability felt too foreign.

The therapist Terry Real described our well-worn behaviors as "our internalized family of origin. It's our repertoire of relational themes." People don't have to tell you their stories with words because they always act them out for you. Often they project negative expectations onto the therapist, but if the therapist doesn't meet those negative expectations, this "corrective emotional experience" with a reliable and benevolent person changes the patients; the world, they learn, turns out *not* to be their family of origin. If Charlotte works through her complicated feelings toward her parents with me, she'll find herself increasingly attracted to a different type, one that might give her the *un*familiar experience she's seeking with a compassionate, reliable, and mature partner. Until then, every time she meets an available guy who might love her back, her unconscious rejects his stability as "not interesting." She still equates feeling loved not with peace or joy but with anxiety.

And so it goes. Same guy, different name, same outcome.

"Did you see her?" Charlotte asked, referring to the woman who came to therapy with the Dude. "She must be his girlfriend." In the quick peek I'd gotten of the two of them, they were sitting in adjoining chairs but not interacting in any way. Like the Dude, the young woman was tall with thick dark hair. She could be his sister, I thought, coming with him for family therapy. But Charlotte was probably right; more likely she was the girlfriend.

And now, in today's session—two months after the Dude's girlfriend became a fixture in the waiting room—Charlotte has pronounced again that I'm going to kill her. I run through the possibilities in my mind, the first of which is that she slept with the Dude, despite the girlfriend. I imagine the girlfriend and the Dude sitting in the waiting room with Charlotte, the girlfriend unaware that Charlotte has slept with her boyfriend. I imagine the girlfriend gradually getting wise to this and dumping the Dude, leaving Charlotte and the Dude free to become a couple. Then I imagine Charlotte doing what she does in relationships (avoiding intimacy) and the Dude doing whatever he does in relationships (only Mike knows), and the whole thing blowing up in a spectacular fashion.

But I'm wrong. Today Charlotte believes that I'm going to kill her because as she was leaving her finance job last night to head out for her very first Alcoholics Anonymous meeting, some coworkers invited her to join them for drinks and she said yes, because she thought it would be a good networking opportunity. Then she tells me, without a trace of irony, that she drank too much because she was upset with herself for not going to the AA meeting.

"God," she says. "I hate myself."

I was once told by a supervisor that every therapist has the experience of seeing a patient with whom the similarities are so striking that this person feels like your doppelgänger. When Charlotte walked into my office, I knew she was that patient—almost. She was the twin of my twenty-year-old self.

It wasn't just that we looked alike and had similar reading habits, mannerisms, and default ways of thinking (over- and negative). Charlotte came to me three years after she had graduated from college, and while everything looked good on the outside—she had friends and a respectable job; she paid her own bills—she was also unsure of her career direction, conflicted about her parents, and generally lost. Granted, I didn't drink too much or sleep with random people, but I'd moved through that decade just as blindly.

It may seem logical that if you identify with a patient, it will make the work easier because you intuitively understand her, but in many ways, this kind of identification makes things harder. I've had to be extra-vigilant in our sessions, making sure that I'm seeing Charlotte as a separate person and not as a younger version of myself that I can go back and fix. More so than with other patients, I've had to resist the temptation to jump in and set her straight too quickly when she plops down in her chair, tells a meandering anecdote, and finishes with a demand couched in a question: "Isn't my manager *unreasonable?*" "Can you *believe* my roommate said that?"

At twenty-five, though, Charlotte has pain but not significant regret. Unlike me, she hasn't had a midlife reckoning. Unlike Rita, she hasn't damaged her children or married someone abusive. She has the gift of time, if she uses it wisely.

Charlotte didn't think she had an addiction when she first entered treatment for depression and anxiety. She drank, she insisted, only "a couple of glasses" of wine each night "to relax." (I immediately applied the standard therapeutic calculation used when somebody seems defensive about drug or alcohol use: whatever the total reported, double it.)

Eventually I learned that Charlotte's nightly alcohol consumption averaged three-quarters of a bottle of wine, sometimes preceded by a cocktail (or two). She said that she never drank during the day ("except on weekends," she added, "because hashtag brunch") and rarely appeared drunk to others, having developed a tolerance over the years—but she did sometimes have trouble recalling events and details the day after drinking.

Still, she believed there was nothing unusual about her "social drinking" and she obsessed about her "real" addiction, the one that increasingly plagued her the longer she stayed in therapy: *me.* If she could, she said, she'd come to therapy every day.

Each week after I'd indicate that our time was up, Charlotte would sigh dramatically and exclaim with surprise, "Really? Are you *serious?*" Then, very slowly, while I stood at the open door, she'd gather her scattered belongings one by one—sunglasses, cell phone, water bottle, hair band—frequently leaving behind something that she'd have to come back for later.

"*See*," she'd say when I'd suggest that her leaving items behind was her way of not leaving her session. "I'm addicted to therapy." She'd use the generic term *therapy* rather than the more personal *you*.

But as much as she disliked leaving, therapy was the perfect setup for somebody like Charlotte, a person who craved connection but also avoided it. Our relationship was the ideal combination of intimacy and distance; she could get close to me but not too close because at the end of the hour, whether she liked it or not, she went home. During the week, too, she could get close but not too close, emailing me articles she read or one-liners about something that had happened between sessions (*My mom called and acted crazy, and I didn't yell at her*), or photos of various things she found amusing (a license plate that read 4EVJUNG—not taken, I hoped, while she was inebriated behind the wheel).

If I tried to talk about these things during our sessions, Charlotte would brush them off. "Oh, I just thought it was funny," she said about the license plate. When she sent an article on an epidemic of loneliness among her age group, I asked about its resonance for her. "Nothing, really," she replied with a perplexed look on her face. "I just thought it was culturally interesting."

Of course, patients think about their therapists between sessions all the time, but for Charlotte, keeping me in mind felt less like a stable connection and more like a loss of control. What if she relied on me too much?

To deal with that fear, she'd already left our therapy and returned twice, always struggling to stay away from what she called her fix. Each time, she quit without notice.

The first time, she announced in session that she "needed to quit and the only way I'll do it is if I leave quickly." Then she literally got up and bolted from the room. (I'd known something was up when she hadn't unpacked the contents of her bag onto the armrests and left the blanket draped over the chair.) Two months later, she asked if she could come back "for one session" to discuss an issue with her cousin, but when she arrived, it was apparent that her depression had returned, so she stayed for three months. Just as she started feeling better and began to make some positive changes, an hour before her session, she sent me an email explaining that once and for all, she needed to quit.

Therapy, that is. The drinking continued.

Then one night Charlotte was driving home from a birthday party and crashed into a pole. She called me the next morning, after the police had issued her a DUI.

"I didn't see it at all," she told me after she arrived wearing a cast. "And I don't just mean the pole." Her car had been totaled but, miraculously, she'd ended up with just a broken arm.

"Maybe," she said, for the first time, "I have a drinking problem, not a therapist problem."

But she was still drinking a year later, when she met the Dude.

29

The Rapist

At John's appointment time, my green light goes on. I walk down the hall to the waiting room, but when I open the door, the chair John usually takes is empty, save for a bag of takeout. For a minute I think he might be in the restroom down the hall, but the public key is still hanging on the hook. I wonder if John's running late—after all, presumably he ordered the food—or if he's decided not to come today because of what happened last week.

That session had started off uneventfully. As usual, the delivery guy brought our Chinese chicken salads, and after John complained about the dressing ("too saturated") and the chopsticks ("too flimsy"), he got right down to business.

"I was thinking," John began, "about the word *therapist*." He took a bite of his salad. "You know, if you break it in two . . ."

I knew where this was going. *Therapist* is spelled the same way as *the rapist*. It's a common joke in the therapy world.

I smiled. "I wonder if you're trying to tell me that sometimes it's hard to be here." I've certainly felt that with Wendell, especially when his eyes seem to bore into me and there's no place to hide. By day, therapists hear people's secrets and fantasies, their shame and their failures, invading the spaces they normally keep private. Then—*boom*—the hour's over. Just like that.

Are we emotional rapists?

"Hard to be here?" John said. "Nah. You can be a pain in the ass, but this isn't the worst place to be."

"So you think I'm a pain in the ass?" It took some effort not to emphasize the *I,* as in "So you think *I'm* a pain in the ass?"

"Of course," John said. "You ask too many damn questions."

"Oh? Like what?"

"Like that."

I nodded. "I can see how that might annoy you."

John brightened. "You can?"

"I can. I think you'd rather keep me at a distance when I'm trying to get to know you."

"And heeeeeere we go again." John rolled his eyes dramatically. At least once a session, I bring up our pattern: my trying to connect with him; his trying to flee. He may be resistant to acknowledging it now, but I welcome his resistance because resistance is a clue to where the crux of the work lies; it signals what a therapist needs to pay attention to. During training, whenever we interns felt frustrated by resistant patients, our supervisors would counsel, "Resistance is a therapist's friend. Don't fight it—follow it." In other words, try to figure out why it's there in the first place.

Meanwhile, I was interested in the second part of what John had said. "Just to be more annoying," I continued, "I'm going to ask you another question. You said this isn't the worst place to be. What's the worst?"

"You don't know?"

I shrugged. *No.*

John's eyes bugged out. "Really?"

I nodded.

"Oh, come on, you know," he said. "Just guess."

I didn't want to get into a power struggle with John, so I took a guess.

"At work when you don't feel that people understand you? At home with Margo when you feel you're disappointing her?"

John made the sound of a game-show buzzer. "Wrong!" He took a bite of salad, swallowed, then lifted his chopsticks into the air to punctuate his words. "I came here, you may or *may not* remember, because I was having trouble sleeping."

I noticed his dig: *May not.*

"I remember," I said.

He let out a huge sigh, as if summoning the patience of Gandhi. "So, Sherlock, if sleeping is a problem for me, where do you think it's hard for me to be right now?"

Here, I wanted to say. *You're having trouble being here. But in good time, we'll talk about that.*

"Bed," I said.

"Bingo!"

I waited for him to elaborate, but he went back to his salad. We sat together while he ate and swore at his chopsticks.

"Aren't you going to say anything?"

"I'd like to hear more," I said. "What are you thinking about as you're trying to fall asleep?"

"Jesus Christ! Is something wrong with your memory today? What do you *think* I'm thinking about—everything I come in here telling you each week! Work, my kids, Margo—"

John went on to relate an argument he'd had with Margo the night before about whether their older daughter should get a cell phone for her eleventh birthday. Margo wanted her to have it for safety, now that Grace was going to be walking home from school with her friends, and John thought that Margo was being overprotective.

"It's two blocks!" John said he told Margo. "Besides, if someone tries to kidnap her, it's not like Grace is going to say, 'Hey, excuse me, Mr. Kidnapper, let me just pause here for a second, get my phone out of my backpack, and call my mom!' And unless the kidnapper is a complete idiot—which he could be, okay, but he's probably just a sick motherfucker—the first thing he's going to do if he steals someone's kid is *look in her backpack for a cell phone* and dump it or destroy it so we can't track her location. So what's the point of the phone?" John's face had turned red. He was really worked up.

Since our Skype call the day after Margo had insinuated that she might leave, things between them had calmed down. As John described it, he tried to listen more. He tried to get home from work earlier. But really, it seemed to me that he was, as he said, "appeasing her," whereas what she likely wanted was the very thing John and I struggled with together: his presence.

John packed the remnants of his lunch into the takeout bag and tossed it across the room, where it landed with a thud in the trash can.

"And that's why I couldn't sleep," he went on. "Because an eleven-year-old doesn't need a cell phone and you know what? She'll get one anyway because if I put my foot down, Margo will sulk and tell me in some passive-aggressive way that she wants to leave again. And you know why *that* is? Because of her IDIOT THERAPIST!"

Wendell.

I tried to imagine Wendell hearing Margo's version of this story: *We were talking about getting Grace a cell phone for her birthday and John just went ballistic.* I pictured Wendell in position C, wearing his khakis and cardigan, giving Margo the head-tilted look. I imagined him asking a Buddha-like question about whether she might be curious why John had had such a strong reaction. I figured that by the time their session was over, Margo would have a slightly different take on John's motives, just as I had come to see Boyfriend's actions as less than sociopathic.

"And you know what else she's going to tell her idiot therapist?" John continued. "She's going to tell him that her fucking husband can't fucking have sex with her, because when I got in bed at the same time she did instead of finishing up my emails—*another* thing I'm doing to make her happy, by the way—I was so pissed off that I wouldn't have sex with her. She approached me but I told her I was tired and didn't feel well. Like a housewife in the fifties with a headache. Jesus Christ, right?"

"Sometimes our emotional states can really affect our bodies," I said, trying to normalize this for John.

"Can we keep my penis out of this? That's not the point of the story."

Sex comes up with almost every patient I see, the same way that love does. Earlier on, I'd asked John about his sex life with Margo, given the difficulties in their relationship. It's a common belief that people's sex lives reflect their relationships, that a good relationship equals a good sex life and vice versa. But that's only true sometimes. Just as often, there are people who have extremely problematic relationships and fantastic sex, and there are people who are deeply in love but who don't click with the same intensity in the bedroom.

John had told me then that their sex life was "okay." When I'd asked what "okay" meant, he said that he was attracted to Margo and enjoyed sex with her but that they went to bed at different times so it was less frequent than in the past. But often he contradicted himself. At one point he said that he tended to initiate sex but Margo didn't want it; another time he said that she often initiated "but only if I do what she wants during the day." Once he said that they'd talked about their sexual desires and needs; another time he said, "We've been having sex with each other for over a decade. What's there to talk about? We know what the other person wants." Now I got the sense that John was having trouble getting an erection and that he felt humiliated.

"The point of the story," John went on, "is that there's a double standard in our house. If Margo's too tired to have sex one night, I let it go. I don't corner her with a toothbrush in her mouth the next morning and say"—here he did the Oprah impression again—"'I'm sorry you weren't feeling well last night. Maybe we can find some time to connect tonight.'"

John looked up at the ceiling and shook his head.

"Men don't talk like that. They don't dissect every little thing and think it has 'meaning.'" He made air quotes when he said the word *meaning*.

"It feels like picking a scab instead of letting it be."

"Exactly!" John nodded. "And now I'm the bad guy unless she gets to make all the decisions! If I have an opinion, I'm not 'seeing'"—more air quotes—"what Margo's 'needs' are. So then Grace gets into this and says that I'm being unreasonable, that 'everyone' has a phone, and that it's two to one, girls win! She actually said that: 'Girls win.'"

He lowered his arms now that he was done with the air quotes. "And that's when I realize that part of what's driving me nuts and making it hard to sleep is that there's too much estrogen in the house and nobody understands my perspective! Ruby's starting elementary school next year but already acts like her older sister. And Gabe's getting so emotional, like a teenager. I'm outnumbered in my own home and everyone wants something from me every minute and nobody understands that *I* might need something too—like peace and quiet and some say in what goes on!"

"Gabe?"

John sat up. "What?"

"You said Gabe was getting so emotional. Did you mean Grace?" I did a quick memory check: his four-year-old's name was Ruby and his older daughter was Grace. Didn't he just say Grace wanted a phone for her birthday? Or did I have that wrong? Was it Gabriella? Gabby shortened to Gabe, the way some girls named Charlotte are called Charlie nowadays? I'd once confused Ruby with Rosie, their dog, but I was pretty sure I had Grace's name right.

"I did?" He seemed flustered but recovered quickly. "Well, I meant Grace. Obviously I'm sleep-deprived. Like I *told* you."

"But you know a Gabe?" Something about John's reaction made me suspect that this wasn't just about insomnia. I wondered if Gabe was somebody significant in his life—one of his brothers, a childhood friend? The name of his father?

"This is an idiotic conversation," John said, looking away. "I meant Grace. Sometimes a cigar is just a cigar, Dr. Freud."

We both sat there.

"Who's Gabe?" I asked gently.

John was quiet for a long while. His face went through a series of expressions in rapid succession, like a time-lapse video of a storm. This was new; he generally had two modes, angry and jokey. Eventually he looked at his shoes—the same checkered sneakers I'd seen on our Skype call—and shifted into the safest gear, neutral.

"Gabe is my son," John said so quietly that I could barely hear him. "How's that for a twist in the case, Sherlock?"

Then he grabbed his phone, walked out the door, and shut it behind him.

Now here I am, a week later, standing in the empty waiting room, and I'm not sure what to make of the fact that our lunches have arrived but John hasn't. I haven't heard from him since the revelation, but I've been thinking about him. *Gabe is my son* rang through my mind at the most random of moments, especially at bedtime.

This felt like a classic example of projective identification. In projection, a patient attributes his beliefs *to* another person; in projective identification, he sends them *into* another person. For instance, a man may feel angry at his boss at work, then come home and say to his spouse, "You seem angry." He's projecting, because the spouse *isn't* angry. In projective identification, on the other hand, the man may feel angry at his boss, return home, and essentially *insert his anger into his partner,* actually making the partner feel angry. Projective identification is like tossing a hot potato to the other person. The man no longer has to feel his anger, since it's now living inside his partner.

I talked about John's session in my Friday consultation group. Just as he had been lying in bed with a metaphorical circus in his mind, I told the group that now I'd been doing the same thing—and since I was holding all of his anxiety, he was probably sleeping like a baby.

Meanwhile, my mind reeled. What to do with this bomb that John had detonated before walking out the door? *John has a son? From his youth? Is he living a double life? Does Margo know?* I flashed back to our session after the Lakers game when he'd commented on the handholding with my son. *Enjoy it while it lasts.*

What John did—the walking-out part, at least—isn't uncommon. Especially in couples therapy, patients occasionally walk out if they feel besieged by intense feelings. Sometimes that person benefits from a phone call from the therapist, particularly if the reason he or she bolted had to do with feeling misunderstood or injured. Often, though, it's best to let patients sit with their feelings, get their bearings, and then work through it with them the following session.

My consultation group believed that if John was already feeling cornered by the people around him, a call from me might be too much. Everyone agreed: Back off. Don't push him. Wait for him to come back.

Except today he's not here.

I pick up the unmarked takeout bag in the waiting room and look to make sure it's ours. Inside are two Chinese chicken salads and John's soda.

Did he forget to cancel the order, or is he using the food to communicate with me, making his absence known? Sometimes when people don't show, they do it to punish the therapist and send a message: *You've upset me.* And sometimes they do it to avoid not just the therapist but themselves, to avoid confronting their shame or pain or the truth they know they need to tell. People communicate through their attendance — whether they're prompt or late, cancel an hour beforehand, or don't show up at all.

I walk back into our suite, place the food bag in the fridge, and decide to use the hour to catch up on chart notes. When I get to my desk, I notice that I have some voicemails.

The first is from John.

"Hi, it's me," his message begins. "Shit, I completely forgot to cancel until my phone beeped just now with our, um, appointment. Usually my assistant schedules everything but since I do the shrink thing myself . . . anyway, I can't make it today. Work is insane and I can't get away. Sorry about that."

My initial thought is that John needs some space and will be back next week. I imagine that he wrestled up to the last minute with whether or not to come today, and that's why he didn't call in advance — and also why the standing food order appeared here without him.

But then I play my next message.

"Hi, it's me again. So, um, I didn't *forget* to call, actually." There's a long pause, so long that I think John may have hung up. I'm about to hit Delete when finally he continues. "I was going to tell you that, um, I'm not going to do therapy anymore, but don't worry, it's not because you're an idiot. I realized that if I'm not sleeping, I should get sleep medication. *Obviously.* So I did and — problem solved! *Better living through chemistry,* ha-ha! And, uh, as for the other stuff we talked about, you know, all the stress I'm under, I guess that's just life and if I get some sleep, I'll be less annoyed by it all. Idiots will always be idiots and there's no pill for that, right? We'd have to medicate half the city if there were!" He laughs at his joke, the same laugh I remember from when he said I'd be like his mistress. His laugh is his shelter.

"Anyway," he goes on, "sorry for the late notice. And I know I owe you for today—don't worry, I'm good for it." He laughs again, then hangs up.

I stare at the phone. That's it? No *Thank you* or even a *Goodbye* at the end, just . . . done? I had expected that something like this might happen after the first few sessions, but now that I've been seeing him for nearly six months, I'm surprised by his sudden departure. In his own way, John seemed to be forming an attachment to me. Or maybe it's that I've been forming an attachment to him. I've come to feel real affection for John, to see flashes of humanity behind his obnoxious façade.

I think about John and his son Gabe, some boy or grown man who may or may not know his father. I wonder if on some level John wants to leave me with the burden of this mystery, a big fuck-you for not helping him feel better quickly enough. *Take that, Sherlock, you idiot.*

I want to let John know that I'm here, to somehow communicate that he—and I—can handle whatever he brings to therapy. I want him to know it's safe to talk about Gabe here, however tricky that situation or relationship might be. At the same time, I want to respect where he is right now.

I don't want to be *the rapist.*

It would be so much better to say all of this in person, though. In my informed-consent paperwork that I give to patients before they start treatment, I recommend that they participate in at least two termination sessions. I discuss this with new patients at the outset so that if something upsets them during treatment, they don't act impulsively to rid themselves of the uncomfortable feelings. Even if they do feel it's best to stop, at least the decision will have been reflected upon so they can leave feeling that they made a thoughtful and considered choice.

As I pull out some patient charts, I remember something John said while making the slip about Gabe. *There's too much estrogen in the house and nobody understands my perspective . . . I'm outnumbered . . . everyone wants something from me . . . nobody understands that I might need something too—like peace and quiet and some say in what goes on!*

Now it makes sense; Gabe could counteract some of the estrogen. Maybe John believes that Gabe understands him—or would, if he were in John's life.

I put down my pen and dial John's number. When his voicemail beeps, I say, "Hi, John. It's Lori. I got your message, and thanks for letting me know. I just put our lunches in the fridge, and I thought of last week when you said that nobody understands that *you* might need something too. I think you're right that you need something, but I'm not so sure that nobody understands this. Everyone needs something—often, lots of things. I'd like to hear what it is that you need. You mentioned needing peace and quiet, and maybe finding peace and quieting down the noise in your head will involve Gabe, and maybe it won't, but we don't have to talk about Gabe if you don't want to. I'm here if you change your mind and decide you want to come in next week to continue our conversation, even if it's just one last time. My door is open to you. Bye for now."

I make a note in John's chart and then close it, but as I lean over the file cabinet, I decide not to move it into the Terminated Patients section today. I remember in medical school how hard it was for us students to accept that somebody had died and that there was nothing else we could do, to have to be the person to "call it"—to say aloud those dreaded words *Time of death* . . . I look at the clock—3:17.

Let's give it one more week, I think. *I'm not ready to call it just yet.*

30

On the Clock

In my final year of graduate school, I was required to do a clinical traineeship. The traineeship is like a baby version of the three-thousand-hour
internship that comes later and is required for licensure. By this point, I'd
taken the necessary coursework, participated in classroom role-play simu-
lations, and watched countless hours of videotape of renowned therapists
conducting sessions. I'd also sat behind a one-way mirror and observed our
most skilled professors in real-time therapy sessions.

Now it was time to get in a room with my own patients. Like most
trainees in the field, I'd be doing this under supervision at a community
clinic, much the way medical interns get their training in teaching hospitals.

On my first day, immediately after the orientation, my supervisor hands
me a stack of charts and explains that the one on top will be my first case.
The chart contains only basic information—name, birth date, address,
phone number. The patient, Michelle, who is thirty and has listed her boyfriend as her emergency contact, will be arriving in an hour.

If it seems strange that this clinic is letting me, a person who has per-
formed exactly zero hours of therapy, take on somebody's treatment, it's
simply the way therapists are trained—by doing. Medical school was also
a trial by fire; in medicine, students learned procedures by the "see one, do
one, teach one" method. In other words, you watched a physician, say, pal-

pate an abdomen, you palpated the next abdomen yourself, and then you taught another student how to palpate an abdomen. *Presto!* You're deemed competent to palpate abdomens.

Therapy, though, felt different to me. I found performing a concrete task with specific steps, like palpating an abdomen or starting an IV, less nerve-racking than figuring out how to apply the numerous abstract psychological theories I'd studied over the past several years to the hundreds of possible scenarios that any one therapy patient might present.

Still, as I make my way to the waiting room to meet Michelle, I'm not terribly worried. This initial fifty-minute session is an intake, which means I'll gather a history and establish some rapport with her. All I have to do is collect information using a specific set of questions as my guide, then I'll bring those results to my supervisor so that we can formulate a treatment plan. I spent years as a journalist asking probing questions and establishing a comfort level with people I didn't know.

How hard, I think, *can this be?*

Michelle is tall and too thin. Her clothes are rumpled, her hair unkempt, her skin pasty. Once we're seated, I open by asking what brings her here, and she tells me that recently she has had trouble doing anything but cry.

Then, as if on cue, she starts crying. And by crying, I mean howling in the way one might if just informed that the person she loves most in the world has just died. There's no warm-up, no wetness in her eyes that leads to a light drizzle and gradually a downpour. This is a level-four tsunami. Her entire body shakes, mucus drips from her nose, wheezy noises emanate from her throat, and, frankly, I'm not sure how she can breathe.

We're thirty seconds in. This isn't how the simulated intakes went at school.

Unless you've sat alone in a quiet room with a sobbing stranger, you don't really know how simultaneously awkward and intimate it feels. To make matters weirder, I have no context for this outburst, because I haven't gotten to the history part yet. I know nothing about this very distressed person sitting five feet away from me.

I'm not sure what to do or even where to look. If I look right at her, will she feel self-conscious? If I look away, will she feel ignored? Should I say something to engage with her or wait for her to finish crying? I'm so uncomfortable that I worry a nervous giggle might erupt. I try to stay focused, thinking about my list of questions, and I know I should be asking how long she's felt this way ("history of present condition"), how severe it's been, whether something happened that brought this on (a "precipitating event").

But I do nothing. I wish that my supervisor were in the room with me right now. I feel totally useless.

The tsunami continues with no sign of letting up. I consider waiting it out, figuring she'll run out of steam soon and then be ready to talk, the way my son would as a toddler after throwing a tantrum. But it just keeps going. And going. Finally I decide to say something, but as the words leave my lips, I'm convinced I've just uttered the dumbest thing that any therapist has ever said in the history of the field.

I say, "Yeah, you seem depressed, all right."

I feel bad for this woman the instant I say it, like I should punctuate it with a big *duh*. This poor, depressed thirty-year-old is in tremendous pain, and she isn't coming here so that a trainee on her first day can state the blatantly obvious. As I try to think how to correct my error, I wonder if she'll request a different therapist. I'm sure she isn't going to want somebody like me in charge of her care.

But instead Michelle stops crying. As quickly as she started, she wipes the tears away with a tissue and takes a long, deep breath. And then she half smiles.

"Yeah," she says. *"I am so fucking depressed."* She seems almost giddy to be saying this aloud. It's the first time, she tells me, that somebody has said the word *depressed* about her condition.

She goes on to explain that she's an architect who's had some success, having been part of a team that designed a few high-profile buildings. She's always been melancholy, she says, but nobody really knows the extent of it because she's generally social and busy. About a year ago, though, she noticed a change. Her energy level decreased, as did her appetite. Just getting out of bed each morning felt like a huge effort. She wasn't sleeping well.

She fell out of love with her live-in boyfriend but wasn't sure if it was because she was so down or because he wasn't the right person for her. In the past few months, she's been secretly crying every night in the bathroom while her boyfriend sleeps, making sure not to wake him. She's never cried in front of anybody the way she has just cried in front of me.

She cries some more, and through her tears, she says, "This is like . . . emotional yoga."

What has brought her here now, she confides, is that her work has started getting sloppy and her boss noticed. She can't concentrate because trying not to cry is taking all of her focus. She looked up the symptoms of depression and ticked off all the boxes. She's never been in therapy before but knows she needs help. Nobody, she says, looking me in the eye—not her friends, not her boyfriend, not her family—knows how depressed she is. Nobody but me.

Me. The trainee who has never done therapy before.

(If you ever want proof that what people present online is a prettier version of their lives, become a therapist and Google your patients. Later, when I Googled Michelle out of concern—I learned quickly never to do this again, to always let patients be the sole narrators of their stories—pages of hits popped up. I saw images of her receiving a prestigious award, smiling at an event standing next to a handsome guy, looking cool and confident and at peace with the world in a magazine photo spread. Online, she bore no resemblance to the person who sat across from me in that room.)

Now I talk to Michelle about her depression, find out if she's contemplating suicide, get a sense of how functional she is, what her support system is like, what she does to cope. I'm mindful of the fact that I've got to bring a history to my supervisor—the clinic needs it for its records—but every time I ask a question, Michelle segues into something that leads us in a completely different direction. I subtly redirect, but that inevitably takes us someplace else, and I'm very aware that I'm getting nowhere with the history.

I decide to just listen for a while, but I can't completely block out my thoughts: *Do the other trainees know how to do this the first time out? Can you get fired from this gig on your first day?* And, when Michelle starts crying again, *Is there anything I can do or say that will help her even the slightest bit before she leaves in . . . wait, how many minutes are left?*

I glance at the clock on the table next to the sofa. Ten minutes have passed.

No, I think. *Surely* we've been in here for more than ten minutes! It seems more like twenty or thirty or . . . I have no idea. Has it been only ten? Now Michelle is going into great detail about all the ways she's screwing up her life. I go back to listening, then glance at the clock again: it's still ten minutes past the hour.

That's when I realize: The clock hands aren't moving! The battery must have died. My cell phone is in another room, and while it's likely that Michelle has one in her bag, I can't exactly ask her what time it is in the middle of her story.

Great.

Now what? Should I arbitrarily say "Our time is up," even though I have no sense of whether twenty or forty or sixty minutes have passed? What if I cut it off way too early or too late? I'm supposed to see my second new patient after this. Is he sitting in the waiting room wondering if I've forgotten his appointment?

Panicking, I'm no longer paying close attention to what Michelle is saying. Then I hear this:

"Is it over already? That went faster than I expected."

"Hmm?" I say. Michelle points to somewhere behind my head and I turn around to look. There's a clock on the wall right behind me so that patients can also see the time.

Oh. I had no idea, and I hope that she has no idea that I had no idea. All I know is that my heart is racing and that, though the session has gone quickly for Michelle, it felt like an eternity to me. It would take practice before I'd come to feel the rhythm of every session by instinct, to know that there was an arc to every hour, with the most intense parts in the middle third, and that you needed about three or five or ten minutes to put the patient back together, depending on the person's fragility, the subject matter, the context. It would take years to learn what should or shouldn't be brought up when and how to work with the time available to get the most out of it.

I walk Michelle out, ashamed about getting flustered and distracted, of not gathering the history and having to report to my supervisor empty-handed. All through graduate school, we students had been awaiting the Big Day when we would lose our therapeutic virginity, and now, I think, mine turned out to be more disgrace than thrill.

Then, relief: Discussing the session that afternoon with my supervisor, she says that, despite my clumsiness, I did just fine. I'd sat with Michelle in her suffering, which for many people can be an unusual and powerful experience. Next time I won't worry so much that I have to do something to stop it. I'd been there to listen when she needed to unload the burdensome secret of her depression. In the parlance of therapeutic theory, I'd "met the patient where she was"—history-taking be damned.

Years later, when I've done thousands of first sessions, and information-gathering has become second nature, I'll use a different barometer to judge how it went: *Did the patient feel understood?* It always amazes me that someone can walk into a room as a stranger and then, after fifty minutes, leave feeling understood, but it happens nearly every time. When it doesn't, the patient doesn't return. And because Michelle did, something had gone right.

As for the clock snafu, though, my supervisor doesn't mince words: "Don't bullshit your patients."

She lets that sink in, then goes on to explain that if I don't know something, I should simply say, "I don't know." If I'm confused about the time, I should tell Michelle that I need to step out of the room for a second to bring in a working clock so that I'm not distracted. If I'm to learn anything in this traineeship, my supervisor emphasizes, it's that I can't help anybody unless I'm authentic in that room. I had cared about Michelle's well-being, I'd wanted to help, I'd done my best to listen—all key ingredients for starting the relationship.

I thank her and start toward the door.

"But," my supervisor adds, "be sure to get that history in the next couple of weeks."

Over the next few sessions, I get what I need for the clinic's intake form, but it's clear to me that's all it is—a form. It takes a while to hear a person's story and for that person to tell it, and like most stories—including mine—it bounces all over the place before you know what the plot really is.

Part Three

What makes night within us may leave stars.

—*Victor Hugo*

31

My Wandering Uterus

I have a secret.

Something is wrong with my body. I could be dying, or maybe it's nothing at all. In which case, there's no reason to disclose my secret.

This question of my illness started a couple of years ago, a few weeks before I met Boyfriend. Or at least I think it did. My son and I were on our summer vacation, spending a relaxing week in Hawaii with my parents. The night before we were to return home, though, a painful, angry rash seemed to appear out of nowhere and devour my body. I spent the plane ride back hopped up on antihistamines and slathered with over-the-counter cortisone cream, scratching myself so hard that my nails were caked in blood by the time we landed. Within a few days, the rash subsided, and my doctor ran some tests and chalked it up to a random allergic reaction. But the rash had felt like an eerie foreboding, a harbinger of what was to come.

Something seemed to be lurking inside me, attacking my body over the next several months while I looked the other way (which was, at the time, directly into Boyfriend's eyes). Yes, I felt fatigued and weak and had an array of disturbing symptoms, but as my condition worsened, I convinced myself that it must be a change in stamina that happens in one's forties. My doctor ran more tests and found some markers for autoimmune disease but none that could be linked to a particular illness like, say, lupus. He sent me to a rheumatologist, who suspected that I might have fibromyalgia, a condition that can't be diagnosed with a specific test. The idea was to treat the symptoms and see if they improved, and that's when the off-label-use antidepressant ended up in my record at the CVS across from my office. Soon I was at that CVS often, picking up cortisone creams for bizarre rashes, antibiotics for unexplained infections, and antiarrhythmics for my irregular heart rate. But my doctors couldn't figure out what was wrong, and I reasoned that this was a good sign; if I *did* have a dangerous illness, my doctors would have found it already. *No news is good news,* I told myself.

Just as with the misery-inducing happiness book, I plugged along, keeping my health worries as private as my writing worries. It wasn't so much that I purposely hid my medical situation from my close friends and family. It was more that I chose to hide it from myself. Like the physician who suspects he has cancer but delays getting scanned, I found it far more convenient to just *not deal.* Even as I no longer had the strength to exercise and inexplicably lost ten pounds—I felt sluggish and weighted down even as I became lighter—I assured myself it must be something benign, like, I don't know, menopause. (Never mind that I wasn't in menopause yet.)

When I did let myself think about it, I'd go online and learn that I was dying of basically everything, only to remember that in medical school, we students suffered from "medical students' disease." This is an actual phenomenon, documented in the literature, in which medical students believe that they're suffering from whatever illnesses they happen to be studying. On the day we studied the lymphatic system, a group of us felt each other's lymph nodes over dinner. One student put her hands on my neck and exclaimed, "Whoa!"

"Whoa what?" I asked.

She made a face. "It feels like lymphoma." I lifted my arms and felt my neck. She was right; I had lymphoma! Several other classmates felt my neck and agreed—I was toast. Better check my white cell count, they said. Let's biopsy those nodes!

In class the next morning, our professor felt my neck. My nodes were big but within the normal range. I didn't have lymphoma; I had medical students' disease.

I probably had nothing now too, I figured. Except deep down, I knew it wasn't normal for somebody in her forties who used to be a runner not to be able to run anymore and to feel sick every day. I'd wake up tingling, my fingers red and thick as sausages, my lips swollen as if stung by bees. My internist ran even more lab tests, some of which came back abnormal or, as he put it, "quirky." He sent me for MRIs and scans and biopsies, some of which were also "quirky." He sent me to specialists to interpret the various quirky labs and scans and signs and symptoms, and I saw so many specialists that I began calling my odyssey the Medical Mystery Tour.

It was indeed a mystery. One doctor thought I had a rare form of cancer (based on lab tests, but the scan ruled this out); another thought it was some kind of virus (starting with the rash); another thought it was a metabolic condition (my eyes were riddled with deposits that nobody could diagnose); and yet another thought I had multiple sclerosis (my brain scan showed spots that weren't typical of MS, but they could be an unusual presentation). At various times it was thought that I might have thyroid disease, scleroderma, or, yes, lymphoma (again, those enlarged glands; did this actually start back then, in medical school, lying dormant until now?).

But all those tests came back negative.

About a year in—by which point I'd developed subtle jaw and hand tremors—one doctor, a neurologist who wore green cowboy boots and spoke with a thick Italian accent, believed he'd figured out my condition. The first time I met him, he walked into the room, logged on to the hospital network's computer, noted the long list of specialists I'd seen ("Well, you've certainly seen everyone in town, haven't you?" he said flippantly, as if I'd been sleeping around), and—skipping the exam—immediately had the diagnosis. He thought I was a modern-day version of Freud's female hysteric, experiencing what's known as conversion disorder.

This is a condition in which a person's anxiety is "converted" into neurologic conditions such as paralysis, balance issues, incontinence, blindness, deafness, tremors, or seizures. The symptoms are often temporary and tend to be related (sometimes symbolically) to the psychological stressor at its root. For instance, after seeing something traumatic (like one's spouse in bed with another person or a grisly murder), a patient might experience blindness. After a terrifying fall, a patient might experience leg paralysis even though there was no functional evidence of nerve damage. Or a man who feels that his anger toward his wife is unacceptable might experience numbness in the arm he fantasized about raising to hit her.

People with conversion disorder aren't faking it—that's called factitious disorder. People with factitious disorder have a need to be thought of as sick and intentionally go to great lengths to *appear* ill. In conversion disorder, though, the patient is actually *experiencing* these symptoms; it's just that there's no identifiable medical explanation for them. They seem to be caused by emotional distress that the patient is completely unconscious of.

I didn't think I had conversion disorder. But then again, if conversion disorder was caused by an *unconscious* process, how could I know?

Conversion disorders have a long history and have been documented as far back as four thousand years ago in ancient Egypt. Like most emotional conditions, they were disproportionately diagnosed in women. In fact, symptoms were thought to be caused by a woman's uterus moving either up or down, a syndrome that came to be known as a "wandering uterus."

The treatment? A woman was to place pleasing aromas or spices near her body in the opposite direction of where the uterus had supposedly wandered. This "cure" was thought to lure the uterus back to its proper location.

In the fifth century BC, however, Hippocrates noted that aromas didn't seem to be working for this malady, which he had named *hysteria,* from the Greek word for "uterus." Accordingly, the treatment for hysterical women went from aromas and spices to exercise, massages, and hot baths. That lasted until the beginning of the thirteenth century, at which point there was thought to be a connection between women and the devil.

The new treatment? Exorcism.

Finally, in the late 1600s, hysteria came to be thought of as related to the brain rather than the devil or the uterus. Today, there's still debate on how to think about symptoms for which we can't find a functional explanation. The current ICD-10 lists "conversion disorder with motor symptom or deficit" as a dissociative disorder (and includes the word *hysterical* in its subtypes), whereas the *DSM-5* classifies conversion disorder as a "somatic symptom disorder."

Interestingly, conversion disorders tend to be more prevalent in cultures with strict rules and few opportunities for emotional expression. Overall, though, their diagnosis has gone down in the past fifty years, for two possible reasons. First, doctors no longer misdiagnose the symptoms of syphilis as a conversion disorder; second, the "hysterical" women who succumbed to conversion disorder in the past tended to be reacting to restrictive gender roles that look very different from the freedoms more women are experiencing now.

Nonetheless, the neurologist in cowboy boots scanned the list of specialists I'd seen, looked up at me, and smiled the way people smile at naive children or delusional adults.

"You worry too much," he said in his Italian accent. Then he asserted that I must be stressed out—being a working single mom and all—and that what I needed was a massage and a good night's sleep. After diagnosing me with conversion disorder (his word: *anxiety*), he prescribed melatonin and told me to make a weekly spa appointment. He said that though I looked "like a Parkinson's patient," with the big bags under my eyes and the tremors, I didn't have Parkinson's; I had sleep deprivation, which could cause those same symptoms. When I explained that the fatigue was making me sleep too much, not too little (leaving Boyfriend to wake up with my son and look at those Legos), Dr. Cowboy Boots grinned. "Ah, but you're not getting *good* sleep."

My internist was certain that I didn't have a conversion disorder, not only because my symptoms were chronic and getting progressively worse, but also because each specialist I saw discovered something wrong (a hyperinflated lung, a grossly elevated level of something in my blood, a swollen tonsil, those deposits scattered throughout my eyes, "extra space" in my brain scan, and, again, those angry skin rashes). They just didn't know how to put the data together. It was possible, some specialists said, that my symptoms were related to my DNA, a glitch in one of my genes. They wanted to sequence my genes to see what they might find, but the insurance wouldn't cover the gene sequencing—even after the doctors appealed several times—because, the insurance company reasoned, if I did have a yet-to-be-discovered genetic disorder, there would be no known treatment.

I'd still be sick.

If it sounds strange that I presented myself as relatively fine to the outside world—I shared little of the Medical Mystery Tour with anyone, even Boyfriend—I had my reasons. First, if I were to tell people what was going on, I wouldn't know how to explain it. It wasn't as though I could say, "I have [X] illness." Even people with depression, a malady that has a name, often have trouble explaining it to others because its symptoms seem vague and intangible to anyone who hasn't experienced them. You're sad? Cheer up!

My symptoms were as nebulous as emotional suffering appeared to outsiders. I imagined people listening to me and wondering how I could have gotten so sick and still not have any answers. How could so many doctors be flummoxed?

In other words, I knew I was at risk of being told it was all in my head, even before the cowboy-boot-wearing neurologist did exactly that. In fact, after my appointment with him, *anxiety* was added to my electronic medical chart, a word that every subsequent doctor would see on the home page of my file. And while technically this was true—I certainly *was* anxious about my miserable happiness book and my poor health (it wouldn't be until later that I'd be anxious about my breakup)—I felt as though there was no way to escape that label as the cause of my symptoms, no way to be believed.

I kept it to myself because I wanted to avoid being a woman suspected of having a wandering uterus.

And then there was this: On one of our early dates, when Boyfriend and I were in the midst of infatuation and had hours-long conversations about anything and everything, he mentioned that before meeting me, he'd gone on a few dates with a woman he really liked but when he'd learned that she had some difficulty with her joints that made it hard for her to go hiking, he'd stopped seeing her. I asked him why. After all, she didn't have an acute illness; it sounded more like a common case of arthritis, and we were middle-aged, after all. Besides, Boyfriend wasn't even a hiker.

"I don't want to have to take care of her if she gets really sick one day," he said over our shared dessert. "If we'd been married for twenty years and *then* she got sick, that's different. But why get into it knowing she's already sick?"

"But any of us could get sick," I said. At the time, I didn't think I fell into that category. I thought that whatever I had was temporary (a bug of some sort) or treatable (a thyroid imbalance). Later, as my Medical Mystery Tour got under way, my denial turned into magical thinking: *As long as I don't have a diagnosis, I can postpone telling Boyfriend the extent of it— indefinitely, and maybe forever—if it turns out that nothing's wrong after all.* He knew (sometimes) that I was having tests done and wasn't feeling "myself," but I also explained away a lot of my fatigue the way Dr. Cowboy Boots had: I was a busy working mom. Other times I'd make jokes about getting older. I wasn't willing to test his love for me by letting him think that either I had some physical illness or I was crazy for believing that I did.

Meanwhile, I was so terrified by whatever was happening to me that I kept hoping my symptoms would simply vanish. I thought, *I'm going into this future with Boyfriend, focus on that.* Which is also why I ignored any hints that we might not be well suited for each other. If that future went away, I would have to contend with an unwritten book and a failing body.

But now that future *has* gone away.

So I wonder: Did Boyfriend leave me because I was sick—or he thought I was paranoid for believing I was? Or did he leave me because I was as dishonest with him as he had been with me about who I was and what I wanted in a partner? It turns out that we weren't that different after all. In the hopes of making it work with a person he genuinely enjoyed, he wanted to postpone his confession for the same reason I did: so that we could continue to be together even though we couldn't. If Boyfriend didn't want to live with a kid under his roof for the next ten years, if what he wanted was freedom, he certainly wouldn't have wanted to take care of me if one day I needed it. And I'd known that about him as early as that dinner-date conversation—just as he'd known I had a kid.

And now I'm doing the same thing—postponing—with Wendell, because the truth comes with a cost: the need to face reality. My patient Julie had said that she always wished she could freeze time in the few days between having a scan and getting the result. Before that call came in, she explained, she could still tell herself everything was fine—but knowing the truth might change everything.

The cost of my telling the truth isn't that Wendell will leave me, as Boyfriend did. It's that he'll make me face this mystery illness head-on instead of pretending it away.

32

Emergency Session

"You sound like Goldilocks," I said to Rita a month after her suicide ultimatum. Despite her tumultuous past, I'd been focusing on Rita's present. It's important to disrupt the depressive state with action, to create social connections and find a daily purpose, a compelling reason to get out of bed in the morning. Mindful of Rita's goals, I tried to help her find ways to live better now, but nearly every suggestion I came up with was a bust.

The first thing Rita did was reject the wonderful psychiatrist I suggested that she see for a medication consultation. She looked him up, noticed that he was in his seventies, and pronounced him "too old to know the latest medications." (Never mind that he teaches psychopharmacology to today's medical students.) So I referred her to a younger psychiatrist, but she, Rita felt, was "too young to understand." Then I referred her to a middle-aged psychiatrist, and although she had no objections ("He's a very attractive fellow," Rita noted), once she started the medication, it made her too sleepy. The psychiatrist changed her medication, but this one made her anxious and worsened her insomnia. She decided she was done with medication.

Meanwhile, Rita told me that a board position had opened up in her apartment building, and I encouraged her to join so that she could get to know her neighbors better. ("No, thank you," she said. "The interesting tenants are too busy to join.")

I'd brainstormed with her about volunteering, perhaps getting involved in the art world or at a museum, since her passions were painting and art history, but she came up with reasons to dismiss these suggestions as well. I talked with her about how she might make contact with her adult children, who had, to this point, shut her out of their lives, but she felt she couldn't handle another failed attempt. ("I'm already deeply depressed.") And I'd suggested the dating apps, which resulted in what she called "the octogenarian brigade."

All this time, what I found more urgent than her birthday-suicide fantasy was the acute level of pain she lived with and had been living with for so long. Part of it was due to circumstances. She'd had a lonely childhood, an abusive husband, and a difficult midlife, and she had certain relational patterns that got in her way. But part of it, I felt as I got to know Rita better, might be something else, and I wanted to confront her about it. I'd come to the conclusion that even if Rita *could* relieve some of her pain, she wouldn't allow herself to be happy. Something was holding her back.

And then she called me for an emergency session.

Rita, it turned out, also had a secret. Recently, there *had* been a man in her life—and now she was in crisis.

Myron, Rita tells me when she arrives for her emergency session, agitated and uncharacteristically disheveled, is "a former friend." At the time of their friendship, she explains, which ended six months ago, he was her only friend. Yes, there were women she'd say hello to in passing at the Y, but they were younger and not interested in befriending "an old lady." She felt, as she had for much of her life, excluded. Invisible.

Myron, though, took notice of Rita. At the beginning of last year, when he was sixty-five, he had relocated from the East Coast and moved into Rita's apartment complex. Three years before, his wife of forty years had died, and his grown children, who lived in Los Angeles, had encouraged him to move west.

They'd met at the mailboxes in the common area of their building. He was leafing through flyers advertising local events—junk mail that Rita always tossed straight into the trash—when he told Rita he was new to town and wondered if any of the listings were nearby. She peered at the flyer. The farmers' market was close, she said, just a few blocks away.

Great, Myron said, will you go with me so I don't get lost?

I'm not dating, Rita said.

I'm not asking you on a date, he said.

Rita thought she might die of embarrassment. *Of course,* she thought. Myron couldn't possibly be attracted to her, standing there in her baggy sweatpants and T-shirt with the hole in it. Her hair was greasy, the unwashed hair of a depressed person, her face sagging with sadness. If he was attracted to anything, she assumed it was her mail: a brochure from the modern art museum, a copy of *The New Yorker,* a magazine about bridge. They apparently had similar interests. Myron was struggling to adjust to the city, and Rita seemed to be about his age. Perhaps, he said, Rita knew people to introduce him to, to get his social life going. (Little did he know that Rita was a friendless hermit.)

At the farmers' market, they talked about old movies, Rita's paintings, Myron's family, and bridge. In the following months, Myron and Rita did things together—took walks, visited museums, went to a few lectures, tried some new restaurants. But mostly, they cooked dinner and watched movies on Myron's couch, both of them chattering throughout. When Myron needed a new outfit for his grandchild's baby-naming ceremony, they went to the mall, and Rita, with her keen artistic eye, found the perfect one. Sometimes if she was at the mall she would pick up a shirt for Myron just because she knew it would look good on him. She also helped furnish his apartment. In return, Myron hung Rita's artwork on her walls with earthquake-proof hardware, and he served as her on-call tech support whenever her computer crashed or she couldn't get a WiFi signal.

They weren't dating, but they spent much of their time together. And while Rita at first found Myron merely "decent-looking" (she had trouble finding men over fifty attractive), one day, as he was showing Rita photos of his grandchildren, something in her stirred. At first she thought it was envy of his close relationship with his family, but she couldn't deny that she was also feeling something else. It surfaced more and more, though she tried not to think about it. After all, she knew from their first mortifying encounter by the mailboxes that her relationship with Myron was a platonic one.

But still. After six months of this, they certainly acted like they were dating. So much so that she considered bringing this up with Myron. She was going to have to, she told herself, because she couldn't sit a foot away from him on the sofa, wineglass in hand, movie flickering in the darkness, and act cool as a cucumber when he accidentally brushed her knee while placing his glass on the coffee table. (*Was* it accidental? she asked herself.) Besides, she thought, it was *she* who'd said she wasn't dating when Myron first approached her. Maybe he'd said he wasn't asking her out only to save face?

She hated the fact that she was almost seventy and still analyzing interactions with men with the same obsessiveness she had in college. She hated feeling like a girl with a crush, foolish and helpless and confused. She hated trying on outfits one after the other, discarding this one, replacing it with that one, her bed littered with evidence of her insecurity and overinvestment. She wanted to will away her feelings, to just enjoy the friendship, but she was worried that she might not be able to handle the tension building up inside her—that she might just plant a wet one on Myron's face if this went on much longer. She'd have to get up the nerve to say something.

Soon. Very soon.

But then Myron met somebody. On Tinder, of all places! ("Revolting!") The woman was, to Rita's disgust, quite a bit younger—in her *fifties!* Mandy or Brandy or Sandy or Candy or some vapid name like that, some name ending in a *y* sound that, Rita guessed, the bimbo would spell with an *ie*. Mandie. Brandie. Sandie. Rita could never remember. All she knew was that Myron had disappeared and left a crater in Rita's life.

That's when Rita made the decision to see a therapist and end it all if nothing improved by her seventieth birthday.

Rita looks up at me as if her story is over. I find it interesting that though Myron was the real impetus for her coming to therapy, she has never mentioned him before. I wonder why she's telling me now and what today's emergency is about.

Rita lets out a long sigh. "Wait," she says glumly. "There's more."

She goes on to explain that while Myron was off dating what's-her-name, Rita still saw him at the Y, where he swam while she took aerobics —but they didn't drive over together anymore, because now he slept at Mandie's/Brandie's/Sandie's. They still saw each other at the mailboxes in the afternoon, where Myron would try to make small talk and Rita would give him the cold shoulder. It was Myron who had asked Rita to join the board at their apartment complex, and it was Myron whose invitation she'd brusquely declined. Once, as she was leaving the building for therapy and found herself in the elevator with Myron, he complimented her on her appearance (she always "put herself together" for our therapy sessions, her one outing each week).

"You look lovely today," he'd said. To which Rita replied, curtly, "Thank you," then stared straight ahead the rest of the ride down. In the evening, she never left her unit, not even to take out the foul-smelling trash on fish night, for fear that she might run into Mandie/Brandie/Sandie with Myron, as she had done a few times, the two of them arm in arm, laughing or, worse, kissing ("Revolting!").

Love is pain, Rita had said after she told me about her failed marriages and again after her encounter with the eighty-year-old. *Why bother?*

But that was also before Myron had ended things with Mandie/Brandie/Sandie; before he had cornered Rita in the parking lot at the Y after she'd spent weeks letting his calls go to voicemail and not answering his texts. (*Can we talk?* to which Rita clicked Delete.) It was before Myron—who, she noted when face-to-face with him in the sunlit parking lot yesterday, "looked like he'd aged a bit"—told her the things he had wanted to tell her for a long time, things he didn't realize, he explained, until three months into his relationship with Randie. (So *that* was her name!)

Here's what Myron realized: He missed Rita. Deeply. He wanted to tell her things—all the time, every day—the way he had wanted to tell his wife Myrna things throughout their marriage. Rita made him laugh and think, and when photos of his grandchildren popped up on his phone, he wanted to show them to Rita. He didn't want to do any of this with Randie in the same way. He loved Rita's sharp intellect and sharper wit, her creativity, her kindness. How she picked up his favorite cheese if she was at the grocery store.

He liked Rita's worldliness and wry observations and wise counsel whenever he asked her advice. He adored her throaty laugh and her eyes that were green in the sunlight and brown indoors and her bright red hair and her values. He loved that if they started a conversation on one topic, it would segue into two or three others before it would loop back around or that sometimes they'd get so immersed in their tangents that they'd forget what they'd been talking about in the first place. Her paintings and sculptures made his heart thrill. He was curious about her, wanted to know more about her kids, her family, her life, *her*. He wanted her to feel comfortable telling him and wondered why she had been like a cipher, revealing so little of her past.

Oh, and he thought she was beautiful. Absolutely stunning. But would she please stop wearing T-shirts that looked like rags?

Myron and Rita stood there in the parking lot of the Y, Myron catching his breath after pouring his heart out and Rita feeling dizzy, unsteady —and angry.

"I'm not interested in staving off your loneliness," she said. "Just because you broke up with gold-digger-what's-her-name. Just because you miss your wife and can't stand to be alone."

"Is that what you think is going on?" Myron asked.

"Obviously," Rita said imperiously. "Yes."

And then he kissed her. An intense, soft, urgent, movie-worthy kiss, a kiss that seemed to go on forever. It finally ended with Rita slapping Myron on the cheek and running to her car, then calling me for an emergency session.

"That's exciting!" I say when Rita finishes telling me the story. I hadn't expected this twist at all, and I'm genuinely thrilled for her. But Rita just makes a snorting sound, and I realize she's missed the forest for the trees.

"What he said was beautiful," I say. "And that kiss—" I see the beginning of a smile before she suppresses it and her expression turns hard, cold.

"Well, that's all fine and good," she says, "but I'm never speaking to Myron again." She unzips her purse, pulls out a wadded-up tissue, and adds resolutely, "I'm completely done with love."

I remember Rita's earlier proclamation: *Love is pain.* The Myron situation has upended her so because when her heart that had been in a decades-long deep freeze finally began to thaw with Myron in her life, she had tasted hope and then lost it. It occurs to me now that when Rita first came to see me, she was desperate not just because she would be turning seventy in a year, as she reported then, but because Myron's disappearance had made her wonder the same thing I was wondering when I first saw Wendell: Had the man who'd just left been the "end of the line," as I'd put it—the last chance at love? Rita, too, has been grieving something bigger.

But now the kiss has presented another crisis for Rita—possibility. And that may feel even more intolerable to her than her pain.

33

Karma

Charlotte is late for today's appointment because somebody hit her car as she was pulling out of the parking lot at work. She's fine, she says, it was a minor fender-bender, but it caused the steaming coffee in her cup holder to spill onto her laptop on which she'd composed her presentation for tomorrow and which she hadn't backed up.

"Do you think I should tell them what happened or just pull an all-nighter?" she asks. "I want it to be good, but I don't want to seem flaky."

The prior week, at the gym, she'd accidentally dropped a weight on her toe. The bruise had gotten worse, and she was still in pain. "Do you think I should get it x-rayed?" she asked.

Before that, her favorite college professor had died in a camping accident ("Do you think I should fly to the funeral, even though my boss will be mad?"), and before that, her wallet had been stolen and she'd spent days combating identity theft ("Should I keep my driver's license locked in the glove compartment of the car from now on?").

Charlotte believes she's been hit with a wave of "bad karma." It seems as if, every other week, there's another crisis—a traffic violation, an incident with her sublet—and while at first I felt bad for her and tried to help her cope, gradually I noticed that we'd stopped doing any therapy at all. And how could we? By focusing on one external calamity after another, Charlotte has been distracting herself from the real crises in her life—the internal ones. Sometimes "drama," no matter how unpleasant, can be a form of self-medication, a way to calm ourselves down by avoiding the crises brewing inside.

She's waiting for me to advise her on what to do about her presentation, but she knows by now that I don't tend to give prescriptive advice. One of the things that surprised me as a therapist was how often people wanted to be told what to do, as if I had the right answer or as if right and wrong answers existed for the bulk of choices people make in their daily lives. Taped up next to my files is the word *ultracrepidarianism,* which means "the habit of giving opinions and advice on matters outside of one's knowledge or competence." It's a reminder to myself that as a therapist, I can come to understand people and help them sort out what *they* want to do, but I can't make their life choices *for* them.

When I first started out, though, occasionally I'd feel pressure to give advice of the benign (or so I believed) sort. But then I realized that people resent being told what to do. Yes, they may have *asked* to be told—repeatedly, relentlessly—but after you comply, their initial relief is replaced by resentment. This happens even if things go swimmingly, because ultimately humans want to have agency over their lives, which is why children spend their childhoods begging to make their own decisions. (Then they grow up and plead with me to take that freedom away.)

Sometimes patients assume that therapists have the answers and we simply aren't telling them—that we're being withholding. But we aren't out to torture people. We hesitate to give answers not only because patients don't really want to hear them, but also because they often misconstrue what they hear (leaving us thinking, for instance, *I never suggested you say that to your mother!*). Most important, we want to support their independence.

But when I'm in Wendell's office, I forget all this, along with everything else I've learned about advice-giving over the years: that the information the patient presents to you is distorted through a particular lens; that the presentation of the information will change over time as it becomes less distorted; that the dilemma may even be about something entirely different that has yet to be uncovered; that the patient is sometimes gunning for you to support a particular choice and this will become more clear as your relationship develops; and that the patient wants others to make decisions so that she doesn't have to take responsibility if things don't work out.

Here are some questions I've asked Wendell: "Is it normal for a fridge to break after ten years? Should I keep this one longer or pay to repair it?" (Wendell: "Are you really here to ask me something you can ask Siri?") "Should I choose this school for my son, or the other one?" (Wendell: "I think you'll benefit more from understanding why this decision is so hard for you.") Once he said, "I only know what *I* would do. I don't know what *you* should do," and instead of absorbing his meaning, I replied, "Okay, then, just tell me—what would *you* do?"

Behind my questions lies the assumption that Wendell is a more competent human being than I am. Sometimes I wonder, *Who am I to make the important decisions in my own life? Am I really qualified for this?*

Everyone wages this internal battle to some degree: Child or adult? Safety or freedom? But no matter where people fall on those continuums, every decision they make is based on two things: fear and love. Therapy strives to teach you how to tell the two apart.

Charlotte once told me about a commercial she saw on television that made her cry.

"It was for a car," she said, then added dryly, "I can't remember *which* car, so clearly the commercial wasn't very effective."

The ad, she said, is set at night, and there's a dog at the wheel. We see the dog driving through a suburban neighborhood, and then the camera pans to the interior, in the back, where there's a puppy in a car seat, barking away. Mommy Dog keeps driving, glancing in the rearview mirror, until the smooth ride lulls the puppy to sleep. Mommy Dog finally pulls into her driveway, lovingly gazing at her sleeping pup, but the second she kills the motor, the puppy wakes up and once again starts barking away. With a resigned look on her face, Mommy Dog turns the car back on and starts driving again. We get the sense she'll be driving around the neighborhood for quite a while.

By the time Charlotte got to the end of this story, she was sobbing, which was unusual for her. Charlotte generally betrays little, if any, real emotion—her face is a mask, her words, diversions. It's not that she's hiding her feelings; it's that she can't access them. There's a word for this kind of emotional blindness: *alexithymia*. She doesn't know what she's feeling or doesn't have the words to express it. Praise from her boss will be reported in a monotone, and I have to probe . . . and probe . . . and probe, until I finally get to a hint of pride. A sexual assault in college—she was drinking, found herself at a party in a strange dorm room, naked, in a bed—will be reported in that same monotone. A retelling of a chaotic conversation with her mom will sound like she's reciting the Pledge of Allegiance.

Sometimes people can't identify their feelings because they were talked out of them as children. The child says, "I'm angry," and the parent says, "Really? Over such a tiny thing? You're so sensitive!" Or the kid says, "I'm sad," and the parent says, "Don't be sad. Hey, look, a balloon!" Or the child says, "I'm scared," and the parent says, "There's nothing to be worried about. Don't be such a baby." But nobody can keep profound feelings sealed up forever. Inevitably, when we least expect it—seeing a commercial, for instance—they escape.

"I don't know why this makes me so sad," Charlotte said about the car commercial.

Watching her cry, I understood not just her pain but the reason she constantly pushed for me to make her decisions. For Charlotte, there had been no Mommy Dog in the driver's seat. With Mom immersed in her depression, taking to her bed between bouts of inebriated late-night partying; with Dad frequently out of town for "business"; with two chaotic parents who argued with abandon and liberal strings of expletives, sometimes so loudly that the neighbors complained—Charlotte had been forced to act as a grownup prematurely, like an underage driver navigating her life without a license. She rarely got to see her parents acting like adults, like her friends' parents.

I imagined her as a child—*What time should I leave for school? How do I deal with a friend who said something mean today? What should I do when I find drugs in my dad's desk drawer? What does it mean when it's midnight and my mom isn't home? How do I apply to college?* She'd had to parent herself, and her younger brother too.

Children, however, don't like having to be hyper-competent. So it's not surprising that Charlotte wants me to be the mother for her now. I can be the "normal" parent who safely and lovingly drives the car, and she can have the experience of being taken care of in a way she never has before. But in order to cast me in the competent role, Charlotte believes she has to cast herself as the helpless one, letting me see only her problems—or, as Wendell once put it in relation to what I do with him: "seduce me with her misery." Patients often do this as a way to ensure that the therapist won't forget about their pain if they mention something positive. Good things happen in Charlotte's life too, but I rarely hear about them; if I do, it's either in passing or months after they occurred.

I think of this misery-seduction dynamic between Charlotte and me, and between a younger Charlotte and her parents. No matter what Charlotte did—getting drunk, staying out late, being promiscuous—it didn't have the desired effect. *This went wrong. That went wrong. Pay attention to me. Can you even hear me?*

Now, after the questions about the laptop and the spilled coffee, Charlotte is asking what she should do with the Dude from the waiting room. She hadn't seen him for a few weeks, then he came with the girlfriend, and today he came alone again. A few minutes ago, in the waiting room, he asked her on a date. Or at least she thinks it's a date. He asked her to "hang out" tonight. She said yes.

I look at Charlotte. *Why on earth would you think* that's *a good idea?*

Okay, I don't say this out loud. But sometimes, and not just with Charlotte, I'll hear something a patient is saying—some self-destructive course of action she's taken or is about to take (for instance, telling her employer how she really feels in the service of "being authentic")—and I'll have to suppress the urge to blurt out, *No! Don't do it!*

But I can't just bear witness to a train wreck either.

Charlotte and I have talked about anticipating the outcome of her decisions, but I know this is more than an intellectual process. <u>Repetition</u>

compulsion is a formidable beast. For Charlotte, stability and its attendant joy isn't to be trusted; it makes her feel queasy, anxious. When you're
a child and your father is loving and playful, then disappears for a while,
and later comes back and acts as if nothing happened—and does this repeatedly—you learn that joy is fickle. When your mother emerges from
her depression and suddenly seems interested in your days and acts the way
you see other kids' moms acting, you don't dare feel joy because you know
from experience that it will all go away. And it does. Every single time. Better to expect nothing too stable. Better to "hang out" with the guy in the
waiting room who either still has a girlfriend or no longer does but flirted
with you when he did.

"I don't know what his deal with the girlfriend is," Charlotte continues.
"You think this is a bad idea?"

"How do you feel about it?"

"I don't know." Charlotte shrugs. "Excited? Scared?"

"Scared of what?"

"I don't know. That he won't like me outside of the waiting room or
that I'm his rebound after his girlfriend. Or that he's fucked up because he
was having problems with his girlfriend in the first place. I mean, why else
would they be coming to therapy?"

Charlotte starts fidgeting, playing with her sunglasses on the arm of
the chair.

"Or," she goes on, "what if he's still with his girlfriend and this isn't a
date but just a friend thing, and I didn't realize that, and then I have to see
him again in the waiting room each week?"

I tell Charlotte that the way she speaks about the Dude reminds me of
how she's described her state of mind before interactions with her parents,
not just as a child, but now, as an adult. *Will it go well? Will they behave
themselves? Will we get into an argument? Will my dad show up or cancel at
the last minute? Will my mom act inappropriately in public? Will we have fun?
Will I be humiliated?*

"Yeah," Charlotte says. "I won't go." But I know she will.

When our time is up, Charlotte goes through her ritual (expressing
disbelief that the hour is over, slowly packing up her belongings, stretch-

ing languidly). She ambles toward the door but stops at the threshold, as she often does to ask me a question or say something she should have said during the session. Like John, she's prone to what we call "doorknob disclosures."

"By the way," she begins casually, although I have a feeling that whatever comes next will be anything but an offhand aside. It's not uncommon for patients to go through an entire session talking about this or that, only to spill something important in the last ten seconds ("I think I'm bisexual," "My biological mother found me on Facebook"). People do this for a variety of reasons—they're embarrassed, they don't want you to have a chance to comment, they want to leave you feeling as unsettled as they do. (*Special delivery! Here's all my turmoil; sit in it all week, will you?*) Or it's a wish: *Keep me in mind.*

This time, though, nothing comes out. Charlotte just stands there. I wonder if she's thinking about something particularly hard for her to address—her drinking, or her hope that her father will pick up the phone when she calls on his birthday next week. Instead she blurts out: "Where did you get that top?"

It seems like such a simple question. I've had an Uber driver, a barista at Starbucks, and a stranger on the street all ask me the same question about this new top—one of my favorites—and each time, I answered without a hint of hesitation. "Anthropologie, on sale!" I'd reply, proud of my good taste and good fortune. But with Charlotte, something stops me. It's not that I'm worried she'll start to dress exactly like me (as one of my patients did). It's that my gut tells me why she's asking; she wants to get it and wear it on her date with the Dude—the date that she's supposedly not going on.

"Anthropologie," I say anyway.

"It's cute," she says, smiling. "See you next week."

And off she goes, but not before I meet her eyes for a split second and she looks away.

We both know what's about to happen.

34

Just Be

About halfway through my traineeship, I got into a conversation with my hairstylist about therapy.

"Why would you want to be a therapist?" Cory asked, scrunching up his nose. He said that often he felt like a therapist, listening to people's problems all day. "It's TMI," he continued. "I'm cutting their hair. Why do they tell me these things?"

"Do they really get that personal?"

"Oh yeah, some do. I don't know how you do it. It's so —" He held up the scissors, searching for the right word. "Draining."

He went back to cutting. I watched him snip my front layers.

"What do you say to them?" I asked. It occurred to me that when people shared their secrets with him, they were probably looking in the mirror, the way we were having our conversation right now — with each other's reflections. Maybe that made it easier, I thought.

"What do I say when I hear all their problems?" he asked.

"Right. Do you try to give them advice, add your two cents?"

"None of that," he said.

"Then what?"

"'Just be,'" he said.

"What?"

"I tell them, 'Just be.'"

"That's what you say?" I started laughing. I imagined saying that in my office. *You've got problems? Just be.*

"You should try it with your patients," he said, smiling back. "It might help them."

"Does it help your clients?" I asked.

Cory nodded. "It's like this. I'll give them a haircut, and they'll come back the next time and say they want something different. 'Why?' I'll ask. 'Was something wrong with the last one?' No, they say. The last one was fabulous! They just want something different. So I give them the *exact same haircut* but they think it's different. And they love it."

I waited for him to say more, but he seemed to be focusing on my split ends. I watched my hair fall to the floor.

"Okay," I said. "But what does this have to do with their problems?"

Cory stopped cutting and looked at me in the mirror.

"Maybe everything they complain about isn't actually a problem! Maybe it's fine the way it is. Maybe it's even great, like their haircut. Maybe they'd be happier if they didn't try to *change* things. Just be."

I considered this. There was certainly some truth here. Sometimes people needed to accept themselves and others the way they were. But sometimes in order to feel better, you need a mirror held up to you, and not the mirror that makes you look pretty, like the one I was looking in now.

"Have you ever been to therapy?" I asked Cory.

"Hell no." He shook his head vigorously. "Not for me."

Despite Cory's objections to TMI, in the years he'd been cutting my hair, he'd told me quite a bit about himself—how burned he'd been by love, how his family had trouble accepting him when he told them he was gay, how his father had been secretly gay his whole life, having affairs with men, but still hadn't come out. I knew, too, that Cory had had multiple cosmetic surgeries and still wasn't satisfied with his looks, that he was preparing to go under the knife yet again. Even as we spoke, he was checking himself out in the mirror and finding himself wanting.

"What do you do when you feel lonely or sad?" I asked.

"Tinder," he said matter-of-factly.

"And hook up?"

He smiled. *Of course.*

"And then you don't see these guys again?"

"Not usually."

"And you feel better?"

"Yeah."

"You mean, until you get lonely or sad again and go back on the app for another fix?"

"Exactly." He exchanged his scissors for the blow dryer. "Anyway, is that any different from people who come to therapy each week for their fix?"

It was. It was different in so many ways. For one, therapists don't provide a simple weekly fix. I once heard a journalist say that doing a proper interview was a little bit like cutting another person's hair: it looked easy until you got the scissors in your hand. The same, I was learning, was true of therapy. But I didn't want to proselytize. Therapy, after all, wasn't for everyone.

"You're right," I said to Cory. "There are many ways to just be."

He turned on the dryer. "You have your therapy," he said, then he nodded toward his cell phone. "And I have mine."

35

Would You Rather?

Julie is cataloging her body parts, deciding which ones to keep.

"Colon? Uterus?" she asks, her eyebrows raised as if telling a joke. "And you're not going to believe this one. *Vagina*. So basically it comes down to, do I want to be able to shit, have babies, or fuck."

I feel a knot form in my throat. Julie looks different from the way she had at Trader Joe's a few months back, or even from what she'd looked like a few weeks ago, when the doctors said that in order to keep her alive, they'd need to take more of her away. She'd soldiered through the first bout of cancer and the recurrence and the death sentence that ended up with a stay of execution and the pregnancy that gave her hope. But after too many *just kidding*s, she's done with the cosmic jokes, worn down by it all. Her skin looks thin and lined, her eyes bloodshot. Now sometimes we cry together, and she hugs me when she leaves.

Nobody at Trader Joe's knows that she's sick, and for as long as she can, she wants to keep it that way. She wants them to know her first as a person, not as a cancer patient, which sounds a lot like how we therapists think about our patients: We want to get to know them before we get to know their problems.

"It's like those 'would you rather' games we played at slumber parties as kids," she says today. "Would you rather die in an airplane crash or a fire? Would you rather be blind or deaf? Would you rather smell bad for the rest of your life or smell bad things for the rest of your life? One time when it was my turn to answer, I said, 'Neither.' And everyone said, 'No, you have to choose one,' and I said, 'Well, I choose neither.' And that kind of blew people's minds, just the concept that when presented with two awful alternatives, maybe *neither* was an option."

In her high-school yearbook, under her name, they'd written *I choose neither.*

She'd used this logic in her grown-up life too. When she'd been asked if she'd rather have a prestigious grad-school opportunity with minimal funding or a fully funded position that was far less interesting, everyone had an opinion about which one she should take. But against all advice, she chose neither. It served her well; soon after, she got an even better grad-school offer in a better location in the same city as her sister, and she'd met her husband there.

Once she got sick, though, *neither* became less of an option: Would you rather have no breasts but live or keep your breasts and die? She chose life. There were many decisions like this, where the answers were difficult yet obvious, and each time, Julie took them in stride. But now, with this particular would-you-rather, this body-part roulette, she didn't know how to choose. She was, after all, still getting over the shock of her recent miscarriage.

Her pregnancy had lasted eight weeks, during which time her younger sister, Nikki, had become pregnant with her second child. Not wanting to announce their news until the end of their first trimesters, the sisters kept each other's secrets, giddily marking the days on a shared online calendar that labeled their progression for twelve weeks. Julie's hash marks were in blue because she guessed she was carrying a boy; she'd nicknamed him BB, for Beautiful Boy. Nikki's were in yellow (nickname: Baby Y), the color she planned to paint the baby's nursery; as with her first pregnancy, she wanted the gender to be a surprise.

At the end of Julie's eighth week, the bleeding started. Her sister was just beginning week six. As Julie was on her way to the ER, a text popped up from Nikki. It was an ultrasound photo with the caption *Hey, look, I have a heartbeat! How's my cousin BB? XO, Baby Y.*

Baby Y's cousin wasn't doing so well. Baby Y's cousin was no longer viable.

But at least I don't have cancer, Julie thought as she left the hospital she knew so well by then. This time, she'd been there for a "normal" problem for people her age. Lots of people miscarried in those early weeks, her obstetrician explained. Julie's body had been through a lot.

"It's just one of those things," her doctor had said.

And for the first time in her life, Julie, who had always lived in the land of rational explanations, was content with this answer. After all, every time the doctors had a *reason* for something, the reason was devastating. Fate, bad luck, probability—any of those seemed like a welcome respite from a dismal diagnosis. Now when her computer crashed or a pipe burst in the kitchen, she'd say, *It's just one of those things.*

The phrase made her smile. It could work both ways, she decided. How many times do *good* things inexplicably come our way too? Just the other day, she told me, some random person walked into Trader Joe's with a homeless woman who'd been sitting in the parking lot and said to Julie, "See that woman over there? I told her to buy herself some food. When she gets to the register, come find me and I'll pay the bill." Relating the story to Matt after work, Julie shook her head and said, *It was just one of those things.*

And, in fact, on her next try, Julie got pregnant again. Baby Y was going to have a *younger* cousin this time. It was just one of those things.

So as not to jinx it, Julie didn't nickname the baby. She sang to it and talked to it and carried around her secret like a diamond that nobody could see. The only people who held the secret with her were Julie's husband, her sister, and me. Even her mother didn't know yet. ("She has trouble keeping good news to herself," Julie said, laughing.) So it was me to whom she reported her progress, me to whom she described the heart-shaped balloon that Matt had brought to their first-heartbeat ultrasound appointment, and me whom she called when, a week later, she miscarried again and tests revealed that Julie's uterus was "inhospitable" due to a fibroid she would need to have removed. Again, a welcome problem because it was so common—and fixable.

"But at least I don't have cancer," Julie said. That had been her and Matt's other refrain. No matter what happened—all the daily annoyances big and small that people tended to complain about—as long as Julie didn't have cancer, all was right with the world. Julie just needed a minor surgery to get rid of the fibroid, and then she could try to get pregnant again.

"Another surgery?" Matt had said.

He worried that Julie's body had gone through enough. Maybe, he suggested, they should adopt or use a surrogate to carry the baby with the embryos they'd frozen. Matt was just as risk-averse as Julie—this had been a point of commonality when they met. With all of her miscarriages, wasn't that a safer idea? Besides, if they went the surrogate route, they had the perfect person in mind.

On the way to the ER during her recent miscarriage, Julie had called Emma, a coworker at Trader Joe's, to see if she could cover Julie's shift. Unbeknownst to Julie, Emma had just signed up with a surrogate agency so that she could pay for college. Emma was a twenty-nine-year-old married mom who wanted to get a college degree, and she loved the idea of giving a family their dream as a way to make her own educational dreams come true. When Julie confided in Emma about her uterus problem, Emma instantly offered her services. Earlier, Julie had encouraged her to go back to school, even helping her with college applications. She and Emma had worked side by side for months and it never occurred to Julie that Emma might one day be pregnant with her child. But if her question in life had always been *Why?*, this time she asked herself, *Why not?*

So Julie and Matt came up with a new plan, as they'd had to do so many times since the beginning of their marriage. She would get her fibroid removed and attempt one more pregnancy. If that didn't work out, they'd ask Emma to carry their baby. And if *that* didn't work out, they'd try to become parents through adoption.

"At least I don't have cancer," Julie had said in my office after she finished explaining the baby setback and the plan forward. Except that while preparing for her fibroid removal, Julie's doctors discovered the fibroid wasn't the only issue. Her cancer was back, and spreading. There was nothing they could do. No more miracle drugs. If she wanted, they would do what they could to prolong her life as long as possible, but she would have to give up a lot along the way.

She was going to have to figure out what she could live with—and without—and for how long.

When the doctors first presented this news, Julie and Matt, sitting side by side in vinyl chairs in a doctor's office, burst out laughing. They laughed at the earnest gynecologist, and then the next day they laughed at the solemn oncologist. By the end of the week, they had laughed at the gastroenterologist, the urologist, and the two surgeons they consulted for second opinions.

Even before they saw the doctors, they were giggling. Whenever the nurses, escorting them to an examination room, asked rhetorically, "How are you two today?" Julie would reply nonchalantly, "Well, *I'm* dying. And how are you?" The nurses never knew what to say.

She and Matt found this hilarious.

They laughed, too, when presented with the possibility of removing body parts where the cancer might grow most aggressively.

"We have no use for a uterus now," Matt said casually while sitting with Julie in one doctor's office. "Personally, I'd vote for keeping the vagina and losing the colon, but I'll leave the colon and vagina up to her."

"'I'll leave the colon and vagina up to her'!" Julie guffawed. "He's so sweet, isn't he?"

At another appointment, Julie said, "I don't know, Doc. What's the point of keeping my vagina if we remove my colon and I've got a bag of poop attached to my body? Not exactly an aphrodisiac." Matt and Julie laughed then too.

The surgeon explained that he could create a vagina out of other tissue, and Julie burst out laughing again. "A custom vagina!" she said to Matt. "How about that?"

They laughed and laughed and laughed.

And then they cried. They cried as hard as they'd laughed.

When Julie told me this, I remembered how I had burst out laughing when Boyfriend said he didn't want to live with a kid under his roof for another ten years. I remembered the patient who laughed hysterically when her beloved mother died, and another who laughed when he learned that his wife had multiple sclerosis. And then I remembered sobbing in Wendell's office for entire sessions, the way my patients had and the way Julie had for the past few weeks.

This was grief: You laugh. You cry. Repeat.

"I'm leaning toward keeping my vagina but dumping the colon," Julie says today, shrugging, as if we're having a normal conversation. "I mean, I just got fake breasts. With a fake vagina, there won't be much difference between me and a Barbie doll."

She's been figuring out how much has to be taken away before she's no longer herself. What constitutes life even if you're alive? I think about how people barely talk about this with their elderly parents, all the would-you-rathers that they'd rather not contemplate. Besides, it's all a thought experiment until you're there. What are your deal-breakers? When your mobility goes? When your mind does? How much mobility? How much cognition? Will it still be a deal-breaker when it actually happens?

Here were Julie's deal-breakers: She'd rather die if she could no longer eat regular food or if the cancer spread to her brain and she couldn't form coherent thoughts. She used to believe that she'd rather die if she had poop traveling through a hole in her abdomen, but now, she just worries about the colostomy bag.

"Matt's going to be repulsed by this, isn't he?"

The first time I saw a colostomy in medical school, I was surprised by how unobtrusive it was. There's even a line of fashionable bag covers adorned with flowers, butterflies, peace signs, hearts, jewels. A lingerie designer dubbed them "Victoria's *Other* Secret."

"Have you asked him?" I say.

"Yes, but he's afraid of hurting my feelings. I want to know. Do you think he'll find it repulsive?"

"I don't think he'll find it repulsive," I say, realizing that I'm being careful with her feelings too. "But he may have to get used to it."

"He's had to get used to a lot," she says.

She tells me about a fight they had a few nights ago. Matt was watching a show, but Julie wanted to talk. Matt was *uh-huh*-ing her, pretending to listen, and Julie got upset. *Look what I found on the internet, maybe we can ask the doctors,* she said, and Matt said, *Not tonight, I'll look tomorrow,* and Julie said, *But this is important and we don't have a lot of time,* and Matt looked at her with an anger she'd never seen in him before.

"Can't we have *one night* off from cancer?" Matt yelled. It was the first time he had been anything but kind and supportive, and Julie, taken aback, snapped at him. "*I* don't get a night off!" she said. "Do you know what *I'd* give for a night off from cancer?" She fled to the bedroom and closed the door, and a minute later, Matt followed, apologizing for his outburst. *I'm stressed,* he said. *This is very stressful for me. But not as stressful as what you're going through, so I'm sorry. I was insensitive. Show me the thing on the internet.* But his words shook her. She knew that it wasn't just her quality of life that was changing. Matt's was, too. And she hadn't been paying attention to that.

"I didn't tell him about the thing on the internet," Julie says. "I felt so selfish. He *should* get a night off from cancer. This isn't what he signed up for when he married me either."

I give her a look.

"Well, sure, the vows say 'in sickness and health' and 'for better or worse' and all that, but that's kind of like clicking *okay* to the terms and conditions when you download an app or sign up for a credit card. You don't think any of that is going to apply to *you.* Or if you do, you don't expect it to happen right after your honeymoon, before you've even had a chance to be married."

I'm glad that Julie is thinking about the impact of her cancer on Matt. It's something she's avoided talking about by changing the subject whenever I mentioned that maybe it was hard for Matt to go through this too.

Julie would shake her head. "Yeah, he's amazing," she'd say. "He's so solid, so there for me. Anyway . . ."

If Julie had any awareness of the depth of Matt's pain, she hadn't been ready to face it. But something shifted with Matt's outburst, forcing her to acknowledge a difficult tension: their togetherness on this unfortunate journey, but also their separateness.

Julie is crying now. "He kept wanting to take back what he'd said, but it was already out there, hanging between us. I understand why he wants a night off from cancer." She pauses. "I'll bet he wishes that I would just die already."

I'll bet sometimes he does, I think for a second. It's hard enough in a marriage to do the give-and-take of putting one's wants and needs aside for another, but here the scales are tipped, the imbalance unrelenting. Yet I also know it's much more complicated than that. I imagine that Matt feels trapped in time, newly married, young, wanting to live a normal life and start a family, all the while knowing that what he has left with Julie is temporary. He sees his future as a widower, then as a father in his forties rather than his thirties. He probably hopes that this doesn't go on for another five years, five years at the prime of his life spent in hospitals, caretaking his young wife whose body is being cut apart. At the same time, I'll bet that he is touched to his core by this experience, that in some ways it makes him feel, as one man told me in the months before his wife of thirty years died, "forever changed and paradoxically alive." I'd wager that, like that man, Matt wouldn't choose to go back in time and marry a different person. But Matt's at a life stage when everyone else is moving forward; the thirties are a decade of building the foundation of the future. He's out of sync with his peers, and in his own way, in his own grief, he probably feels completely alone.

I don't think it would be helpful for Julie to know every detail, but I believe that their time together will be richer if there's space for Matt to show more of his humanity during this process. And if they can have a deeper experience of each other in the time that they have left together, Julie will live more fully within Matt after she's gone.

"What do you think Matt meant by wanting the night off from cancer?" I ask.

Julie sighs. "All the doctor appointments, the lost pregnancies, everything I want a night off from too. He wants to talk about how his research is going and the new taco place down the street and . . . you know, the *normal* things people our age talk about. The whole time I've been going through this, all we cared about was finding a way for me to live. But now, he can't make plans with me for even a year from now, and he can't go meet someone else. The only way he can move forward is if I die."

I hear what she's getting at. Underlying their ordeal is a fundamental truth: For all of the ways that Matt's life has changed, it will eventually return to some kind of normal. And that, I suspect, pisses Julie off. I ask if she's angry with Matt, envious.

"Yes," she whispers, as though she's sharing a shameful secret. I tell her it's okay. How could she not be envious of the fact that he gets to live?

Julie nods. "I feel guilty for putting him through this and jealous that he gets a future," she says, adjusting a pillow behind her back. "And then I feel guilty for being jealous."

I think about how common it is, even in everyday situations, to be jealous of a spouse and how taboo it is to talk about that. Aren't we supposed to be happy for their good fortune? Isn't that what love is about?

In one couple I saw, the wife got her dream job on the same day that her husband was let go from his, which made for extreme awkwardness every night at the dinner table. How much should she share of her days without inadvertently making her husband feel bad? How could he manage his envy without raining on her parade? How noble can people reasonably be expected to be when their partners get something they desperately want but can't have?

"Matt came home from the gym yesterday," Julie says, "and he said that he had a fantastic workout, and I said, 'That's great,' but I felt so sad, because we used to go to the gym together. He'd always tell people that I was the one with the stronger body, the marathon runner. 'She's the superstar, I'm the wimp!' he'd say, and the people we became friends with at the gym started calling us that.

"Anyway, we used to have sex a lot after the gym. So yesterday when he gets back, he comes over and kisses me, and I start kissing him back, and we have sex, but I'm out of breath in a way I've never been before. I don't let on, though, so Matt gets up to shower, and as he's walking into the bathroom, I look at his muscles and think, *I used to be the one with the stronger body.* And then I realize that it's not just Matt who's watching me die. It's me, too. I'm watching myself die. And I'm so angry at everyone who gets to live. My parents will outlive me! My *grandparents* might too! My sister's having a second baby. But me?"

She reaches for her water bottle. After Julie recovered from her initial cancer treatment, her doctors told her that drinking water flushes out toxins, so Julie began carrying a sixty-four-ounce bottle everywhere she went. Now it's no longer useful but it's become a habit. Or a prayer.

"It's hard to see what's still there," I say, "and to let it in when you're grieving for your own life."

We sit in silence for a while. Finally, she wipes her eyes and the slip of a smile forms on her lips. "I have an idea."

I look at her expectantly.

"You'll tell me if it's too wacky?"

I nod.

"I was just thinking," she begins, "that instead of spending my time being jealous of everyone else, maybe part of my purpose for the time I have left could be helping the people I love to move forward."

She shifts on the couch, getting excited. "Take Matt and me. We won't grow old together. We won't even grow middle-aged together. I've been wondering if, for Matt, my death will feel more like a breakup than the end of a marriage. Most of the women in the cancer group who talk about leaving their husbands behind are in their sixties and seventies, and the one in her forties has been married for fifteen years, and she and her husband have two kids. I want to be remembered as a wife and not an ex-girlfriend. I want to *behave* like a wife and not an ex-girlfriend. So I'm thinking, *What would a wife do?* Do you know what these wives say about leaving their husbands behind?"

I shake my head.

"They talk about making sure their husbands are going to be okay," she says. "Even if I'm jealous of his future, I want Matt to be okay." Julie looks at me like she just said something I'm supposed to understand, but I don't.

"What would make you feel that he'll be okay?" I ask.

She shoots me a grin. "As much as this makes me want to vomit, I want to help him find a new wife."

"You want to let him know it's okay to love again," I say. "That doesn't sound wacky at all." Often a dying spouse wants to give the surviving one this blessing—to say that it's okay to hold one person in your heart and fall in love with another, that our capacity for love is big enough for both.

"No," Julie says, shaking her head. "I don't want to just give him my blessing. I want to actually *find him a wife*. I want that gift to be part of my legacy."

As when Julie first suggested the Trader Joe's idea, I feel myself recoil. This seems masochistic, a form of torture in an already torturous situation. I think about how Julie would *not* want to see this, could not bear this. Matt's future new wife will have his babies. She'll go on long hikes and climb mountains with him. She'll cuddle up with him and laugh with him and have passionate sex with him the way Julie once did. There's altruism and love, sure, but Julie's also human. And so is Matt.

"What makes you think he'll *want* this gift?" I ask.

"It's crazy, I know," Julie says. "But there's a woman in my cancer group whose friend did that. She was dying, and her best friend's husband was dying, and she didn't want her husband or her best friend to be alone, and she knew how well they got along—they'd been good friends for decades. So her dying wish was that they would go on a date after the funeral. One date. So they did. And now they're engaged." Julie's crying again. "Sorry," she says. Almost every woman I see apologizes for her feelings, especially her tears. I remember apologizing in Wendell's office too. Perhaps men apologize preemptively, by holding their tears back.

"I mean, not sorry, just sad," Julie says, echoing a phrase I shared with her earlier.

"You're going to miss Matt a lot," I say.

"I am," she squeaks out. "Everything about him. The way he gets so excited about little things, like a latte or a line in a book. The way he kisses me, and the way his eyes take ten minutes to open if he wakes up too early. How he warms my feet in bed and looks at me when we're talking, like his eyes are soaking up everything I'm saying as much as his ears are." Julie pauses to catch her breath. "And you know what I'm going to miss most of all? His *face*. I'm going to miss looking at his beautiful face. It's my favorite face in the entire world."

Julie is crying so hard that no sound comes out. I wish that Matt could have been here for this.

"Have you told him?" I ask.

"All the time," Julie says. "Every time he holds my hand, I say, 'I'm going to miss your hands.' Or when he's whistling around the house—he's an amazing whistler—I'll tell him how much I'm going to miss that sound. And he always used to say, 'Jules, you're still here. You can hold my hands and hear me whistle.' But now—" Julie's voice cracks. "Now he says, 'I'm going to miss you just as much.' I think he's starting to accept the fact that I'm really dying this time."

Julie wipes her upper lip.

"You want to hear something?" she continues. "I'm also going to miss myself. All those insecurities I'd spent my life wanting to change? I was just getting to a place where I really like myself. *I like me.* I'm going to miss Matt, and my family, and my friends, but I'm also going to miss *me.*"

She goes on to name all the things she wishes she'd appreciated more before she got sick: Her breasts, which she used to think weren't perky enough until she had to give them up; her strong legs, which she often thought were too thick, even though they served her well in marathons; her quiet way of listening, which she feared some might find boring. She's going to miss her distinctive laugh that a boy in fifth grade called "a squawk," a comment that somehow stuck like a burr inside her for years until that laugh made Matt glance her way in a crowded room and then make a beeline for her to introduce himself.

"I'm going to miss my freaking colon!" she says, laughing now. "I didn't appreciate it enough before. I'm going to miss sitting on a toilet and *shitting.* Who thinks they'll miss *shitting?*" Then come the tears—angry ones.

Every day is another loss of something she took for granted until it was gone, like what happens to the couples I see who take each other for granted and then miss each other when the marriage seems to be dying. Many women, too, have told me that they loathed getting their menstrual periods but grieved the loss of them when they reached menopause. They missed bleeding the way Julie will miss shitting.

Then, in almost a whisper, Julie adds, "I'm going to miss *life.*

"Fuck, fuck, fuck, fuck, *fuck!*" she says, starting soft and getting louder, surprising herself with her volume. She looks at me, embarrassed. "Sorry, I didn't mean—"

"It's okay," I say. "I agree. It fucking sucks."

Julie laughs. "And now I got my therapist to say *fuck!* I never used to swear like this. I don't want my obituary to read, 'She swore like a sailor.'"

I wonder what she *does* want her obituary to say, but time is almost up and I make a mental note to come back to this next time.

"Oh, who cares, that felt good. Let's do it again," Julie says. "Will you do it with me? We've got a minute left, right?"

At first I don't know what she's talking about—do what? But she has that mischievous look again, and then it clicks.

"You want us to—"

Julie nods. The rule-follower is asking me to yell obscenities with her. Recently in my consultation group, Andrea had said that while we need to hold hope for our patients, we have to hope for the right thing. If I can no longer hold hope for Julie's longevity, Andrea said, I have to hold hope for something else. "I can't help her in the way that she wants," I'd said. But sitting here now, I see that maybe I can, at least for today.

"Okay," I say. "Ready?"

We both yell, "FUCK, FUCK, FUCK, FUCK, FUCK, FUCK, FUCK!" When we're done, we catch our breath, exhilarated.

Then I walk her to the door, where, as usual, she hugs me goodbye.

In the hallway, other patients are leaving their sessions, doors opening at ten to the hour like clockwork. My colleagues look at me questioningly as Julie leaves. Our voices must have carried into the corridor. I shrug, close my door, and start laughing. *That was a first,* I think.

Then I feel the tears well up. Laughter to tears—grief. I'm going to miss Julie and I'm having a hard time with this myself.

Sometimes the only thing to do is yell, "*Fuck!*"

36

The Speed of Want

After completing my traineeship year, I began my internship at a nonprofit clinic located in the basement of a sleek office building. Upstairs, the light-filled suites had views of Los Angeles's mountains to one side and beaches to the other, but downstairs was another story. In cramped, cave-like, windowless consultation rooms furnished with decades-old chairs, broken lamps, and torn sofas, we interns thrived on patient volume. When a new case came in, we all vied for it, because the more people we saw, the more we learned and the closer we came to finishing our hours. Between back-to-back sessions, clinical supervision, and mounds of paperwork, we didn't pay much attention to the fact that we were living underground.

Sitting in the break room (aroma: microwaved popcorn and ant spray), we would scarf down some food (lunch was always eaten "al desco") and commiserate about our lack of time. But despite our gripes, our initiation as therapists felt exhilarating—partly because of the steep learning curve and our wise supervisors (who gave us advice like "If you're talking that much, you can't be listening" and its variant "You have two ears and one mouth; there's a reason for that ratio"), and partly because we knew this phase was blessedly temporary.

The light at the end of the years-long tunnel was licensure, when we imagined we could improve people's lives by doing the work we loved but with reasonable hours and a less frenetic pace. As we hunkered down in that basement, doing our charts by hand and searching for reception on our phones, we didn't realize that upstairs, a revolution was under way, one of speed, ease, and immediate gratification. And that what we were being trained to offer—gradual but lasting results that required some hard work —was becoming increasingly obsolete.

I'd seen hints of these developments in my patients at the clinic but, focused on my own harried existence, I failed to see the bigger picture. I thought: *Of course these people have trouble slowing down or paying attention or being present. That's why they're in therapy.*

My life wasn't much different, of course, at least during this phase. The faster I finished my work, the sooner I'd get to spend time with my son, and then the quicker we could do the bedtime routine, the quicker I could get to bed so that I could wake up the next day and hurry all over again. And the quicker I moved, the less I saw, because everything became a blur.

But this would end soon, I reminded myself. Once I finished my internship, my *real* life would begin.

One day I was in the break room with some fellow interns, and we once again started counting our required number of hours and calculating how old we'd be when we finally got licensed. The higher the number, the worse we felt. A supervisor in her sixties walked by and overheard the conversation.

"You'll turn thirty or forty or fifty anyway, whether your hours are finished or not," she said. "What does it matter what age you are when that happens? Either way, you won't get today back."

We all went quiet. *You won't get today back.*

What a chilling idea. We knew that our supervisor was trying to tell us something important. But we didn't have time to think about it.

Speed is about time, but it's also closely related to endurance and effort. The faster the speed, the thinking goes, the less endurance or effort required. Patience, on the other hand, *requires* endurance and effort. It's defined as "the bearing of provocation, annoyance, misfortune, or pain without complaint, loss of temper, irritation, or the like." Of course, much of life is made up of provocation, annoyance, misfortune, and pain; in psychology, patience might be thought of as the bearing of these difficulties for long enough to work through them. Feeling your sadness or anxiety can also give you essential information about yourself and your world.

But while I was down in that basement rushing toward licensure, the American Psychological Association published a paper called "Where Has All the Psychotherapy Gone?" It noted that 30 percent fewer patients received psychological interventions in 2008 than they had ten years earlier and that since the 1990s, the managed-care industry—the same system that my medical-school professors had warned us about—had been increasingly limiting visits and reimbursements for talk therapy but not for drug treatment. It went on to say that in 2005 alone, pharmaceutical companies spent $4.2 billion on direct-to-consumer advertising and $7.2 billion on promotion to physicians—nearly twice what they spent on research and development.

Of course, it's a lot easier—and quicker—to swallow a pill than to do the heavy lifting of looking inside yourself. And I had nothing against patients using medication to feel better. Just the opposite; I was, in fact, a strong believer in the tremendous good it often did in the right situations. But did 26 percent of the general population in this country really need to be on psychiatric medications? After all, it wasn't that psychotherapy didn't work. It was that it didn't work *fast enough* for today's patients, who were now, tellingly, called "consumers."

There was an unspoken irony to all of this. People wanted a speedy solution to their problems, but what if their moods had been driven down in the first place by the hurried pace of their lives? They imagined that they were rushing now in order to savor their lives later, but so often, later never came. The psychoanalyst Erich Fromm had made this point more than fifty years earlier: "Modern man thinks he loses something—time—when he does not do things quickly; yet he does not know what to do with the time he gains except kill it." Fromm was right; people didn't use extra time earned to relax or connect with friends or family. Instead, they tried to cram more in.

One day, as we interns begged to be given more new cases despite our full caseloads, our supervisor shook her head.

"The speed of light is outdated," she said dryly. "Today, everybody moves at *the speed of want.*"

Indeed, I sped through. Before long, I completed my internship, passed my board exams, and moved upstairs into an airy office with a view of the world around me. After two false starts—Hollywood, medical school—I was ready to begin a career I felt passionate about, and my being older also gave it a sense of urgency. I had taken a circuitous route, arriving late to the game, and though now I could finally slow down and appreciate the hard-won fruits of my labor, I still felt as rushed as I had in my internship —this time, I felt rushed to enjoy it. I sent out an email announcement introducing my practice and did some networking. After six months, I had a smattering of patients, but then the number seemed to plateau. Everyone I spoke to was having a similar experience.

I joined a consultation group for new therapists, and one night, after we'd discussed our cases, the conversation turned to the state of our practices—were we imagining things, or was our generation of therapists doomed? Somebody said she had heard about branding specialists specifically for therapists, professionals who could help to bridge the gap between the culture's need for speed and ease and what we were trained to do.

We all laughed—branding consultants for *therapists?* How ludicrous. The influential therapists of the past that we admired would be turning in their graves! But secretly, she got my attention.

A week later, I found myself on the phone with a branding consultant for therapists.

"Nobody wants to buy therapy anymore," the consultant said matter-of-factly. "They want to buy a solution to a problem." She made some suggestions about positioning myself for this new marketplace—even proposing that I should offer "text therapy"—but the whole thing made me uncomfortable.

Still, she was right. The week before Christmas, I got a call from a man in his early thirties about coming in for therapy. He explained that he wanted to figure out whether to marry his girlfriend, and he hoped we could "resolve this" quickly because Valentine's Day was coming up and he knew he had to produce a ring or she'd bail. I explained that I could help him with clarity but couldn't guarantee his timeline. It was a big life question, and I didn't know anything about him yet.

We set up an appointment, but the day before he was to come in, he called and told me he'd found someone else to help sort things out. She'd given him a guarantee that they'd resolve the issue in four sessions, which would meet his Valentine's Day deadline.

Another patient who genuinely wanted to find a life partner told me that she was going through people on the dating apps so fast that several times she had contacted a guy only to have him reply that they'd already *met*. She'd actually spent an hour having coffee with this person, but she was cycling through her options so quickly that she couldn't keep track.

Both of these patients were examples of, as my supervisor had put it, "the speed of want" — *want* in the sense of a desire. But I also began to think of the term slightly differently, as referring to the other sort of want — a lack or deficit.

If you'd asked me when I started as a therapist what most people came in for, I would have replied that they hoped to feel less anxious or depressed, to have less problematic relationships. But no matter the circumstances, there seemed to be this common element of loneliness, a craving for but a *lack* of a strong sense of human connection. A *want*. They rarely expressed it that way, but the more I learned about their lives, the more I could sense it, and I felt it in many ways myself.

One day at my new practice, in the long lull between patients, I found a video online of MIT researcher Sherry Turkle talking about this loneliness. In the late 1990s, she said, she had gone to a nursing home and watched a robot comfort an elderly woman who had lost a child. The robot looked like a baby seal, with fur and large eyelashes, and it processed language well enough to respond appropriately. The woman was pouring her heart out to this robot, and it seemed to follow her eyes, to be listening to her.

Turkle went on to say that while her colleagues considered this seal robot to be great progress, a way to make people's lives easier, she felt profoundly depressed.

I gasped in recognition. Just the day before, I'd joked to a colleague, "Why not have a therapist in your iPhone?" I didn't know then that soon there *would* be therapists in smartphones—apps through which you could connect with a therapist "anytime, anywhere . . . within seconds" to "feel better now." I felt about these options the way Turkle felt about the woman with the robotic seal.

"Why are we essentially outsourcing the thing that defines us as people?" Turkle asked in the video. Her question made me wonder: Was it that people couldn't tolerate being alone or that they couldn't tolerate being with other people? Across the country—at coffee with friends, in meetings at work, during lunch at school, in front of the cashier at Target, and at the family dinner table—people were texting and Tweeting and shopping, sometimes pretending to make eye contact and sometimes not even bothering.

Even in my therapy office, people who were paying to be there would glance at their phones when they buzzed just to see who it was. (These were often the same people who later admitted that they also glanced at pinging phones during sex or while sitting on the toilet. Upon learning this, I placed a bottle of Purell in my office.) To avoid distraction, I'd suggest turning off their phones during sessions, which worked well, but I noticed that before patients even reached the door at the end of the session, they'd grab their phones and start scrolling through their messages. Wouldn't their time have been better spent allowing themselves just one more minute to reflect on what we had just talked about or to mentally reset and transition back to the world outside?

The second people felt alone, I noticed, usually in the space between things—leaving a therapy session, at a red light, standing in a checkout line, riding the elevator—they picked up devices and ran away from that feeling. In a state of perpetual distraction, they seemed to be losing the ability to be with others and losing their ability to be with themselves.

The therapy room seemed to be one of the only places left where two people sit in a room together for an uninterrupted fifty minutes. Despite its veil of professionalism, this weekly I-thou ritual is often one of the most human encounters that people experience. I was determined to establish a flourishing practice, but I wasn't willing to compromise this ritual in order to make that happen. It may have seemed quaint, if not downright inconvenient, but for those patients I *did* have, I knew there was a tremendous payoff. If we create the space and put in the time, we stumble upon stories that are worth waiting for, the ones that define our lives.

And my own story? Well, I wasn't really allowing the time and the space for *that*—gradually, I became too busy listening to the stories of others. But beneath the hectic bustle of therapy sessions and school drop-offs, of doctor appointments and romance, a long-repressed truth was percolating beneath the surface and just beginning to make itself felt when I arrived in Wendell's office. *Half my life is over,* I would say, seemingly out of nowhere, in our very first session—and Wendell would jump right on this. He was picking up where my internship supervisor had left off years earlier.

You won't get today back.

And the days were flying by.

37

Ultimate Concerns

I'm soaked when I get to Wendell's office this morning. During my short walk across the street from the parking lot to his building, the winter's first downpour began unannounced. Having no umbrella or coat, I threw my cotton blazer over my head and ran.

Now my blazer is dripping, my hair is frizzing, my makeup is running, and my wet clothes are sticking to my body like leeches in the most unfortunate places. Too damp to sit, I'm standing by the waiting-room chairs, wondering how I'm going to make myself presentable for work, when the door to Wendell's inner office opens and out comes the pretty woman I've seen before. Again, she's wiping her tears. She lowers her head and rushes past the paper screen, and I hear the *click-clack* of her boots echoing down the building's corridor.

Margo?

No—it's coincidence enough that she's also seeing Wendell, but to have our weekly appointments back to back? I'm being paranoid. Then again, as the writer Philip K. Dick put it, "Strange how paranoia can link up with reality now and then."

I stand there shivering like a wet puppy until Wendell's door opens again, this time to let me in.

I drag myself to the sofa and settle into position B, arranging the familiar mismatched pillows behind my back in the way I've become accustomed. Wendell quietly closes the office door, walks across the room, lowers his tall body into his spot, and crosses his legs when he lands. We begin our opening ritual: our wordless hello.

But today I'm getting his sofa wet.

"Would you like a towel?" he asks.

"You have *towels?*"

Wendell smiles, walks over to his armoire, and tosses me a couple of hand towels. I dry my hair with one and sit down on the other.

"Thanks," I say.

"You're welcome," he says.

"Why do you have towels here?"

"People get wet," Wendell replies with a shrug, as if towels are an office staple. How strange, I think—and yet I feel so taken care of, like when he tossed me the tissues. I make a mental note to store towels in my office.

We look at each other in silent greeting again.

I don't know where to start. Lately I've been anxious about pretty much everything. Even little things like making small commitments have left me paralyzed. I've become cautious, afraid of taking risks and making mistakes because I've made so many already and I fear I won't have time to clean up the mistakes anymore.

The night before, as I tried to relax in bed with a novel, I came across a character who described his constant worry as "a relentless need to escape a moment that never ends." *Exactly,* I thought. For the past few weeks, every second has been linked to the next by worry. I know the anxiety is front and center because of what Wendell said at the end of our last session. I'd had to cancel my next appointment to go to an event at my son's school, then Wendell was away the following week, so I've been sitting with Wendell's words for three weeks now. Me: *What fight?* Him: *Your fight with death.*

The skies opening up on me on my way in today felt appropriate. I take a deep breath and tell Wendell about my wandering uterus.

Until today, I've never told this story from beginning to end. If before

I'd been embarrassed by it, now, as I say it aloud, I realize how truly ter-rified I've been. Layered on top of the grief Wendell had mentioned early on—that half my life is over—has been the fear that I, like Julie, might be dying much sooner than expected. There's nothing scarier to a single mom than contemplating leaving her young child on this earth without her. What if the doctors are missing something that could be treated if found promptly? What if they find the cause but it can't be treated?

Or what if this *is* all in my head? What if the person who can cure my physical symptoms is none other than the person I am sitting with right now, Wendell?

"That's quite a story," Wendell says when I'm done, shaking his head and blowing out some air.

"You think it's a story?" *Et tu, Brute?*

"I do," Wendell says. "It's a story about something frightening that's been happening to you over the past couple of years. But it's also a story about something else."

I anticipate what Wendell will say: It's a story about avoidance. Every-thing I've told him since coming to therapy has been about avoidance, and we both know that avoidance is almost always about fear. Avoidance of seeing the clues that Boyfriend and I had irreconcilable differences. Avoid-ance of writing the happiness book. Avoidance of talking about not writ-ing the happiness book. Avoidance of thinking about my parents getting older. Avoidance of the fact that my son is growing up. Avoidance of my mysterious illness. I remember something I learned during my internship: "Avoidance is a simple way of coping by not having to cope."

"It's a story about avoidance, isn't it?" I say.

"Well, in some ways, yes," Wendell replies. "Though I was going to say uncertainty. It's also a story about uncertainty."

Of course, I think. *Uncertainty.*

I've always thought about uncertainty in terms of my patients. Will John and Margo stay together? Will Charlotte stop drinking? But now so much seems uncertain in my own life. Will I be healthy again? Will I find the right partner? Will my writing career go up in flames? What will

the next half of my life—if I even have that long—look like? I'd once told
Wendell that it was hard to walk around those prison bars when I didn't
know where I was headed. I might be free, but which way should I go?

I remember a patient who had pulled into her garage at the end of an
ordinary workday and was greeted by an intruder with a gun. The intruder's accomplice, she would soon learn, was in the house with her children
and their babysitter. After a horrific ordeal, they were saved when a neighbor called the police. My patient told me that the worst thing about this
incident was that it had shattered her smug sense of safety, however illusory
it might have been.

And yet, whether she realized it or not, she still held on to that illusion.

"Do you worry about pulling into your new garage?" I asked when the
family, too traumatized to live at the scene of the crime, had moved into
a new home.

"Of course not," she said, as if it were an absurd question. "Like this
would happen twice? What are the chances of *that?*"

I tell Wendell this story and he nods. "How do you make sense of her
response?" he asks.

Wendell and I rarely talk about my work as a therapist, and now I feel
self-conscious. Sometimes I wonder how Wendell would be with my patients, what he would say to Rita or John. Therapy is a completely different experience with a different therapist; no two are exactly the same. And
because Wendell has been doing this much longer than I have, I feel like
the student to his teacher, Luke Skywalker to his Yoda.

"I think we want the world to be rational, and it was her way of having control over how uncertain life is," I say. "Once you know a truth, you
can't *un*know it, but at the same time, to protect herself from that knowledge, she convinces herself she could never be assaulted again." I pause.
"Did I pass the test?"

Wendell starts to open his mouth but I know what he's about to say:
This isn't a test.

"Well," I say, "was that what you were thinking? How would you make
sense of her certainty in the face of uncertainty?"

"The way you did with her," he says. "The same way I'd make sense of it with you."

Wendell goes through the concerns I've brought to him: my breakup, my book, my health, my father's health, my son's rapid ascent through childhood. The seemingly offhand observations I'd pepper our conversations with, like "I heard on the radio that about half of today's Americans weren't *alive* in the 1970s!" Everything I talk about is shaded with uncertainty. How much longer will I live, and what will happen in that time before I die? How much control will I have over any of it? But, Wendell says, like my patient, I've come up with my own way to cope. If I screw up my life, I can engineer my own death rather than have it happen to me. It may not be what I want, but at least I'll choose it. Like cutting off my nose to spite my face, this is a way to say, *Take that, uncertainty.*

I try to wrap my mind around this paradox: self-sabotage as a form of control. *If I screw up my life, I can engineer my own death rather than have it happen to me.* If I stay in a doomed relationship, if I mess up my career, if I hide in fear instead of facing what's wrong with my body, I can create a living death—but one where I call the shots.

Irvin Yalom, the scholar and psychiatrist, often talked about therapy as an existential experience of self-understanding, which is why therapists tailor the treatment to the individual rather than to the problem. Two patients might have the same problem—say, they have trouble being vulnerable in relationships—but the approach I take with them will vary. The process is highly idiosyncratic because there's no cookie-cutter way to help people through what are at the deepest level existential fears—or what Yalom called "ultimate concerns."

The four ultimate concerns are death, isolation, freedom, and meaninglessness. Death, of course, is an instinctive fear that we often repress but that tends to increase as we get older. What we fear isn't just dying in the literal sense but in the sense of being extinguished, the loss of our very identities, of our younger and more vibrant selves. How do we defend against this fear? Sometimes we refuse to grow up. Sometimes we self-sabotage. And sometimes we flat-out deny our impending deaths. But as Yalom wrote in *Existential Psychotherapy,* our awareness of death helps us live more fully—and with less, not more, anxiety.

Julie, with the "wacky" risks she's been taking, is a perfect example of this. I never paid attention to my own death until I embarked on the Medical Mystery Tour—and even then, Boyfriend allowed me to distract myself from my fears of extinction, both professional and actual. But he also offered me an antidote to my fear of isolation, another ultimate concern. There's a reason that solitary confinement makes prisoners literally go crazy; they experience hallucinations, panic attacks, obsessional behavior, paranoia, despair, difficulty with focus, and suicidal ideation. When released, these people often struggle with social atrophy, which renders them unable to interact with others. (Perhaps this is simply a more intense version of what happens with our increasing *want,* our loneliness, created by our speedy lifestyles.)

And then there's the third ultimate concern: freedom, and all the existential difficulties that freedom poses for us. On the surface, it's almost laughable how much freedom I have—if, as Wendell pointed out, I'm willing to walk around those bars. But there's also the reality that as people get older, they face more limitations. It becomes harder to change careers or move to a different city or marry a different person. Their lives are more defined, and sometimes they crave the freedom of youth. But children, bound by parental rules, are really free only in one respect—emotionally. For a while, at least, they can cry or laugh or have tantrums unselfconsciously; they can have big dreams and unedited desires. Like many people my age, I don't feel free because I've lost touch with that emotional freedom. And that's what I'm doing here in therapy—trying to free myself emotionally again.

In a way, this midlife crisis may be more about opening up than shutting down, an expansion rather than a constriction, a rebirth rather than a death. I remember when Wendell said that I wanted to be saved. But Wendell isn't here to save me or solve my problems as much as to guide me through my life *as it is* so that I can manage the certainty of uncertainty without sabotaging myself along the way.

Uncertainty, I'm starting to realize, doesn't mean the loss of hope—it means there's possibility. *I don't know what will happen next—how potentially exciting!* I'm going to have to figure out how to make the most of the life I have, illness or not, partner or not, the march of time notwithstanding.

Which is to say, I'm going to have to look more closely at the fourth ultimate concern: meaninglessness.

38

Legoland

"You know why I'm late?" John says as soon as I open the door to the waiting room. It's fifteen minutes past the hour, and I'd assumed he wasn't coming. A month went by before he responded to my message after his no-show—he'd unexpectedly resurfaced and asked to come in. But maybe, I thought before he arrived, he got cold feet. Indeed, on the walk down the hallway, John goes on to say that after he pulled into the building's parking lot, he sat in his car, debating whether to come upstairs. The attendant asked for his keys, but John said he needed a minute, so the attendant told him to pull over toward the exit, and by the time John decided to stay, the attendant informed him that the lot was full. John had to find a spot on the street and sprint the two blocks to my building.

"Can't a person have a minute to sit in his own car and collect his thoughts?" John asks.

As we enter my office, I think about how beleaguered he tends to feel. Today he looks ragged, exhausted. So much for his sleep medication.

John lowers himself onto the couch, kicks off his shoes, then stretches out, lies down, and adjusts his head on the pillows. Usually he sits cross-legged on the sofa, so this is a first. I notice, too, that there's no food today.

"Okay, you win," he begins with a sigh.

"Win what?" I ask.

"The pleasure of my company," he deadpans.

I raise my eyebrows.

"The explanation to the mystery," he continues. "I'm going to tell you the story. So, lucky you—you win."

"I didn't know we were competing," I say. "But I'm glad you're here."

"Oh, for Chrissake," he says. "Let's not analyze everything, okay? Let's just do this, because if we don't start now, I'm two seconds away from leaving."

He rolls over to face the back of the couch, and then, very quietly, says to the fabric, "So, uh, we were going on a family trip to Legoland."

According to John, he and Margo were driving down the California coast with the kids to Legoland, a theme park in Carlsbad, for a long weekend away when they had a disagreement. It had been their policy never to argue in front of the children, and up to that point, they'd both kept their promise.

At the time, John was in charge of his first television show, which meant that he was on call day and night in order to get each week's episode out. Margo also felt overwhelmed, taking care of two young kids and trying to keep up with her graphic-design clients, but while John got to interact with adults all day, Margo was either "in Mommy-land," as she put it, or working at her home computer.

Margo looked forward to seeing John at the end of the day, but at dinner he would answer calls while she gave him what he termed the *death stare*. When things got so busy that John couldn't make it home for dinner, Margo would ask him to turn off his cell at bedtime so that they could catch up and relax together without interruption. But John insisted that he couldn't be unreachable.

"I didn't work this hard all these years only to get this opportunity and see my show fail," he told her. And, indeed, it was off to a rocky start. The ratings were disappointing, but critics raved about the show, so the network agreed to give it more time to find an audience. The reprieve was a short one, though; if the ratings didn't improve quickly, the show would be canceled. John doubled his efforts and made some changes (including "firing some idiots"), and the show took off.

The network had a hit on its hands. And John had a very angry wife on his.

With the show's success, John got even busier. Did he remember that he had a wife? Margo asked him. What about his kids, who, when Margo called out, "Daddy's here!" ran to the computer instead of the front door because they were so used to talking to Daddy on a screen? The younger one had even begun calling the computer Daddy. Yes, Margo conceded, John spent time with them on weekends, playing with them in the park for hours, taking them on outings, and horsing around with them at home. But even then, the ringing phone never left his side.

John didn't understand why Margo was making such a big deal out of this. When he became a father, he was surprised at how intense and immediate the bond was. His connection with his babies felt so powerful—fierce, even. It reminded him of the love he'd had as a boy for his mother before she died. It was a kind of love he didn't even experience with Margo, though he loved her deeply, despite their disagreements. The first time he'd seen her, she was standing across the room at a party, laughing at something some doofus had said. Even from afar, John could see that it was the laugh of somebody being polite but thinking, *What an idiot.*

John was smitten. He walked over to Margo, made her laugh for real, and married her a year later.

Still, the way he loved his wife was different from the way he loved his kids. If his love for his wife was romantic and warm, his love for his kids was like a volcano. When he read *Where the Wild Things Are* to them, and they asked why the Wild Things wanted to *eat* the kid, he knew exactly why. "Because of how much they *love* him!" he said, pretending to swallow them as they giggled so hard they could barely breathe. He understood that devouring love.

So what if he took calls when he was with his kids? He spent time with them, they adored him, and it was his professional success, after all, that provided them with the kind of financial security that he wished he'd had growing up as the son of two teachers. Yes, John was under a lot of pressure at work, but he loved creating characters and making up entire worlds as a writer—the very craft that his father had always aspired to. Whether by luck or talent or a combination, John had achieved both his and his father's dreams. And he couldn't be two places at once. The cell phone, he told Margo, was a gift.

"A *gift?*" Margo had said.

Yes, replied John. *A gift.* It allowed him to be at work and at home at the same time.

Margo thought that was precisely the problem. *I don't want you to be at work and at home at the same time. We aren't your coworkers. We're your family.* Margo didn't want to be midsentence or mid-kiss or mid-whatever with John, only to be interrupted by Dave or Jack or Tommy from the show. *I didn't invite them into our home at nine p.m.,* she said.

The night before the trip to Legoland, Margo asked John if he would please stay off the phone during their vacation. It was family time away, and it was just three days.

"Unless someone's dying," Margo had pleaded—which John took to mean *Unless there's an emergency*—"please don't pick up the phone on this trip."

To avoid another fight, John agreed.

The kids couldn't wait to go to Legoland—they'd been talking about it for weeks. On the drive down, they wriggled in their seats, asking every few minutes, "How much longer?" and "Are we *almost* there?"

The family had decided to take the scenic route along the beach instead of the freeway, and John and Margo distracted the kids by having them count the boats in the ocean and play a game in which they'd make up silly songs together, each person adding a lyric more hilarious than the last until they were all cracking up.

John's phone was quiet. The night before, he'd warned the show's crew not to call.

"Unless someone's dying," he'd told them, quoting Margo, "find a way to handle it yourselves." They weren't complete idiots, he assured himself. The show was doing well. They could manage whatever came up. It was three fucking days.

Now, making up silly songs in the car, John glanced over at Margo.

She was laughing the way she'd laughed with him at the party where they'd met. He hadn't seen her laugh like that in—well, he couldn't remember how long. She placed her hand on his neck, and he melted into it, responding in a way he hadn't in—again, he couldn't remember how long. The kids were jabbering away in the back. He felt a sense of peace, and an image popped into his mind. He imagined that his mom was looking down from heaven or wherever the hell she was, smiling at how well things had turned out for her youngest son, the one he'd always believed was her favorite. Here John was, with his wife and kids, now a successful television writer, heading to Legoland in a car full of laughter and love.

He remembered sitting in the back seat himself as a young boy, squeezed in the middle between his two older brothers, his parents in the front, his dad driving, his mom riding shotgun and navigating, all of them making up song lyrics and laughing their heads off. He remembered trying to keep up with his older brothers when it was his turn to add a line, and how his mom delighted in his wordplay.

"So precocious!" she'd exclaim each time.

John didn't know what *precocious* meant. He assumed it was a fancy way of saying "precious"—and he knew that, to his mom, he was the most precious of the boys, not the "mistake" his brothers teasingly called him because he was so much younger than they were but instead, as his mom said, a "special surprise." He remembered seeing his mom put her hand on the back of his father's neck, and now Margo was doing this for him. He felt optimistic; he and Margo would find their way back to each other.

Then John's phone rang.

The ringing phone was sitting on the console between him and Margo. John glanced at it. Margo gave him the death stare. John remembered his instructions to his staff to call only in case of emergency—*unless someone's dying*. He knew that today's shoot was on location. Had something gone wrong?

"Don't," Margo said.

"I just need to check who it is," John replied.

"God damn it," Margo hissed, the first time she'd sworn in front of the kids.

"Don't 'God damn it' me," John hissed back.

"We've been away only two hours," Margo said, her voice rising, "and you promised you wouldn't do this!"

The kids went silent, and so did the phone. The call had gone to voicemail.

John sighed. He asked Margo to look at the caller ID and tell him who had called, but she shook her head and turned away. John reached for the phone with his right hand. Then they collided with a black SUV coming straight at them.

Strapped in their booster seats were five-year-old Gracie and six-year-old Gabe. Irish twins, born just a year apart and inseparable. The loves of John's life. Gracie survived along with John and Margo. Gabe, seated directly behind John and at exactly the point of impact, died at the scene.

Later, the police would try to piece together what had caused the tragedy. The two witnesses from nearby cars weren't much help. One said that the SUV veered across the lane, taking the curve too quickly. The other said that John's car didn't adjust to the position of the SUV coming around the curve. The police determined that the driver of the SUV had a blood-alcohol level above the legal limit, and he was put in jail. Manslaughter. But John didn't feel absolved. He knew that at the very moment the SUV had rounded the curve, he'd looked away for a millisecond—or he possibly had, though he thought his eyes had stayed on the road as he felt for the phone with his hand. Margo didn't see the SUV coming either. She was looking out the passenger window, toward the ocean, fuming at John while refusing to check his phone.

Gracie couldn't remember a thing, and the only person who saw what was about to happen seemed to be Gabe. The last time John heard his son's voice, it was a piercing scream with one long word: *"Daddyyyyyyy!"*

The phone call, by the way, was a wrong number.

As I listen, I'm overwhelmed with heartbreak—not just for John but for his entire family. I'm holding back tears, but John, on the couch, has turned to face me now, and I see that his eyes are dry. He seems removed, distant, just as he had when he told me about his mother's death.

"Oh, John," I say, "that's—"

"Yeah, yeah," he interrupts, his tone a taunt, "it's so sad. I know. It's so fucking sad. That's all everyone said when it happened. My mom dies. *It's so sad.* My kid dies. *It's so sad.* Obviously. But that doesn't change anything. They're still dead. Which is why I don't tell people. And why I didn't tell you. I don't need to hear how fucking sad it is. I don't need to see people's faces get that sad, stupid look of *pity.* The only reason I'm telling you is that I had a dream the other night—you shrinks like dreams, right? And I haven't been able to get it out of my head and I thought—"

John stops, sits up.

"Margo heard me scream last night. I woke up screaming at four in the fucking morning. And I can't be doing shit like that."

I want to say that what John sees in me isn't pity at all—that it's compassion and empathy and even a kind of love. But John doesn't let anyone touch or be touched by him, which leaves him alone in already isolating circumstances. Losing somebody you love is such a profoundly lonely experience, something only you endure in your own particular way. I think about how gutted and alone John must have felt as a six-year-old when his mom died and then again as a dad when his own six-year-old died. But I don't say that right now. I can tell that John's feeling what therapists call *flooded,* meaning that his nervous system is in overdrive, and when people feel flooded, it's best to wait a beat. We do this with couples when one person is so overwhelmed by anger or hurt that all he can do is lash out or shut down. The person needs a few minutes for his nervous system to reset before he can take anything in.

"Tell me about the dream," I say.

Miraculously, he doesn't balk. I notice that John isn't fighting me right now, and he hasn't once looked over at his phone today. He hasn't even taken it out of his pocket. He simply sits up, folds his legs under him, takes a breath, and begins.

"So, Gabe is sixteen. I mean, he *was,* in the dream—"

I nod.

"Okay, so he's sixteen and he's taking his driving test. He's been waiting for this day and now it's here. We're standing outside by the car in the parking lot at the DMV and Gabe looks so confident. He's started to shave, and I see some stubble, and I notice how grown up he's become." John's voice breaks.

"What was that like, seeing him so grown up?"

John smiles. "I felt proud. So proud of who he was. But also, I don't know, sad. Like he was going to leave for college soon. *Did I spend enough time with him? Had I been a good father?* I was trying not to cry—in the dream, I mean—and I didn't know if these were tears of pride or regret or . . . who the fuck knows. Anyway—"

John looks away, like he's trying not to cry now.

"So we're talking about what he's going to do after the test—he says he's going out with some friends—and I'm telling him to make sure never to get in the car if he's been drinking or if his friends have. And he says, 'I *know*, Dad. I'm not an *idiot*.' The way teenagers do, you know? And then I go on to tell him never to text and drive."

John laughs, a dark laugh. "How on the nose is this dream, Sherlock?"

I don't smile. I bring him back by waiting.

"Anyway," he continues, "the examiner walks over, and Gabe and I give each other a thumbs-up—like the day I dropped him off at kindergarten right before he walked into his classroom. A quick *You'll do great.* But something about the examiner makes me nervous."

"How so?" I ask.

"I just have a bad feeling about her. Unsettling. I don't trust her. Like she's got it in for Gabe and he won't pass the test. Anyway, I watch them pull away. I see Gabe make his first right turn out of the driveway and it goes well. So I start to relax, but then Margo calls. She says that my mom keeps calling and Margo wants to know if she should pick up the phone. In the dream my mom is still alive, and I don't know why Margo's asking me this, why she doesn't just answer the goddamned phone. Why the hell wouldn't she pick up? So she says, 'Remember, we agreed, don't pick up the phone unless somebody's dying?' And all of a sudden I think that if Margo picks up the phone, it means my mom is dying. That she'll die. But if Margo *doesn't* pick up, nobody's dying—my mom's not dying.

"So I say, 'You're right. Whatever you do, *don't* pick up the phone. Let it ring.'

"So we hang up and I'm still waiting for Gabe at the DMV. I look at my watch. Where are they? They said they'd be back in twenty minutes. Thirty minutes go by. Forty. Then the examiner returns but Gabe isn't there. She walks toward me, and I know.

"'I'm sorry,' she says. 'There's been an accident. A man on his cell phone.' And that's when I see that the examiner is *my mom*. She's the one telling me that Gabe is dead. And that's why she was calling Margo over and over, because somebody *was* dying—it was Gabe. Some idiot on a cell phone killed him while he was taking his driving test!

"So I say, 'Who is this man? Have you called the police? I'll murder him!' And my mom just looks at me. And I realize that the man is me. *I* killed Gabe."

John takes a breath, then continues his story. After Gabe died, he says, he and Margo bitterly blamed each other. In the emergency room, Margo growled at John, "A gift? You said the phone was a gift? *Gabe was the gift, you fucking moron.*" Later, after the toxicology report indicated that the driver was drunk, Margo apologized to John, but he knew that deep down, Margo still blamed him. He knew because, deep down, John blamed *her.* Part of him felt that *she* was responsible, that if she hadn't been so stubborn and had just looked at the caller ID, John would have had his hand on the wheel and reacted more quickly to the swerving drunk driver, getting them out of harm's way.

The terrible thing, he says, is that nobody will ever know who was responsible. The driver might have hit them anyway, or they might have avoided him if they hadn't been distracted by their argument.

It's the not knowing that torments John.

I think about how it's the not knowing that torments all of us. Not knowing why your boyfriend left. Not knowing what's wrong with your body. Not knowing if you could have saved your son. At a certain point, we all have to come to terms with the unknown and the unknowable. Sometimes we'll never know why.

"Anyway," John says, returning to the dream, "at that point I wake up screaming. And you know what I say? I yell, '*Daddyyyyyyy!*' Gabe's last word. And Margo hears this and freaks out. She runs into the bathroom and cries."

"Did you?" I say.

"What?"

"Cry."

John shakes his head.

"Why not?"

John sighs, as if the answer's obvious. "Because Margo's in the bathroom having a breakdown. What am I gonna do, have a breakdown too?"

"I don't know. If I had that kind of dream and woke up screaming, I might be pretty shaken by it. I might feel all kinds of things—rage, guilt, sadness, despair. And I might need to let some of it out, open the pressure valve a bit. I don't know what I'd do. Maybe I'd do what you did, which is also a reasonable reaction to an intolerable situation—numb out, try to ignore what I felt, hold it together. But I think at some point I'd just explode."

John shakes his head. "Let me tell you something," he says, locking his eyes on mine. There's an intensity in his voice. "I'm a parent. I have two girls. I won't let them down. I *will not* be a basket case and ruin their childhoods. I *will not* leave them with two parents who are haunted by the ghost of their son. They deserve better than that. What happened isn't their fault. It's *ours*. And it's our responsibility to be there for them, to have our shit together for them."

I think about his idea of having his shit together for his kids. How he feels that he failed Gabe and doesn't want to fail the others. How he feels that keeping the pain locked up will protect them. And I decide to tell him about my father's brother, Jack.

Until he was six years old, the age that John was when his mother died and the age Gabe was when he died, my father believed that he and his sister were their parents' only kids. Then one day, my father was rummaging around in the attic and came across a box of photos of a little boy, from birth all the way to about school age.

"Who's that?" he asked his dad. The boy was my father's brother, Jack, who had died at age five from pneumonia. Jack had never been mentioned before. My father was born a few years after his death. His parents believed that not talking about Jack was a way of keeping their shit together for their kids. But their six-year-old was shocked and confused. He wanted to talk about Jack—Why didn't they tell him? What happened to Jack's clothes? His toys? Were they in the attic with the photos? Why didn't they ever talk about Jack? If he—the little boy who would one day be my father—died, would they forget all about him too?

"You're so focused on being a good dad," I say to John, "but maybe part of being a good dad is allowing yourself the full range of human emotions, of really living, even if living fully can sometimes be harder than not. You can feel your feelings privately, or with Margo, or here with me—you can let them out in the adult sphere—and doing that might allow you to be more alive with your kids. It might be a different way of keeping your shit together for them. It might even be confusing for them if Gabe is never mentioned. And allowing yourself to rage or cry or sit with the despair at times might be more manageable if Gabe were given some air in your household and not tucked away in a box in the proverbial attic."

John shakes his head. "I don't want to be like Margo," he says. "She cries at the slightest things. Sometimes it seems like she'll never stop crying, and I can't live that way. It seems like nothing has changed for her and at some point, you have to make a decision to move on. I've chosen to move on. Margo hasn't."

I picture Margo sitting on the couch near Wendell, hugging my favorite pillow and telling him how alone she feels in her pain, how she's bearing it all herself while her husband is in his closed-off world. And then I think about how alone John must feel, watching his wife's pain and not being able to bear the sight of it.

"I know it looks that way," I say finally. "But I wonder if part of why Margo is like this is that she's been doing double duty. Maybe all of this time, she's been crying for both of you."

John's forehead furrows, then he looks down at his lap. A few tears land on his black designer jeans, slowly at first, then quickly, like a waterfall, faster than he can wipe them, and finally he stops trying. These are the tears he's been holding in for the past six years.

Or maybe more than thirty.

While he's crying, it occurs to me that what I'd seen as a theme with John—the argument with Margo about letting their daughter have a cell phone, the back-and-forth with me about using it in my office—had far deeper meaning than I'd realized. I remember holding hands at the Lakers game with my son—*Enjoy it while it lasts*—and John's comment when he arrived today. "You win . . . the pleasure of my company." But perhaps he won the pleasure of mine. After all, he chose to come here today and tell me all of this.

I think, too, about how there are many ways to defend oneself from the unspeakable. Here's one: you split off unwanted parts of yourself, hide behind a false self, and develop narcissistic traits. You say, *Yeah, this catastrophic thing has happened, but I'm A-Okay. Nothing can touch me because I'm special. A special surprise.* When John was a boy, wrapping himself in the memory of his mother's delight was a way to shield himself from the horror of life's utter unpredictability. He may have comforted himself this way as an adult too, clinging to how special he was after Gabe died. Because the one certainty that John can count on in this world is that he is a special person surrounded by idiots.

Through his tears, John says that this is exactly what he didn't want to happen, that he didn't come here to have a breakdown.

But I assure him that he's not breaking down; he's breaking open.

39

How Humans Change

Theories involving stages abound in psychology, no doubt because their order, clarity, and predictability are appealing. Anyone who has taken an introductory psychology course has likely encountered the developmental-stage models posited by Freud, Jung, Erikson, Piaget, and Maslow.

But there's one stage model I keep in mind nearly every minute of every session—the stages of change. If therapy is about guiding people from where they are now to where they'd like to be, we must always consider: How do humans actually change?

In the 1980s, a psychologist named James Prochaska developed the transtheoretical model of behavior change (TTM) based on research showing that people generally don't "just do it," as Nike (or a new year's resolution) might have it, but instead tend to move through a series of sequential stages that look like this:

Stage 1: Pre-contemplation
Stage 2: Contemplation
Stage 3: Preparation
Stage 4: Action
Stage 5: Maintenance

So let's say you want to make a change—exercise more, end a relationship, or even try therapy for the first time. Before you get to that point, you're in the first stage, pre-contemplation, which is to say, you're not even thinking about changing. Some therapists might liken this to denial, meaning that you don't realize you might have a problem. When Charlotte first came to me, she presented herself as a social drinker; I realized that she was in the pre-contemplation stage as she talked about her mother's tendency to self-medicate with alcohol but failed to see any connection to her own alcohol use. When I challenged her on this, she shut down, got irritated ("People my age go out and drink!"), or engaged in "what-aboutery," the practice of diverting attention from the difficulty under discussion by raising a different problematic issue. ("Never mind X, what about Y?")

Of course, therapists aren't persuaders. We can't convince an anorexic to eat. We can't convince an alcoholic not to drink. We can't convince people not to be self-destructive, because for now, the self-destruction serves them. What we can do is try to help them understand themselves better and show them how to ask themselves the right questions until something happens—either internally or externally—that leads them to do their own persuading.

It was Charlotte's car accident and DUI that moved her into the next stage, contemplation.

Contemplation is rife with ambivalence. If pre-contemplation is denial, contemplation might be likened to resistance. Here, the person recognizes the problem, is willing to talk about it, and isn't opposed (in theory) to taking action but just can't seem to get herself to do it. So while Charlotte was concerned by her DUI and the subsequent mandate to participate in an addiction program—which she grudgingly attended and only after failing to take the course in time and having to hire a lawyer (at great expense) to get her deadline extended—she wasn't ready to make any changes to her drinking.

People often start therapy during the contemplation stage. A woman in a long-distance relationship says that her boyfriend keeps delaying his planned move to her city, and she acknowledges that he's probably not coming—but she won't break up with him. A man knows that his wife has been having an affair, but when we talk about it, he comes up with excuses for where she might be when she's not answering her texts so that he doesn't have to confront her. Here people procrastinate or self-sabotage as a way to stave off change—even positive change—because they're reluctant to give something up without knowing what they'll get in its place. The hiccup at this stage is that change involves the loss of the old and the anxiety of the new. Although often maddening for friends and partners to witness, this hamster wheel is part of the process; people need to do the same thing over and over a seemingly ridiculous number of times before they're ready to change.

Charlotte talked about trying to "cut back" on her drinking, about having two glasses of wine each night instead of three or skipping cocktails at brunch if she would be drinking again at dinner (and, of course, *after* dinner). She could acknowledge the role that alcohol was playing in her life, its anxiety-muting effects, but she couldn't find an alternative way to manage her feelings, even with medication prescribed by a psychiatrist.

To help with her anxiety, we decided to add a second therapy session each week. During this time, she drank less, and for a while she believed that this would be enough to control her drinking. But coming twice a week created its own problems—Charlotte was once again convinced that she was addicted to me—so she went back to the once-a-week schedule. When, in an opportune moment (say, after she'd mentioned getting drunk on a date), I'd bring up the idea of an outpatient treatment program, she'd shake her head. No way.

"Those programs make you stop completely," she'd say. "I want to be able to have a drink at dinner. It's socially awkward not to drink when everyone else is."

"It's socially awkward getting drunk too," I'd say, to which she'd reply, "Yeah, but I'm cutting back." And by then it was true; she *was* cutting back. And she was reading up on addiction online, landing her in stage three, preparation. For Charlotte, it was hard to concede the lifelong fight she'd been in with her parents: "I won't change, Mom and Dad, until you treat me the way I want to be treated." She'd made a subconscious bargain that she'd change her habits only if her parents changed theirs, a lose-lose pact if there ever was one. In fact, her relationship with her parents couldn't change until she had something new to bring to it.

Two months later, Charlotte waltzed in, unpacked the contents of her bag onto the arms of her throne, and said, "So, I have a question." Did I know of any good outpatient alcohol-treatment programs? She had entered stage four, action.

In the action stage, Charlotte dutifully spent three nights per week in an addiction-treatment program, using the group as a substitute for the wine drinking she used to do at that time. She stopped drinking entirely.

The goal, of course, is to get to the final stage, maintenance, which means that the person has maintained the change for a significant period. That's not to say that people don't backslide, like in a game of Chutes and Ladders. Stress or certain triggers for the old behavior (a particular restaurant, a call from an old drinking buddy) can result in relapse. This stage is hard because the behaviors people want to modify are embedded in the fabric of their lives; people with addiction issues (whether that addiction is to a substance, drama, negativity, or self-defeating ways of being) tend to hang out with other addicts. But by the time a person is in maintenance, she can usually get back on track with the right support.

Without wine or vodka, Charlotte was able to focus better; her memory improved, and she felt less tired and more motivated. She applied to graduate school. She got involved with a charitable organization for animals that she felt passionate about. She was also able to talk with me about her difficult relationship with her mother for the first time in her life and begin to interact with her in a calmer, less reactive way. She stayed away from "friends" who invited her out to have just one birthday drink—"Because you only turn twenty-seven once, right?" Instead, she spent the night of her birthday with a new group of friends who served her her favorite meal and toasted her with a creative assortment of festive nonalcoholic drinks.

But there was one addiction she couldn't quite kick: the Dude.

Full disclosure: I disliked the Dude. His swagger, his dishonesty, his dicking Charlotte around—literally and figuratively. One week he was with his girlfriend, the next he wasn't. One month he was with Charlotte, the next he wasn't. *I'm onto you* I wanted my look to say when I opened the waiting-room door and saw him sitting near Charlotte. I felt protective, like the mommy dog in the driver's seat in the car commercial. But I stayed out of the fray.

Charlotte would often wiggle her thumbs in the air while narrating the latest installment: "And then I said . . ." "And then he's like . . ." "And then I'm like . . ."

"You had this conversation in text?" I asked, surprised, the first time she did this. When I suggested that discussing the state of their relationship via text might be limiting—you can't look into somebody's eyes or take someone's hand to offer reassurance even though you're upset—she replied, "Oh, no, we use emojis too."

I thought of the deafening silence and twitching foot that clued me in to Boyfriend's desire to break up; had we been texting about the movie tickets that night, he might have waited months more to tell me. But with Charlotte, I knew I sounded like an old fogy; her generation wasn't going to change, so *I'd* have to change to keep up with the times.

Today Charlotte's eyes are red. She found out on Instagram that the Dude is back with his supposedly *ex*-girlfriend.

"He keeps saying he wants to change, but then this happens," she says, sighing. "Do you think he'll ever change?"

I think about the stages of change—where Charlotte is, where the Dude might be—and about how Charlotte's father's constant disappearing act is being replayed with the Dude. It's hard for her to accept that while *she* might change, other people might not.

"He won't change, will he?" she says.

"He may not want to change," I say gently. "And your father might not either."

Charlotte squeezes her lips together, as if considering a possibility that had never occurred to her before. After all of her efforts to try to get these men to love her the way she wants to be loved, she can't change them because *they don't want to change*. This is a familiar scenario in therapy. A patient's boyfriend doesn't *want* to stop smoking pot and watching video games on weekends. A patient's child doesn't *want* to study harder for tests at the expense of doing musical productions. A patient's spouse doesn't *want* to travel less for work. Sometimes the changes you want in another person aren't on that person's agenda—even if he tells you they are.

"But—" she says, then stops herself.

I watch her, sensing the shift happening inside her.

"I keep trying to get them to change," she says, almost to herself.

I nod. He won't change, so she'll have to.

Every relationship is a dance. The Dude does his dance steps (approach/retreat), and Charlotte does hers (approach/get hurt)—that's how they dance. But once Charlotte changes her steps, one of two things will happen—the Dude will be forced to change his steps so that he doesn't trip and fall down, or he'll simply walk off the dance floor and find somebody else's feet to stomp on.

Charlotte's first drink after four months of sobriety happened on Father's Day, when her dad was supposed to fly into town to be with her but canceled at the last minute. That was three months ago. She didn't like that dance, so she changed her steps. She hasn't had a drink since.

"I need to stop seeing the Dude," she says now.

I smile as if to say, *That sounds familiar.*

"No, really—I mean it this time," she says, but she smiles too. It's been her mantra for months while in preparation. "Can I change the time of my appointment?" she asks. Today she's ready for action.

"Of course," I say, recalling that I'd suggested this before so that Charlotte wouldn't have to sit with the Dude in the waiting room each week, but Charlotte hadn't been ready to consider it. I offer her a different day and time and she puts the appointment into her phone.

At the end of our session, Charlotte gathers up her myriad belongings, walks to the door, and, as always, stops, stalling. "Well, see you on *Monday*," she whispers, knowing we've pulled one over on the Dude, who will likely wonder why Charlotte's not there at their regular Thursday time. *Let him wonder,* I think.

As Charlotte heads down the hallway, the Dude comes out of his session, and Mike and I nod hello, poker-faced.

Maybe the Dude told Mike about the girlfriend, and they spent the session talking about his tendency to juggle people, to mislead, to cheat.

("Oh, so *that's* his issue," Charlotte once said after he'd done this to her twice.) Or maybe the Dude didn't mention it to Mike at all. Maybe he's not ready to change. Or maybe he's just not interested in changing.

When I bring this up in my consultation group the next day, Ian says simply, "Lori, three words: *not your patient.*"

And I realize that, like Charlotte, I need to release the Dude too.

40

Fathers

During a belated New Year's cleaning, I come across my grad-school course-work on the Austrian psychiatrist Viktor Frankl. Scanning my notes, I begin to remember his story.

Frankl was born in 1905, and as a boy, he became intensely interested in psychology. By high school, he began an active correspondence with Freud. He went on to study medicine and lecture on the intersection of psychology and philosophy, or what he called *logotherapy,* from the Greek word *logos,* or "meaning." Whereas Freud believed that people are driven to seek pleasure and avoid pain (his famous pleasure principle), Frankl maintained that people's primary drive isn't toward pleasure but toward finding meaning in their lives.

He was in his thirties when World War II broke out, putting him, a Jew, in jeopardy. Offered immigration to the United States, he turned it down so as not to abandon his parents, and a year later, the Nazis forced Frankl and his wife to have her pregnancy terminated. In a matter of months, he and other family members were deported to concentration camps, and when Frankl was finally freed, three years later, he learned that the Nazis had killed his wife, his brother, and both of his parents.

Freedom under these circumstances might have led to despair. After all, the hope of what awaited Frankl and his fellow prisoners upon their release was now gone—the people they cared about were dead, their families and friends wiped out. But Frankl wrote what became an extraordinary treatise on resilience and spiritual salvation, known in English as *Man's Search for Meaning*. In it, he shares his theory of logotherapy as it relates not just to the horrors of concentration camps but also to more mundane struggles.

He wrote, "Everything can be taken from a man but one thing: the last of the human freedoms—to choose one's attitude in any given set of circumstances."

Indeed, Frankl remarried, had a daughter, published prolifically, and spoke around the world until his death at age ninety-two.

Rereading these notes, I thought of my conversations with Wendell. Scribbled in my grad-school spiral were the words *Reacting vs. responding = reflexive vs. chosen.* We can choose our response, Frankl was saying, even under the specter of death. The same was true of John's loss of his mother and son, Julie's illness, Rita's regrettable past, and Charlotte's upbringing. I couldn't think of a single patient to whom Frankl's ideas didn't apply, whether it was about extreme trauma or an interaction with a difficult family member. More than sixty years later, Wendell was saying I could choose too—that the jail cell was open on both sides.

I particularly liked this line from Frankl's book: "Between stimulus and response there is a space. In that space is our power to choose our response. In our response lies our growth and our freedom."

I'd never emailed Wendell for anything other than scheduling issues, but I was so stunned by the parallel that I wanted to share it with him. I pulled up his email and typed, *This is what we were talking about. The trick, I suppose, is to find that elusive "space."*

A few hours later, he replied.

I've always appreciated Frankl. Beautiful quote. See you Wednesday.

It was typical Wendell—warm and genuine but clearly stating that therapy takes place face-to-face. I remembered our first phone call, when he'd said almost nothing, and how surprisingly interactive he was once we met.

Still, I carried around his reply in my head all week. I could have sent that quote to various friends who would have appreciated it too, but it wouldn't have been the same. Wendell and I existed in a separate universe where he saw me in ways that even those close to me didn't. Of course, it's also true that my family and friends saw aspects of me that Wendell would never see, but nobody would quite understand the subtext of my email as precisely as Wendell would.

The following Wednesday, Wendell brings up the email. He tells me that he shared the quote with his wife, who, he says, is going to use it for a talk she's giving. He's never mentioned his wife, though I know everything about her from my long-ago Google binge.

"What does your wife do?" I ask as if I haven't seen her LinkedIn profile. He tells me about her work at a nonprofit.

"Oh, interesting," I reply, but the word *interesting* sounds unnaturally high-pitched.

Wendell watches me. I quickly change the subject.

For a split second, I think about what I might do if I were the therapist here. Sometimes I want to say, *I wouldn't do it that way,* but I know that's like back-seat driving. I need to be the patient, which means I need to relinquish control. It may seem like the patient controls the session, deciding what to say or not, setting the agenda or topic. But therapists pull the strings in our own ways—in what we say or don't say, what we respond to or hold on to for later, what we give attention to and what we don't.

Later in the session, I'm talking about my father. I tell Wendell that he'd been in the hospital again due to his heart condition, and though he's okay now, I'm afraid of losing him. I'm aware in a new way of just how frail he is, and I'm starting to absorb the reality that he won't be here forever.

"I can't picture a world without him in it," I say. "I can't imagine not being able to call and hear his voice or ask his advice or laugh together about something we both find funny." I think about how there's nothing in the world like laughing with my dad. I think about how knowledgeable he is on almost any topic and how fully he loves me and how kind he is— not just to me, but to everyone. The first thing people say about my father isn't how smart or funny he is, though he is both. The first thing they say is "He's so sweet."

I tell Wendell about the time I was in college on the East Coast, missing home and unsure if I wanted to stay there. My father heard the pain in
my voice and got on a plane and flew three thousand miles to sit with me
on a park bench across from my dorm, in the cold winter weather, and just
listen. He listened to me for two more days, and I felt better, and he went
home. I haven't thought about this in years.

I also recount what happened this past weekend after my son's basketball game. As the boys ran off to celebrate their victory, my father took me
aside and told me that he'd just been at a friend's funeral the day before.
After the funeral, he explained, he'd gone up to the friend's daughter, now
in her thirties, and said, "Your father was so proud of you. Every conversation we had, he'd say, 'I'm so proud of Christina,' and he'd tell me about
all you were doing!" This was absolutely true, but Christina was shocked.

"He never told me that," she said, bursting into tears. My father was
floored until he realized that he wasn't sure if he'd told *me* how he felt about
me. Had he done it at all—or enough?

"So," my father said outside the gym, "I want to make sure that I've
told you how proud of you I am. I want to make sure *you know*." He said
it in such a shy way, obviously uncomfortable having this kind of interaction; he was used to listening to others but keeping his emotional world
to himself.

"I know," I said, because my father had communicated his pride to
me in countless ways, though I wasn't always listening as well as I should
have been. But that day I couldn't help hearing the subtext: *I'm going to die
sooner rather than later.* We stood there, the two of us, hugging and crying
as people passing by tried not to stare, because we both knew that this was
the beginning of my father's goodbye.

"As your eyes are opening, his are beginning to close," Wendell says
now, and I think about how bittersweet but true that is. My awakening is
happening at an opportune moment.

"I'm so glad I have this time with him and that it can be so meaningful," I say. "I wouldn't want him to abruptly die one day and feel like it's
too late, that I waited too long for us to really see each other."

Wendell nods, and I feel queasy. All of a sudden I remember that Wendell's father had died ten years ago very unexpectedly. In my Google search, I'd come across his father's obituary after I read the story of his death in his mother's family interview. Apparently, Wendell's father had been in seemingly perfect health when he'd collapsed at dinner. I wonder if my talking about my father this way might be painful for him. I also worry that if I say any more, I'll give away how much I know. So I pull back, ignoring the fact that therapists are trained to listen for what patients aren't saying.

A few weeks later, Wendell comments that for the past couple of sessions, I seem to have been editing myself—ever since, he adds, I sent him the Viktor Frankl quote and he'd mentioned his wife. He wonders (what would we therapists do without the word *wonder* to broach a sensitive topic?) how the mention of his wife has affected me.

"I haven't really thought about that," I say. It's true—I've been focused on hiding my internet search.

I look at my feet, then at Wendell's. Today's socks are a blue chevron pattern. When I lift my head, I see that Wendell is looking at me with his right eyebrow raised.

And then I realize what Wendell is getting at. He thinks that I'm jealous of his wife, that I want him all to myself! This is called romantic transference, a common reaction patients have to their therapists. But the idea that I have a crush on Wendell strikes me as hilarious.

I look at Wendell, in his beige cardigan and khakis and funky socks, his green eyes staring back at me. For a second, I imagine what it must be like to be married to Wendell. In a photo I'd found of him and his wife, they were at a charity event, arm in arm and all dressed up, Wendell smiling at the camera and his wife looking at him adoringly. I remember feeling a twinge of envy when I saw that photo, not because I was envious of his wife but because they seemed to have the kind of relationship I wanted for myself—with someone else. But the more I deny the romantic transference, the less Wendell will believe me. *The lady doth protest too much.*

There are about twenty minutes left in the session—even as a patient, I can feel the rhythm of the hour—and I know that this façade can't last forever. There's only one thing to do.

"I Googled you," I say, looking away. "I stopped stalking Boyfriend, and I ended up stalking you. When you mentioned your wife, I already knew all about her. And your mother." I pause, especially mortified by this last part. "I read that long interview with your mom."

I get ready for . . . I don't know what. Something bad to happen. A tornado to enter the room and alter our connection in some intangible but irreparable way. I wait for everything to feel distant, different, changed between us. But instead, the opposite happens. It feels as though the storm came in, passed through the room, and left not ruins but a clearing in its wake.

I feel lighter, relieved of a burden. Sharing difficult truths might come with a cost—the need to face them—but there's also a reward: freedom. The truth releases us from shame.

Wendell nods, and we sit there in a wordless conversation. Me: *I'm sorry. I shouldn't have done that. That was so invasive.* Him: *It's okay. I understand. It's natural to be curious.* Me: *I'm happy for you—for the loving family that you have.* Him: *Thank you. I hope you will have this one day too.*

And then we have a version of that conversation aloud. We also talk about my curiosity. Why I kept it a secret. What it was like to hold that secret and also know so much about him. What I imagined would happen between us if I revealed it—and how it feels now that I have. And because I'm a therapist—or maybe because I'm a patient and I just need to know—I ask him what it's like to learn that I stalked him. Is there anything I found that he wishes I didn't know? Does he feel different about me, about us?

Only one of his answers shocks me: He has never seen the interview with his mother! He didn't know it existed online. He knew that his mother had done an interview for that organization, but he thought it was for their internal archives. I ask if he worries that other patients might come across it and he sits back and takes a breath. For the first time, I see his forehead scrunch up.

"I don't know," he says after a beat. "I'll have to think about it."

Frankl's quote pops into my mind again. He's making space between stimulus and response in order to choose his freedom.

Our time is up, so Wendell gives his legs the usual two pats and stands. We head for the exit, but at the threshold, I stop.

"I'm sorry about your father," I say. After all, the jig is up. He knows I know the whole story.

Wendell smiles. "Thank you."

"Do you miss him?" I ask.

"Every day," he says. "Not a day goes by that I don't miss him."

"Not a day will go by that I won't miss my father either," I say.

He nods, and we stand there, thinking about our fathers together. When he steps back to open the door for me, I see a hint of moisture in his eyes.

There's so much more I want to ask him. Is he at peace with where things were left when his father collapsed? I think about the ways in which sons and fathers can get tangled up in expectations and yearnings for approval. Did his father ever tell him he was proud of him, not despite his rejecting the family business and carving out his own path but *because* of it?

I won't learn more about Wendell's father, but we'll have many discussions in the coming weeks and months about mine. And through these discussions, it will become clear that by seeking a male therapist, I had hoped to get an objective opinion on the breakup, but instead, I got a version of my father.

Because my father, too, shows me how it feels to be exquisitely seen.

41

Integrity Versus Despair

Rita is sitting across from me in her smart slacks and sensible shoes giving a detailed commentary on why her life is hopeless. Her session, like most of her sessions, feels like a dirge, which is all the more confounding because between bouts of insisting that nothing will ever change, she has been making changes both minute and monumental.

Back when she and Myron were friends, pre-Randie, Myron had made Rita a website so that she could catalog her art online. This way, he said, she could keep her pieces organized and also share them with others. But Rita didn't think she needed a website. "Who's going to look at it?" she asked.

"I will," Myron said. Three weeks later, Rita had a website with exactly one visitor. Well, two, if you counted Rita who, truth be told, loved it. It looked so *professional*. Those first weeks, she spent hours each day clicking around on her site, coming up with ideas for new projects, imagining them on display. But her excitement waned when Myron started dating Randie. Why bother posting anything new now? She didn't know how to work the darn thing anyway.

Then one afternoon, Rita ran into Myron and Randie holding hands in the lobby, and, to make herself feel better, she hightailed it to the art-supply store and splurged on materials. Carrying the goods up to her apartment, she tripped over a couple of kids who darted out from nowhere. The

bags of brushes, acrylics, and gouaches, the canvases and cartons of clay—
all of it came tumbling down, along with Rita, who was caught at the last
second by a strong pair of hands.

The hands belonged to the kids' father, Kyle, whom Rita had seen
many times through her peephole but had never met. He was the dad from
the "Hello, family" apartment across from hers, and he'd saved his neighbor from a potential broken hip.

After Kyle asked the kids to apologize for not looking where they were
going, they all gathered up Rita's supplies and carried them into her apartment. There, in her living room turned art studio, they saw Rita's work
covering the entire space—portraits and abstracts on easels, ceramics near
a potter's wheel, charcoals in progress hanging from a board on the wall.
The kids were in heaven. And Kyle was stunned. *You have talent,* he said.
Real talent. You should sell these.

They went back to their apartment, and shortly after, when Kyle's wife,
Anna, arrived home ("Hello, family!"), the kids begged their mom to go
across the hall with them to see "the art lady's" living room. Rita was sta-
tioned, as usual, at the peephole, and the knock came before Rita had a
chance to back away. She counted to five, asked, "Who is it?" and greeted
them with mock surprise.

Soon Rita was teaching art to Sophia and Alice, ages five and seven,
and often joined the "Hello, family" for, well, family dinner. One afternoon, Anna came home and yelled, "Hello, family!" to Sophia and Alice,
who were painting in Rita's living room. The kids called back, "Hello!"
and then Alice turned to Rita and asked why she didn't answer when their
mom said hello.

"I'm not family," Rita said matter-of-factly, to which Alice replied, "Yes,
you are. You're our California grandma!" The girls' grandparents lived in
Charleston and Portland. They visited often, but it was Rita who saw them
nearly every day.

Anna, meanwhile, had hung one of Rita's paintings over the sofa in
the family's living room. Rita also painted two custom pieces for the kids'
room—a dancer for Sophia and a unicorn for Alice. The girls were elated.
Anna tried to pay Rita for her work, but Rita refused, insisting they were

gifts. Finally, Kyle, a computer programmer, convinced Rita to let him add a feature to her website, an online store. He sent out an email to the parents of Sophia's and Alice's classmates, and soon Rita was taking orders for children's custom portraits. One parent also purchased ceramics for her dining room.

Given all of these developments, I had expected Rita's mood to improve. She was coming alive, leading a less constricted life. She had people to talk to every day. She was sharing her artistic talent with others who admired it. She wasn't invisible in the same way she'd been when she first came to see me. But still, her pleasure or joy or whatever she felt ("It's nice, I suppose," was the most she would say) lived beneath a dark cloud, a running litany of how if Myron really meant what he'd said in the parking lot at the Y, he would have dated Rita instead of that disgusting Randie in the first place, how no matter how kind they were, the hello-family weren't really her family, and how she would still die alone.

She seemed to be stuck in what the psychologist Erik Erikson termed *despair*.

In the mid-1900s, Erikson came up with eight stages of psychosocial development that still guide therapists in their thinking today. Unlike Freud's stages of psycho*sexual* development, which end at puberty and focus on the id, Erikson's psycho*social* stages focus on personality development in a social context (such as how infants develop a sense of trust in others). Most important, Erikson's stages continue throughout the entire lifespan, and each interrelated stage involves a crisis that we need to get through to move on to the next. They look like this:

Infant (hope) — trust versus mistrust
Toddler (will) — autonomy versus shame
Preschooler (purpose) — initiative versus guilt
School-age child (competence) — industry versus inferiority
Adolescent (fidelity) — identity versus role confusion
Young adult (love) — intimacy versus isolation
Middle-aged adult (care) — generativity versus stagnation
Older adult (wisdom) — integrity versus despair

The eighth stage is where people Rita's age generally find themselves. Erikson maintained that, in later years, we experience a sense of integrity if we believe we have lived meaningful lives. This sense of integrity gives us a feeling of completeness so that we can better accept our approaching deaths. But if we have unresolved regrets about the past—if we think that we made poor choices or failed to accomplish important goals—we feel depressed and hopeless, which leads us to despair.

It seemed to me that Rita's current despair about Myron was tied to an old despair, and that was why it was hard for her to enjoy any of the ways her life had expanded. She was used to viewing the world from a place of deficit, and as a result, joy felt foreign to her. If you're used to feeling abandoned, if you already know what it's like for people to disappoint or reject you—well, it may not feel good, but at least there are no surprises; you know the customs in your own homeland. Once you step into foreign territory, though—if you spend time with reliable people who find you appealing and interesting—you might feel anxious and disoriented. All of a sudden, nothing's familiar. You have no landmarks, nothing to go by, and all of the predictability of the world you're used to is gone. The place you came from may not be great—it might, in fact, be pretty awful—but you knew exactly what you'd get there (disappointment, chaos, isolation, criticism).

I've talked about this with Rita, about how for so much of her life she wanted not to be invisible, to be *seen,* and now this was happening—in her relationship with her neighbors, in the people who bought her art, and in Myron's declaration of his romantic interest. These people enjoyed her company, admired her, desired her, *saw* her—and yet she seemed unable to acknowledge that anything positive was happening.

"Are you waiting for the other shoe to drop?" I ask. There's a term for this irrational fear of joy: *cherophobia* (*chero* is the Greek word for "rejoice"). People with cherophobia are like Teflon pans in terms of pleasure—it doesn't stick (though pain cakes on them as if to an ungreased surface). It's common for people with traumatic histories to expect disaster just around the corner. Instead of leaning into the goodness that comes their way, they become hypervigilant, always waiting for something to go wrong. That might be why Rita still fumbled for tissues in her purse even though she knew a fresh box was beside her on the table. Better not to get used to a full box of tissues, or a surrogate family next door, or people purchasing your art, or the man you're dreaming about giving you a big fat kiss in the parking lot. *Don't delude yourself, sister!* The second you get too comfortable—whoosh!—it will all go away. For Rita, joy isn't pleasure; it's anticipatory pain.

Rita looks up at me, nodding. "Exactly," she says. "The other shoe always drops." It did when she got to college, when she married an alcoholic, when she had two more chances at love and those went out the window too. It did when her father died and she finally—finally!—started to have a relationship with her mother, only to have her mother diagnosed with Alzheimer's, after which Rita had to care for this woman who no longer recognized her for twelve long years.

Of course, Rita didn't *have* to bring her mother into her apartment during those years—she chose to because somehow her misery served her. At the time it never occurred to her to ask if she had an obligation to take care of her mother when her mother hadn't taken care of her while she was growing up. She didn't grapple with that toughest of tough questions: *What do I owe my parents, and what do they owe me?* She could have gotten outside help for her mother. Rita considers this as we talk, but then she says that if she had to do it over, she'd do it all the same.

"I got what I deserved," she explains. She *deserves* this misery for all of her crimes—ruining her kids' lives, lacking compassion for her second husband's grief, never getting her own life together. What feels horrible to her are her recent glimmers of happiness. She feels like a fraud, like somebody who won the lottery but stole the ticket. If the people who have come into her life lately really knew her, they would be disgusted. They would run for the hills! *She's* disgusted. And even if she were to somehow fool them for a time, a few months, a year, who knows, how can she be happy when her kids are so sad—and because of her? That doesn't seem fair, does it? How can someone have done something so awful and still be asking for love?

This, she says, is why there's no hope for her. She balls up a tissue in her hand. Too much has happened. Too many mistakes were made.

I look at Rita and notice how young she appears as she tells me this —her cheeks puffed out, her arms folded across her chest. I picture her as a girl in her childhood home, her red hair pulled back neatly with a headband, wondering if she was at fault for her parents' distance from her, brooding over it alone in her room. *Are they mad at me? Have I done something to upset them, to cause them to take so little interest in me?* They'd waited so long to finally have a child; had she not lived up to what they had hoped for?

I think, too, of Rita's four children. Of their father, the lawyer, who could be so fun one minute and drunk and abusive the next. Of their mother, Rita, removed, making excuses for their father, offering promises on his behalf that they knew were lies. How confusing and harrowing their childhoods must have been. How furious they must be now. How they must not want to deal with their mother coming to them, as she had several times over the years, crying and begging for a relationship. Whatever she wants, they'd likely think, it was for one reason and one reason only: for her sake, always for her sake. My guess was that Rita's children wouldn't talk to her because they couldn't give her the one thing she seemed to want even if she'd never asked for it directly: forgiveness.

Rita and I had talked about why she hadn't protected her children, why she'd let her husband hit them, why she'd spent her time reading or painting or playing tennis or bridge instead of being present for them. And once we got past the explanations she'd given herself for years, we arrived at something she hadn't been aware of: Rita envied her children.

Rita wasn't unusual in this. Take the case of a mother who came from a household with little money and who now admonishes her child every time she gets a new pair of shoes or a new toy by saying, "Don't you realize how lucky you are?" A gift wrapped in a criticism. Or consider the father who takes his son to visit prospective colleges and spends the entire tour of the college that he himself dreamed of attending but was rejected from making negative comments about the tour guide, the curriculum, the dorms—not only embarrassing his son but possibly hurting his chances of admission.

Why do parents do this? Often, they envy their children's childhoods

—the opportunities they have; the financial or emotional stability that the parents provide; the fact that their children have their whole lives ahead of them, a stretch of time that's now in the parents' pasts. They strive to give their children all the things they themselves didn't have, but they sometimes end up, without even realizing it, resenting the kids for their good fortune.

Rita envied her kids their siblings, their comfortable childhood home with the pool, their opportunities to go to museums and travel. She envied their young, energetic parents. And it was, in part, her unconscious envy —her fury at the unfairness of it all—that kept her from allowing them to have the happy childhood she didn't, that kept her from saving them in the way she so badly wanted to be saved when she was young.

I'd brought up Rita in my consultation group. Despite her gloomy, Eeyore-like exterior, I told my colleagues, she was warm and interesting, and because I was free of the history her kids shared with her, I could enjoy Rita the way I'd enjoy a friend of a parent. I liked her quite a bit. But could her children really be expected to forgive her?

Did *I* forgive her? the group asked. I thought of my son and felt sick at the idea of anyone hitting him, of my ever allowing that to happen.

I wasn't sure.

Forgiveness is a tricky thing, in the way that apologies can be. Are you apologizing because it makes you feel better or because it will make the other person feel better? Are you sorry for what you've done or are you simply trying to placate the other person who believes you *should* be sorry for the thing you feel completely justified in having done? *Who is the apology for?*

There's a term we use in therapy: *forced forgiveness.* Sometimes people feel that in order to get past a trauma, they need to forgive whoever caused the damage—the parent who sexually assaulted them, the burglar who robbed their house, the gang member who killed their son. They're told by well-meaning people that until they can forgive, they'll hold on to the anger. Granted, for some, forgiveness can serve as a powerful release—you forgive the person who wronged you, without condoning his actions, and it allows you to move on. But too often people feel pressured to forgive and then end up believing that something's wrong with them if they can't quite get there—that they aren't enlightened enough or strong enough or compassionate enough.

So what I say is this: You can have compassion without forgiving. There are many ways to move on, and pretending to feel a certain way isn't one of them.

I once had a client named Dave who had a problematic relationship with his father. His father was, by his account, a bully—demeaning, critical, and full of himself. He had alienated both of his sons from a young age and had a distant and contentious relationship with them as adults. When his father was dying, Dave was fifty years old, married with children of his own, and he struggled with what to say at his father's funeral. What would ring true? And then he told me that as his father lay on his deathbed, he had reached out for his son's hand and said, out of the blue, "I wish I'd treated you better. I was a prick."

Dave was livid—did his father expect absolution now, at the eleventh hour? The time to make repairs, he felt, was long before you left this earth, not on the eve of your departure; you don't automatically get the gift of closure or forgiveness from a deathbed confession.

He couldn't help himself. "I don't forgive you," Dave told his dad. He hated himself for saying this, regretted it the second it came out. But after all the pain his father had put him through and all the work he'd done to create a good life for himself and his family, he'd be damned if he was going to soothe his father now with a sugary lie. He'd spent his childhood lying about how he felt. Still, Dave wondered, what kind of person says this to his dying father?

Dave had started to apologize, but his father interrupted him. "I understand," he said. "If I were you, I wouldn't forgive me either."

And then the strangest thing happened, Dave told me. Sitting there holding his father's hand, Dave felt something shift. He felt, for the first time in his life, genuine compassion. Not forgiveness, but compassion. Compassion for the sad dying man who must have had his own pain. And it was that compassion that allowed Dave to speak authentically at his father's funeral.

It was compassion, too, that helped me help Rita. I didn't have to forgive her for what she'd done with her children. As with Dave's father, that was up to Rita to reckon with. We may want others' forgiveness, but that comes from a place of self-gratification; we are asking forgiveness of others to avoid the harder work of forgiving ourselves.

I thought of something Wendell had said to me after I'd listed my own regrettable missteps that I took great pleasure in punishing myself for: "How long do you think the sentence for this crime should be? A year? Five? Ten?" Many of us torture ourselves over our mistakes for decades, even after we've genuinely attempted to make amends. How reasonable is that sentence?

It's true that in Rita's case, her children's lives were significantly affected by their parents' failures. She and her children would always feel the pain of their shared pasts, but shouldn't there be some redemption? Did Rita deserve to be persecuted day after day, year after year? I wanted to be realistic about the considerable scars they all bore, but I didn't want to be Rita's warden.

I can't help but think about her evolving relationship with the hello-family girls next door; what if she had been able to offer her four children what she offers them?

I put the question to Rita: "What should your sentence be, as you approach seventy, for the crimes you committed in your twenties and thirties? They were significant crimes, yes. But you've felt remorse for decades, and you've tried to make repairs. Shouldn't you have been released by now, or at least out on parole? What do you think is a fair sentence for your crimes?"

Rita considers this for a moment. "Life in prison," she says.

"Well," I say. "That's what you got. But I'm not sure that a jury that included Myron or the hello-family would agree."

"But the people I care most about, my kids—they'll never forgive me."

I nod. "We don't know what they're going to do. But it doesn't help them in any way for you to be miserable. Your misery doesn't change *their* situation. You can't lessen their misery by carrying it for them inside you. It doesn't work that way. There are ways for you to be a better mother to them at this point in all of your lives. Sentencing yourself to life in prison isn't one of them." I notice that I have Rita's attention. "There's only one person in this entire world who benefits from you not being able to enjoy anything good in your life."

Rita's forehead becomes a series of lines. "Who?"

"You," I say.

I point out to her that pain can be protective; staying in a depressed place can be a form of avoidance. Safe inside her shell of pain, she doesn't have to face anything, nor does she have to emerge into the world, where she might get hurt again. Her inner critic serves her: *I don't have to take any action because I'm worthless.* And there's another benefit to her misery: she may feel that she stays alive in her kids' minds if they relish her suffering. At least *somebody* has her in mind, even in a negative way—and in this sense, she's not completely forgotten.

She looks up from her tissue, as if considering the pain that she's carried for decades in an entirely new way. For maybe the first time, Rita seems to see the crisis she has been in the midst of—the battle between what Erik Erikson called integrity and despair.

Which, I wonder, will she choose?

42

My *Neshama*

I'm at lunch with my colleague Caroline.

We're catching up, talking about our practices, when Caroline asks if the Wendell referral she gave me a while back ever worked out for my friend. As an aside, she says that our call brought back memories from when she and Wendell were in graduate school together. A classmate of theirs had a massive crush on him, but it wasn't reciprocated, and Wendell actually started dating another—

Whoa! I stop her. I can't hear this. The referral, I admit, was for me.

Caroline looks shocked for a second, and then she laughs and iced tea begins spurting from her nose. "Sorry," she says, wiping her face with a napkin. "I thought I was referring a married guy to him. I just can't imagine *you* with Wendell." I understand what she means. It's hard to envision somebody you know as the patient of somebody else you know, especially if you knew that person back in graduate school. You know too much about both of them.

I tell her I was ashamed back then—about my breakup, my book fiasco, my health issues—and she shares her own struggles with trying to conceive a second child. Near the end of our lunch, she also tells me about a difficult patient and how she had no idea during the initial consultation how difficult this patient would be—how abrasive, demanding . . . entitled.

"I have one too," I say, thinking about John, "but over time, I've come to like him quite a bit—to care about him deeply."

"I hope mine works out that way," Caroline says. Then, an afterthought: "But if not, could I send her to you? Do you have the time?" I can tell from her tone that she's kidding—mostly. I remember talking to my consultation group early on about John and his enormous ego and constant put-downs. Ian had quipped: "Well, if it doesn't work out, just make sure you refer him to somebody you dislike."

"Oh, no," I say now, shaking my head. "Don't send her to me."

"Then I'll refer her to Wendell!" Caroline says. And we laugh.

"So," I say to Wendell the following Wednesday morning. "I had lunch with Caroline last week."

He's silent, but his magnet eyes are on me. I start telling him how Caroline felt about her patient and how sometimes I feel that way about patients, how every therapist does, but still, I say, it bothers me. Are we judging people too harshly? Do we not have enough empathy?

"I can't pinpoint why," I continue, "but I've felt strange about that conversation all week. It makes me uncomfortable in a way it hadn't at lunch, and—"

Wendell's brow is furrowed, as though he's trying to follow my train of thought.

"I think as a profession," I say, attempting to clarify, "we can't keep it all inside, but at the same time—"

"Do you have a question for me?" Wendell asks, interrupting.

I realize I do. I have many: Does Wendell talk about me with his colleagues at lunch? Do I *still* feel to him like my patient Becca felt to me before I stopped seeing her?

Wendell had used the singular, though—not "Do you have *questions* for me?" but "Do you have *a question* for me?" He did that, I recognize, because all of my questions boil down to an essential one, a question so loaded that I don't know how to say it aloud. Is there anything that makes us feel more vulnerable than asking someone, *Do you like me?*

It seems that being a therapist hasn't made me immune to responding to Wendell in the ways that patients respond to me. I get frustrated with him. I resent being charged for a cancellation when I'm sick (even though I have the same cancellation policy). I don't always tell him everything I should, and I unwittingly (or wittingly) distort what he says. I've always assumed that when Wendell closed his eyes in our sessions, it was to give him space to think something through. But now I wonder if it's more of a reset button. Perhaps he's saying to himself, *Have compassion, have compassion, have compassion,* the way I used to do with John.

Like most patients, I want my therapist to enjoy my company and have respect for me, but, ultimately, I want to *matter* to him. Feeling deep in your cells that you matter is part of the alchemy that takes place in good therapy.

The humanistic psychologist Carl Rogers practiced what he called client-centered therapy, a central tenet of which was *unconditional positive regard.* His switch from using the term *patient* to *client* was representative of his attitude toward the people he worked with. Rogers believed that a positive therapist-client relationship was an essential part of the cure, not just a means to an end—a groundbreaking concept when he introduced it in the mid-twentieth century.

But unconditional positive regard doesn't mean the therapist necessarily *likes* the client. It means that the therapist is warm and nonjudgmental and, most of all, genuinely believes in the client's ability to grow if nurtured in an encouraging and accepting environment. It's a framework for valuing and respecting the person's "right to determination" even if her choices are at odds with yours. Unconditional positive regard is an attitude, not a feeling.

I want more than Wendell's unconditional positive regard—I want him to like me. My question, it turns out, isn't only about discovering whether I matter to Wendell. It's also about acknowledging how much he matters to me.

"Do you like me?" I squeak out, feeling pathetic and awkward. I mean, what can he possibly say? He's not going to say no. Even if he doesn't like me, he could throw it back to me by asking, "What do you think?" or "I wonder why you're asking this now?" Or he could say what I might have said to John if he'd asked me this question early on. I would have told him the truth of my experience, which might have been less about whether I liked him and more about how hard it was to get to know him when he kept me at arm's length.

But Wendell does none of that.

"I do like you," he says in a way that makes me feel he means it. It sounds neither rote nor gushy. It's so simple—and so unexpectedly moving in its simplicity. *Yes, I like you.*

"I like you too," I say, and Wendell smiles.

Wendell says that while I want to be liked for being smart or funny, he was talking about liking my *neshama*, which is the Hebrew word for "spirit" or "soul." The concept registers instantly.

I tell Wendell about a recent college graduate who, considering a career as a therapist, asked if I liked my patients, because, after all, that's who therapists spend their time with each day. I said that sometimes patients seem one way on the outside, but that's often because they're confusing me with others from their past who may not have seen them the way I do. Even so, I told this young woman, I feel genuine affection for my patients all the time—their tender places, their bravery, their souls. For, as Wendell is saying, their *neshamot*.

"But in a professional way, right?" the young woman persisted, and I knew that she didn't quite understand, because before I met my patients, I didn't understand either. And as a patient myself, it was hard to remember. But Wendell has just reminded me.

43

What Not to Say to
a Dying Person

"That's not a thing!" Julie says. She's talking about a coworker who had a miscarriage—a fellow cashier at Trader Joe's—and how another coworker, trying to console her, said, "Everything happens for a reason. This one just wasn't meant to be."

"'Everything happens for a reason' is not a thing!" Julie repeats. "There's no divine plan if you miscarry or have cancer or your child is murdered by a lunatic!" I know what she means. People make misguided comments about all kinds of misfortune, and Julie has been toying with the idea of writing a book she plans to call *What Not to Say to a Dying Person: A Guide for the Well-Meaning but Clueless.*

According to Julie, here are a few things not to say: *Are you* sure *you're dying? Have you gotten a second opinion? Be strong. What are your odds? You need to be less stressed. It's all about attitude. You can beat this! I know somebody who took vitamin K and was cured. I read about this new therapy that shrinks tumors—in mice, but still. You really have no family history of this?* (If Julie did, the person asking would feel safer; it could be explained by genetics.) The other day, someone told Julie, "I knew a woman who had the same kind of cancer as you." "*Knew?*" Julie said. "Um, yes," the person replied sheepishly. "She, uh, died."

As Julie goes through her list of things not to say, I think about other patients who've complained about comments people make at various difficult times: *You can still have another child. At least he lived a long life. She's in a better place now. When you're ready, you can always get another dog. It's been a year; maybe it's time to move on.*

To be sure, these comments are meant to comfort, but they're also a way of protecting the speakers from the uncomfortable feelings that somebody else's bad situation stirs up. Platitudes like these make a terrible circumstance more palatable for the person saying the words but leave the person experiencing the adversity feeling angry and alone.

"People think that if they talk about me dying, it'll become a reality when it already *is* a reality," Julie says, shaking her head. I've seen this to be true too, and not just about death. Not speaking about something doesn't make it less real. It makes it scarier. For Julie, the worst thing is the silence, people who avoid her so that they don't have to get into a conversation and say those awkward things in the first place. She'd choose awkward over ignored.

"What do you wish people would say?" I ask.

Julie thinks about this. "They can say, 'I'm so sorry.' They can say, 'How can I be helpful?' Or 'I feel so helpless but I care about you.'"

She shifts on the couch, her thinner frame not quite filling out her clothes. "They can be honest," she continues. "One person blurted out, 'I have no idea how to say the right thing here,' and I was so relieved! I told her that before I got sick, I wouldn't have known what to say either. At work when my grad students first heard, they all said, 'What will we do without you?' and that felt good, because it was an expression of how they feel about me. People have said, 'Noooooo!' and 'I'm always a phone call away if you want to talk or just go do something fun.' They remember that I'm still *me*—that I'm still their friend and not just a cancer patient, and they can talk to me about their relationships and work and the latest episode of *Game of Thrones*."

One thing that has surprised Julie about going through the process of watching herself die is how vivid her world has become. Everything that she used to take for granted produces a sense of revelation, as if she were a child again. Tastes—the sweetness of a strawberry, its juice dripping onto her chin; a buttery pastry melting in her mouth. Smells—flowers on a front lawn, a colleague's perfume, seaweed washed up on the shore, Matt's sweaty body in bed at night. Sounds—the strings on a cello, the screech of a car, her nephew's laughter. Experiences—dancing at a birthday party, people-watching at Starbucks, buying a cute dress, opening the mail. All of this, no matter how mundane, delights her to no end. She's become hyper-present. When people delude themselves into believing they have all the time in the world, she's noticed, they get lazy.

She hadn't expected to experience this pleasure in her grief, to find it invigorating, in a way. But even as she's dying, she's realized, life goes on—even as the cancer invades her body, she still checks Twitter. At first she thought, *Why would I waste even ten minutes of the time I have left checking Twitter?* And then she thought, *Why wouldn't I? I like Twitter!* She also tries not to dwell on what she's losing. "I can breathe fine now," Julie says, "but it'll get harder, and I'll grieve for that. Until then, I breathe."

Julie gives more examples of what helps when she tells people she's dying. "A hug is great," she says. "So is 'I love you.' My absolute favorite is just a plain 'I love you.'"

"Did anyone say that?" I ask. Matt did, she says. When they found out she had cancer, his first words weren't "We'll beat this!" or "Oh, fuck!" but "Jules, I love you so much." That was all she needed to know.

"Love wins," I say, referencing a story Julie once told me about the time her parents went through a rough patch and separated for five days when Julie was twelve. By the weekend, they were back together, and when she and her sister asked why, her father looked at her mother with such affection and said, "Because at the end of the day, love wins. Always remember that, girls."

Julie nods. *Love wins.*

"If I write this book," she says, "maybe I'll say that the best responses I've gotten have been from people who were genuine and didn't edit themselves." She looks at me. "Like you."

I try to remember what I'd said when Julie told me she was dying. I remember feeling uncomfortable the first time, devastated the second. I ask Julie what she remembers me saying.

She smiles. "Both times you said the same thing, and I'll never forget it, because I wasn't expecting that from a therapist."

I shake my head. Expecting what?

"You spontaneously said, in this quiet, sad voice, 'Oh, Julie'—which was the perfect response, but it's what you *didn't* say that meant the most. You teared up, but I figured that you didn't want me to see it, so I didn't say anything."

The memory takes shape in my mind. "I'm glad that you saw my tears, and you could have said something. I hope from now on, you will."

"Well, now I would. I mean, now that we've done my *obituary* together, I think I'm pretty much an open book."

A few weeks ago, Julie finished writing her obituary. We were in the midst of some important conversations at the time, talking about how she wanted to die. Who did she want with her? Where did she want to be? What would she want for comfort? What was she afraid of? What kind of memorial service or funeral did she want? What did she want people to know and when?

Even as she'd discovered hidden parts of herself since the cancer diagnosis—more spontaneity, more flexibility—she was still, at heart, a planner, and if she was going to have to contend with her early death sentence, she would do as much of it as she could the way she wanted.

In considering her obituary, we talked about what meant the most to her. There was her professional success and her passion for her research and her students. There was her Saturday-morning "home" at Trader Joe's and the sense of freedom she found there. There was Emma, who, with Julie's help in the financial-aid application process, was able to cut down her hours at Trader Joe's so that she could attend college. There were the friends she had run marathons with and the ones she did book club with. At the top of the list was her husband ("The best person in the world to go through life with," she said, "but also the best to go through death with"), her sister, and her nephew and newborn niece (Julie was their godmother).

There were her parents and four grandparents—all of whom couldn't understand how in a family with such longevity, Julie was dying so young.

"It's like we've done therapy on steroids," Julie said of everything that had happened since we met. "Like the way Matt and I say that we're doing our marriage on steroids. We have to cram it all in as quickly as possible." Julie realized, when she talked about cramming it all in, that if she was pissed off about having such a short life, it was only because it had been such a good one.

Which is why, in the end, after several drafts and revisions, Julie decided to keep her obituary simple: "For every single day of her thirty-five years," she wanted it to read, "Julie Callahan Blue was loved."

Love wins.

44

Boyfriend's Email

I'm at my desk, working on my happiness book, slogging through another chapter. I motivate myself with this thought: *If I turn in this book, next time I'll get to write something that matters (whatever that is). The sooner I finish this, the sooner I can get myself back on fresh ground (wherever that is).* I'm embracing uncertainty. And I'm actually writing the book.

My friend Jen calls, but I don't pick up. Recently I've filled her in on the missing parts of my health situation, and she's been helpful in the way Wendell has—not by finding a diagnosis but by helping me cope with a lack of one. I've been learning how to be okay with not being totally okay while also arranging consults with specialists who might take my condition more seriously. No more wandering-uterus doctors for me.

Right now, though, I have to finish this chapter—I've blocked out two hours to write. I type words and they appear on my screen, filling up page after page. I knock out the chapter the way my son does the occasional busywork at school—workmanlike, as the means to an end. I keep going until I get to the chapter's last line, then give myself a reward: I can check email *and* call Jen! I'll take a fifteen-minute break before moving ahead to the next chapter. The end is in sight—just one final section to go.

I'm chatting with Jen and scanning my emails when suddenly I gasp. In bold letters, Boyfriend's name appears in my box. I'm amazed; I haven't heard from Boyfriend in eight months, ever since I tried to get answers and brought pages of notes from those calls to Wendell's office.

"Open it!" Jen says when I tell her, but I just stare at Boyfriend's name. My stomach tightens, though in a different way than it did when I kept hoping he'd change his mind. It tightens because even if he were to say he's had some sort of epiphany and wants to be together after all, I would, without question, say no. My gut is telling me two things—that I don't want to be with him anymore and that, even so, the memory of what happened still stings. Whatever he has to say, it might upset me, and I don't want to get sidetracked by this right now. I have to finish this book I care nothing about so I can write something I *do* care about. Maybe, I tell Jen, I'll read Boyfriend's email after I crank out another chapter.

"Then send it to me and *I'll* read it," she says. "You can't make me wait like this!"

I laugh. "Fine. For *you*, I'll open it."

The email is shocking and predictable at the same time.

You won't believe who I ran into today. Leigh! She just joined the firm.

I read it to Jen. Leigh is someone that Boyfriend and I both know independently and secretly find irritating; if we were still dating, of course he'd share this juicy piece of news. But *now?* It's so out of context, so devoid of acknowledgment of what happened between us and where our conversations left off. It feels as though Boyfriend still has his head in the sand—and I'm poking mine out.

"That's it?" Jen asks. "That's all the Kid Hater has to say?"

She goes silent, waiting for my reaction. I can't help it; I'm thrilled. To me, his email is reassuringly poetic, a beautiful summary of everything I've discovered about avoidance in Wendell's office. It even reads like a haiku: three lines of five, seven, and five syllables, respectively.

You won't believe who
I ran into today. Leigh!
She just joined the firm.

But Jen's not amused; she's furious. No matter what I've told her about my role in our breakup—that while Boyfriend could have been more up-front with himself and with me early on, I could have been more upfront with myself and with him about what I wanted, what I was hiding from, and whether we were really a match after all—she still thinks he's an ass-hole. I remember trying to convince Wendell that Boyfriend was an ass-hole; nowadays I find myself trying to convince everyone else that he's *not*.

"What does that even *mean?*" Jen asks about the email. "How about 'How are you *doing?*' Is he really that emotionally stunted?"

"It means nothing," I say. "It's meaningless." There's no point in try-ing to analyze it, to give it meaning. Jen is outraged, but I'm surprised to find that I'm not upset by this after all. Instead, I'm relieved. My gut un-clenches.

"You're not going to respond to this, I hope," Jen says, but I almost want to—to thank Boyfriend for breaking up with me and not wasting even more of my time. Maybe his email *did* have meaning—or at least, my receiving it on this particular day had meaning for me.

I tell Jen I have to get back to writing my book, but after we hang up, that's not what I do. Nor do I write Boyfriend back. Just as I don't want a meaningless relationship, I don't want to write a meaningless book, even though by now I'm three-fourths done. If death and meaninglessness are "ultimate concerns," it makes sense that this book I care little about has plagued me—and also that I turned down the lucrative parenting book before that. Though I didn't fully acknowledge my failing body back then, somewhere in my cells I must have become aware that my time was lim-ited, so how I spent it would matter. I remember my conversation with Julie, and another thought occurs to me now: When I die, I don't want to leave behind my equivalent of Boyfriend's email.

For a while, I've thought that walking around those prison bars meant finishing the book so that I could keep my advance and have the oppor-tunity to write another. But Boyfriend's email makes me wonder if I'm still shaking those same bars. Wendell has helped me to let go of the story that everything would have worked out for me if I'd married Boyfriend, and there's no point in holding on to the parallel story that the parenting

book would have made everything work out for me too—both are fantasies. Certain things would have been different, sure. Ultimately, though,
I'd still be itching for meaning, for something deeper. Just like I am now,
with this stupid happiness book that my agent says I have to write for all
kinds of practical reasons.

But what if that story's wrong too? What if I *don't*, in fact, have to write
this book that my agent says I must or face disaster? On some level, I suspect I've known this answer for a while, and now, all of a sudden, I know
it in a different way. I think about Charlotte and the stages of change. I'm
ready, I decide, for "action."

I place my fingers on the keyboard again, this time to type a letter to
my editor at the publishing house: *I want to cancel my contract.*

After a brief hesitation, I take a deep breath then push Send, and off it
goes—my truth, finally, hurtling through cyberspace.

45

Wendell's Beard

It's a sunny Los Angeles day and I'm in a good mood as I park my car across the street from Wendell's office. I almost hate being in too good of a mood on therapy days—what's there to talk about?

Actually, I know better. It turns out that sessions to which patients come with neither a crisis nor an agenda tend to be the most revelatory ones. When we give our minds space to wander, they take us to the most unexpected and interesting places. As I cross from the parking lot to Wendell's building, I hear a song blasting from someone's car: Imagine Dragons' "On Top of the World." Walking down the corridor to Wendell's office, I start humming along—but as soon as I open the door to the waiting room, I go silent, confused.

Whoops—this isn't Wendell's waiting room. Caught up in the song, I'd opened the wrong door! I laugh at my mistake.

I walk out and shut the door, then look around to get my bearings. I check the nameplate on the door, which confirms that I am, indeed, in the right place. Once more, I open the door, but what I see looks nothing like the room I know. For a moment, I panic, as if in a dream: Where am I?

Wendell's waiting room has been completely transformed. There's new paint, new flooring, new furniture, and new art—striking black-and-white photos. Gone are what I assumed to be the hand-me-downs from his parents' house. Gone is the vase with the cheesy fake flowers and in its place is a ceramic pitcher and cups for water. The only thing that remains is the noise machine that ensures no one can hear what's being said on the other side of the wall. It feels like I've walked into the finished product on one of those home-improvement shows where a space becomes unrecognizable from its original unfortunate state. I want to *Ooh* and *Aah* the way the owners do on these shows. It looks beautiful—simple and uncluttered and also a bit quirky, like Wendell.

My usual chair is gone, so I take a seat in one of the new ones with funky steel legs and a leather back. I haven't seen Wendell for two weeks —I'd assumed his being out of the office meant that he was on vacation, maybe even at the cabin from his childhood with his large extended family. I had imagined all of his siblings and nieces and nephews I'd discovered online and tried to picture Wendell with them, goofing around with his kids or kicking back with a beer by the lake.

But now I realize that this renovation was also taking place. My good mood is dissipating and I start to question if my contentment was real or if I was experiencing a "flight to health" in Wendell's absence. A flight to health is a phenomenon in which patients convince themselves that they're suddenly over their issues because, unbeknownst to them, they can't tolerate the anxiety that working through these issues is bringing up.

Typically, a patient might have a difficult session about a childhood trauma, then come in the next week and announce that therapy is no longer needed. *I feel great! That session was cathartic!* A flight to health is especially common when the therapist or patient has been away and in that break, the person's unconscious defenses take hold. *I did so well the past few weeks. I don't think I need therapy anymore!* Sometimes this change is genuine. Other times, patients abruptly leave—only to come back.

Flight to health or not, I'm feeling disoriented. Despite the room's vast improvement, I sort of miss the old crappy furniture—much the way I've felt about the inner transformations I've been going through. Wendell was the makeover show that came in and launched my internal renovation, and while I feel so much better now—in the "during," because unlike décor makeovers, there's no such thing as "after" until we're dead—sometimes I think of the "before" with a weird kind of nostalgia.

I wouldn't want it back, but I'm glad I remember it.

I hear the click of Wendell's office door and then his footsteps on the new maple floors as he walks out to greet me. I look up and do another double take. Before I didn't recognize his waiting room, and now I almost don't recognize Wendell. It's like somebody's playing a prank on me. *Surprise! Just kidding!*

In his two weeks off, he has grown a beard. He's also ditched the cardigan for a smart button-down, traded his worn loafers for the same trendy slip-ons John wears, and looks like a completely different person.

"Hi," he says, as usual.

"Wow," I say, a little too loudly. "So many changes." I gesture to the waiting room but I'm staring at his beard. "Now you *really* look like a therapist," I add as I stand up, making a joke to cover my shock. In fact, his beard looks nothing like those stodgy ones in the long tradition of well-known therapists. Wendell's beard is stylish. Scruffy. Unkempt. Rakish.

He looks . . . attractive?

I remember my earlier denial of any romantic transference with him. And I'd been truthful—as far as I was aware. But why was I so profoundly uncomfortable right now? Had my unconscious been having a passionate affair with Wendell behind my back?

I step toward his office but stop short at the doorway. His therapy room has also been redone. The layout is the same—the L-shaped couch configuration, the desk, the armoire, the bookshelf, the table with the tissues—but the paint, flooring, rug, art, sofas, and pillows have all changed. It looks amazing! Stunning. Gorgeous. The *office*, I mean. The office looks gorgeous.

"Did you use a decorator?" I ask, and he says he did. I figured. If the earlier furniture was his doing, he clearly needed a professional for this. Still, it fits Wendell perfectly. The new Wendell. The spruced-up but still unpretentious Wendell.

I go to position B, examine the new pillows, and arrange them behind my back on the new couch. I remember how unnerved I felt the first time I sat this close to Wendell, how it seemed too close, too exposed. Now it feels that way again. *What if I'm attracted to Wendell?*

My attraction wouldn't be uncommon. After all, if people find themselves attracted to their colleagues, friends' spouses, and a variety of men and women they see or meet in the course of a day, why not their therapists? Especially their therapists. Sexual feelings abound in therapy, and how could they not? It's easy to conflate the intimate experience of romance or sex with the intimate experience of having somebody pay undivided attention to the details of your life, accept you fully, support you without competing agendas, and know you so deeply. Some patients even flirt overtly, often unaware of ulterior motives (throwing the therapist off balance; deflecting from difficult topics; regaining power if feeling powerless; repaying the therapist in the only way the patient knows how to given his or her history). Other patients don't flirt but vehemently deny any attraction, like John telling me that I wasn't the kind of person he'd choose as his mistress. ("No offense.")

But John often took note of my appearance: "Now you're looking more like a *real* mistress" (when I got highlights in my hair); "You better watch out, some people might see some cleavage" (when I wore a V-neck blouse); "Are those your fuck-me shoes for after work?" (when I wore heels). Each time, I'd try to talk about his "jokes" and the feelings underlying them.

And now here I am, making a stupid joke with Wendell and smiling dumbly. He asks if I'm having a reaction to his beard.

"I'm just not used to it," I say. "But it looks good on you. You should keep it." *Or maybe you shouldn't,* I think. *Maybe I'll be too attrac . . . I mean,* dis*tracted.*

He raises his right eyebrow, and I notice that his eyes look different today. Brighter? And did he always have that dimple? What's going *on?* "I'm asking because how you respond to me is related to how you respond to men—"

"You're not a *man,*" I interrupt, laughing.

"I'm not?"

"No!" I say.

Wendell feigns surprise. "Well, last time I checked—"

"Right, but you know what I mean. You're not a *man*-man. You're not a *guy*. You're a *therapist*." I realize with horror that I sound just like John again.

A few months earlier, I'd found myself struggling to dance at a wedding because of some muscle weakness in my left foot from this mysterious medical condition. At the following week's session, I told Wendell how sad I had been, watching everyone else dancing. Wendell replied that I could still dance with my good foot, I just needed a partner.

"Well," I said. "Isn't the loss of a partner how I landed here in the first place?"

But Wendell didn't mean a romantic partner. He said I could ask anyone—that I could lean on people if I needed support, dancing or otherwise.

"I can't just ask anyone," I insisted.

"Why not?"

I rolled my eyes.

"You can ask me," he said, shrugging. "I'm a good dancer, you know." He added that he'd studied dance seriously while growing up.

"Really? What kind of dance?" I didn't know if he was kidding. I tried to picture gawky Wendell dancing. I imagined him getting all tangled up and tripping.

"Ballet," he said, without a trace of embarrassment.

Ballet?

"But I can do any kind of dance," he continued, smiling at my incredulity. "I also do swing, modern. What would you like to dance to?"

"No way," I said. "I'm not dancing with my therapist."

I wasn't concerned that he was being sexually suggestive or creepy; I knew that he had no intention of that. It was more that I didn't want to use my therapy time that way. I had *things to talk about,* like how I was coping with my medical condition. But part of me also knew that this was just an excuse I was giving myself, that this intervention could be useful, that the movement of dance allows our bodies to express our emotions in a way that words sometimes can't. When we dance, we express our buried feelings, talking through our bodies instead of our minds — and that can help us get out of our heads and to a new level of awareness. That's partly what dance therapy is about. It's another technique some therapists use.

But still — no.

"I'm your therapist *and* a guy," Wendell says today, adding that we all interact with people in different ways based on any number of things we notice about them. Political correctness aside, we aren't emotionally blind to qualities like appearance, wardrobe, gender, race, ethnicity, or age. That's the way transference works. If my therapist were a woman, he says, I'd react to her based on the ways I relate to women. If Wendell were short, I'd react to him as somebody who's short rather than tall. If . . .

As he talks, I can't stop staring at the "new" him, trying to make the adjustment. It occurs to me that it wasn't just that I hadn't been attracted to Wendell earlier. It was that I hadn't been attracted to *anyone*. I was grieving, and it's only upon my gradual emergence that I've begun to feel attraction in the world again.

Sometimes when a new patient comes in, I ask not just "What brings you here?" but "What brings you here now?" The *now* is the key. *Why this year, this month, this day, have you decided to come talk to me?* It seemed like the breakup was my answer to "Why now?" but underneath it was my stuckness and my grief.

"I wish I could stop crying!" I'd told Wendell early on when I felt like a human fire hydrant.

But Wendell saw it differently. He'd given me permission to feel and also a reminder that, like so many people, I'd been mistaking feeling *less* for feeling *better*. The feelings are still there, though. They come out in unconscious behaviors, in an inability to sit still, in a mind that hungers for the next distraction, in a lack of appetite or a struggle to control one's appetite, in a short-temperedness, or — in Boyfriend's case — in a foot that twitched under the covers as we sat in that heavy silence under which lay the feeling that he'd kept to himself for months: whatever he wanted, it wasn't me.

And still people try to suppress their feelings. Just a week before, a patient had told me that she couldn't go a single night without turning on her TV, falling asleep to it, and waking up hours later. "Where did my evening go?" she asked from my couch. But the real question was, where had her feelings gone?

Another patient recently lamented, "Wouldn't it be nice to be one of those people who doesn't overthink anything, who just goes with the flow —who lives the unexamined life?" I remember saying that there was a difference between examining and dwelling, and if we're cut off from our feelings, just skating on the surface, we don't get peace or joy—we get deadness.

So it's not that I'm in love with Wendell. The fact that I'm finally noticing him not just as a therapist but as a man is simply evidence that our work together has helped me rejoin the human race. I feel attraction again. I've even begun dating, dipping my toe in the water.

Before I leave, I ask about the "Why now?" of Wendell's office renovation, of his beard.

"What made you do all this?" I ask.

The beard, he says, was the result of being out of the office and not needing to shave; when it was time to come back, he decided he liked it. As for the office makeover, he says simply, "It was time."

"But why *now?*" I ask, trying to phrase my next question graciously. "It seems like you'd had that furniture for, um . . . a long while?"

Wendell laughs. I didn't hide the subtext very well. "Sometimes," he says, "change is like that."

Back in the waiting area, I move past the new modern-looking screen separating the exit from the seating. Outside, heat mirages rise on the sidewalk, and as I wait for the light, the Imagine Dragons song pops into my head again. *I've been waiting to smile, 'ey, been holding it in for a while.* When the light turns green, I cross and head toward the parking lot but today I don't go straight to my car. I keep walking up the street until I'm in front of a glass storefront—a salon.

I catch sight of myself in the window's reflection and stop to adjust my top—the one from Anthropologie, which I'd chosen for tonight's date— and then hurry inside.

I'm just in time for my appointment at the waxing place.

Part Four

Though we travel the world over to find the beautiful,

we must carry it with us, or we find it not.

—*Ralph Waldo Emerson*

46

The Bees

A minute before Charlotte's appointment, I get a text from my mother. *Please call me.* She doesn't normally send texts like this, so I dial her cell. She answers on the first ring.

"Don't be alarmed," she says, which always means that something alarming has happened. "But Dad's in the hospital."

My hand tenses on the phone.

"He's fine," she says quickly. *Fine people aren't admitted to the hospital,* I think. "What happened?" I ask.

Well, she says, they don't know yet. She explains that my father was eating lunch when he said he didn't feel well. Then he started shaking and had trouble breathing, and now they're at the hospital. It looks like he has an infection but they don't know if it's related to his heart or something else. *He's fine,* she keeps repeating. *He'll be fine.* I think she says this as much for herself as for me. We both want—need—my father to be fine.

"Really," she says, "he's fine. Here, see for yourself." I hear her mumble something to my father as she hands him the phone.

"I'm fine," he says by way of hello, but I can hear his labored breathing. He tells me the same story about having lunch and not feeling well, leaving out the shaking and difficulty-breathing parts. He'll probably be out by tomorrow, he says, once the antibiotics kick in, though when my mom gets back on the phone, we wonder whether it's something more serious. (Later that night, when I go to the hospital, I'll see that my father looks pregnant—his abdomen filled with fluid—and that he's on several different IV antibiotics because a serious bacterial infection has spread throughout his body. He will be hospitalized for a week, the fluid around his lungs aspirated, his heart rate stabilized.)

But right now, getting off the phone with my parents, I realize that I'm twelve minutes late for Charlotte's appointment. I try to shift focus as I head to the waiting room.

Charlotte jumps up from her seat when I open the door. "Oh, phew!" she says. "I thought maybe I had the wrong time, but this is always my time, and then I thought I had the wrong *day,* but no, it's Monday"—she holds up her phone to show me the date—"so then I thought maybe, I don't know, but here you are."

This all comes out as one long sentence. "Anyway, hi," she says, moving past me into my office.

This may seem surprising, but when therapists are late, many patients are shaken. Though we try to avoid this, every therapist I know has let a patient down this way. And when we do, it can bring up old experiences of distrust or abandonment, leaving patients feeling anything from discombobulated to enraged.

In my office, I explain that I was on an urgent phone call and apologize for the delay.

"It's fine," Charlotte says nonchalantly, but she seems out of sorts. Or maybe I am, after the call with my father. *I'm fine,* he had said. Just like Charlotte says it's fine. Are they both really fine? Charlotte fidgets in her chair, twirling her hair, looking around the room. I try to help her locate herself by meeting her eyes, but they're darting from the window to a picture on the wall to the pillow she always keeps on her lap. One leg is crossed over the other, and she's rapidly kicking that leg in the air.

"I wonder what it was like for you, not knowing where I was," I say, remembering how, a few months ago, I'd been in the same position, sitting in Wendell's waiting room and wondering where *he* was. Killing time on my phone, I noticed that he was four minutes late, then eight. After ten minutes, the thought crossed my mind that maybe he'd been in an accident or fallen ill and was at this moment in the emergency room.

I debated whether to call and leave a message (to say what, I'm not sure. *Hi, it's Lori. I'm sitting in your waiting room. Are you in there, on the other side of the door, writing chart notes? Eating a snack? Have you forgotten me? Or are you dying?*). And just as I was thinking about how I'd need to find a new therapist, in no small part to process my *old* therapist's death, the door to Wendell's office opened. Out walked a middle-aged couple, the man saying "Thank you" to Wendell and the woman smiling tightly. A first session, I speculated. Or the disclosure of an affair. Those sessions tend to run over.

I breezed past Wendell and took my place perpendicular to him.

"It's fine," I said when he apologized for the delay. "Really," I continued, "my sessions go over sometimes too. It's fine."

Wendell looked at me, his right eyebrow raised. I raised my eyebrows back, trying to preserve my dignity. *Me, get all worked up because my therapist was late? C'mon.* I burst out laughing, and then some tears escaped. We both knew how relieved I was to see him and how important he had become to me. Those ten minutes of waiting and wondering were definitely not "fine."

And now—with a forced smile on her face, her leg jerking like she's having a seizure—Charlotte is reiterating how fine it was to wait for me.

I ask Charlotte what she thought had happened when I wasn't there.

"I wasn't worried," she says, even though I said nothing about worry. Then something catches my eye through the large wall-to-wall window.

Flying in dizzyingly fast circles a few feet behind the right side of Charlotte's head are a couple of very kinetic bumblebees. I've never seen bees out my window, several stories high, and these two look like they're hopped up on amphetamines. Maybe it's a bee mating dance, I think. But then a few more fly into view, and within seconds, I see a swarm of bees buzzing in circles, the only thing separating us from them being a huge sheet of glass. Some are starting to land on the window and crawl around.

"So, you're going to kill me," Charlotte begins, apparently unaware of the bees. "But, um, I'm going to take a break from therapy."

I look away from the bees and back to Charlotte. I'm not expecting this today, and it takes a moment for what she just said to register, especially because there's so much movement in my peripheral vision and I can't help but follow it. Now there are hundreds of bees, so many that my office has become darker, the bees pressed up against the windowpanes and blocking out the light like a cloud. Where are they coming from?

The room is so dark that Charlotte now notices. She turns her head in the direction of the window and we sit there, saying nothing, staring at the bees. I wonder if she'll be upset by the sight of them, but instead she seems mesmerized.

My colleague Mike used to see a family with a teenage girl at the same time I saw a couple. Every week about twenty minutes in, this couple and I would hear an eruption from Mike's office, the teenager screaming at her parents, storming out, slamming the door; the couple yelling after her to come back; her yelling "*No!*" and then Mike coaxing her back, calming everyone down. The first few times this happened, I thought it would be upsetting for the couple in my office, but it turned out it made them feel better. *At least that's not us,* they thought.

I'd hated the disturbance, though—it always broke my focus. And in the same way, I'm hating these bees. I think about my dad in the hospital, ten blocks away. Are these bees a sign, an omen?

"I once thought about becoming a beekeeper," Charlotte says, breaking the silence, and this is less surprising to me than her sudden wish to leave. She finds terrifying situations thrilling—bungee jumping, skydiving, swimming with sharks. As she tells me about her beekeeper fantasy, I think that the metaphor is almost too neat: this job that would require her to wear head-to-toe protective clothing so she wouldn't get stung and would allow her to master the very creatures that might hurt her, harvesting their sweetness in the end. I can see the appeal of having that kind of control over danger, especially if you grew up feeling like you had none.

I can also imagine the appeal of saying you're leaving therapy if you were inexplicably left in the waiting room. Has Charlotte been planning to leave, or is this an impulsive reaction to the primal fear she felt a few minutes ago? I wonder if she's drinking again. Sometimes people drop out of therapy because it makes them feel accountable when they don't want to be. If they've started drinking or cheating again—if they've done or failed to do something that now causes them shame—they may prefer to hide from their therapists (and themselves). What they forget is that therapy is one of the safest of all places to bring your shame. But faced with lying by omission or confronting their shame, they may duck out altogether. Which, of course, solves nothing.

"I decided before I came in today," Charlotte says. "I feel like I'm doing well. I'm still sober, work is going fine, I'm not fighting as much with my mom, and I'm not seeing the Dude—I even blocked him on my phone." She pauses. "Are you mad?"

Am I mad? I'm certainly surprised—I thought she'd moved past her fear of being addicted to me—and I'm frustrated, which I admit to myself is a euphemism for *mad*. But underneath the anger is the fact that I worry for her, perhaps more than I should. I worry that until she has had practice being in a healthy relationship, until she can find more peace with her dad than bouncing between pretending he doesn't exist and becoming devastated when he shows up and inevitably disappears again, she'll struggle and miss out on much of what she wants. I want her to work through this in her twenties rather than her thirties; I don't want her to squander her time. I don't want her to one day panic, *Half my life is over.* And yet I also don't want to discourage her independence. Just as parents raise their kids to leave them one day, therapists work to lose patients, not retain them.

Still, something feels rushed about this decision and perhaps comfortably dangerous for her, like jumping out of a plane with no parachute.

People imagine they come to therapy to uncover something from the past and talk it through, but so much of what therapists do is work *in the present,* where we bring awareness to what's going on in people's heads and hearts in the day-to-day. Are they easily injured? Do they often feel blamed? Do they avoid eye contact? Do they fixate on seemingly insignificant anxieties? We take these insights and encourage patients to practice making use of them in the real world. Wendell once put it this way: "What people do in therapy is like shooting baskets against a backboard. It's necessary. But what they need to do then is go and play in an actual game."

The one time Charlotte got close to having a real relationship, about a year into her therapy, she abruptly stopped seeing this guy but refused to tell me why. Nor would she tell me why she didn't want to talk about it. I was less interested in what had happened than in what made *this*—of all the things she'd told me about herself—the Thing That Cannot Be Discussed. I wonder, today, if she's leaving because of that thing.

I remember how she'd wanted to hold on to this Thing—to say no to my request. "It's hard for me to say no," she explained, "so I'm practicing in here." I told her that regardless of whether she talked about the breakup, I thought it was equally hard for her to say yes. The inability to say no is largely about approval-seeking—people imagine that if they say no, they won't be loved by others. The inability to say yes, however—to intimacy, a job opportunity, an alcohol program—is more about lack of trust in oneself. *Will I mess this up? Will this turn out badly? Isn't it safer to stay where I am?*

But there's a twist. Sometimes what seems like setting a boundary—saying no—is actually a cop-out, an inverted way of avoiding saying yes. The challenge for Charlotte is to get past her fear and say yes—not just to therapy, but to herself.

I glance at the bees pressed up against the glass and think of my father again and how once, when I was complaining about the way a relative would try to make me feel guilty, my father quipped, "Just because she sends you guilt doesn't mean you have to accept delivery." I think about this with Charlotte: I don't want her to feel guilty for leaving, to feel that she has let me down. All I can do is let her know that I am here for her either way, share my perspective and hear hers, and set her free to do as she wishes.

"You know," I tell Charlotte as I watch some of the bees begin to disperse, "I agree that things are better in your life, and that you've worked hard to make that happen. I also have the sense that you're still struggling with getting close to people and that the parts of your life that might be related to this—your dad, the conversation about the guy that you don't want to have—feel too painful to talk about. By not talking about them, part of you might believe that you can still hold out hope that things might be different—and you wouldn't be alone in that way of thinking. Some people hope that therapy will help them find a way to be heard by whoever they feel wronged them, at which point those lovers or relatives will see the light and become the people they'd wished for all along. But it rarely happens like that. At some point, being a fulfilled adult means taking responsibility for the course of your own life and accepting the fact that now you're in charge of your choices. You have to move to the front seat and be the mommy dog driving the car."

Charlotte has been looking at her lap while I speak, but she sneaks a glance at me during that last part. The room is brighter now, and I notice that most of the bees have left. Just a few stragglers remain, some still on the glass, others circling each other before flying away.

"If you stay in therapy," I say softly, "you might have to let go of the hope for a better childhood—but that's only so that you can create a better adulthood."

Charlotte looks down for a long time, then says, "I know."

We sit together in the silence.

Finally she says, "I slept with my neighbor." She's talking about a guy in her apartment building who had been flirting with her but also said that he wasn't looking for anything serious. She'd decided she was only going to date men who were looking for a girlfriend. She wanted to stop dating emotional versions of her dad. She wanted to stop being like her mom. She wanted to start saying no to those things and yes to becoming neither parent but instead the person she has yet to discover.

"I figured if I left therapy, I could just keep sleeping with him," she says.

"You can do whatever you want," I say, "whether you're in therapy or not." I watch her hear what she already knows. Yes, she has given up drinking and the Dude and has begun to give up the fight with her mom too, but the stages of change are such that you don't drop all of your defenses at the same time. Instead, you release them in layers, moving closer and closer to the tender core: your sadness, your shame.

She shakes her head. "I just don't want to wake up five years from now and never have had any kind of relationship," she says. "Five years from now, a lot of people my age won't be single anymore, and I'll be the girl who hooks up with a guy in the waiting room or her neighbor and then tells the story at a party like it's just another adventure. Like I don't even care."

"The cool girl," I say. "The one who has no needs or feelings and just goes with the flow. But you *do* have feelings."

"Yeah," she says. "Being the cool girl feels like shit." She's never admitted this before. She's taking off her beekeeper suit. "Is 'like shit' a feeling?" she asks.

"It sure is," I say.

And so it begins, at last. Charlotte doesn't leave this time. Instead, she stays in therapy until she learns to drive her own car, navigating her way through the world more safely, looking both ways, making many wrong turns but finding her way back, always, to where she truly wants to go.

47

Kenya

I'm getting a haircut and telling Cory my news about canceling my book contract with the publisher. I explain that now I might spend years repaying the publisher its money, and I might not be able to get another book contract after backing out of this one so late in the game, but I feel like an albatross has been removed from around my neck.

Cory nods. I see him check out his tattooed biceps in the mirror.

"You know what *I* did this morning?" he says.

"Hmm?" I say.

He combs out my front layers and checks that they're even. "I watched a documentary on Kenyans who can't get clean water," he says. "They're dying, and many of them are traumatized by war and sickness, and they're being thrown out of their homes and villages. They're wandering around just trying to find some water to drink that won't kill them. None of them go to therapy or owe their publishers money." He pauses. "Anyway, that's what I did this morning."

There's an awkward silence. Cory and I find each other's eyes in the mirror, and then, slowly, we begin to laugh.

We're both laughing at me, and I'm laughing too at the ways people rank their pain. I think about Julie. "At least I don't have cancer," she'd say, but that's also a phrase that healthy people use to minimize their own suffering. I remember how, initially, John's appointment was scheduled after

Julie's and how I regularly made an effort to remember one of the most important lessons from my training: There's no hierarchy of pain. Suffering shouldn't be ranked, because pain is not a contest. Spouses often forget this, upping the ante on their suffering—*I had the kids all day. My job is more demanding than yours. I'm lonelier than you are.* Whose pain wins —or loses?

But pain is pain. I'd done this myself, too, apologizing to Wendell, embarrassed that I was making such a big deal about a breakup but not a divorce; apologizing for suffering from anxiety about the very real financial and professional consequences of an unmet book contract but that, nonetheless, were in no way as serious as the problems facing, well, the people in Kenya. I even apologized for talking about my health concerns—like when a patient noticed my tremor and I didn't know what to say—because, after all, how bad was my suffering if I didn't even have a diagnosis, much less a diagnosis that ranked high on the "acceptable problems to suffer from" scale? I had an unidentified condition. I didn't—knock on wood —have Parkinson's. I didn't—knock on wood—have cancer.

But Wendell told me that by diminishing my problems, I was judging myself and everyone else whose problems I had placed lower down on the hierarchy of pain. You can't get through your pain by diminishing it, he reminded me. You get through your pain by accepting it and figuring out what to do with it. You can't change what you're denying or minimizing. And, of course, often what seem like trivial worries are manifestations of deeper ones.

"You still doing Tinder therapy?" I ask Cory.

He rubs some product into my hair. "Hell, yeah," he says.

48

Psychological
Immune System

"Congratulations, you're not my mistress anymore," John says dryly as he walks in carrying a bag with our lunches.

I wonder if this is his way of saying goodbye. Has he decided to stop therapy right when we've just genuinely begun?

He walks to the couch and makes a show of silencing his cell phone before tossing it onto a chair. Then he opens the takeout bag and hands me my Chinese chicken salad. He reaches in again, pulls out some chopsticks, and holds them up: *Want these?* I nod: *Thanks.*

Once we're settled, he looks at me expectantly, tapping his foot.

"Well," he says, "don't you want to know why you're no longer my mistress?"

I look back at him: *I'm not playing this game.*

"Okay, fine." He sighs. "I'll tell you. You're not my mistress anymore because I came clean to Margo. She knows that I'm seeing you." He takes a bite of his salad, chews. "And you know what she did?" he continues.

I shake my head.

"She got mad! *Why would you keep this a secret? How long has this been going on? What's her name? Who else knows?* You'd think you and I were fucking or something, right?" John laughs to make sure I know how out-landish he considers that possibility.

"To her, it might feel like that," I say. "Margo feels left out of your life and now she's hearing that you've been sharing it with somebody else. She craves that closeness with you."

"Yeah," John says, and he seems lost in thought for a bit. He takes more bites of his salad, looks at the floor, then rubs his forehead as if whatever's going on in there is draining him. Finally he looks up.

"We talked about Gabe," he says quietly. And then he starts crying, a guttural wail, raw and wild, and I recognize it instantly. It's the sound I heard in the ER back in medical school from the parents of the drowned toddler. It's a love song to his beloved son.

I have a flash to another ER, on the night when my son was a year old and he had to be rushed by ambulance to the hospital after he spiked a fever of 104 and began seizing. By the time the paramedics arrived at my house, his body was limp, his eyes closed, and he was unresponsive to my voice. As I sit with John, I feel again in my body the terror of seeing my son lifeless, me on the gurney with him on my torso, the EMTs flanking us, the sirens a surreal soundtrack. I hear the sound of him howling for me as they strapped him into the x-ray contraption, forcing him to be still, his eyes open now, terrified, beseeching me to hold him as he squirmed violently to reach me. His screams, in their intensity, sounded much like John's wail now. Somewhere in the hospital's hallway, I remember seeing what looked like an unconscious child—or a dead one—being wheeled by. *This could be us,* I thought at that moment. *This could be us by the morning. We could be leaving here like this too.*

But it wasn't us. I got to go home with my beautiful boy.

"I'm sorry, I'm sorry, I'm so, so sorry," John is saying through his tears, and I don't know if he's apologizing to Gabe or Margo or his mother—or to me, for his outburst.

All of the above, he says. But mostly, he's sorry that he can't remember. He wanted to block out the unfathomable—the accident, the hospital, the moment he learned that Gabe had died—but he couldn't. What he'd give to forget hugging his son's dead body, Margo's brother pulling them both away, and John punching him, screaming, "I will not leave my son!" How he'd like to erase the scene of telling his daughter that her brother had died and of the family's arrival at the cemetery, Margo falling to the ground, unable to walk in — but those memories, unfortunately, remain vividly intact, the stuff of his waking nightmares.

What's fuzzier, he says, are the happy memories. Gabe in his twin bed in his Batman pajamas ("Snuggle me, Dada"). Rolling around in wrapping paper after opening his birthday presents. The way Gabe strode confidently into his preschool class like a big kid, only to turn around at the door and blow a furtive kiss. The sound of his voice. *I love you to the moon and back.* The smell of his head when John bent down to kiss him. The music of his giggle. His animated facial expressions. His favorite food or animal or color (Was it blue or "rainbow" before he died?). All of these memories feel, to John, as if they're fading into the distance — that he's losing the details of Gabe, much as he wants to hold on to them.

All parents forget these details about their kids as they grow, and they mourn that loss too. The difference is that as the past recedes in their memories, the present is right in front of them. For John, the loss of his memories brings him closer to the loss of Gabe. And so at night, John tells me, while Margo seethes, assuming that he's working or watching porn, he's hiding out with his laptop watching videos of Gabe, thinking about how these are the only videos he'll ever have of his son, just as the memories John has of Gabe are the only memories he'll ever have. There will be no more memories made. And while the memories might get blurry, the videos won't. John says that he's watched these videos hundreds of times and can no longer tell the difference between his actual memories and the videos. He watches obsessively, though, "to keep Gabe alive in my mind."

"Keeping him alive in your mind is your way of not abandoning him," I say.

John nods. He says that he pictures Gabe alive all the time — what he would look like, how tall he would be, what interests he'd have. He still sees the neighbor boys who were Gabe's friends as toddlers and imagines Gabe hanging out with them now in middle school, having crushes on girls, eventually shaving. He also imagines the possibility that Gabe would have gone through a phase of butting up against John, and when John hears other parents complain about their high-schoolers, he thinks about what a luxury it would be to have the chance to nag Gabe about his homework or find weed in his room or catch him doing any of the pain-in-the-ass things that teens tend to do. He'll never get to meet his son the way other parents meet their kids at different stages along the way, when they're the same people they've always been but both thrillingly and sadly different.

"What did you and Margo talk about?" I ask.

"When Margo was interrogating me about therapy," he says, "she wanted to know why. Why I was here. Was it about Gabe? Did I talk about Gabe? And I told her that I didn't come to therapy to talk about Gabe. I was just stressed out. But she wouldn't let it go. She was incredulous. 'So you haven't talked about Gabe *at all*?' I told her that what I talked about was private. I mean, can't I talk about what I want in my own therapy? What is she, the therapy police?"

"Why do you suppose it's important to her that you talk about Gabe?"

He considers this. "I remember after Gabe died, Margo wanted me to talk about Gabe and I just couldn't. She didn't understand how I could go to barbecues and Lakers games and seem like a normal person, but that first year I was in shock. Numb. I told myself, *Keep moving, don't stop*. But the next year, when I woke up I'd want to die. I kept my game face on but I was bleeding internally, you know? I wanted to be strong for Margo and Gracie, and I had to keep a roof over our heads, so I couldn't let anyone see the bleeding.

"Then Margo wanted another baby, and I said, fuck it, okay. I mean, Jesus, I was in no shape to be a new father, but Margo was adamant that she didn't want Gracie to grow up alone. It wasn't just that *we* had lost a child. Gracie had lost her only sibling. And the house did seem different than it had when we had two kids running around. It didn't feel like a kid house anymore. The stillness was a reminder of what was missing."

John sits forward, puts the cover on his salad, tosses it across the room into the trash bin. *Swish*. It always goes right in. "Anyway," he says, "the pregnancy seemed to be good for Margo. It brought her back to life. But not me. I kept thinking that nobody could replace Gabe. Besides, what if I killed this one too?"

John told me that when he first heard that his mother had died, he was sure he had killed her. Before she'd left to go to rehearsal that night, he'd begged her to rush home so she'd be there in time to tuck him in. *She must have died rushing home in her car,* he thought. Of course, his father told him that she died while trying to push one of her students out of harm's way, but John was certain this was a cover story to protect his feelings. It wasn't until he saw the headline in the local paper—he had just learned to read—that he knew it was true, he hadn't killed his mother. But he also knew that she would have died for him in a heartbeat, just like he would have done for Gabe or Gracie and just as he would now for Ruby. But would he do it for Margo? He's not so sure. Would she do it for him? He's not sure either.

John pauses, then quips to break the tension. "Wow, this is getting heavy. I think I'll lie down." He stretches out on the couch, tries to fluff a pillow behind his head, and makes a disgruntled sound. ("What's this filled with, cardboard?" he once complained.)

"In a weird way," he continues, "I was worried I might love the new baby *too much*. Like I'd be betraying Gabe. I was so glad it wasn't another boy. I didn't think I could handle a baby boy without him reminding me of Gabe—what if he liked the same fire trucks that Gabe did? Everything would be an agonizing memory, and that would be unfair to the kid. I was so worried about this that I did research on when to have sex so you had the best chance of a girl—it was on the show."

I nod. It was in a subplot with a couple who were later written out, season three, I think. They were always having sex at the wrong time because one or the other of them couldn't control themselves and wait. I remember how funny it was. I had no sense of the pain that inspired it.

"The point," John says, "is that I didn't tell Margo. I just made sure to have sex only on the day that we'd have the best chance of a girl. Then I sweated it out until the ultrasound. When the OB said it looked like a girl, Margo and I both said, 'Are you *sure?*' Margo wanted a boy because she loved raising a boy and we already had a girl, so she was disappointed that first night. 'I'll never get to raise a boy again,' she said. But I was fucking ecstatic! I felt like I could be a better father to a girl, under the circumstances. And then, when Ruby was born, I thought I'd *shit my pants*. The second I saw her, I fell madly in love."

John's voice catches and he stops.

"What happened to your grief then?" I ask.

"Well, it got better at first—which, in a strange way, made me feel worse."

"Because the grief had connected you to Gabe?"

John looks surprised. "Not bad, Sherlock. Yeah. It was almost like my pain was evidence of my love for Gabe, and if it let up, it meant I was forgetting about him. That he didn't matter as much to me."

"That if you were happy, you couldn't also be sad."

"Exactly." He looks away. "I still feel that way."

"What if it's both?" I say. "What if your sadness—your grief—is what allowed you to love Ruby with so much joy when you first saw her?"

I remember a woman I treated whose husband had died. When she fell in love a year later—a love all the more sweet because of the loss of her husband—she worried that others would judge her. (*So soon? Didn't you love your husband of thirty years?*) In fact, her friends and family were excited for her. It wasn't *their* judgment she was hearing—it was her own. What if her happiness was an insult to her husband's memory? It took her a while to see that her happiness didn't diminish her love for her husband —it honored it.

John tells me he finds it ironic that Margo used to be the one who wanted to talk about Gabe and John couldn't; later, if John made a rare reference to Gabe, Margo would get upset. Would their family always be haunted by this tragedy? Would his marriage? "Maybe we remind each other of what happened—like our mere presence is some kind of sick memento," John says.

"What we need," he adds, looking up at me, "is some kind of closure."

Ah, closure. I know what John means, and yet I've always thought that "closure" was an illusion of sorts. Many people don't know that Elisabeth

Kübler-Ross's familiar stages of grieving—denial, anger, bargaining, depression, acceptance—were conceived in the context of terminally ill patients learning to accept their *own* deaths. It wasn't until decades later that the model came to be used for the grieving process more generally. It's one thing to "accept" the end of your own life, as Julie is struggling to do. But for those who keep on living, the idea that they should be getting to acceptance might make them feel worse ("I should be past this by now"; "I don't know why I still cry at random times all these years later"). Besides, how can there be an endpoint to love and loss? Do we even *want* there to be? The price of loving so deeply is feeling so deeply—but it's also a gift, the gift of being alive. If we no longer feel, we *should* be grieving our own deaths.

The grief psychologist William Worden takes into account these questions by replacing *stages* with *tasks* of mourning. In his fourth task, the goal is to *integrate* the loss into your life and create an ongoing connection with the person who died while also finding a way to continue living.

But many people come to therapy seeking closure. *Help me not to feel.* What they eventually discover is that you can't mute one emotion without muting the others. You want to mute the pain? You'll also mute the joy.

"You're both so alone in your grief," I say. "And in your joy."

In our sessions, John had dropped occasional hints of his joy: his two girls; his dog, Rosie; writing a killer show; winning another Emmy; a boys' trip with his brothers. Sometimes, John says, he can't believe that he's capable of feeling joy. After Gabe died, he thought he'd never live through it. He'd go on, he figured, but like a ghost. And yet, just a week after Gabe's death, he and Gracie were playing together, and for a second—maybe two—he felt okay. He smiled and laughed with her, and the fact that he laughed amazed him. Just one week ago his son had died. Was that sound really coming from him?

I tell John about what's known as the psychological immune system. Just as your physiological immune system helps your body recover from physical attack, your brain helps you recover from psychological attack. A series of studies by the researcher Daniel Gilbert at Harvard found that in responding to challenging life events from the devastating (becoming handicapped, losing a loved one) to the difficult (a divorce, an illness), people do better than they anticipate. They believe that they'll never laugh again, but they do. They think they'll never love again, but they do. They go grocery shopping and see movies; they have sex and dance at weddings; they overeat on Thanksgiving and go on diets in the New Year—the day-to-day returns. John's reaction while playing with Grace wasn't unusual; it was the norm.

There's another related concept that I share with John: impermanence. Sometimes in their pain, people believe that the agony will last forever. But feelings are actually more like weather systems—they blow in and they blow out. Just because you feel sad this minute or this hour or this day doesn't mean you'll feel that way in ten minutes or this afternoon or next week. Everything you feel—anxiety, elation, anguish—blows in and out again. For John, on Gabe's birthday, on certain holidays, or simply running in the background, there will always be pain. Hearing a certain song in the car or having a fleeting memory might even plunge him into momentary despair. But another song, or another memory, might minutes or hours later bring intense joy.

Where, I wonder, is John's shared joy with Margo? I ask him what he imagines would have happened with Margo had the car crash not happened. What would their marriage be like today?

"Oh, for God's sake," he says, "now you think I can rewrite history?" He looks out the window, at the clock, at his sneakers, which he had slipped off when he lay down on the couch. Finally he looks at me.

"Actually, I think about that a lot lately," he says. "Sometimes I think about how we were a young family and my career was taking off and Margo was taking care of the kids and trying to run a business, and how we'd lost touch with each other, the way people do at that stage of life. I think about how things might have changed once both kids were in school and we were farther ahead in our careers. You know, life would normalize. But maybe it wouldn't have. I used to be so sure that she was the right person for me and I was the right person for her, but we make each other so unhappy, and I don't even remember when that started. Everything I do is wrong in her eyes. Maybe we would have been divorced by now. People say that marriages fall apart after a child's death, but maybe we stayed together because of what happened to Gabe." He laughs. "Maybe Gabe saved our marriage."

"Maybe," I say. "Or maybe you stayed together because you both want to rediscover the parts of yourselves that seemed to have died along with Gabe. Maybe you both believe you can find each other again—or for the first time."

I think about the family of the drowned toddler in the ER. What are they doing right now? Did they have another child? Their baby, the one whose diaper was being changed while their three-year-old ran outside and drowned, would now be in college. Maybe that couple is long divorced and living with their new spouses. Or maybe they're still together, stronger than ever, perhaps taking a hike on the scenic trails near their home on a peninsula south of San Francisco, reminiscing about the past, remembering their beloved daughter.

"It's funny," John says. "I guess we're finally both ready to talk about Gabe at the same time. And now that we are, I feel better. I mean, I also feel like shit, but it's okay, if you know what I mean. It's not as bad as I thought it would be."

"It's not as bad as it was *not* talking about Gabe," I suggest.

"Like I said, you're good, Sher—" We share a smile. He's stopped himself from calling me Sherlock, from using the caricature as a space keeper between us. Letting Gabe become more real in his life is allowing him to let others be more real too.

John sits up and starts fidgeting; our session is about to end. As he slips on his sneakers and stands to retrieve his phone, I think back to his earlier comment about telling Margo he came to therapy due to stress and how often he's told me the same thing.

"John," I say, "do you really think you came here because of stress?"

"What are you, an idiot?" he says, a twinkle in his eye. "I came here to talk about Margo and Gabe. Boy, are you dim sometimes."

When he leaves, there's no wad of cash at the door for his "hooker." "You can bill me," he says. "No more skulking around. We're legit now."

49

Counseling Versus Therapy

"Are you asking for counseling or therapy?" Wendell says at today's session after I tell him that I have a professional question. He knows I'll understand the distinction because he's offered professional guidance twice before. Do I want advice (counseling) or self-understanding (therapy)?

The first time I asked Wendell such a question, I'd been talking about my frustration with people choosing the quick fix over the deeper work of psychotherapy. As a relatively new therapist, I was curious how someone more seasoned—specifically Wendell—dealt with this. It was one thing to hear what older colleagues had to say, but from time to time, I couldn't help but wonder how Wendell handled the frustrations of the profession.

I doubted he would answer my question directly—he would more likely express empathy for my predicament. In fact, I knew I was putting him in the classic Catch-22 position in which therapists often find themselves: *I want empathy, but if you give it to me, I'll feel angry and hopeless, because empathy alone won't solve my very real problem, so what good are you anyway?* I was thinking that he might even say something about this Catch-22 (because the best way to defuse an emotional land mine is to expose it).

Instead, he looked at me and asked, "Would you like a practical suggestion?"

I wasn't sure I'd heard him correctly. A *practical* suggestion? Are you kidding me? My therapist was going to give me a concrete piece of advice? I moved closer.

"My father was a businessman," Wendell began quietly. At that time, I hadn't yet fessed up to my Google-binge, so I nodded, pretending this information was new. He told me that when he was starting out, his father suggested that he make an offer to prospective patients: They could try a session, and if they chose not to continue to work with Wendell after that, the session would be free. Since many people were nervous about starting therapy, this risk-free session would give them the opportunity to see what therapy was about and how Wendell might help them.

I tried to picture Wendell having this conversation with his father. I imagined the pleasure his father might have gotten from finally giving professional advice to his gentler son. His suggestion wasn't groundbreaking in the world of business, but therapists don't often think of what we do as a business. And yet we *do* run small businesses, and Wendell's father must have realized that his son, despite leaving the family's company, had actually become a businessman after all. Maybe he took great joy in having that connection with his son. And maybe it meant a lot to Wendell, which is why he was willing to pass this wisdom along to other therapists like me.

In any event, his father was smart. As soon as I implemented this offer, my practice filled up.

But his second piece of counseling—which I not only asked for, but pushed for—flopped. While I was grappling with my happiness-book dilemma, I kept agitating for Wendell to tell me what to do. I pushed so hard and so often that finally, Wendell (who, of course, had no knowledge of the publishing business) gave in near the end of one session. "Well, I don't know what else there is to say about this," he replied to my eighty-seventh query on that topic. "It sounds like you'll just have to find a way to write this so that you can write what you want next time." Then he patted his legs twice and stood, signaling our time was up.

Sometimes a therapist will deliberately "prescribe the problem" or symptom that the patient wants to resolve. A young man who keeps putting off finding a job might be told in therapy that he *can't* look for a job; a woman who won't initiate sex with her partner might be told *not* to initiate it for a month. This strategy, in which the therapist instructs patients not to do what they're already not doing, is called a *paradoxical intervention*. Given the ethical considerations involved, a therapist has to be well trained on how and when to use paradoxical directives, but the idea behind them is that if patients believe that a behavior or symptom is beyond their control, then making it voluntary, something they can choose whether or not to do, calls that belief into question. Once patients realize that they're choosing a behavior, they can examine the secondary gains—the unconscious benefits it offers (avoidance, rebellion, a cry for help).

But Wendell hadn't been doing that. He was just reacting to my endless complaints. If I came in upset because my agent once more insisted that nothing could be done and that I had to write this book or I'd never get another book contract, Wendell would question why I couldn't get a second opinion—or another agent—and I would explain that I couldn't approach other agents because I had nothing to offer them other than the mess I was currently in. Wendell and I had some version of this conversation often, and finally I convinced both of us that there was just one way out: to keep writing. So I trudged on, now blaming not just myself but also him for my predicament. Of course, I didn't realize I was blaming Wendell, but my resentment surfaced the week after I emailed my editor and told her I wouldn't be finishing the book. I'd been edgy all session, unable to share this milestone with him.

"Are you angry with me?" Wendell asked, picking up on my vibe, and suddenly it hit me: Yes! I was *furious* with him, I replied. And, I added, guess what—I had canceled my book contract, finances and consequences be damned! I was walking around those prison bars! Especially given my mysterious medical condition and its debilitating fatigue, I wanted to be sure that I was using the "good" time I had in a meaningful way. Julie had once said that she finally understood the meaning of the phrase "living on borrowed time": our lives are literally on loan to us. Despite what we think in our youth, none of us have all that much time. Like Julie, I told Wendell, I was starting to strip my life down to its essentials rather than sleepwalking my way through it, so who was *he* to tell me to hunker down and write this book? All therapists make mistakes, but when it happened with Wendell, I felt irrationally betrayed.

When I finished talking, he looked at me thoughtfully. He didn't get defensive, though he could have. He simply apologized. He'd failed, he said, to see something important that was going on between us. In trying to convince him how trapped I was, I left him feeling trapped as well, imprisoned by my perceived imprisonment. And in his frustration, like me in mine, he'd taken the easiest way out: *Fine, you're screwed—write the damn book.*

"The counseling I want today is about a patient," I say now.

I tell Wendell that I have a patient whose wife sees *him,* Wendell, and that every time I come here, I think about whether she's the woman I've seen leaving his office. I tell him that I know he can't say anything about a patient to me, but still I wonder if she's mentioned the name of her husband's therapist—me—to him. And how should we handle this coincidence? As a patient, I can say whatever I want about any aspect of my life, but I don't want to cloud his patient's therapy with my private knowledge of her husband.

"This is the counseling you want?" Wendell asks.

I nod. Given the earlier fiasco, I imagine he's being extra-careful in how he responds.

"What can I tell you that will be useful to you?" he asks.

I think about this. He can't answer my question about whether Margo has the appointment before mine or even say if he's aware that we're talking about Margo. He can't tell me if the fact that I see his patient's husband is new information or if he's known all along. He can't tell me what Margo may or may not have said about me. And I know if I were ever to say anything about John, Wendell would handle it professionally and we'd talk about it in the moment. Maybe I want his advice on whether I did the right thing by telling him about the situation.

"Do you ever wonder if I'm a good therapist?" I ask instead. "I mean, given all you've seen in here?" I remember my earlier "Do you like me?," but this time I'm asking something different. Then I was saying, *Do you love me as a child, love my* neshama? Now I'm saying, *Can you picture me as an adult, as a competent grownup?* Of course, Wendell has never seen me do therapy, has never supervised my work. How can he have any opinion at all on the matter? I start to say this but Wendell stops me.

"I *know* you are," he says.

At first I don't understand. He knows I'm a good therapist? Based on wha—*oh!* So Margo thinks things are getting better with John.

Wendell smiles. I smile. We both know what he can't tell me.

"I have one more question," I say. "Given the situation, how do we lessen the awkwardness?"

"Maybe you just did," he says.

And he's right. In couples therapy, therapists talk about the difference between privacy (spaces in people's psyches that everyone needs in healthy relationships) and secrecy (which stems from shame and tends to be corrosive). Carl Jung called secrets "psychic poison," and after all of the secrets I've kept from Wendell, it feels good to have this final secret out in the open.

I don't ask for counseling again because the truth is that Wendell has been counseling me from day one, in the sense that therapy is a profession you learn by doing—not just the work of being a therapist, but also the work of being a patient. It's a dual apprenticeship, which is why there's a saying that therapists can take their patients only as far as they've gone in their own inner lives. (There's much debate about this idea—like my colleagues, I've seen patients reach heights I can only aspire to. But still, it's no surprise that as I heal inside, I'm also becoming more adept at healing others.)

On a practical level, too, I've taken Wendell's lessons straight to my office.

"I'm reminded of a cartoon of a prisoner, shaking the bars . . ." I said to John early on, in a Hail Mary attempt to help him see that the "idiot" he was talking about that day wasn't his jailer after all.

When I got to the punch line—the bars are open on each side—John smiled for a second in what seemed like recognition but then batted it back at me. "Oh, give me a break," he said, rolling his eyes. "Do other patients actually fall for this?" But he was the outlier. The intervention has worked beautifully with everyone else.

Still, the most important skill I've learned from Wendell is how to remain strategic while also bringing my personality into the room. Would I kick a patient to make a point? Probably not. Would I sing? I'm not sure. But I might not have yelled "*Fuck!*" with Julie had I not seen Wendell be so utterly himself with me. In internships, therapists learn how to do therapy by the book, mastering the fundamentals the way you have to master scales when learning to play piano. For both, once you know the basics, you can skillfully improvise. Wendell's rule isn't as simple as "There are no rules." There *are* rules, and we're trained to adhere to them for a reason. But he has shown me that when rules are bent with thoughtful intention, it broadens the definition of what effective treatment can be.

Wendell and I don't talk about John or Margo again, but a few weeks later, as I settle into my chair in the waiting room, Wendell's door opens and I hear a male voice. "So this time next Wednesday?"

"Yes, see you then," replies Wendell, then his door clicks shut.

Past the screen, a guy in a suit slips out the door to the hall. *Interesting,* I think. Maybe the woman before me ended her therapy, or maybe she *was* Margo, and Wendell engineered the switch to protect my privacy in case Margo eventually figured it out. I don't ask, though, because it doesn't matter anymore.

Wendell was right: The awkwardness had disappeared. The secret was out, the psychic poison diluted.

I'd gotten all the counseling—or was it therapy?—I needed.

50

Deathzilla

It's ten minutes before Julie's session, and I'm mainlining pretzels in our suite's kitchen. I don't know when our last session will be. If she's late, I think the worst. Should I check on her between sessions or let her call if she needs me (knowing she has trouble asking for help)? Should therapists' boundaries be different—looser—with terminally ill patients?

The first time I saw Julie at Trader Joe's, I'd been reluctant to get in her line, but every time after that, if I happened to be there when she was, Julie would wave me over and I'd happily go. If my son was with me, he'd get an extra sheet of stickers and a high five. And when Julie wasn't there anymore, he noticed.

"Where's Julie?" he asked, scanning the counters for her as we approached the checkout. It wasn't that I wouldn't talk about death with him —a close childhood friend of mine had died of cancer a few years before, and I had told Zach the truth about her illness. But because of confidentiality, I couldn't reveal more about Julie. One question would lead to another, to lines I couldn't cross.

"Maybe she changed days," I said, as if I knew her only as the clerk at Trader Joe's. "Or maybe she got another job."

"She wouldn't get another job," Zach said. "She *loved* her job!" I was struck by his response: even a young child could tell.

Without Julie there anymore, we've been going in Emma's line—the woman who offered to carry Julie's baby. Emma also gives him extra stickers.

But back at my office, waiting for Julie to arrive, I ask the same question Zach did: "Where's Julie?"

There's a word we use for the end of therapy: *termination.* I've always found it to be oddly harsh-sounding for what's ideally a warm, bittersweet, and moving experience, much like a graduation. Generally, when the therapy is coming to an end, the work moves toward its final stage, which is saying goodbye. In those sessions, the patient and I consolidate the changes made by talking about "process and progress." What was helpful in getting to where the person is today? What wasn't? What has she learned about herself—her strengths, her challenges, her internal scripts and narratives—and what coping strategies and healthier ways of being can she take with her when she leaves? Underlying all this, of course, is how do we say goodbye?

In our daily lives, many of us don't have the experience of meaningful goodbyes, and sometimes we don't get goodbyes at all. The termination process allows someone who has spent a great deal of time working through a significant life issue to do more than simply leave with some version of "Well, thanks again—see ya!" Research shows that people tend to remember experiences based on how they end, and termination is a powerful phase in therapy because it gives them the experience of a positive conclusion in what might have been a lifetime of negative, unresolved, or empty endings.

Julie and I have been preparing for another kind of termination, though. We both know that her therapy won't end until she dies; I made her that promise. And our process lately has consisted of more and more silence, not because we're avoiding saying something, but because this is how we're facing each other most honestly. Our silences are rich, our emotions swirling in the air. But the silences are also about her declining state. She has less energy, and talking can take a toll. Jarringly, Julie looks healthy, if thin, on the outside, which is why so many people have trouble believing that she's dying. Sometimes I do too. And in a way, our silences serve another purpose: They give us the illusion of stopping time. For fifty blissful minutes, we're both granted a respite from the outside world. She feels safe here, she told me, not having to worry about people worrying about her, having their own feelings.

"But *I* have feelings about you too," I said the day that Julie brought this up.

She thought about this for a second and then said simply, "I know."

"Would you like to know what they are?" I asked.

Julie smiled. "I know that too." And then we went back to silence.

Of course, between the silences, Julie and I have also been talking. Recently, she said she was thinking about time travel. She'd heard a radio show about it and shared a quote she loved, a description of the past as "a vast encyclopedia of calamities you can still fix." She'd memorized it, she said, because it made her laugh. And then it made her cry. Because she'll never live long enough to have this list of calamities that other people acquire by the time they reach old age—relationships they'd want to mend, career paths they'd want to take, mistakes that they'd go back and "get right" this time.

Instead, Julie has been time-traveling to the past to relive parts of her life that she's enjoyed: birthday parties as a child, vacations with her grandparents, her first crush, her first publication, her first conversation with Matt, one that lasted until dawn and still hasn't ended. But even if she were healthy, she said, she'd never want to travel to the future. She wouldn't want to know the plot of the movie, to hear the spoilers.

"The future is hope," Julie said. "But where's the hope if you already know what happens? What are you living for then? What are you striving for?"

I immediately thought of a difference between Julie and Rita, between young and old, but flip-flopped. Julie, who was young, had no future but was happy with her past. Rita, who was old, had a future but was plagued by her past.

It was that day that Julie fell asleep in session for the first time. She dozed off for a few minutes, and when she woke up and realized what had happened, she made a joke, out of embarrassment, about how I must have been time-traveling while she was sleeping, wishing I were someplace else.

I told her I wasn't. I was remembering hearing what must have been the same show she'd heard on the radio, and I was thinking about an observation made at the end of that segment—that we're all time-traveling into the future and at exactly the same rate: sixty minutes per hour.

"Then I guess we're fellow time travelers in here," Julie said.

"We are," I said. "Even when you're resting."

Another time Julie broke our silence to tell me that Matt thought she was being a Deathzilla—going crazy with the death-party planning, the way some brides become over-the-top Bridezillas with their weddings. She'd even hired a party planner to help carry out her funeral-party vision ("It's *my* day, after all!"), and despite his initial discomfort, Matt was now fully onboard.

"We planned a wedding together and now we're planning a funeral together," Julie said, and it has been, she told me, one of the most intimate experiences of their lives, full of deep love and deep pain and gallows humor. When I asked what she wanted that day to be like, first she said, "Well, I'd rather not be dead that day," but failing *that,* she didn't want it to be all "sugarcoated" and "cheery." She liked the idea of a "celebration of life," which the party planner told her was all the rage nowadays, but she didn't like the message that came with it.

"It's a funeral, for God's sake," she said. "All these people in my cancer group say, 'I want people to celebrate! I don't want people to be sad at my funeral.' And I'm like, 'Why the fuck not? You *died!*'"

"You want to have touched people and for them to be affected by your death," I said. "And for those people to remember you, to keep you in mind."

Julie told me that she wanted people to keep her in mind the way she keeps me in mind between sessions.

"I'll be driving, and I'll panic about something, but then I'll hear your voice," she explained. "I'll remember something you said."

I thought about how I did this with Wendell—how I'd internalized his lines of questioning, his way of reframing situations, his voice. This is such a universal experience that one litmus test of whether a patient is ready for termination is whether she carries around the therapist's voice in her head, applying it to situations and essentially eliminating the need for the therapy. "I started to get depressed," a patient might report near the end of treatment, "but then I thought of what you said last month." I've had entire conversations in my head with Wendell, and Julie has done the same with me.

"This might sound crazy," Julie said, "but I know that I'll hear your voice after I die—that I'll hear you wherever I am."

Julie had told me that she'd begun thinking about the afterlife, a concept she insisted that she didn't completely believe in but nonetheless contemplated, "just in case." Would she be alone? Afraid? Everyone she loved was still alive—her husband, her parents, her grandparents, her sister, her nephew and niece. Who would keep her company there? And then she realized two things: first, that her babies from her miscarriages might be there, wherever "there" was, and second, that she was coming to believe that she would hear, in some unknowable spiritual way, the voices of those she loved.

"I would never say this if I weren't dying," she said shyly, "but I include you in those I love. I know you're my therapist, so I hope you don't think it's creepy, but when I tell people that I love my therapist, I really mean I *love* my therapist."

Though I'd come to love many patients over the years, I'd never used those words with any of them. In training, we're taught to be careful with our words to avoid misinterpretations. There are many ways to convey to patients how deeply we've come to care about them without getting into dicey territory. Saying "I love you" isn't one of those ways. But Julie had said she loved me, and I wasn't going to stand on professional ceremony and reply with a watered-down response.

"I love you too, Julie," I said to her that day. She smiled, then closed her eyes and dozed off again.

Now, as I stand in the kitchen waiting for Julie, I think about that conversation and about the ways I know that I'll hear her voice too, long after she's gone, especially at certain times, like while shopping at Trader Joe's or folding laundry and seeing that pajama top with NAMAST'AY IN BED in the pile. I'm saving that top not to remember Boyfriend anymore, but to remember Julie.

I'm still munching on pretzels when my green light goes on. I pop one more into my mouth, rinse my hands, and breathe a sigh of relief.

Julie's early today. She's alive.

51

Dear Myron

Rita is carrying an artist's portfolio, a large black case with nylon handles that's at least three feet long. She's begun teaching art at the local university, the one from which she would have graduated had she not dropped out to get married, and today she brought in her own work to share with her students.

Her portfolio holds sketches for the prints that she's selling on her website, a series based on her own life. The images are visually comical and even cartoonish, but their themes—regret, humiliation, time, eighty-year-old sex—reveal their darkness and depth. She's shown me these before, but now when Rita reaches into her portfolio, she takes out something else: a yellow legal pad.

She hasn't spoken to Myron since the kiss more than two months ago —has avoided him, in fact, going to a different class at the Y, ignoring his knocks on her door (she uses the peephole for screening purposes now, not for spying on the hello-family), going into stealth mode when moving about the building. She's been taking time to craft a letter, obsessing over every line. She tells me she has no idea if her words make sense anymore, and after reading it again this morning, she's not convinced she should send it at all.

"Can I read it to you before I make an absolute fool of myself?" she asks.

"Of course," I say, and she places the yellow pad on her lap.

I can see her handwriting from where I'm sitting—not the specific letters, but the shapes. An artist's handwriting, I think. Gorgeous cursive, the loops perfectly formed but with an added flair. It takes her a minute to start. She breathes in, sighs, almost begins, breathes in, and sighs again. Finally, she speaks.

"'Dear Myron,'" she reads off the page, then looks up at me. "Is that too formal—or too intimate, perhaps? Do you think I should start with 'Hi'? Or just the more neutral 'Myron'?"

"I think if you worry too much about the details, you might miss the big picture," I say, and Rita makes a face. She knows that I'm talking about more than her salutation.

"All right, then," she says, looking back at the lined pad. Still, she grabs a pen, crosses out the word *dear*, then takes a breath and begins again.

"'Myron,'" she reads. "'I'm sorry for my inexcusable behavior in the parking lot. It was completely uncalled for, and I owe you an apology. I certainly owe you an explanation, and you deserve one. So I'm going to give you that here, and then I'm sure you'll be done with me.'"

I must have made a sound—an involuntary *mmm*—because Rita looks up and asks, "What? Too much?"

"I was thinking about the prison sentence," I say. "I was just noticing that you're assuming Myron abides by your same punishment system." Rita thinks about that, crosses something out, then continues reading.

"'Honestly, Myron,'" she continues from the legal pad, "'at first I didn't know why I slapped you. I thought it was because I was angry that you'd been dating that woman, who was, quite frankly, so beneath you. But more important, I couldn't understand why we had been acting like a couple for months—why you would allow me to misperceive the situation in this way only to dispose of me. I know that you've since offered your reasons. You were afraid to start something romantic with me because if it turned out badly, you would lose our friendship. You were afraid that if it didn't work out, we would feel awkward living in the same building—as if it weren't tremendously awkward seeing you with that woman, whose cackle I could hear two floors up, even with my television on.'"

Rita looks up at me, raises her eyebrows in a question, and I shake my head. She strikes something out.

"'But now, Myron,'" Rita goes on, "'you say you want to take that risk. You say that I am worth that risk. And when you said that in the parking lot, I had to run because, believe it or not, I felt sorry for you. I felt sorry for you because you have no idea what kind of risk you'd be taking by getting involved with me. It wouldn't be fair to let you take that risk without telling you who I really am.'"

A tear rolls down Rita's face, then another, and she reaches for a side pocket in her artist's portfolio, where she's stuffed a bunch of tissues. As always, a box of tissues sits within arm's reach, and it still makes me crazy that she won't just *take the tissues*. She cries for a few moments, stuffs the used tissues into the pocket of the portfolio, then looks back at the pad.

"'You think you know my past,'" she reads. "'My marriages, the names and ages of my children, and the cities they live in, and that I don't see them much. Well, *much* wasn't accurate. I should have said that I don't see them at all. Why? Because they hate me.'"

Rita chokes up, then composes herself and goes on.

"'What you don't know, Myron—what even my second and third husbands didn't fully know—is that their father, my first husband, Richard, drank. And when he drank, he hurt our children, *my* children—sometimes with words, sometimes with his hands. He would hurt them in ways I can't get myself to write here. Back then I would scream at him to stop, pleading, and he would yell back at me, and if he was very drunk, he'd hurt me too, and I didn't want the children to see that, so I would stop. You know what I did instead? I would go in the other room. Did you read that, Myron? *My husband would be hurting my children and I would go in the other room!* And I would think, about my husband, *You are ruining them forever, hurting them beyond repair,* and I would know that I was ruining them too, and I would cry and do nothing.'"

Rita is crying so hard now she can no longer speak. She's crying into her hands, and when she calms down, she unzips the portfolio's pocket, pulls out the soiled tissues, wipes her face, licks her finger, and turns the page on the pad.

"'Why didn't I report it to the police, you may wonder. Why didn't I leave and take the children with me? At the time, I told myself that there would be no way to survive, to take care of the children and get a decent job with no college degree. Every day, I would look at the want ads in the newspaper and think, *I could be a waitress or a secretary or a bookkeeper, but could I make the hours and the pay work? Who would pick up the kids from school? Make them dinner?* I never called to find out, because the truth is— and you have to hear this, Myron—the truth is that I didn't want to find out. That's right: *I didn't want to.*'"

Rita looks at me as if to say, *See? See what a monster I am?* This part is new to me too. She holds up a finger—a signal for me to wait for her to collect herself—then reads on.

"'I had felt so alone as a child—and this is no excuse, just an explanation—that the idea of being alone with four kids and working eight hours each day at a dead-end job, well, I just couldn't bear it. I'd seen what happened to other divorcées, the ways they were ostracized, like lepers, and I thought, *No, thank you.* I imagined I would have no adults to talk to, and that, perhaps even worse, I'd lose my one salvation. I'd have neither the time nor the resources to paint, and I worried that under these circumstances, taken together, I would be tempted to kill myself. I justified my staying by reasoning that if the children had a depressed mother, that would be better than a dead mother. But here's another truth, Myron: I didn't want to lose Richard.'"

A dark sound emerges from Rita, and then tears. She wipes her eyes with the dirty tissues.

"'Richard—I hated him, yes, but I also loved him or, rather, the version of him when he wasn't drinking. He was brilliant and witty, and as strange as this sounds, I knew I would miss his companionship. Besides, I would worry about the kids spending time alone with Richard, given his drinking and his temper, so I would have fought to keep them with me all the time, and with him being at work every day, often going to late dinners, he would have agreed. And the thought of him getting off easy like that made me horribly resentful.'"

Rita licks her finger to turn the page again, but the paper sticks and it takes several attempts before she extricates the single sheet from the rest.

"'Once, when I was very courageous, I told him I was leaving. I meant it, Myron, it wasn't an empty threat. I resolved that I was done. So I told him, and Richard just looked at me, stunned at first, I think. But then a smile formed on his face, the most evil smile I had ever seen, and he said, slowly, deliberately, in a voice that I can only describe as a growl, "If you leave, you will have *nothing*. The kids will have *nothing*. So, be my guest, Rita. Leave!" And then he started laughing, and there was venom in his laugh, and I knew right then it was a silly idea. I knew I would stay. But in order to stay, to live with the situation, I told myself all kinds of lies. I told myself it would stop. That Richard would stop drinking. And sometimes he would, at least for a while. But then I'd find his hiding places, bottles peeking out from behind his law books on the shelf in the den or rolled up in blankets on the top of the kids' closets, and we'd be back in hell.

"'I imagine what you're thinking right now—that I'm making excuses. That I'm playing the victim. It's all true. But I've also thought a lot about how a person can be one thing and another thing, both at the same time. I've thought about how much I loved my children despite what I let happen to them, and how Richard, believe it or not, loved them too. I've thought about how he could hurt them and hurt me and also love us and laugh with us and help the kids with their schoolwork and coach their Little League games and give them thoughtful advice when they had disagreements with their friends. I've thought about how Richard would say he would change, and how much he wanted to change, and how he still wouldn't change, at least not for long, and how despite all of this, none of what he said was ever a lie.

"'When I finally left, Richard cried. I'd never seen him cry before. He begged me to stay. But I saw my children, now teenagers or about to be, getting into drugs and harming themselves, wanting to die like me. My son almost overdosed, and a switch flipped, and I said, *Enough*. Nothing—not poverty, not giving up my art, not the fear of being alone for the rest of my life—nothing could stop me from taking the kids and leaving. The morning of the evening I told Richard I was leaving, I withdrew money from our bank account, applied for a job, and rented a two-bedroom apartment, one room for me and my daughter, the other for the boys, and we left.

"'But it was too late. The kids were a mess. They hated me, and, strangely, they wanted to be back with Richard. Once we left, Richard was on his best behavior, and he provided for them financially. He would show up at my daughter's college and take her and her friends out for fancy meals. And the kids soon remembered him differently—especially the youngest, who missed playing ball with him. The youngest would beg to stay with him. And I would feel guilty for leaving. I would doubt myself. *Had* it been the right decision?'"

Rita stops. "Hold on," she says to me, "I lost my place." She turns some pages, then picks up again.

"'Anyway, Myron,'" she reads, "'eventually my children cut me out of their lives entirely. By the time of my second divorce, they said they had no respect for me. They kept in touch with Richard periodically, and he would send them money, but when he died, his new wife somehow got all the money, and the children were angry. Just livid! And suddenly they remembered more clearly what he had done to them, but they weren't enraged just at him—they were still enraged at *me* for letting it happen. They blocked me out, and the only time I heard from them was when they were in trouble. My daughter was in an abusive relationship and needed money to leave, but she wouldn't give me any details. *Just send the money,* she said, so I did. I sent her money to rent an apartment and buy food. And, of course, she didn't leave, and far as I know, she's still with that man. Then my son needed money for rehab but wouldn't let me visit.'"

Rita glances at the clock. "I'm getting to the end," she says. I nod.

"'I lied to you about something else, Myron. I said that I couldn't be your bridge partner because I wouldn't be very good, but I used to be an excellent bridge player. I declined your offer because I imagined it would put me in a situation where I'd have to tell you what I'm telling you now —that we'd travel to a tournament in a city where one of my children lives and you would ask why we weren't visiting them, and I would make something up, say they were out of town, or ill, or what have you, but that wouldn't work every time. You would get suspicious, and sooner or later, I knew, you would put the pieces together and realize that something had gone dreadfully wrong. You would say to yourself, *Aha! This woman I'm dating is not at all as she seems!*'"

Rita's voice quivers and then breaks as she tries to get this last part out.

"'So that's me, Myron,'" she reads, so quietly I can barely hear her. "'That's the person you kissed in the parking lot at the Y.'"

As Rita looks down at the letter, I'm floored by how clearly she's spelled out the contradictions of her history. When she first came to me, she mentioned that I made her think of her daughter, whom she missed terribly. She said that her daughter had at one point talked about wanting to become a psychologist and had volunteered to work in a treatment center but then got sidetracked by her volatile relationship.

What I didn't tell Rita was that she, in some ways, reminded me of my mother. Not that my mother's adult life looked anything like Rita's—my parents have had a long, stable, and loving marriage, and my father is the kindest possible husband. It's that both Rita and my mother came from difficult and lonely childhoods. In my mother's case, her father died when she was just nine years old, and though her mother did her best to raise her and her sister, who was eight years older, my mother suffered. And her suffering affected the way she interacted with her own children.

So, like Rita's children, I went through a period where I shut my mom out. And while that had long passed, as I sit with Rita and hear her story, I have the urge to cry—not for *my* pain, but for my mother's. As much as I've thought about my relationship with my mother over the years, I've never considered her experience in exactly the way I am now. I have the fantasy that all adults should be given the opportunity to hear parents—not their own—rip themselves open, become completely vulnerable, and give their versions of events, because in seeing this, you can't help but come to a newfound understanding of your own parents' lives, whatever the situation.

While Rita read her letter, I wasn't just listening to her words; I was also observing her body, seeing how at times, it would crumple in on itself, how sometimes her hands would tremble and her lips would become pinched and her leg would shake and her voice would quaver, how she'd shift her weight when she paused. I'm watching her body now too, and sad as she seems, her body appears, if not at peace, the most relaxed I've seen it. She leans back on the couch, recovering from the exertion of the reading.

And then something astounding happens.

She reaches over to the tissue box on my side table and pulls one out. A clean, fresh tissue! She opens it up, blows her nose, then takes another from the box and blows her nose again. It's all I can do not to break into applause.

"So," she asks, "do you think I should send this?"

I picture Myron reading Rita's letter. I wonder how he'll respond as a father and grandfather, as somebody who was married to Myrna, likely a very different kind of mother to their now happily grown children. Will he accept who Rita is, all of her? Or will this information be too much, something he can't get past?

"Rita," I say, "that's a decision only you can make. But I'm curious—is this a letter for Myron or for your children?"

Rita pauses for a second, looks at the ceiling. Then she looks back at me, nods, but says nothing, because we each know the answer is *Both*.

52

Mothers

"So," I'm telling Wendell, "we get back from a late dinner with friends and I ask Zach to take his shower, but he wants to play, and I tell him we can't because it's a school night. And then he has this complete overreaction and whines, 'You're so mean! You're the meanest!'—which isn't like him at all —but also this anger just boils up inside *me*.

"So I say something petty like, 'Oh, really? Well, maybe next time I shouldn't take you and your friends out to dinner, if I'm so mean.' Like I'm five years old! And he says, 'Fine!' and slams his door—he's never slammed his door before—and gets in the shower and I go to my computer planning to answer emails but instead I'm having a conversation in my head about whether I really *am* mean. *How could I have responded that way? I'm the adult, after all.*

"And then all of a sudden I remember a frustrating phone conversation I'd had with my mother that morning and it clicks. I'm not angry with Zach. I'm angry with *my mom*. It was classic displacement."

Wendell smiles as if to say, *Displacement's a bitch, isn't it?* We all use defense mechanisms to deal with anxiety, frustration, or unacceptable impulses, but what's fascinating about them is that *we aren't aware of them in the moment*. A familiar example is *denial*—a smoker might cling to the belief that his shortness of breath is due to the hot weather and not his cigarettes. Another person might use *rationalization* (justifying something shameful) — saying after he's rejected for a job that he never really wanted the job in the first place. In *reaction formation,* unacceptable feelings or impulses are expressed as their opposite, as when a person who dislikes her neighbor goes out of her way to befriend her or when an evangelical Christian man who's attracted to men makes homophobic slurs.

Some defense mechanisms are considered *primitive* and others *mature.* In the latter group is *sublimation,* when a person turns a potentially harmful impulse into something less harmful (a man with aggressive impulses takes up boxing) or even constructive (a person with the urge to cut people becomes a surgeon who saves lives).

Displacement (shifting a feeling toward one person onto a safer alternative) is considered a neurotic defense, neither primitive nor mature. A person who was yelled at by her boss but could get fired if she yelled back might come home and yell at her dog. Or a woman who felt angry at her mother after a phone conversation might displace that anger onto her son.

I tell Wendell that when I went to apologize to Zach after his shower, I discovered that he, too, was displacing his anger onto me — some kids at recess had kicked Zach and his friends off the basketball courts. When the yard teacher said that everyone could play, the boys wouldn't pass the ball to Zach or his friends, and apparently some "mean" things were said. Zach was furious with those boys, but it was safer to be furious at his mom who wanted him to take a shower.

"The irony of the story," I continue, "is that we both launched our anger at the wrong target."

From time to time, Wendell and I have discussed the ways parental relationships evolve in midlife as people shift from blaming their parents to taking full responsibility for their lives. It's what Wendell calls "the changing of the guard." Whereas in their younger years, people often come to therapy to understand why their parents won't act in ways they wish, later on, people come to figure out how to manage what *is.* And so my question about my mother has gone from "Why can't she change?" to "Why can't I?" How is it, I ask Wendell, that even in my forties, I can be affected so deeply by a phone call from my mother?

I'm not asking for an actual answer. Wendell doesn't need to tell me that people regress; that you might astonish yourself with how far you've come, only to slip back into your old roles.

"It's like the eggs," I say, and he nods in recognition. I once told Wendell that Mike, my colleague, had said a while back that when we feel fragile, we're like raw eggs—we crack open and splatter if dropped. But when we develop more resilience, we're like hard-boiled eggs—we might get dinged up if dropped, but we won't crack completely and spill all over the place. Over the years, I've gone from being a raw egg to a hard-boiled egg with my mother, but sometimes the raw egg in me emerges.

I tell Wendell that later that night my mom apologized and we worked it out. Before that, though, I'd gotten caught up in our old routine—her wanting me to do something the way she wanted it done, me wanting to do it the way I wanted. And perhaps Zach perceives me the same way, trying to control him by getting him to do things the way I want too—all in the name of love, of wanting the best for our children. As much as I claim to be dramatically different from my mother, there are times when I'm eerily similar.

Now, talking about my phone conversation, I don't bother telling Wendell what my mom said or what I said because I know that's not the point. He won't position me as victim and my mom as aggressor. Years ago I might have deconstructed our pas de deux, trying to garner sympathy for my predicament: *Can't you see? Isn't she difficult?* But now I find his more clear-eyed approach comforting.

Today I tell Wendell that I've begun saving my mom's phone messages to my computer, the warm and sweet ones that I'll want to hear, that my son may want so that he can hear his grandmother's voice when he's my age—or, later, when we're both gone. I tell him that I'm also noticing that the nagging I do as a parent isn't for Zach as much as it is for me; it's a distraction from my awareness that he'll be leaving me one day, from my sadness, despite my wanting him to do the healthy work of what's called "separation and individuation."

I try to imagine Zach as a teenager. I remember my mom dealing with me as a teenager and finding me as alien as I might one day find Zach. It seems not that long ago that he was in preschool, and my parents were healthy, and I was healthy, and the neighborhood kids all ran outside to play every evening after dinner, and the only thought I had about the future at all was the sense of *Things will be easier, I'll have more flexibility, more sleep.* I never thought about what would be lost.

Who knew that a phone call with my mother could bring all this to the surface—that underneath the old mother-daughter frustration was not a wish for her to go away but a longing for her to stay forever?

I think of something else Wendell once said: "The nature of life is change and the nature of people is to resist change." It was a paraphrase of something he'd read that had resonated with him both personally and as a therapist, he told me, because it was a theme that informed nearly every person's struggles. The day before he said this, I had been told by my eye doctor that I had developed presbyopia, which happens to most people in their forties. As people age, they become farsighted; they have to hold whatever they're reading or looking at farther away in order to see it clearly. But maybe an emotional presbyopia happens around this age too, where people pull back to see the bigger picture: how scared they are to lose what they have, even if they still complain about it.

"And my mother!" Julie exclaims in my office later that day, recalling her own morning conversation with her mom. "This is so hard on her. She said her job as a parent was to make sure that her children were safe when *she* left the planet, but now she's making sure *I'm* leaving the planet safely."

Julie tells me that when she was in college, she got in a fight with her mom about Julie's boyfriend. Her mother thought that Julie had lost her natural buoyancy and that the boyfriend's behaviors—canceling plans at the last minute, pressuring Julie to edit his papers, demanding that Julie spend the holidays with him instead of with her own family—were the reason. Julie's mom suggested that she check out the campus counseling center to talk this over with a neutral party, and Julie exploded.

"There's nothing wrong with our relationship!" Julie shouted. "If I go to a counselor, it will be to talk about *you*, not him!" She didn't go to a counselor, though now she wishes she had. A few months later, the boyfriend dumped her. And her mom loved her enough *not* to say *I told you so*. Instead, when Julie called crying, her mom sat on the phone and simply listened.

"Now," Julie says, "my mom will have to go to a therapist to talk about *me*."

Recently, one of my lab tests came back positive for a marker for Sjögren's syndrome, an autoimmune disease most common in women over forty, but even so, my doctors aren't sure I have this because I don't have its chief symptoms. "It could be an unusual presentation," one doctor explained, then went on to say that I may have Sjögren's *and* something else or just something else that hasn't—still—been determined. Sjögren's, it turns out, is difficult to diagnose, and nobody knows what causes it—it could be genetic, environmental, triggered by a virus or bacteria, or some combination of those factors.

"We don't have all the answers," this doctor said, and while the prospect of still not knowing scared me, another doctor's comment frightened me even more: "Whatever it is will present itself eventually." That week, I'd told Wendell again that my greatest fear is leaving Zach without a mother, and Wendell said that I had two choices: I could give Zach a mother who's constantly worried about leaving him motherless, or I could give him a mother whose uncertain health makes her more acutely aware of the preciousness of their time together.

"Which scares you less?" he'd asked rhetorically.

His question made me think of Julie and how initially I'd hesitated when she asked if I would see her through her death. It wasn't just my inexperience that gave me pause, I realized later—it was that Julie would force me to face my own mortality, something I wasn't ready to do. Even after agreeing to her request, I'd been keeping myself safe in that relationship by never comparing my mortality to hers. After all, nobody has put a time limit on my lifespan in the same way. But Julie had learned to live with who she was and what she had—which was, in essence, what I'd helped her to do and what we all need to do. There's so much about our lives that remains unknown. I would have to cope with not knowing what my future held, manage my worry, and focus on living *now*. This couldn't be just a piece of advice I'd given Julie. It was time for me to take my own medicine.

"The more you welcome your vulnerability," Wendell had said, "the less afraid you'll feel."

This isn't how we tend to view life when we're younger. Our younger selves think in terms of a beginning, middle, and some kind of resolution. But somewhere along the way—perhaps in that middle—we realize that everyone lives with things that may not get worked out. That the middle has to *be* the resolution, and how we make meaning of it becomes our task. Although time feels like it's slipping away and I just can't hold on to it, something else is true too: My illness has sharpened my focus. It's why I couldn't write the wrong book. It's why I'm dating again. It's why I'm soaking in my mother and looking at her with a generosity I have for so long been unable to access. And it's why Wendell is helping me examine the mothering I'll leave Zach with someday. Now I keep in mind that none of us can love and be loved without the possibility of loss but that there's a difference between knowledge and terror.

As Julie imagines her mother in therapy, I wonder what Zach might say to a therapist about me when he's grown.

And then I think: *I hope he finds his Wendell.*

53

The Hug

I'm curled up on the couch—my living-room couch, that is—with Allison, my college friend who's in town from the Midwest. We're surfing channels after dinner and land on John's show. She has no idea that John is my patient. I keep going, wanting to watch something light and breezy.

"Wait," Allison says, "go back!" Turns out she loves John's show.

I click back with the remote. I haven't seen the show in a while, so I try to catch up. Some of the people have changed; their relationships are new. I'm half watching, half dozing, content to be relaxing with my longtime friend.

"She's so great, isn't she?" Allison says.

"Who?" I ask sleepily.

"The therapist character."

I open my eyes. The main character is in what appears to be a therapist's office. The therapist is a petite brunette in glasses—but in typical Hollywood fashion, she's stunning in an intellectual way. *Maybe* that's *the kind of woman John would take as a mistress,* I think. The main character is getting up to leave. He appears troubled. She walks him to the door.

"You look like you need a hug," the main character says to the therapist.

The therapist seems surprised for a split second, then shifts into neutral. "Are you saying you'd like a hug?" she asks.

"No," he says. There's a beat, and then suddenly he leans down and hugs her. It's not sexual, but it's intense. The camera moves in on the character's face: his eyes are closed, but a tear escapes. He rests his head on her shoulder and seems at peace. Then the camera pans around to the therapist's face, and her eyes are open wide, bulging, as if she wants to bolt. It's like those scenes in romantic comedies after two people have finally slept together and one person has a look of utter bliss while the other looks completely freaked out.

"I think we both feel better now," the character says, letting go of the embrace and turning to leave. He walks away, and the scene ends on the therapist's expression: *What the hell just happened?*

It's a funny moment and Allison laughs, but I'm as confused as the therapist in the show. Is John acknowledging his affection for me? Is he making fun of himself, of the way he projects his needs onto others? Television shows are written months in advance. Was he aware back then of how obnoxious he can be? Is he now?

"So many shows have therapists lately," Allison says. She starts talking about her favorite TV therapists: Jennifer Melfi from *The Sopranos,* Tobias Fünke from *Arrested Development,* Niles Crane from *Frasier,* even the goofy Marvin Monroe on *The Simpsons.*

"Did you ever watch *In Treatment?*" I ask. "The Gabriel Byrne character?"

"Oh, yeah—loved him," she says. "But this one's more realistic."

"You think so?" I say, wondering now whether this character is modeled after me or after the "nice, but an idiot" therapist John saw before me. Shows are staffed by a dozen or so writers who are assigned their own episodes, so it's also possible that this character was created by another writer altogether.

I keep the show on through the credits, though I know exactly what they'll say. This episode was written by John.

"I watched your show last week," I tell John at our next session.

John shakes his head, mixes his salad with his chopsticks, takes a bite, chews.

"Fucking network," he says, swallowing. "They made me do it."

I nod.

"They said everyone likes therapists."

I shrug. *Oh, well.*

"They're like sheep," John continues. "One show has a therapist, *every* show has to have one."

"It's your show," I observe. "Couldn't you say no?"

John thinks about this. "Yeah," he says. "But I didn't want to be an asshole."

I smile. *He didn't want to be an asshole.*

"And now," John goes on, "because of the ratings, I'll never get rid of her."

"You're stuck with her," I say. "Because of the ratings."

"Fucking network," he repeats. John takes another bite, curses the chopsticks. "It'll be okay, though," he says. "She's kind of growing on me. We have some good ideas for next season." He wipes his mouth with his napkin, first the left corner of his lips, then the right. I watch him.

"What?" he says.

I raise my eyebrows.

"Oh, no, no, no," he says, protesting. "I know what you're thinking. You're thinking that there's some 'connection'"—he puts air quotes around the word *connection*—"between the therapist and you. It's fiction, okay?"

"All of it?" I say.

"Of course! It's a story, a *show*. God, if I took any dialogue from here, it would kill the ratings. So, no, obviously it's not you."

"I'm thinking about the emotions more than the dialogue," I say. "Maybe there's some truth in them."

"It's a *show*," he repeats.

I give John a look.

"I mean it. That character has no more to do with you than the main character has to do with me. Other than his good looks, of course." He laughs at his joke. At least, I think it's a joke.

We sit in silence as John glances around the room—at the pictures on the wall, at the floor, at his hands. I remember his "One Mississippi, two Mississippi," back before he could tolerate the wait. After a couple of minutes, he speaks up.

"I want to show you something," he says, then adds sarcastically, "Can I get a permission slip to use my phone?"

I nod. He grabs his phone, scrolls through it, then hands it over to me. "That's my family." On the screen is a photo of a pretty blonde and two girls who appear to be cracking up as they do bunny ears on their mom —Margo, Gracie, and Ruby. (Turns out Margo wasn't the patient before me at Wendell's.) Next to Ruby is Rosie, the ugly dog that John loves dearly, with a pink bow on her patchy-furred head. After hearing so much about them, here they are, a mesmerizing tableau. I can't stop staring at them.

"Sometimes I forget how lucky I am," he says quietly.

"You have a lovely family," I say. I tell him how moved I am that he shared this picture with me. I start to hand the phone back, but John stops me.

"Wait," he says. "Those are my girls. But here's my boy."

I feel a pinch in my gut. He's about to show me Gabe. As the mom of a boy myself, I don't know if I can look without crying.

John scrolls through some photos, and there he is: Gabe. He's so adorable I feel like my heart might split in half. He has John's thick, wavy hair and Margo's bright blue eyes. He's sitting in John's lap at a Dodgers game, and he's got a ball in his hand, mustard on his cheek, and a look on his face like he's just won the World Series. John tells me that they'd just caught a ball up in the stands and Gabe was ecstatic.

"I'm the luckiest person in the whole wide world!" Gabe had said that day. John tells me that Gabe said it again when he got home and showed the ball to Margo and Gracie and then again when he was snuggling with John at bedtime. "The luckiest person in the whole world, the entire galaxy and beyond!"

"He *was* the luckiest that day," I say, and I can feel my eyes get wet.

"Oh, for Christ's sake, don't cry on me," John says, looking away. "Just what I need, a therapist who cries."

"Why not cry in response to sadness?" I say pointedly. John takes his phone back and types something in.

"As long as you're letting me use my phone," he says, "there's something else I want to show you." Now that I've seen his wife, his daughters, his dog, and his dead son, I wonder what else he wants to share.

"Here," he says, extending his arm in my direction. I take the phone and recognize the *New York Times* website. There's a review of the new season of John's show.

"Check out the last paragraph," he says.

I scroll to the end, where the reviewer waxes poetic about the direction the show has taken. The main character, the reviewer writes, has begun to share glimpses of his underlying humanity without losing his edge, and this makes him all the more interesting, his moments of compassion a delightful twist. If viewers used to be riveted by his perverse lack of regard for others, the reviewer contends, now we can't stop watching him struggle to reconcile this with what's buried beneath. The review concludes with a question: What might we discover if he continues to reveal himself?

I look up from the phone and smile at John. "I agree," I say. "Especially with the question posed at the end."

"It's a nice review, huh?" he says.

"It is—and more."

"No, no, no—don't start making this like he's talking about me again. It's the *character.*"

"Okay," I say.

"Good," he says. "Just so we're straight on that."

I catch John's eye. "Why did you want me to see this?"

He looks at me like I'm an idiot. "Because it's a great review! It's the fucking *New York Times*!"

"But why that specific paragraph?"

"Because it means we'll go into syndication. If this season is doing so well, the network can't not give us another pickup."

I think about how hard it is for John to be vulnerable. How ashamed and needy it makes him feel. How scary connection seems.

"Well," I say, "I look forward to seeing where 'the character'"—I make air quotations like John did—"goes in the next season. I think the future holds a lot of possibility."

John's body responds for him; he blushes. Caught, he blushes even more. "Thanks," he says. I smile and meet his eyes, and he manages to meet mine and hold my gaze for a good twenty seconds before glancing toward his feet. Looking down, he whispers, "Thanks for . . . you know" —he searches for the right word—"everything."

My eyes tear up again. "You're so welcome," I say.

"Well," John says, clearing his throat and folding his pedicured feet onto the couch. "Now that the preliminaries are over, what the fuck should we talk about today?"

54

Don't Blow It

There are two main categories of people who are so depressed that they contemplate suicide. One type thinks, *I had a nice life, and if I can just emerge from this terrible crisis*—the death of a loved one; extended un-employment—*I'll have something to look forward to. But what if I can't?* The other type thinks, *My life is barren, and there's nothing to look forward to.*

Rita fell into the second category.

Of course, the story a patient comes into therapy with may not be the story she leaves with. What was included in the telling at first might now be written out, and what was left out might become a central plot point. Some major characters might become minor ones, and some minor char-acters might go on to receive star billing. The patient's own role might change too—from bit player to protagonist, from victim to hero.

A few days after her seventieth birthday, Rita comes in for her regular ses-sion. Instead of marking the occasion with her suicide, she's brought me a present.

"It's my birthday gift to you," she says.

Rita's gift is beautifully wrapped, and she asks me to open it in front of her. The box is heavy, and I try to figure out what it is. Bottles of my favor-ite tea that she had seen and commented on in my office? A large book? A set of the darkly comic mugs that she's begun selling on her website? (I'm hoping for these.)

I dig through the tissue paper and feel something ceramic (the mugs!), but as I lift the object out, I look at Rita and smile. It's a tissue-box cover painted with the words RITA SAYS — DON'T BLOW IT. The design is at once bold and unassuming, like Rita herself. I turn the box over and notice her logo with her business's name: It Ain't Over Till It's Over, Inc.

I begin to thank her but she interrupts me.

"It was inspired by our conversations about my not taking the tissues," Rita says, as if I might not get the reference. "I used to think, *What is* with *this therapist, harping on which tissues I use?* I never understood it until one of the girls" — she means one of the hello-family girls — "saw me take a tissue from my purse and said, 'Ewwww! Our mom says you should never use dirty tissues!' And I thought, *So does my therapist. Everybody needs a fresh box of tissues. And why not add a classy cover?*" She says the word *classy* with a wink in her voice.

Rita's being here today doesn't signal the end of her therapy, nor do I measure the therapy's success by the fact that she's alive. After all, what if Rita had chosen not to kill herself on her seventieth birthday but was still severely depressed? What we're celebrating today isn't her continued physical presence so much as her still-in-progress emotional revival — the risks she's taken to begin to move from a position of ossification to one of openness, from self-flagellation to something closer to self-acceptance.

Though we have a lot to celebrate today, Rita's therapy will continue because old habits die hard. Because pain abates but doesn't vanish. Because broken relationships (with herself, with her children) require sensitive and intentional rapprochement, and new ones need support and self-awareness to flourish. If Rita is going to be with Myron, she'll have to better acquaint herself with her projections, her fears, her envy, her pain and past crimes, so that this next marriage, her fourth, becomes her last and first great love story.

Myron, it turns out, didn't respond to Rita's letter for a full week. She had handwritten her missive and stuffed it through a slit on the side of the communal bank of metal boxes into his, and at first Rita agonized about what might have happened. Her eyesight wasn't as good as it used to be, and her arthritis made it difficult to push the letter through the slightly rusted opening. Had she accidentally slipped it into the adjacent box, the one that belonged to the hello-family? How mortifying that would be! She obsessed about this possibility all week, tormenting herself in a spiral I call *catastrophizing*, until a text arrived from Myron.

In my office, Rita had read me the text: "'Rita, thank you for sharing yourself with me. I want to talk with you, but there's a lot to absorb, and I need a bit more time. Back in touch soon, M.'

"A lot to absorb!" Rita exclaimed. "I know what he's *absorbing*—what a monster I am and how grateful he is to have spared himself! Now that he knows the truth, he's *absorbing* how he can retract everything he said when he *mauled* me in the parking lot!"

I noted how assaulted she felt by Myron's perceived abandonment, how quickly a romantic kiss had turned into a mauling.

"That's one explanation," I said. "But another is that you've hidden yourself from him so deliberately and for so long that he needs some time to take in this new part of the picture. He kissed you in the parking lot, poured his heart out to you, and you've avoided him ever since. And now he gets this letter. That *is* a lot to absorb."

Rita shook her head. "You see," she went on as if she hadn't heard a word I said, "this is exactly why it's better to keep my distance."

I told Rita what I tell everyone who's afraid of getting hurt in relationships—which is to say, everyone with a heartbeat. I explained to her that even in the best possible relationship, you're going to get hurt sometimes, and no matter how much you love somebody, you will at times hurt that person, not because you want to, but because you're human. You will inevitably hurt your partner, your parents, your children, your closest friend —and they will hurt you—because if you sign up for intimacy, getting hurt is part of the deal.

But, I went on, what was so great about a loving intimacy was that there was room for repair. Therapists call this process *rupture and repair,* and if you had parents who acknowledged their mistakes and took responsibility for them and taught you as a child to acknowledge your mistakes and learn from them too, then ruptures won't feel so cataclysmic in your adult relationships. If, however, your childhood ruptures didn't come with loving repairs, it will take some practice for you to tolerate the ruptures, to stop believing that every rupture signals the end, and to trust that even if a relationship doesn't work out, you will survive that rupture too. You will heal and self-repair and sign up for another relationship full of its own ruptures and repairs. It's not ideal, opening yourself up like this, putting your shield down, but if you want the rewards of an intimate relationship, there's no way around it.

Still, Rita called me every day to let me know that Myron hadn't responded. "Radio silence," she'd say into my voicemail, then add sarcastically, "He must still be *absorbing*."

I urged her to stay connected to all the good in her life despite her anxiety around Myron, to not withdraw into hopelessness because something was painful, not to be like the person on a diet who messes up once and says, "Forget it! I'll never lose weight," and then binges for the rest of the week, making herself feel ten times worse. I told her to report to me on my voicemail what she was doing each day, and, dutifully, Rita would tell me that she had dinner with the hello-family, created the syllabus for her college class, took "the grandkids" — her honorary granddaughters — to the museum for an art lesson, filled orders from her website. But without fail, she'd end with a caustic crack about Myron.

Secretly, of course, I too was hoping that Myron would rise to the occasion and that he'd do so sooner rather than later. Rita had gone out on a limb by revealing herself to him, and I didn't want the experience to confirm her deeply held belief that she was unlovable. As the days wore on, Rita got more antsy to hear from Myron — but so did I.

At our next session, I was relieved to hear that Rita and Myron had talked. And, indeed, he'd been taken aback by all that Rita had shared — and by the fact that she'd concealed so much. Who was this woman to whom he was drawn so strongly? Was this kind and caring person the same one who'd fled in fear while her husband hurt their children? Could this woman who doted on the hello-family kids be the same one who neglected her own? Was this funny, artistic, and whip-smart woman the same one who'd wiled away her days in a haze of depression? And if so, what did this mean? What effect might it have not just on Myron, but on his children and grandchildren? After all, he reasoned, whomever he dated would be woven into the fabric of his close-knit family.

During that week of "absorbing," Myron confessed to Rita, he spoke to Myrna, his deceased wife, whose counsel he had always relied on. He still talked to her, and now, she was telling him not to be so judgmental —to be cautious but not closed-minded. After all, had she not been fortunate enough to have loving parents and a wonderful husband, who knows what *she* would have done under the circumstances? He also called his brother back east, and he said, "Have you told her about Dad?" By which he meant, *Have you told her about Dad's deep depression after Mom died? Have you told her that you were afraid of the same thing happening to you after Myrna died?*

Finally, he'd phoned his best buddy from childhood, who listened intently to Myron's story and then said, "My friend, all you do is talk about this woman. At our age, who *doesn't* come with enough baggage to bring down an airplane? You think you've got nothing? You've got a dead wife you talk to every day and an aunt in the loony bin that nobody mentions. You're a good catch, but c'mon. Who do you think you are, Prince Charming?"

But most important, Myron spoke to himself. His voice inside said, *Take a risk. Maybe our pasts don't define us but inform us. Maybe all she's been through is exactly what makes her so interesting—and so caring now.*

"Nobody's ever called me caring before," Rita said in my office, tearing up as she related the conversation with Myron. "I was always called selfish and demanding."

"But you're not like that with Myron," I said.

Rita thought about that. "No," she said slowly. "I'm not."

Sitting with Rita, I was reminded that the heart is just as fragile at seventy as it is at seventeen. The vulnerability, the longing, the passion— they're all there in full force. Falling in love never gets old. No matter how jaded you are, how much suffering love has caused you, a new love can't help but make you feel hopeful and alive, like that very first time. Maybe this time it's more grounded—you have more experience, you're wiser, you know you have less time—but your heart still leaps when you hear your lover's voice or see that number pop up on your phone. Late-in-life love has the benefit of being especially forgiving, generous, sensitive—and urgent.

Rita told me that after her talk with Myron, they went to bed, and she enjoyed what she called "an eight-hour orgasm," just what her skin hunger craved. "We slept in each other's arms," Rita said, "and that felt just as good as the several orgasms that came before it." Over the past couple of months, Rita and Myron have become life partners and bridge partners; they won their first travel tournament. She still gets pedicures, not just for the foot massages but because somebody other than her actually sees her toes now.

That's not to say that Rita doesn't struggle; she does, sometimes mightily. While the changes in her life have added much-needed color to her days, she still experiences what she calls "pinches": sadness over her children as she watches Myron with his; anxiety that comes with the novelty of being in a trusting relationship after her unstable history.

More than once, Rita has been on the verge of reading something negative into something Myron has said, of sabotaging her relationship so that she could punish herself for her happiness or retreat to the familiar safety of loneliness. But each time, she has worked hard to reflect before acting; she channels our conversations and tells herself, like on her tissue-box cover, "Don't blow it, girl." I've told her about the many relationships I've seen implode simply because one person was terrified of being abandoned and so did everything in his or her power to push the other person away. She is starting to see that what makes self-sabotage so tricky is that it attempts to solve one problem (alleviate abandonment anxiety) by creating another (making her partner want to leave).

Seeing Rita in this phase of her life reminds me of something I once heard, though I can't recall from where: "Every laugh and good time that comes my way feels ten times better than before I knew such sadness."

· · ·

For the first time in forty years, Rita tells me after I open her gift, she had a birthday party. Not that she expected one. She assumed she'd celebrate quietly with Myron, but when they walked into the restaurant, she found a group of people waiting for her—surprise!

"You can't do that to a seventy-year-old," Rita says today, relishing the memory. "I almost went into cardiac arrest."

Standing in the crowd, clapping and laughing, were the hello-family —Anna, Kyle, Sophia, and Alice (the girls made paintings as gifts); Myron's son and daughter and their children (who are gradually becoming another set of honorary grandchildren); and a few students from the college class she's teaching (one student told her, "If you want to have an interesting conversation, talk to an *old* person"). Also there were fellow members of her apartment board (after finally agreeing to join, Rita spearheaded a replacement of the rusted mailboxes) and some bridge-group friends that she and Myron had made recently. Nearly twenty people had come to celebrate a woman who a year earlier hadn't had a friend in the world.

But the biggest surprise had come that morning, when Rita got an email from her daughter. After writing to Myron, she had sent a well-thought-out letter to each of her kids, to which she'd received the usual nonresponses. But that day, there was an email from Robin, which Rita reads to me in session.

> Mom: Well, you're right, I don't forgive you, and I'm glad you aren't asking me to. Honestly, I almost deleted your email without reading it because I thought it would be the usual bullshit. And then, I don't know why—maybe because we hadn't been in touch in so long—I thought I should at least open it and make sure that you weren't writing to say you were dying. But I wasn't expecting anything like this at all. I kept thinking, Is this my mom?
>
> Anyway, I took your letter to my therapist—yes, I'm in therapy now; and no, I haven't dumped Roger yet—and I told her, "I don't want to turn out like this." I don't want to be stuck in an abusive relationship and making excuses not to leave, thinking it's too late or that

I can't start over or God knows what I tell myself when Roger tries to rope me back in. I told my therapist that if you're finally able to be in a healthy relationship, I can do this too, and I don't want to wait until I'm seventy. Did you notice the email address I'm sending this from? It's my secret job-hunting email.

Rita cries for a while, then continues reading.

You know what's funny, Mom? After I read her your letter, my therapist asked if I had any positive memories of my childhood, and I couldn't think of anything. But then I started having dreams. I had a dream about going to a ballet and when I woke up, I realized that I was the ballerina in the dream, and you were the teacher, and I remembered that time when I was maybe eight or nine and you took me to a ballet class I was dying to go to, and they said I didn't have enough experience, and I cried, and you hugged me and said, "Come on, I'll teach you," and we went into an empty studio and pretended to do ballet for what seemed like hours. I remember laughing and dancing and wishing each moment would last forever. And there were more dreams after that, dreams that brought back positive memories from childhood, memories I didn't even know I had.

I guess I'm saying that I'm not ready to talk or try to have any kind of relationship right now, or maybe ever, but I wanted you to know that I remembered you at your best, which wasn't nearly enough, but it was something. For what it's worth, all of us were shocked by your letter. We all talked about it and agreed that even if we never have a relationship with you, we need to get our lives together because, like I said, if you can, so can we. My therapist said that maybe I don't want to get my life together because then you would win. I didn't know what she meant, but I think now I do. Or I'm starting to.

Anyway, happy birthday.

From,

Robin

P.S. Nice website.

Rita looks up from the email. She's not sure what to make of it. She wishes her sons had also replied, because she worries deeply about all of her kids. About Robin, who still hasn't left Roger. The boys—one still struggling with addiction issues, one divorced for the second time from a "nasty, critical woman who tricked him into marriage with a fake pregnancy," and the little one, who left college because of a learning disability, and has jumped from job to job ever since. Rita says she's tried to help, but they won't talk to her, and besides, what could she do for them now anyway? She's given financial help when asked, but that's all the contact they want.

"I worry about them," she says. "I worry all the time."

"Maybe," I say, "instead of worrying about them, you can love them. All you can do is find a way to love them that's about what they need from you and not what you need from them right now."

I think about what it must have been like for her kids to receive her letter. Rita had wanted to tell them about her relationship with the hello-family kids, to show them that she's changed, to let them see her loving maternal side that she'd like to offer them too. But I suggested that she leave that out for now. I imagined that they'd feel resentful, like the patient who told me about his father who left the family and married a younger woman and had kids with her. *His* father had been cranky and emotionally absent, but the kids in family number two got the Dad of the Year— he coached their soccer teams, attended their piano recitals, volunteered in their schools, took them on vacations, knew the names of their friends. My patient felt like an outsider, an unwanted visitor in family number two, and he was, like many people with similar stories, deeply hurt at seeing his dad become the father he wanted—but to different children.

"It's an opening," I say of the letter.

Eventually, two of the boys reach out to Rita and meet Myron. For the first time in the boys' lives, they start to form a relationship with a reliable, loving father figure. The youngest, though, remains hobbled by his anger. All of her children are distant and furious, but that's okay—at least this time, Rita is able to hear them without shielding herself with defensiveness or tears. Robin moved into a studio apartment and got an administrative job at a mental-health clinic. Rita had encouraged her to move west to be close to her and Myron, to provide some community as she rebuilds her life after Roger, but Robin doesn't want to leave her therapist (or, Rita suspects, Roger)—not yet.

It's not an ideal family, or even a functional one, but it's family. Rita revels in it but also reckons with the pain of all that she cannot fix.

And though Rita's days are finally full, she does have time to add a few more products to her website. One is a welcome sign that can be hung in people's entryways. It consists of two large words surrounded by various stick figures who all look unhinged in their own ways. The sign reads HELLO, FAMILY!

The second is a print she created for Myron's daughter, a teacher, who saw this message on a Post-it above Rita's desk and asked if she'd make an artistic version for her classroom to teach kids resilience. It reads FAILURE IS PART OF BEING HUMAN.

"I must have read that somewhere," she told me, "but I couldn't find an attribution." In fact, it was something I had said to her in session once, but I don't mind that she doesn't remember. Irvin Yalom, the psychiatrist, wrote that it was "far better that [a patient make progress but] forget what we talked about than the opposite possibility (a more popular choice for patients)—to remember precisely what was talked about but to remain unchanged."

Rita's third addition is a small print featuring two abstract gray-haired people, their bodies entwined and in motion, surrounded by cartoon-like exclamations: *Ouch . . . my back! Slow down . . . my heart!* In elegant calligraphy above the bodies, she wrote, OLD PEOPLE STILL FUCK.

It's her best-selling piece to date.

55

It's My Party and You'll Cry if You Want To

The email arrives and my fingers freeze on the keyboard. The subject line reads *It's a party . . . wear black!* The sender is Matt, Julie's husband, and I decide to let the email sit there until I'm finished with patients for the day. I don't want to open Julie's funeral invitation just before going into session.

I think again about the hierarchy of pain. When I first started seeing Julie, I imagined that it would be hard going from hearing about her CT scans and tumors to listening to "So, I think the babysitter is stealing from me" and "Why do *I* always have to initiate sex?"

You think you *have problems?* I worried I'd say in my head.

But it turned out that being with Julie made me more compassionate. Other patients' problems mattered too: their betrayal by the person who'd been trusted to watch their child; their feelings of shame and emptiness when rejected by their spouses. Underneath these details were the same essential questions Julie had been forced to face: How do I feel safe in a world of uncertainty? How do I connect? Seeing Julie called forth in me an even greater sense of responsibility to my other patients. Every hour counts for all of us, and I want to be fully present in the therapy hour I spend with each one.

After my last patient leaves, I slowly write my chart notes, procrastinating before finally opening the email. The invitation includes a note from Julie explaining that she wants people to come to a "cry-your-eyes-out goodbye party" and that she hopes her single friends might take advantage of the gathering "because if you meet at a funeral you'll always remember how important love and life are, and to let the small stuff go." It also contains a link to the obituary that Julie had crafted in my office.

I send my condolences to Matt, and a minute later, I get another email that he indicates Julie left for me. *Because I'm dead, I'll cut to the chase,* it says. *You said you'd come to my goodbye party. I'll know if you're not there. Remember to be my sister's buffer for Aunt Aileen, the one who always . . . well, you know the story. You know all my stories.*

There's a P.S. from Matt: *Please be there with us.*

Of course I want to be there, and I'd considered the potential complications before I made my promise to Julie. Not every therapist would make the same choice. Some worry that this might be crossing a line—being overly invested, as it were. And while in some instances that might be true, it seems odd that in a profession dedicated to the human condition, therapists are expected to compartmentalize their humanity when it comes to their patients' deaths. This doesn't apply to other professionals in the person's life: Julie's attorney, chiropractor, oncologist. Nobody blinks if *they* attend the funeral. Therapists, though, are expected to keep their distance. But what if their being there would comfort their patients' families? And what if it would comfort the therapists themselves?

Most of the time, therapists grieve their patients' deaths in private. Who could I talk to about Julie's death other than my colleagues in my consultation group or Wendell? And even then, none of them knew her the way I did or the way her family and friends (who get to grieve together) did. The therapist is left to grieve alone.

Even at the funeral, there are confidentiality issues to consider. Our duty to protect our patients' confidentiality doesn't end with death. A wife whose husband has committed suicide, for instance, may call up her husband's therapist to get some answers, but therapists can't breach that code. Those files, those interactions, are protected. Similarly, if I attend a patient's funeral and somebody asks how I knew the deceased, I can't say I was the therapist. These issues come up more in unexpected deaths—suicide, overdose, heart attack, car accident—than in situations like Julie's. After all, as therapists, we discuss things with patients—and Julie and I had discussed her wish that I attend the funeral.

"You promised you'd stay with me to the end," she'd said with a sideways grin about a month before she died. "You can't abandon me at my own funeral, can you?"

In Julie's last weeks, we talked about how she wanted to say goodbye to her family and friends. *What do you want to leave with them? What do you want them to leave you with?*

I wasn't talking about transformative deathbed conversations—those are mostly fantasies. People may seek peace and clarity, understanding and healing, but deathbeds themselves are often a stew of drugs, fear, confusion, weakness. That's why it's especially important to be the people we want to be *now*, to become more open and expansive while we're able. A lot will be left dangling if we wait too long. I remember a patient who, after years of indecisiveness, finally reached out to his biological father who had been seeking a relationship, only to be devastated to learn that he was lying unconscious, in a coma, and would die within a week.

We also place undue pressure on those last moments, allowing them to supersede whatever came before. I had a patient whose wife collapsed and died in midconversation, as he was being defensive about not doing his share of the laundry. "She died mad at me, thinking I was a schmuck," he said. In fact, they'd had a strong marriage and loved each other deeply. But because this one argument became enshrined as the final words they exchanged, it took on a significance that it wouldn't otherwise have had.

Near the end, Julie fell asleep more often during our sessions, and if before it seemed like time stopped whenever she came to see me, now it felt like a dress rehearsal for her death; she was "trying on" what it would feel like in the stillness without the terror she had of being alone.

"Almost is always the hardest, isn't it?" she said one afternoon. "Almost getting something. Almost having a baby. Almost getting a clean scan. Almost not having cancer anymore." I thought about how many people avoid trying for things they really want in life because it's more painful to get close to the goal but not achieve it than not to have taken the chance in the first place.

During those luxuriously quiet sessions, Julie said that she wanted to die at home, and for our last few sessions, that's where I saw her. She had surrounded her bed with photos of everyone she loved, and she played Scrabble and watched *The Bachelor* reruns and listened to her favorite music and received visitors.

Finally, though, even enjoying those pleasures became difficult. Julie told her family, "I want to live, but I don't want to live like this," and they understood this to mean that she would stop eating. She was no longer able to eat most foods anyway. When she decided the life she had left wasn't enough of a life to sustain, her body naturally followed suit, and she was gone within days.

We didn't have a profound "grand finale," as Julie had been calling our final session. Her last words to me were about steak. "God, what I would give for a steak!" she said, her voice weak and barely audible. "They better have steak wherever I'm going." And then she fell asleep. It was an ending not unlike our sessions, where even though "our time is up," the conversation lingers. In the best goodbyes, there's always the feeling that there's something more to say.

I'm astounded—though I shouldn't be—by the turnout at Julie's funeral party. There are hundreds of people here from all parts of her life: her childhood friends, her summer-camp friends, her marathon-training friends, her book-club friends, her college friends, her graduate-school friends, her work friends and colleagues (from both the university and Trader Joe's), her parents, both sets of grandparents, Matt's parents, both of their siblings. I know who they are because people from all of these groups get up and talk about Julie, telling stories of who she was and what she meant to them.

When it's Matt's turn, everyone goes silent, and sitting in the back row, I look down at my iced tea and the napkin in my hand. IT'S MY PARTY AND YOU'LL CRY IF YOU WANT TO! it says. Earlier I'd noticed a big banner that read I STILL CHOOSE NEITHER.

Matt takes some time to settle himself before he speaks. When he does, he shares an anecdote about how Julie had written a book for him to have after she was gone, and she titled it, *The Shortest Longest Romance: An Epic Love and Loss Story*. He loses it here, then slowly composes himself and keeps going.

He explains that in the book, he was surprised to find that near the end of the story—*their* story—Julie had included a chapter on how she hoped Matt would always have love in his life. She encouraged him to be honest and kind to what she called his "grief girlfriends"—the rebound girlfriends, the women he'll date as he heals. *Don't mislead them,* she wrote. *Maybe you can get something from each other.* She followed this with a charming and hilarious dating profile that Matt could use to find his grief girlfriends, and then she got more serious. She wrote the most achingly beautiful love letter in the form of another dating profile that Matt could use to find the person he'd end up with for good. She talked about his quirks, his devotion, their steamy sex life, the incredible family he inherited (and that, presumably, this new woman would inherit), and what an amazing father he'd be. She knew this, she wrote, because they got to be parents together —though in utero and for only a matter of months.

The people in the crowd are simultaneously crying and laughing by the time Matt finishes reading. *Everyone should have at least one epic love story in their lives,* Julie concluded. *Ours was that for me. If we're lucky, we might get two. I wish you another epic love story.*

We all think it ends there, but then Matt says that he feels it's only fair that Julie have love wherever she is too. So in that spirit, he says, he's written *her* a dating profile for heaven.

There are a few chuckles, although they're hesitant at first. *Is this too morbid?* But no, it's exactly what Julie would have wanted, I think. It's out-there and uncomfortable and funny and sad, and soon everyone is laugh-sobbing with abandon. *She hates mushrooms,* Matt has written to her heavenly beau, *don't serve her anything with mushrooms.* And *If there's a Trader Joe's, and she says that she wants to work there, be supportive. You'll also get great discounts.*

He goes on to talk about how Julie rebelled against death in many ways, but primarily by what Matt liked to call "doing kindnesses" for others, leaving the world a better place than she found it. He doesn't enumerate them, but I know what they are—and the recipients of her kindnesses all speak about them anyway.

I'm glad I came, glad that I got to fulfill my promise to Julie and also see a side of her that I can never know about any of my patients—what their lives look like outside of the therapy office. One on one, therapists get depth but not breadth, words without illustrations. Despite being the ultimate insider in terms of Julie's thoughts and feelings, I'm an outsider here among all these people I don't know but who knew Julie. We're told, as therapists, that if we do attend a patient's funeral, we should stay off to the side, avoid interacting. I do this, but just as I'm about to leave, a friendly couple starts talking to me. They say that Julie is responsible for their marriage—she set them up on a blind date five years ago. I smile at their story, then try to excuse myself, but before I can, the woman in the couple asks, "And how did you know Julie?"

"She was a friend," I say reflexively, mindful of confidentiality, but the moment I say it, I realize it also feels true.

"Will you think about me?" Julie used to ask me before she went in for her various surgeries, and I always told her I would. The assurance soothed her, helped her stay centered in the midst of her anxiety about going under the knife.

Later, though, when it became clear that Julie would die, that question took on another meaning: *Will a part of me remain alive in you?*

Julie had recently told Matt that she felt horrible for dying on him, and the next day he sent her a note with a lyric from the musical *The Secret Garden.* In it, the ghost of a beloved wife asks her grieving husband if he could forgive her, if he could hold her in his heart and "'find some new way to love me/Now that we're apart.'" Matt had written, *Yes*. He added that he didn't believe that people disappeared but that something in us was eternal and survived.

Walking to my car that day, I hear Julie's question: *Will you think about me?*

All these years later, I still do.

I remember her most in the silences.

56

Happiness Is Sometimes

"Honestly, don't hold back. Do you think I'm an asshole?" John asks as he sets down the bag with our lunches. He's brought his dog Rosie to session today—her "danny" was ill and Margo's out of town—and she's on John's lap, sniffing the takeout containers. Now John's eyes are on me, as are Rosie's beady ones, as if they're both awaiting my response.

I'm caught off guard by his question. If I say yes, I might hurt John, and the last thing I want to do is hurt him. If I say no, I might be condoning some of his more asshole-like behaviors instead of creating awareness around them. The second-to-last thing I want to do is to be John's yes-man. I could turn the question around on him: *Do* you *think you're an asshole?* But I'm more interested in something else: Why is he asking—and why now?

John flicks off his slip-on sneakers, but instead of arranging himself cross-legged on the couch, he leans forward, elbows on knees. Rosie jumps down, positions herself on the floor, and looks up at John. He hands her a treat. "Here you go, my little princess," he croons.

"You're not going to believe this," he says, looking back at me, "but I made a, uh, *unfortunate* comment to Margo a few nights ago. She said that her therapist recommended a couples therapist for us, and I said that I wanted to get a referral from you because I don't necessarily trust her idiot therapist's suggestion. I knew the second it came out of my mouth that

I should have filtered, but it was too late, and Margo just tore into me. '*My* idiot therapist?' she said. '*Mine?*' She said that if my therapist can't see what an asshole I am, then *I'm* going to the idiot therapist. I apologized for calling her therapist an idiot and she apologized for calling me an asshole, and then we both started laughing, and I can't remember the last time we laughed like that together. We couldn't stop, and the girls heard us and they came in and looked at us like we were a couple of crazy people. 'What's so funny?' they kept asking but we couldn't explain it. I don't think we even *knew* what was so funny.

"Then the girls started laughing and we were all laughing about the fact that we couldn't stop laughing. Ruby got on the floor and started rolling around, and then so did Gracie, and then Margo and I looked at each other and we got on the floor and all four of us were rolling around on our bedroom floor and laughing. And then *Rosie* runs over to see what all the commotion's about, and when she sees us rolling around the floor, she freezes, right there in the doorway. She just stands there shaking her head, like, *You humans are too much.* And then she runs away. And then we laughed at Rosie, and as I was rolling around on the floor with my wife and my kids and the dog is barking at us from the other room, I watched the scene, almost from above, like I was observing it and living it at the same time, and I thought, *I love my fucking family.*"

He basks in the thought for a second before continuing.

"I felt the happiest I've been in a long time," he says. "And you know what? Margo and I actually had a really nice night together after that. So much of the tension that's normally between us was gone." John smiles at the memory. "But then," John continues, "I don't know what happened. I've been sleeping much better, but that night I was up for hours thinking about what Margo said about my being an asshole. I couldn't get it out of my head. Because I know you don't think I'm an asshole. I mean, *you* obviously like me. So then I thought, *Wait, what if Margo's right?* What if I'm an asshole but you can't see it? Then you really *are* an idiot therapist. So which is it—am I an asshole, or are you an idiot?"

What a trap, I think. *Either I say he's an asshole or I claim I'm an idiot.* I think of Julie and the phrase that her friends wrote in her high-school year-book: *I choose neither.*

"Maybe there's a third possibility," I suggest.

"I want the truth," he says adamantly. A mentor once remarked that often in therapy, change happens "gradually, then suddenly," and that might be true for John too. I imagine that as John tossed and turned in bed, unable to sleep, the house of cards he'd built for himself about how everyone else was an idiot came crashing down, and now he's left with the wreckage: *I'm an asshole. I'm not better than everyone else — special. My mom was wrong.*

But that's not the truth either. It's simply the collapse of the narcissistic defense in the form of an overcorrection. John started out with the belief that "I'm good and you're bad," and now it's being turned upside down — "You're good and I'm bad." Neither is right.

"The truth as I see it," I say honestly, "is not that I'm an idiot or you're an asshole but that sometimes in order to protect yourself, you act like one."

I watch John for his reaction. He takes a breath and seems like he's about to say something flip but then decides not to. He's quiet for a minute, gazing at Rosie, who has fallen asleep.

"Yeah," he says. "I do act like an asshole." Then he smiles and adds, "*Sometimes.*"

Recently John and I talked about the beauty of the word *sometimes,* how *sometimes* evens us out, keeps us in the comfortable middle rather than dangling on one end of the spectrum or the other, hanging on for dear life. It helps us escape from the tyranny of black-or-white thinking. John said that when he was struggling with the pressure of his marriage and his career, he used to think that there'd be a point when he'd be happy again, and then when Gabe died, he thought he'd never be happy again. Now, he says, he's come to feel it's not either/or, yes or no, always or never.

"Maybe happiness is sometimes," he says, leaning back on the sofa. It's an idea that brings him relief. "I guess it couldn't hurt to try that couples therapist," John adds, referring to the one Wendell apparently suggested. Margo and John had gone to couples therapy for a few sessions after Gabe died, but they were both so furious and ashamed—alternately blaming each other and themselves—that even when the therapist brought up the police report on the drunk driver as a contributing factor in the accident, John had no interest in what he called the "pointless postmortem." If Margo wanted therapy, he was all for it, but he saw no reason to prolong his own torture for an hour each week.

But now, he explains, he's agreeing to couples therapy because he's lost so much—his mom, his son, maybe even himself—and he wants to fight to keep Margo before it's too late.

In that spirit, recently he and Margo have begun—tentatively, delicately—to talk about Gabe, but also about many other things. They're learning who they are at this point in their lives and what that means going forward. And whatever the outcome, maybe, John reasons, a couples therapist can help.

"But if the guy's an idiot—" John starts, and I stop him.

"If you begin to feel that way," I say, "I'm going to encourage you to hang in there until you have more information. If the therapist is any good, the process might make you uncomfortable, and we can talk about that discomfort in here. Let's understand it together before you make a determination." I think about when I doubted Wendell, when I projected my discomfort onto him. I remember wondering what he was smoking when he first talked about my grief. I remember finding him corny at times and being skeptical of his competence at others.

Maybe we all need to doubt, rail against, and question before we can really let go.

John tells me that when he was having trouble falling asleep the other night, he started thinking about his childhood. Ever since he was a boy, he says, he wanted to be a doctor, but his family didn't have enough money to send him to medical school.

"I had no idea," I say. "What kind of doctor?"

John looks at me like the answer is evident. "Psychiatrist," he says.

John, a psychiatrist! I try to picture John seeing patients: *Your mother-in-law said* that? *What an idiot!*

"Why a psychiatrist?"

John rolls his eyes. "Because I was a kid whose mother died, *obviously*, and I want to save her or myself or something." He pauses. "That and I was too lazy to be a surgeon."

I'm fascinated by his self-awareness, even if he still covers his vulnerability with a joke.

Anyway, he continues, he had applied to medical school with the hope of substantial financial aid. He knew he would graduate with tremendous debt, but he figured that on a doctor's salary, he'd be able to pay it off. He did well in college, majoring in biology, but because he had to work twenty hours a week for his tuition, his grades weren't as good as they might have been. Certainly not as good as those of his fellow premed students, the gunners who pulled all-nighters and competed for top scores.

Still, he got interviews at several schools. Inevitably, though, the interviewer would make some "backhanded crack" about how great his application essays were and then try to manage his expectations, given his good-but-not-exceptional GPA. "You should be a writer!" more than one interviewer said, kidding but not. John was furious. Couldn't they see from his application that he had been working a job while doing a premed curriculum? Didn't that show his dedication? His work ethic? His ability to power through? Couldn't they see that a handful of Bs and that fucking C minus weren't indicators of his aptitude but of the fact that he never had time to study, much less stay after class if the labs went long?

In the end, John got into one medical school, but he wasn't given enough financial aid to live on. And since he knew he couldn't work his way through medical school the way he'd worked his way through college, he declined the offer and planted himself in front of the television set, despairing about his future. His father, a teacher like his late mother, suggested that John become a science teacher, but John kept thinking about the famous saying "Those who can't do, teach." John *could* do—he knew he could do the science classes in medical school—he just needed the money. And then, as he sat in front of the TV and cursed his dismal predicament, an idea came to him.

He thought, *Hey, I can write this crap.*

In short order, John bought a book on scriptwriting, cranked out an episode, sent it to an agent whose name he got from a directory, and was hired as a staff writer on a show. The show, he says, was "absolute garbage," but his plan was to write for three years, make some real money, then reapply to medical school. A year later, though, he was hired on a much better show, and the following year, he was hired on a hit show. By the time he'd saved up the money to get himself through medical school, John had an Emmy award on the mantel in his studio apartment. He decided not to reapply. What if he got into zero schools this time? Besides, he wanted to make money—the crazy money he could make in Hollywood—so his future kids wouldn't have to face those kinds of choices. Now, he says, he has so much money, his daughters could go to medical school many times over.

John stretches his arms, rearranges his legs. Rosie opens her eyes, sighs, closes them again. He goes on to say that he remembers standing on the awards stage with the show's staff and thinking, *Ha! Take this, you morons! You can take your rejection letters and shove them up your asses! I've got a fucking Emmy!*

Every year, as his show garnered more awards, John would feel a perverse sense of satisfaction. He'd remember all those people who hadn't believed he was good enough, but now here he was, with an office full of Emmys, a bank account full of cash, a portfolio full of retirement funds, and he'd think, *They can't take any of this away from me.*

I think about how "they" had taken away his mother.

"Who's 'they'?" I ask John.

"The fucking med-school interviewers," he says. It's clear that his success was driven as much by revenge as passion. And I wonder who "they" are for him now. Most of us have a "they" in the audience, even though nobody's really watching, at least not how we think they are. The people who *are* watching us—the people who really see us—don't care about the false self, about the show we're putting on. Who are *those* people for John?

"Oh, come on," he says. "Everyone cares about the show we put on."

"You think I do?"

John sighs. "You're my *therapist.*"

I shrug. *So?*

John relaxes into the couch.

"When I was rolling on the floor with my family," he says, "I had the strangest thought. I was thinking that I wished you could see us. I wanted you to see me in that moment because I felt so much like a person you don't really know. Because in here, you know, it's all doom and gloom. But driving over here today, I thought, *Maybe she does know.* Maybe you do have, like, some kind of therapist's sixth sense about people. Because—and I'm not sure if it's all of your annoying questions or the sadistic silences you put me through—but I feel like you *get me,* you know? And I don't want your head to get too big or anything, but I thought, you have a more complete picture of my total humanity than anyone else in my life."

I'm so moved I can't speak. I want to tell John how touched I am, not just by how he feels, but by his willingness to tell me. I want to tell him that I don't think I'll ever forget this moment, but before my voice returns John exclaims, "Oh, for Christ's sake, don't fucking cry on me again."

I chuckle, and so does John. And then I tell him what I was too choked up to say a minute ago. Now John is tearing up. I remember an earlier session when John said that Margo always cries, and I'd floated the idea that Margo was doing double duty, crying for both of them. Maybe you can let Margo cry, I'd suggested, and maybe you can let yourself cry too. John hasn't been ready to let Margo see him cry. Not yet. But given that he'll let me see it, I feel hopeful about their couples therapy.

John points to his tears. "See?" he says. "My fucking humanity."

"It's magnificent," I say.

We never open the takeout bag. We don't need the food between us anymore.

A few weeks later, I'm on the couch at home, bawling like a baby. I'm watching John's show, and the sociopathic character who's become softer around the edges is talking to his brother—a person we hadn't known existed until a couple of episodes ago. The sociopathic character and his brother had apparently been estranged, and the audience is learning in a flashback what the estrangement has been about: the brother blames the sociopathic character for *his* son's death.

It's a wrenching scene, and I think about John's childhood dream of becoming a psychiatrist and how his grasp of exquisite pain is what makes him such a powerful writer. Was this a gift left by the pain of his mother's death and, later, by Gabe's? Or was it the legacy of the relationships he shared with them while they were alive?

Gain and loss. Loss and gain. Which comes first?

In our next session, John will tell me that he watched this episode with Margo and that they talked about it with their couples therapist, who, so far, seems "not particularly idiotic." He'll tell me that as the episode began, he and Margo sat in their den on opposite ends of their couch, but when the flashback sequence began, he didn't know why, it was instinct or love or both, but something propelled him to get up and move right next to her so that their legs touched, and he wrapped his legs around hers as they both sobbed through the scene. As he tells me this, I'll think about how far away I sat from Wendell on that very first day and how long it was until I finally felt comfortable enough to move closer. John will say in this session that I was right—that it was, in fact, okay to cry with Margo, and that instead of drowning them both in a flood of tears, it brought them safely onto land.

When he says this, I'll imagine myself, John and Margo, and millions of viewers around the world lying on our couches, cracked open by his words—and I'll think how, for all of us, John made it okay to cry.

57

Wendell

"I've been calling you Wendell," I tell my therapist, whose real name, I must confess, isn't actually Wendell.

I've just made an announcement in our session: I started writing again, a book of sorts, and he—my therapist, now called "Wendell"—plays a prominent role.

I hadn't planned to do this, I explain. A week ago, pulled to my desk by what felt like a gravitational force, I fired up my laptop, opened a blank document, and wrote for hours, as if a dam had broken. I felt like myself again, but different—more free, more relaxed, more alive—and I was experiencing what the psychologist Mihaly Csikszentmihalyi calls "flow." It wasn't until I began yawning that I stepped away, noticed the time, and climbed into bed. I was tired, but in an energized way, ready for rest after having been awakened.

I got up the next morning refreshed, and that night, the mysterious force drew me again to my laptop. I thought about John's plan to become a psychiatrist. For many people, going into the depths of their thoughts and feelings is like going into a dark alley—they don't want to go there alone. People come to therapy to have somebody to go there with, and people watch John's show for a similar reason: it makes them feel less alone, allows them to see a version of themselves muddling through life on the screen.

Maybe in this way, he *is* a psychiatrist to many—and maybe his bravery in writing about his own loss had inspired me to write about mine.

All week, I wrote about my breakup, my therapist, my mortality, our fear of taking responsibility for our lives and the need to do so in order to heal. I wrote about outdated stories and false narratives and how the past and the future can creep into the present, sometimes eclipsing it entirely. I wrote about holding on and letting go and how hard it is to walk around those prison bars even when freedom isn't just right in front of us but literally *inside of us,* in our minds. I wrote about how no matter our external circumstances, we have choices about how to live our lives and that, regardless of what has happened, what we've lost, or how old we are, as Rita put it, it ain't over till it's over. I wrote about how sometimes we have the key to a better life but need somebody to show us where we left the damn thing. I wrote about how for me, that person has been Wendell, and how for others, that person is sometimes me.

"Wendell . . ." Wendell says, trying on the name to see if it fits.

"Because I come here on Wednesdays," I say. "You know, *Wednesdays with Wendell* could be the title. The alliteration sort of sings, doesn't it? But mine's too personal to publish. It's just for me. It feels great to write again."

"It has meaning," he says, referring to our earlier conversations. It's true—I couldn't write the happiness book because I wasn't actually searching for happiness. I was searching for *meaning*—from which fulfillment and, yes, occasionally happiness ensue. And I couldn't get myself to cancel the book contract for so long because if I did, I'd have to let go of my crutch—the I-should-have-written-the-parenting-book litany that shielded me from examining anything else. Even after I canceled the contract, for weeks I held on to my regret and the fantasy of how much easier my life would have been had I written the original book. Like Rita, I was reluctant to give light and space to the triumph, still spending more time thinking about how I'd failed rather than how I'd freed myself.

But I got a second chance too. Wendell once pointed out that we talk to *ourselves* more than we'll talk to any other person over the course of our lives but that our words aren't always kind or true or helpful—or even respectful. Most of what we say to ourselves we'd never say to people we love or care about, like our friends or children. In therapy, we learn to pay close attention to those voices in our heads so that we can learn a better way to communicate with ourselves.

So today, when Wendell says, "It has meaning," I know that by "it," he's also referring to us, our time together. People often think they go to therapy for an explanation — say, why Boyfriend left, or why they've become depressed — but what they're really there for is an *experience*, something unique that's created between two people over time for about an hour each week. It was the meaning of this experience that allowed me to find meaning in other ways.

Months will pass before I'll toy with the idea of turning these late-night laptop sessions into a real book, before I'll decide to use my own experience to help others find meaning in their lives too. And once I get up the courage to expose myself in this way, that's what it will become: the book you are reading right now.

"Wendell," he says again, letting the name sink in. "I like it."

But there's one more story to tell.

"I'm ready to dance," I said to Wendell a few weeks before, surprising not just me, but him. I'd been thinking about the comment Wendell had made months earlier after I told him that I felt betrayed by my body on the dance floor at the wedding, by my foot that had lost its strength. He had offered to dance, to show me that I could both reach out for help and take a risk, and in doing so, I realized later, *he* had taken a risk. Therapists take risks all the time on behalf of their patients, making split-second decisions on the presumption that these risks will do far more good than harm. Therapy isn't a paint-by-numbers business, and sometimes the only way to move patients beyond their stuckness is by taking a risk in the room, by going out of the therapist's own comfort zone to teach by example.

"I mean, if the offer's still on the table," I added. Wendell paused. I smiled. It felt like a role reversal.

"It is," Wendell said, after the briefest of hesitations. "What would you like to dance to?"

"How about 'Let It Be'?" I suggested. I'd been playing the Beatles tune on the piano recently and it popped into my head before I realized it wasn't exactly a dance song. I considered changing it to something by Prince or Beyoncé, but Wendell got up and grabbed his iPhone from his desk drawer, and within a minute the room filled with those iconic opening chords. I stood, but immediately got cold feet, stalling with words, telling Wendell that we needed something more clubby and danceable, something like . . .

That's when the song's chorus erupted—*Let it be, let it be, let it be, let it be*—and Wendell started rocking out like a teenager at a heavy-metal concert, exaggerating for comic effect. I watched in amazement. There was buttoned-up Wendell, doing air guitar and all.

The song went on to its quieter, poignant second verse about the brokenhearted people, but Wendell was still rocking the hell out of this, as if to say, *Prince or Beyoncé be damned. Life doesn't have to be perfect.* I watched his tall, skinny frame jiving across the room, the courtyard a backdrop through the windows behind him, as I tried to get out of my head and just, well, let it be. I thought of my hairstylist Cory. *Could* I "just be"?

The chorus started up again and suddenly I was jiving across the room, too, laughing self-consciously at first, twirling in circles as Wendell went even crazier. But his dance training was apparent—or maybe it was less about his training and more about his sense of self. He wasn't doing anything fancy; he just seemed wholly at home in his skin. And he was right: despite the problems with my foot, I needed to get out on the dance floor anyway.

Now we were both dancing and singing out loud together—about the light that shines in the cloudy night—belting out the verses at the top of our lungs as if we were at a karaoke bar, dancing exuberantly in the same room in which I'd fallen apart in despair.

There will be an answer, let it be

The music ended sooner than I'd expected, just as our sessions sometimes did. But rather than feeling like I needed more time, I found something satisfying about our time being up.

Not long before this, I'd told Wendell that I'd begun thinking about what it would be like to stop coming to therapy. So much had changed over the course of the year, and I was feeling not just better equipped to handle life's challenges and uncertainties but also more peaceful inside. Wendell had smiled—it was the smile I'd seen recently that seemed to mean *I'm delighted for you*—then asked if we should talk about termination.

I wavered. Not yet.

Now, though, as Wendell placed his iPhone back in his drawer and returned to his spot on the couch, the time seemed right. There's a biblical saying that translates roughly as "First you will do, then you will understand." Sometimes you have to take a leap of faith and experience something before its meaning becomes apparent. It's one thing to talk about leaving behind a restrictive mindset. It's another to stop *being* so restrictive. The transfer of words into action, the freedom of it, made me want to carry that action outside the therapy room and into my life.

And with that, I was ready to set a date to leave.

58

A Pause in the Conversation

The strangest thing about therapy is that it's structured around an ending. It begins with the knowledge that our time together is finite, and the successful outcome is that patients reach their goals and leave. The goals are different for each person, and therapists talk to their patients about what those goals are. Experiencing less anxiety? Relationships going more smoothly? Being kinder to yourself? The endpoint depends on the patient.

In the best case, the ending feels organic. There might be more to do, but we've done a lot, enough. The patient feels good — more resilient, more flexible, more able to navigate daily life. We've helped them hear the questions they didn't even know they were asking: *Who am I? What do I want? What's in my way?*

It seems silly, though, to deny that therapy is also about forming deep attachments to people and then saying goodbye.

Sometimes therapists find out what happens afterward, if patients come back at a later point in their lives. Other times we're left to wonder. How are they doing? Is Austin thriving after leaving his wife and coming out as a gay man in his late thirties? Is Janet's husband with Alzheimer's still alive? Did Stephanie stay in her marriage? There are so many stories left unfinished, so many people I think about but will never see again.

"Will you remember me?" Julie had asked, but the question wasn't unique to her situation.

And today I'm saying goodbye to Wendell. We've been talking about this goodbye for weeks, but now that it's here, I don't know how to thank him. As an intern, I was taught that when patients thank us, it helps to remind them that they did the hard work.

It's all you, we tend to say. *I was just here to guide you.* And in a sense, that's true. The fact that they picked up the phone and decided to come to therapy and then work through things every week is something no one else could do for them.

But we're also taught something else that we can't really understand until we've done thousands of hours of sessions: We grow in connection with others. Everyone needs to hear that other person's voice saying, *I believe in you. I can see possibilities that you might not see quite yet. I imagine that something different can happen, in some form or another.* In therapy we say, *Let's edit your story.*

Early on, when I was talking about Boyfriend, in my view an open-and-shut case of I'm-the-innocent-injured-party-here, Wendell said, "You want me to agree with you." I said that I didn't want him to agree with me (though I did!), I just wanted him to be sensitive to the shock I was experiencing, and then I proceeded to tell him exactly *how* I wanted him to do that. At that point he said that I was trying to "control the therapy" and that my attempts to bend situations to my liking might have played a part in my being blindsided by Boyfriend. Wendell didn't want to do therapy the way I wanted him to. Boyfriend didn't want to live in contented domesticity the way I wanted him to. Boyfriend tried to accommodate me until he couldn't anymore. Wendell wouldn't waste my time that way, he explained; he didn't want to say two years in, like Boyfriend did, *Sorry, I can't do this.*

I remember how I both loved and hated Wendell for saying that. It's like when somebody finally has the guts to tell you that you have a problem and you feel both defensive and relieved that this person is telling it like it is. That's the delicate work that therapists do. Wendell and I worked on my grief but also my self-imprisonment. And we did it together—it wasn't all me. Therapy can only work if it's a joint endeavor.

Nobody is going to save you, Wendell had said. Wendell didn't save me, but he did help me to save myself.

So when I express my gratitude to Wendell, he doesn't push away the compliment with a trite line of humility.

He says, "It's been my pleasure."

Recently John observed that a good television series leaves viewers feeling like the time between weekly episodes is simply a pause in the story. Similarly, he said, he began to realize that each of our sessions wasn't a discrete conversation but a continuing one and that the time between sessions was just a pause, not a period. I share this with Wendell as the minutes wind down in our final session. "Let's consider this a pause in the conversation," I say. "Like every week, but longer."

I tell him I may come back one day, because it's true; people leave and come back at different times in their lives. And when they do, the therapist is still there, sitting in the same chair, holding all of their shared history.

"We can still consider it a pause," Wendell replies, then adds the part that's hardest to say. "Even if we don't meet again."

I smile, knowing exactly what he means. Relationships in life don't really end, even if you never see the person again. Every person you've been close to lives on somewhere inside you. Your past lovers, your parents, your friends, people both alive and dead (symbolically or literally)—all of them evoke memories, conscious or not. Often they inform how you relate to yourself and others. Sometimes you have conversations with them in your head; sometimes they speak to you in your sleep.

In the weeks leading up to this session, I've been having dreams about my leaving. In one, I imagine seeing Wendell at a conference. He's standing with somebody I don't know and I'm not sure if he's seen me. I feel a yawning distance between us and all that once lived between us. And then it happens: He looks over. I nod. He nods. There's a hint of a smile that only I can see.

In another dream, I'm visiting a friend at her therapy office—who this friend is isn't clear—and as I exit the elevator on her floor, I see Wendell leaving the suite. I wonder if he's there to meet with colleagues for a consultation group. Or maybe he has just left his own therapy session. I'm fascinated; Wendell's therapist! Is one of these therapists Wendell's? Is *my friend* Wendell's therapist? Either way, he's not self-conscious about it. "Hi," he says warmly on his way out. "Hi," I say on my way in.

I wonder what these dreams mean. I'm always embarrassed as a therapist when I can't understand my own dreams. I bring them to Wendell. He doesn't know what they mean either. We come up with theories, two therapists analyzing one therapist's dreams. We talk about how I felt during the dreams. We talk about how I feel now—both anxious and excited to move on. We talk about how hard it can be to get attached and say goodbye.

"Okay," I say now in Wendell's office. "A pause."

We have about a minute left, and I try to take in the moment, memorize it. Wendell with his crossed and impossibly long legs, his stylish button-down and khakis, and today's trendy blue lace-ups over socks with patterned squares. His face—curious, compassionate, present. His beard with the flecks of gray. The table with the tissues between us. The armoire, the bookshelf, and the desk that always has his laptop on it and nothing else.

Wendell pats his legs twice and stands but doesn't say his usual "See you next week" at the door.

"Bye," I say.

"Bye," he says and he reaches his hand out to shake mine.

When I release his hand, I turn and walk through the waiting room with the funky chairs and black-and-white photos and humming noise machine, then head down the corridor toward the building's exit. As I approach the main door, a woman enters from the street. She's holding her phone to her ear with one hand, pulling the door open with the other.

"I have to go. Can I call you in an hour?" she says into her phone. I hang back, watching her move down the hall. Sure enough, she opens the door to Wendell's office. I wonder what they'll talk about. I wonder if they'll ever dance.

I think about our conversation, wondering how the pause will hold.

Once outside, I quicken my step as I head to my car. I have patients to see at the office, people like me, all of us trying our best to get out of our own ways. The light on the corner is about to change so I run to catch it, but then I notice the warmth on my skin and I stop at the curb, tilting my face to the sun, soaking it in, lifting my eyes to the world.

Actually, I've got plenty of time.

Acknowledgments

There's a reason I ask patients early on how their lives are peopled—if I've said it a million times, I'll say it a million and one: we grow in connection with others. It turns out that books grow in the same way. I am so grateful to the following people:

First and foremost, my patients are the reason I do what I do and my admiration for them is endless. Each week, they push themselves harder than Olympic athletes, and it's a privilege to be a part of that process. I hope that I've done justice to their stories, and honored their lives in these pages. They teach me so much.

Wendell—thank you for seeing my *neshama,* even (and especially) when I couldn't. It's an understatement to say that I feel so lucky to have landed in your office when I did.

Therapy is so many things, including a craft that's honed over the years. I've had the great fortune to learn from the best. Harold Young, Astrid Schwartz, Lorraine Rose, Lori Karny, and Richard Dunn helped me from the very beginning. Lori Grapes has been a wise mentor and generous supporter, always making herself available for a quick consult between sessions. My consultation group has provided the most supportive place to do the hard work of examining myself as well as my patients.

Gail Ross made this entire thing possible, launching me into the capable hands of Lauren Wein, a serendipitous match for many reasons, just one of which is that she also happens to be the daughter-in-law of a therapist, so she understood exactly what I was trying to do in these pages. Her "in conversation with" comment was the inspiration that made it all click and, in innumerable ways, she has guided this project with an enthusiasm that authors only dream of. Bruce Nichols and Ellen Archer have been wonderfully encouraging and hands-on from up on high, and have supported and championed this project literally every step of the way. Pilar Garcia-Brown was a wizard behind the scenes; I wish I were half as capable and efficient at making things happen as she is. When it came time to work with the rest of the HMH team, I couldn't believe how much talent there was under one roof. My immense gratitude goes to Lori Glazer, Maire Gorman, Taryn Roeder, Leila Meglio, Liz Anderson, Hannah Harlow, Lisa Glover, Debbie Engel, and Loren Isenberg. Their brilliance and creativity astound me. Martha Kennedy (thank you for the gorgeous cover design) and Arthur Mount (thank you for the office illustrations) made the book look beautiful, inside and out.

Tracy Roe, MD, wasn't just an exacting copyeditor who saved me (and my readers) from countless grammatical disasters. We also discovered many parallel experiences, and her hilarious comments in the margins made this process a delight (for me; my lax pronoun use might have driven her right back to her patients in the ER). Dara Kaye helped navigate the maze of international paperwork for our foreign editions, and here in Los Angeles, Olivia Blaustein's and Michelle Weiner's expert care at CAA has been icing on the cake.

When Scott Stossel first told me about Alice Truax, he used the word "legendary," and he was right. Her clarity, guidance, and wisdom were indeed legendary. She saw connections between my life and my patients' lives that even I hadn't; answered emails at all hours of the night; and like a good therapist, asked discerning questions, pushed me to go deeper, and encouraged me to reveal myself more fully than I ever intended. Alice is, quite simply, all over this book.

Back when my first draft was an obscene 600 pages, a small army of very honest and very generous souls volunteered to offer feedback. Each of one of them helped to improve the book dramatically, and if I had the ability to hand out good karma for life, I'd give it to them: Kelli Auerbach, Carolyn Carlson, Amanda Fortini, Sarah Hepola, David Hochman, Judith Newman, Brett Paesel, Kate Phillips, David Rensin, Bethany Saltman, Kyle Smith, and Miven Trageser.

Anat Baron, Amy Bloom, Taffy Brodesser-Akner, Meghan Daum, Rachel Kauder-Nalebuff, Barry Nalebuff, Peggy Orenstein, Faith Salie, Joel Stein, and Heather Turgeon all provided moral and practical support and/or hilarious title ideas *(There's Dust Under That Couch; My Couch, or Yours?)*. Taffy also launched her truth bombs my way when I needed them most. The savvy Jim Levine encouraged me at a key moment, and his support meant the world. Emily Perl Kingsley offered her gracious blessing when I asked to reprint her beautiful essay "Welcome to Holland" in these pages. Carolyn Bronstein listened . . . and listened . . . and listened.

When you're writing a book, it takes a long time before you have the privilege of connecting with readers, but when you write a weekly column, your readers are right there with you. Huge thanks to my "Dear Therapist" readers, and to the *Atlantic*'s Jeffrey Goldberg, Scott Stossel, Kate Julian, Adrienne LaFrance, and Becca Rosen for giving me the opportunity and trusting me to have candid conversations with the brave readers who write in for that candor. Thanks to Joe Pinsker, a dream editor in every way, for making sure that what I write makes sense and sounds so much better. It's always a joy to work with all of you.

My greatest thanks go to my family. Wendell only had to see me once a week; you have to see me all the time. Your love, support, and understanding are everything. Extra special thanks to the "whole package," Zach, for adding daily magic to all of our lives, and for your helpful thoughts on what to say in my advice column and what to title my book. It's not easy having a mom who's a therapist, and it's not easy having a mom who's a writer. You got a double dose, ZJ, and have handled it all with astonishing grace. You give meaning to the word *meaning,* and, as always, I love you "infinity to the infinity power."